KU-167-611

Arthur Hugh *Clough*

A Poet's Life

ANTHONY KENNY

continuum
LONDON • NEW YORK

Continuum
The Tower Building, 11 York Road, London SE1 7NX
15 East 26th Street, New York NY 10010

www.continuumbooks.com

British Library Cataloguing-in-Publication Data
A catalogue record for this book is available from the British Library.

ISBN: 0–8264–7382–2 (hardback)

Typeset by Kenneth Burnley, Wirral, Cheshire
Printed and bound in Great Britain by MPG Books Ltd, Bodmin, Cornwall

Contents

I have known Tennyson, Browning, the 'naughty' Swinburne and M. Arnold, but I have never seen any trace of the poet's life in his poetry, or of his poetry in his life, except in Clough.

Benjamin Jowett to Florence Nightingale, 1 August 1869

Preface

My interest in Arthur Hugh Clough goes back to 1979. At a luncheon in the Master's Lodgings at Balliol the novelist Graham Greene, the Oxford publisher Dan Davin and I, all three of us Catholics who had lapsed to different degrees, were discussing the question: since, to the unbeliever, faith is a delusion, why do those who have given up their faith feel a sense of loss? Greene quoted the words:

> Of all the creatures under heaven's wide cope
> We are most hopeless who had once most hope
> We are most wretched that had most believed.

I did not recognize the quotation and Greene told me it came from Clough's *Easter Day*. Davin was shocked to learn that I knew only two of Clough's short poems. He took my education in hand and sent me the definitive edition of Clough's poetry, recently published by Oxford University Press. Since then the book has been one of my greatest favourites.

In 1988 I published a book *God and Two Poets*, discussing the religious poetry of Clough and Hopkins: both had similar backgrounds, both had followed the same courses at Balliol within a few years of each other, one had become a Jesuit and the other an agnostic. In the course of researching for that book I discovered that Balliol possessed a number of unpublished Oxford diaries, and in 1990 I published these with OUP. I continued to be interested in Clough's life as well as his poetry: as a Liverpool man with a classical education and an Oxford career, and having followed a similar religious trajectory, I feel a certain kinship with him as well as a keen appreciation of his poetry. The present biography, therefore, is the fruit of a long period of admiration.

In writing it I have incurred debts to many people. The first is to the late Miss Katherine Duff, Clough's great-niece, who long ago gave me permission to publish his Balliol remains. I am grateful to Robin Baird-Smith who agreed with enthusiasm to the proposal that I should write a full-length biography, and to his colleagues at Continuum who assisted it to press. Ben Hayes has been most helpful and I was fortunate to have Christine Ranft as copy-editor.

I am indebted to Mark Bostridge and to Gill Sutherland for suggesting sources of information and for saving me from a number of factual errors. I was fortunate to enjoy the encouragement of Professor Patrick Scott, doyen of Clough scholars. I am grateful to the ever-helpful librarians at Balliol College, Dr P. Bulloch and Mr Alan Tadiello. The staff at the Honnold Library in Claremont California made me warmly welcome to study the vast collection of Clough material assembled by the late F. L. Mulhauser, editor of his poems and correspondence. I owe a debt to Mr Philip Stewart who first persuaded me to take *Mari Magno* seriously. And I am indebted more often than is explicitly acknowledged in the text to Clough's previous biographers, from his wife Blanche onwards. My own wife nobly read the manuscript daily as it came into existence, and suggested frequent improvements, for which I am very grateful.

ANTHONY KENNY
April 2005

Abbreviations

Works cited are identified by the following abbreviations:

B Correspondence of Arthur and Blanche Clough in the Bodleian Library (MSS Eng. Lett. c.189–90, d.175–9, e.74–84). Cited by the number of the letter in the *Catalogue of All Known Letters* appended to Mulhauser's edition of the correspondence (= M below).

K *The Oxford Diaries of Arthur Hugh Clough*, edited by A. Kenny, Oxford 1990.

L *The Letters of Matthew Arnold*, edited by Cecil Y. Lang, University Press of Virginia, six volumes 1996–2002.

M *The Correspondence of Arthur Hugh Clough*, edited by F. L. Mulhauser, Oxford, Clarendon Press 1957 (there are two volumes, but a single page numeration runs through both).

OA *The Oxford Authors: Matthew Arnold*, edited by Miriam Allott and Robert H. Super, Oxford 1986.

P *The Poems of Arthur Hugh Clough*, second edition, edited by F. L. Mulhauser, Oxford, Clarendon Press 1974. References to poems are given by page numbers of this edition.

PPR *The Poems and Prose Remains of Arthur Hugh Clough*, edited by his wife, in two volumes, London, Macmillan & Co. 1869.

RD Rugby Diaries of Arthur Hugh Clough, in Balliol College Oxford.

Chapter One

Childhood and Boyhood

The Cloughs were Welsh, Anglican, Tory and prolific. They prided themselves on their descent from Sir Richard Clough, a prosperous Tudor merchant who claimed kinship by birth with John Calvin and kinship by marriage with Elizabeth I. In the eighteenth century the head of the family was Hugh Clough, of Plas Clough in Denbighshire. He fathered 13 children, of whom the youngest, a parson called Roger, married Ann Jemima Butler, a Sussex heiress. This couple, who lived at Castle House, Denbigh, had in their turn ten children, and in this generation the family spread out. Several of the daughters set up house together in Chester, one of the sons, Alfred, became a don at Jesus College in Oxford, and another, James Butler, moved to Liverpool and became a cotton merchant. He married Ann Perfect, the daughter of a Yorkshire banker, and had four children of whom the second, Arthur Hugh, was born on New Year's Day in 1819.

Arthur was born in Rodney Street, where, just nine years earlier, William Ewart Gladstone had been born. Liverpool had recently become the pre-eminent commercial city of industrial Lancashire, and Rodney Street – later to become the Harley Street of the North – was lined with fashionable town houses inhabited by prosperous merchants. James Clough's mercantile career had been unstable – a period between 1806 and 1810 as an exporter in America had ended in bankruptcy – but by 1819 he was seeing the benefits of the boom in the cotton trade that followed the end of the Napoleonic wars. His children were born into a comfortable home, and shortly after the birth of the youngest of them he felt confident enough to expand his business.

In December 1822 the family migrated to Charleston, South Carolina. They moved into a large red-brick seaside house on East Bay Street, which Anne Jemima, Arthur's slightly younger sister, found ugly after the elegance of Rodney Street. All the members of the family had to live above the business offices, but they were prosperous enough to be able to avoid the heat of the next three summers by sailing to the Northern States. They visited New York and spent part of one summer in fashionable Newport, Rhode Island. Friends owned a house in upstate New York on the banks of the Hudson, and in the garden there the four-year-old Arthur learnt to read.

Merchant's house in Rodney Street, Liverpool

St Michael's Church, Charleston

Towards the end of 1825 James Clough was called back to England on business; he took with him his eldest son Charles, two years Arthur's senior, to put him to school. Arthur already stood out in the family by his precocious intelligence, and according to his sister 'he was a beautiful boy with soft, silky, almost black hair, and shining dark eyes, and a small delicate mouth'. Now, at the age of seven, he found himself promoted, during the year of his father's absence, to temporary head of the family and main support of his mother.

Ann Perfect Clough was a sensitive, pious and austere person, who never found it easy to mingle in society. In Charleston she was more than ever dependent for company on her own family. She was anxious to prevent her children from becoming Americanized, and educated them at home. With Arthur she read English and European history and poetry; she shared with him the novels of Walter Scott and Pope's translations of the *Odyssey* and the *Iliad*. She taught him French, and encouraged him to brandish a Union Jack. The family refused to join in prayers for the president in St Michael's church; on the other hand, they celebrated the Fourth of July even after their return to England.

In summer 1826 there was no escape from the Southern heats: the family spent their holiday in a cottage on Sullivan Island, six miles away. James Clough returned in November, and began to take a hand in the education of Arthur, listening to his Latin lessons early each morning, and watching him doing sums lying on cotton baling. Arthur accompanied his father on business along the wharves and on board the merchantmen, and he was allowed to join his parents in the evening in entertaining visiting sea-captains. When the family returned to Sullivan Island, he began to distance himself from the younger children, refusing to take off his shoes and socks while his brother and sister paddled on the soft white sand. In the hot afternoons he preferred to lie abed and read travel literature. But the sailing ships that bustled in the rivers and the bay during these Charleston summers were to provide a lifetime source of poetic imagery.

James Clough's business fortunes were erratic. For a while he ran a ferry service between Charleston and Sullivan Island, making use of a steamboat he had acquired in lieu of a bad debt. But the boat's boilers burst when the engineer in charge of the vessel got drunk. Profits on cotton trading were variable. Nonetheless, the Cloughs acquired a certain standing in the community. Unlike many Charleston families, they did not keep slaves. But when a black servant of theirs hid a runaway slave, James was able to prevent her from being flogged.[1]

In June 1838 the entire family sailed to England. On the voyage the children were cared for by their father, since their mother was constantly seasick, but they were much spoilt by their fellow-passengers. On arrival in Liverpool, since the Cloughs no longer had a house there, the children were packed off to Wales, where they found a bewildering network of cousins, maiden aunts and clerical uncles.

The first stop was at the vicarage in Beaumaris, presided over by Dr Richard Howard DD, canon of Bangor, a cousin by marriage. His children were too many to count. Anne Jemima, years later, could not remember whether there were nine or ten; Arthur, in a semi-autobiographical poem 'Primitiae' written in the last year of his life, puts down the number of cousins as six, all female. The poem's hero Edmund tells us

> I and my cousin Emily
> Were cousins in the third degree . . .
>
> Such an amount of girls there were
> At first one really was perplexed.
> 'Twas Patty first, and Lydia next,
> And Emily the third, and then,
> Philippa, Phoebe, Mary Gwen.
> Six were they, you perceive, in all;
> And portraits fading on the wall,
> Grandmothers, heroines of old,
> And aunts of aunts, with scrolls that told
> Their names and dates, were there to show
> Why these had all been christened so.[2] (P, 398)

The fictional Edmund, at twelve, enjoys being kissed by all six girls; he teaches them chess, is taught to draw by the eldest of them, and at the seashore rescues Emily from an overwhelming wave, which leads to further kissing and an exchange of Valentines in the following year. The actual Arthur, not quite nine, had a less blissful induction into the world of cousins. Accustomed to adult companionship, he could not, his sister tells us, enter into the boys' rough games. Among all the houses he visited in this first Welsh sojourn the one he preferred was the vicarage of his widower Uncle Charles at Mold. There he used to spend time drawing in quiet solitude (M, 6). In October, father, mother and younger siblings sailed back to America, and Arthur was placed in school at Chester with his elder brother Charles.

During their year at Chester, the brothers took it in turns to write home. Arthur's first surviving letter dates from March 1829. Much of it is a boyish description of a travelling menagerie which included a performing elephant, a quagga, a boa constrictor, and, most splendid of all, a ferocious lion named Wallace. But the letter is framed in a very old-fashioned way. 'As it happens to be my turn to address some of you at Charleston I take up my pen to write to you' he begins; and having told the story of a regimental officer injured in a fall from a window he concludes 'I believe no hopes are entertained of his recovery' (M, 2).

Two months later he informs his nine-year-old sister:

> We have bought a book entitled the 'Newtonian System of Philosophy' which treats chiefly on the power and weight of air, the cause of volcanoes, earthquakes, and other phenomena of nature, such as lightning, the Aurora Borealis, also a description of the sun, planets, their moons or satellites, constellations, comets, and other heavenly bodies, likewise of air guns, balloons, air pumps, also a very pleasing one of snow, hail, and vapours. (M, 2)

In the same letter he announces that after the summer vacation he and his brother are to be conducted by either Uncle Charles or Uncle Alfred to Rugby school. To the modern reader mention of Rugby school instantly evokes the name of its most famous headmaster, Dr Thomas Arnold. But at this period Arnold was known to few outside the circle of liberal Oxford intellectuals, the 'Noetics', into which he had entered when he became a fellow of Oriel in 1814 at the age of 19. In May 1828 he had been headmaster for less than a year, and had not yet established the reforms that were to make Rugby a paradigm for the Victorian public school. The Clough boys were sent to Rugby not because of the reputation of its new headmaster, but because that was where their uncles had been educated in the first decade of the century. Indeed the more conservative members of the family, when they discovered what kind of liberal Christianity Arnold held out to his pupils, wished Arthur had been sent to Shrewsbury school instead.

The choice of Rugby, nonetheless, was a happy one. In the first place, the school under Arnold was comparatively humane and enlightened at a time when most English public schools had the reputation of being seminaries of brutality and nurseries of vice. Secondly, Arnold himself treated these young children of expatriates with extraordinary attention and kindness, welcoming them into the warmth of his own large and lively family.

At Rugby Arnold strove to establish a tone of moral earnestness, and insisted on the serious study of classics, mathematics, modern history and science. He encouraged competitive sport in order to promote physical fitness, courage and endurance. The schooling was set in the context of a traditional Christianity interpreted in a liberal mode. The ritual and dogmatic aspect of Church teaching was emphasized less than strict cultivation of conscience and unselfish service of one's neighbour. Discipline was severe and enforced by flogging, but there was less arbitrary beating than elsewhere; and senior pupils were encouraged to take their part in enforcing the school ethos. Arnold summed up as follows his aims for the school: 'What we must look for here is

1st, religious and moral principles; 2ndly gentlemanly conduct; 3rdly, intellectual ability.' The schoolboy Arthur accepted his headmaster's priorities, and strove to achieve perfection under each of these three heads.

Before coming to Rugby, Arthur had imbibed the religious principles of his uncles and the moral principles of his mother. Late in life, he painted this portrait of the cousin who was vicar of Beaumaris.

> The vicar was of bulk and thews
> Six feet he stood without his shoes,
> And every inch of all a man;
> Ecclesiast on the ancient plan,
> Unforced by any party rule
> His native character to school;
> In ancient learning not unread,
> But had few doctrines in his head;
> He ne'er was bitter or unkind,
> But positively spoke his mind.
> Dissenters truly he abhorred,
> They never had his gracious word.
> Their piety he could not bear,
> A sneaking, snivelling set they were:
> Their tricks and meanness fired his blood;
> Up for his church he stoutly stood.
>
> (P, 379)

The Clough children were brought up in the Tory high churchmanship of their father's family, rather than in the more puritan tradition of the maternal Perfects. But it was from his mother that Arthur acquired the highly sensitive conscience that was to be characteristic of him throughout life. Reflecting in middle age on his schooldays, he maintained that there was no real need for a schoolmaster to tenderize the consciences of his charges. 'As for the conscience, mamma, I take it – such as mammas are now-a-days at any rate – has probably set that a-going fast enough already' (epilogue to *Dipyschus*; P, 293).

While at school, however, Clough was happy to let Arnold refine his already sensitive conscience. He set himself very high standards of behaviour, and he scrutinized each action to detect any unworthiness of motive. On the other hand, under the influence of Arnold's passionate but undogmatic Christianity, he moved away from Tory churchmanship and became more sympathetic to nonconformist dissent. He absorbed Arnold's 1833 pamphlet *Principles of Church Reform*, and took up with enthusiasm the idea that there should be a unified national Church, with a single set of buildings shared by all sects (except, of course, Roman Catholics and Quakers). It was this that most shocked his High Church aunts (M, 5, Blanche Clough 1897, 1903: 17).

Arnold's code did not draw a sharp line between the area of moral principle and that of gentlemanly conduct. A gentleman did not have to be a member of the gentry – the majority of Rugby schoolboys came from middle-class families – but he must have certain clearly defined qualities of character. A gentleman did not steal or cheat, or tell lies; most importantly, in the school context, a gentleman did not bully. A gentleman took his part in school games, displaying courage when called for and uncomplaining when buffeted and battered; he did not try to monopolize the game or draw attention to his own exploits rather than to the achievements of his team. A gentleman might, on occasion, fight with his fists; but he must fight fair and he must never be the aggressor. Even quite a young gentleman would drink – bottled beer as well as the house ale – but whatever he drank he must know how to hold his liquor. One question of conscience much exercised Arnold's pupils: did a gentleman schoolboy, when other schoolboys behaved in an ungentlemanly or immoral fashion, report their names to the schoolmasters?

Rugby's code was made familiar to many generations of English schoolboys by *Tom Brown's Schooldays*, the best-seller written by Thomas Hughes, who entered the school one year after Clough. The hero of that book, at first swept up in a whirl of misbehaviour by his profane, pugnacious, pea-shooting peers, as he moves up the school comes to respect Arnold's ideals, stands up to the bully Flashman, and takes under his protection a younger boy – named, as it happens, Arthur – whose piety makes him ripe for persecution.

Tom Brown's Schooldays, while strong on morality and gentlemanliness, has little to say about the third of Arnold's goals: the nurturing of intellectual ability. The school curriculum was packed: in the third form, for instance, the eleven-year-old Arthur had to begin Greek grammar, write Latin prose, ingest six books of the Bible, study physical geography, master vulgar fractions, compute interest, and learn sufficient French irregular verbs to read an improving work in that language.[3] Academic industry was fostered by an elaborate system of prizes. Clough's earliest surviving letter to his mother from Rugby describes, in a tone of awe, the conferment of these awards at an Easter speech-day (M, 3).

In the following year, when his family returned to England from June to December, Arthur began to win prizes himself. He rushed home to Liverpool at the end of term, his sister tells us, to show his mother his prize copy of Johnson's *Lives of the Poets* (PPR, 11). His own poetic talent had yet to develop, but his resolutely British mother will no doubt have been rejoiced by the painfully patriotic poem he had sent her a year earlier on the occasion of the death of King George IV. It began:

O Muse of Britain teach me now to sing
In verses sad of our late, noble King.

and contained the memorable lines

At George's death sure Eton will be sad
And sorrow mark the mein of every lad.
(P, 453)

At Rugby, school life passed through three stages: the lower forms, the fifth form (upper and lower) and the sixth form which included the prefects (called 'prepostors') on which Arnold relied greatly for the good conduct of the school. The minimum age for entry into the sixth form was sixteen, but in the lower forms pupils of all ages were positioned in classes according to their ability in different subjects. Thus when Charles and Arthur arrived at Rugby they were both placed in the same third form in spite of the age difference between them. Their company would have included precocious young sparks of eight or nine as well as elderly dunces who had failed to qualify for promotion. The system did not suit Charles, and he left after a year to continue his education at Karlsruhe in Germany.

All the boys below the fifth form were grouped in local parlance as 'fags', for they were obliged to fag, that is to perform menial tasks, whenever required to do so by the senior boys in the sixth form. They fetched their fag-masters' food and drink, cleaned their rooms and shoes and even (until Arnold stopped it) collected their fishing lines at dead of night from the nearby river Avon. Those in the fifth form, in theory, neither fagged nor were fagged for; but they often made imperative demands on the younger boys.

In 1832 Clough moved into the fifth form himself. He now had his own study and bedroom, instead of, as hitherto, sleeping in a dormitory and learning his lessons in a hall called Big School. Later he wrote to a schoolfriend 'I let myself be thoroughly corrupted during my first year and a half in the Fifth' (M, 40). He gave no details of his corruption, however, and given the sensitive nature of his conscience it is unlikely to have gone beyond uncharitable thoughts and schoolboy mischievousness. At the end of the school year he was again united with members of his family. James Clough crossed the Atlantic to bring his eldest son home and to place his youngest son George in school – without his wife, however, who had had enough of seasickness.

Arthur met his father and George when they arrived at Liverpool in July 1834 and the three crossed the channel for a visit to Paris where Charles joined them from Germany. France, Arthur told Annie, cured him of his John Bull prejudices. For the time being, he rated a stay in Paris above equal time in London or even a jaunt to the Lake District. From France he brought back

From *Tom Brown's Schooldays*: Dr Arnold rebuking defaulters

Big School at Rugby

Dr Arnold

Matthew Arnold

Tom Arnold the Younger

Jane Arnold

samples of chalk for the Rugby museum, to demonstrate the continuation of the chalk stratum under the Channel (M, 5).

When James and Charles sailed home young George was left, lonely and unhappy, at King William's School in the Isle of Man. Arthur returned to Rugby, in high hopes of rapid advancement to the sixth form, since he was now ninth in the fifth form, and ten of the sixth-form prepostors were due to leave in October. However, when at 15 he became headboy of the fifth he was too young for promotion, and had to wait until the second half of the academic year 1834–5 before he joined the sixth.

Impatient of the delay, and with no prospect of seeing his family again for another two years, Arthur became very homesick. Writing to Annie in September 1834 he recalled a period in the school sickroom in the previous term. 'I was in a room looking on Arnold's garden, and I saw all his children at their play, and I was quite by myself, and how could I help thinking of you all, and I put my feelings into verse that I might remember them afterwards, and since then I have often looked at them and added on a patch' (M, 8).

The verses survive. Written in irregular iambic hexameters, they begin:

> I watched them from the window, thy children at their play,
> And I thought of all my own dear friends, who were far, oh! far away

The poet recalls rambling on the beach with brother and sister, and tells of memories:

> Of my mother's gentle voice, and my mother's beckoning hand,
> And all the tales she used to tell of the far, far English land
> And the happy, happy evening hours when I sat on my father's knee –
> Oh! many a wave is rolling now betwixt that seat and me!

Nostalgia for England has now given way to nostalgia for Charleston.

> I used to think when I was there that my own true home was here –
> But home is not in land or sky, but in those whom each holds dear;
> The evening's cooling breeze is fanning my temples now,
> But then my frame was languid and heated was my brow,
> And I longed for England's cool and for England's breezes then,
> But now I would give full many a breeze to be back in the heat again.
> (P, 471)

Eighteen months later, Arthur published his poem in the school magazine: he signed it T.Y.C. which stood for his school nickname 'Tom Yankee Clough' (PPR, 10).

While waiting for promotion to the sixth form, Arthur devoted himself to the welfare of his younger brother, George. We know little about George, except that he had a distaste for reading and a passion for ships. Arthur regarded himself as *in loco parentis* in the absence of the family. 'To my own father I feel' he noted 'more like a chosen friend and confidant, his representative as it were in England, and the natural director and guardian of my brother.' In letters to the Isle of Man he offered various kinds of comfort.

> I believe that King William's College is worse than many places, but even here at Rugby, the best of all public schools, which are the best kind of schools, – even here there is a vast deal of bad. It was but a few nights ago that a little fellow not more than 13 years old at the very most was quite drunk and that for the second time in the last year. (M, 9)

Mainly he proffered Christian encouragement of a bracing sort:

> Do take the medicine God is giving you; it will be for your good, if you do take it, both here and hereafter . . . When tempted just think what would Papa and Mama think of me for this and above all what would God? Remember always that God is watching over far more tenderly than even Mama or Papa or any one else would when you were very ill and with far greater power to help you too. (M, 12)

At the end of the academic year 1834–5 James Clough took pity on his son's misery and moved him to a private school in Liverpool, kept by a Mr Prince. Here too, George felt frail and lonely in a godless atmosphere. Arthur urged him to accept it as a challenge:

> You are now in a very important situation; you are the only one it seems of a set of boys, who knows God, and wishes to serve him. So that you are in some manner responsible; I mean you will have to answer for some of their sins, if you do not exert yourself in their behalf, to make them better. (M, 18)

Arthur's exhortations sound today impossibly priggish; but they were in no way hypocritical. He was making no demands on George that he did not make on himself. 'You and I' he wrote 'are both placed in our different schools to do good.' George, moreover, was not the least offended or repelled by his brother's sermons. Indeed, he was so grateful that when he spent the next Christmas with Arthur at Mold, he took the savings of six years from his bank to buy a gold watch as a present (M, 31). Arthur treasured the gift and made regular notes of its timekeeping. It gained on the

Rugby college clock at a rate of 11 minutes a week: running almost as fast as its owner's conscience.

Arthur celebrated his sixteenth birthday on New Year's Day 1835 and moved into the sixth form when he returned to Rugby . It was a central feature of Arnold's system of school governance that the sixth formers should take a large part of the responsibility for imposing the school ethos. They supervised the dormitories where the youngsters slept, and helped the masters to monitor the studies in Big School. They were supposed to repress drunkenness and to prevent fighting among the boys. Clough took these responsibilities with high seriousness. An essay he wrote on school governance begins 'The character of the school depends on that of the sixth, in morality, industry, honour and Christianity' (RD, 24/3/36).

In March 1835 Clough began to keep a diary which he maintained, on and off, until he left Rugby for Oxford in August 1837. The entries vary in length and style. Sometimes there will be no more than a schedule of work done or to be done. At other times there will be details of appointments with masters, conversations with friends, walks taken and games played. Many an entry is an examination of conscience, a list of faults followed by self-reproach and resolutions of amendment. Thus, the very first entry, for 22 March, records 'too large a partaking of pancakes at dinner', followed by 'unseemly shying of lemons'. A day or two later he reproaches himself for putting off the study of Pindar because he had become fascinated by Spenser.

From the outset it is clear that Clough at this time saw his future career as lying within the Church. 'I have looked forward so long so continually to God's service, to a parish and its duties that they seem fixed as destiny could make them.' A year earlier he had written to Annie 'It would be no bad thing if you and I in some future time were to live together in some quiet Vicarage' (M, 7). When a Rugby nurse asked him if he was adequately prepared to be a clergyman, he reflected 'how unfit I must be for the spirituality and continual communing about religious things' (RD, 10/9/35).

It was not surprising that Clough saw his future as an ecclesiastical one. Not only did he owe much of his upbringing to clerical uncles, but all his closest friends at Rugby were destined for careers in the Church. The person he was later to describe as his oldest schoolfriend was John Nassau Simpkinson, future rector of many a country parish. His most poetical comrade Thomas Burbidge, the son of the town clerk of Leicester, was to have an unorthodox clerical career which took him to Malta and Palermo as Anglican chaplain. William Charles Lake, a close but difficult and sarcastic member of Arthur's circle, was to end his life as Dean of Durham.

All of Clough's close friends at Rugby were older than him. John Philip Gell, for instance, a future headmaster in Tasmania, was three years his senior. It was he who taught Arthur how to shave, and 'until he was proficient at it shaved him himself'. Most senior in age was Arthur Penrhyn Stanley, the future biographer of Thomas Arnold and Dean of Westminster. Already in the fifth form when the Cloughs arrived at Rugby, he carried off a series of College prizes.

The most potent clerical influence was, of course, Dr Arnold himself. A year after becoming headmaster he had taken over the office of chaplain, and his Sunday sermons burnt themselves into the memories of many of his pupils. Thomas Hughes recalled, from these years:

> The oak pulpit standing out by itself above the School seats. The tall gallant form, the kindling eye, the voice, now soft as the low notes of a flute, now clear and stirring as the call of a light infantry bugle, of him who stood there Sunday after Sunday, witnessing and pleading for his Lord, the King of righteousness and love and glory, with whose spirit he was filled, and in whose power he spoke. The long lines of young faces, rising tier above tier down the whole length of the chapel, from the little boy's who had just left his mother to the young man's who was going out next week into the great world.[4]

Clough was to say that during his first year in the sixth he was weak, foolish and narrow-minded, and preserved from ruin only by reading and hearing Arnold's sermons. He took them immediately to heart. For instance, in June 1835, after a sermon on charity to widows and orphans, he began a course of visits to the indigent. He did not, however, romanticize the objects of his philanthropy. Recovering from a bout of ill-health, he reflected that rather than take pills he should 'get up and visit the poor – the simple unintellectual unsophisticated poor' and 'force myself to make allowances for their faults, their murmurings and grumblings' (RD, 28/6/35).

The early months of 1835 were spent working for Rugby prizes – the English essay prize on the topic 'The English Language' and the English verse prize on the topic 'The Close of the Eighteenth Century'. For the verse prize Clough submitted an elaborate piece of work: 20 nine-line stanzas, each of eight pentameters followed by an alexandrine, with the rhyme scheme ABABCDCDD. The eighteenth century, the poem tells us, was for England a time of degrading sleep during which self and sensuality kept up a carnival of sin and shame. The revolutionary and Napoleonic wars were a summons from slumber.

> Wake, Europe, wake, the dying Age hath spoken
> The dying Century bids thee sleep no more

The blood of millions is spilt, but the peace of 1815 ushers in a period of divine deliverance. The new era is to be free both from the ferocity of battle and from the delusions of the Enlightenment, 'bewildered wisdom's atheist form'.

The writing of this poem, learning it by heart, and reciting it to the school wore Clough out. After winning the prize on 22 April he took to his bed for more than a week (M, 13). When the poem was printed he sent copies to members of his family in America, where its chauvinistic and anti-Enlightenment stance was not well received. Maria Lance, the daughter of a Charleston lawyer, complained to Annie that the poem made no mention of the United States. Clough replied that if he had to write the poem again he would certainly mention the rise of a European State in the West, and would speak with high hope of its people, 'though they be so many of them such money-getting rogues and such cut-throats'.

> With the march of intellect no doubt all foolish prejudices will be worn away, and the elevation of the fair sex to the highest honours and duties of the state will be held perfectly rational and consistent with wisdom and good sense, and in those happy times I hope Maria Lance when she becomes Lady President will do away with, and utterly abolish all such evil customs, and also that she will introduce the system of fagging into all large schools of the United States. (M, 32)

In the meantime, he believed, the US suffered from the lack of an established Church, which would provide an antidote to the terrible new ideas of every man's liberty and independence of all but himself. However, the Church must be a broad Arnoldian one. Every man had a right to his own opinions, and this inevitably led to a variety of sects within Christianity. Whatever bigots might say, members of these sects were true Christians, and could be saved; and so it was wrong to exclude them from the Church.

> So that the only alternative is to admit all such sects as are Christian sects, and believe in the essentials of Christianity, meaning by essentials, those points without which no one can be saved, and thus we shall form into one body all Christians, and all of the Kingdom, and the State would become at least completely Christian externally. (M, 33)

Banal and derivative as it is in both sentiment and expression, *The Close of the Eighteenth Century* inaugurated in Clough a passion for the writing of verse. Henceforth, the list of sins occurring in his diary regularly includes the spending of too much time producing poems.

> How well I remember the night when I sat up till 12 to write out what I had composed that evening. That excitement I shall never forget, it was indeed rich and overflowing excitement – my head troubled with aching and my eyes were half sealed up, but I went on – on – on till it was all done. (RD, 24/5/35)

Continual brooding and poring over one's own writings, he told himself, was bad, bad in the extreme for health of mind and body.

Nonetheless, as the year went on, Clough produced a sizeable crop of poems in various styles and metres, which show a notable improvement on his prize poem. He wrote a pair of competent but excessively Wordsworthian sonnets, pinning moral reflections upon the beauty of the night sky. In imitation of Macaulay he composed two solemn celebrations of Protestant heroes, Maurice of Nassau and Count Egmont (P, 461–2, 468–71). More successful than any of these was *The Poacher of Dead Man's Corner or The Legend of Devil's Turning*. This poem of 200 lines tells the story, in stanzas of varying length and metre, of a Warwickshire poacher who died of terror two days after seeing a night vision of his mother and brothers attending his own funeral. The poem contains many lines which might well be spared, but the central sections are successful in creating an eerie and macabre effect. More significantly for the future, the poet, for the first time, turns his back on solemnity and begins to experiment with wit and irony. Thus the ballad begins:

> Reader (if such blest being shall appear)
> A lay to thee – a simple lay I bring;
> A simple tale, as simply told, is here;
> No faery sprites have I whereof to sing
> Nor headless dames, nor riders quaint and queer,
> Nor elves all dancing in the faery ring –
> Mine is a humbler muse, yet do not scorn her
> Albeit she sing the tale of Dead Man's Corner . . .
>
> Gentles that do, and gentles that do not
> Believe in ghosts, to what suits both I call you.
> Ye that strong nerves, and ye that weak have got,
> Nor sentiment nor horror shall befall you.
> Ye that do shoot, and ye that never shot,
> To please you both I come with naught to gall you
> O be ye sad or glad, or grave or gay,
> Come, gentles all, come listen to my lay.
>
> (P, 462–3)

The apprentice poet is now trying out the tools of Byron as well as those of Wordsworth and Macaulay.

These poems appeared in July 1835 in the first issue of a new Rugby magazine, of which Clough was for practical purposes the editor. Nowadays the CV of every Oxbridge candidate will contain a stint of editorial work on a school magazine, but in the 1830s school magazines were new and rare things. The Rugby magazine was not a record of the academic and sporting achievements of pupils, nor was it aimed only at present and past members of the school. It was much more ambitious: in its content and in its target public it attempted to emulate, so far as schoolboy talent and interests would allow, the literary quarterlies of the age. Clough was himself a major contributor, the most prolific of all with the exception of his poetic friend Thomas Burbidge.

The high hopes which Clough entertained for the venture appear in a prayer which he composed asking God that his work on the magazine might be an instrument of good to the school and to all boys elsewhere. His two principal objects at this time, he told his brother George, were '1st, the improvement of the school. 2nd, the publication and telling abroad of the merit of the School by means of the Magazine' (M, 19). He regarded the editing of the magazine as a solemn and religious task; this did not prevent him from rebuking himself regularly in his diary for spending too much time on 'Maga' and too little on his studies.

In the summer vacation of 1835 Clough was, as usual, passed like a parcel throughout the Clough cousinage. Years later, writing to his fiancée, he recalled:

> Holiday after holiday, when I was at school, after a week or so of recreation, which very seldom came in an enjoyable form to me, the whole remaining 5 or 6 weeks I used to give to regular work at fixed hours. That wasn't so very easy, you know, for a schoolboy spending holidays, not at home, but with Uncles and Aunts, and Cousins. (M, 310)

This summer he spent some time at Oxford with his Uncle Alfred at Jesus, visiting the Cheltenham races with him. Then he took a coach from Shrewsbury to Beaumaris. There he rearranged the furniture in his bedroom to make it resemble a Rugby study, urging his mother to advertise the magazine in Charleston (M, 15–17). A few weeks later he migrated to Min-y-Don, a hundred yards from the sea by Colwyn Bay, the home of his three maiden aunts Jemima, Martha Matilda and Anna Maria, and of a cousin Margaret Marshall Clough, who had lost both her parents. Min-y-Don was the lodging he hated most. Visiting it years later he told his fiancée 'to me as a boy it was intolerable when I thought of course that there was no exit out of it'. He could hope, however, that this would be his last homeless summer: the family were planning to return in the following year and settle once again in Liverpool.

At Rugby Arthur was more lonely than ever. All his close Rugby friendships had been formed with boys older than himself, and by the time he returned to school for the year 1835–6 these had all gone on elsewhere. Stanley had gone up to Balliol on a scholarship the previous year; now he was followed there by Lake. Burbidge and Gell and Simpkinson had all gone away to Cambridge. Of all these departed ones, it was Simpkinson whom Clough missed most. 'I am now quite alone' he wrote to Annie when Simpkinson left 'and am doomed so to remain for two long years' (M, 19). To Simpkinson he wrote 'I don't know which to think greatest, the blessing of being under Arnold, or the curse of being without a home' (M, 24).

Simpkinson's departure meant that Clough was now the head of the School-house, 'an office' he explained to young George 'of considerable trust and great difficulty' (M, 21). The other houses at Rugby each had as housemaster an assistant master, after whom the house would be named: 'Anstey's', 'Bird's' and so on. The School-house, which contained 60 or 70 boarders, was the one house which was presided over by the headmaster himself. The sixth-former who was head of the School-house was therefore, of all the boys in the school, the one closest to Arnold. 'When I have confidence in the Sixth' Arnold famously said 'there is no post in England which I would exchange for this; but if they do not support me, I must go.'[5] Clough bent every nerve to make the form of which he was the head worthy of Arnold's confidence (M, 35).

He found it a painful task. 'There are a great many unprincipled fellows in the Sixth now' Clough wrote to Gell in October 1835. The form, as he saw it, was divided into two camps. The members of his own camp, he believed, were superior in intellect and full of good intentions, but there was a great deal of weakness and want of gentlemanly manner. On the other side lay the physical strength of the school, the greater part of its gentlemanliness, and the advantage of numbers. Every day there were desertions from the better side. The good characters were industrious, and the bad ones idle, 'so that when a fellow wants a companion he is much more likely to pitch on a bad than a good one' (M, 23).

Clough could, of course, rely on the support of Arnold, who always backed up his prepostors – often excessively so. Several such occasions are reported in a letter to Stanley at Balliol. For example, on Guy Fawkes night, 5 November, persons unknown let off some fireworks despite an express prohibition. A prepostor identified seven culprits and reported them to Arnold, who took his word that they were guilty, and threatened flogging and expulsion. It turned out that every one of the seven was innocent (M, 30).

Arnold's support, in fact, was a mixed blessing for someone like Clough who wished to win over the schoolboys' hearts and minds. After two successful issues of the Rugby magazine in July and October, the editorial committee considered prefacing the third number, due out in January 1836, with a dedication to the headmaster. The decision to do so was taken only after long debate on the prior question 'whether the opinion of Arnold's being disliked is more prevalent or that of his being idolized' (RD, 7/9/35).

As 1835 drew to its close Clough's attention focused less on the magazine and more on the end-of-term oral examinations. He was placed in the first class for each of the mainline subjects of Composition, Divinity, Classics, and History, besides winning a prize for the Greek, Latin and English prose and verse submitted during the previous term (M, 28, 34).

The Christmas vacation was, for the last time, a peripatetic one. Arthur left Rugby on 16 December, stopped at Leicester to review magazine proofs with Burbidge and then, with his brother George, spent Christmas with Uncle Charles at Mold, and the early days of the new year at Min-y-don. On 13 January he parted with George and stayed out the rest of the vacation at Chester. A visit with cousins to a New Year's ball made a deep impression on the 17-year-old, recalled a quarter of a century later in the last year of his life.

The reader will recall that the hero of the semi-autobiographical poem *Primitiae*, Edmund, had struck up, at the age of 12, a childish friendship with his slightly older cousin Emily at Beaumaris. The poem records a second visit five years later to the same family of cousins, who have now moved inland to a country parsonage, near to the rectory of the hero's uncle. Summoned to a ball, Edmund is far from enchanted by the prospect.

> A schoolboy still, but now, indeed
> About to college to proceed,
> Dancing was, let it be confessed,
> To me no pleasure at the best:
> Of girls and of their lovely looks
> I thought not, busy with my books.
> (P, 382)

Nonetheless, he accepts the invitation, and on arrival finds the younger girls as warm and affectionate as ever. Emily, however, now a lofty 19, is changed almost out of recognition and puts the schoolboy out of countenance. He takes no pleasure at all in the dance.

> The music scarcely touched my ears,
> The figures fluttered me with fears.
> I talked, but had not aught to say,
> Danced, my instructions to obey;
> E'en when with beautiful good will

Emilia through the long quadrille
Conducted me, alas the day,
Ten times I wished myself away.

Emily, to be sure, cuts a magnificent figure, mingling serenely in the dance:

Not stately she, nor grand, nor tall
Yet looked as if controlling all
The fluctuations of the ball . . .
(P, 383)

She dances twice with Edmund, asks him about the prizes he has won, congratulates him on his learning, and warns him against overwork. Despite this flattering attention, Edmund remains tongue-tied, and counts the moments until, at one o'clock, he can make his escape from the ball, long before it is over.

Once he is safely in bed, however, a change comes over him.

[T]he brief sleep of closing night,
Brought a sensation of delight
Which, when I woke, was exquisite.
The music moving in my brain
I felt; in the gay crowd again
Half felt, half saw the girlish bands,
On their white skirts their white-gloved hands,
Advance, retreat, and yet advance,
And mingle in the mingling dance.
The impulse had arrived at last,
When the opportunity was past.
(P, 384)

The morning after the ball Edmund is persuaded to stay on for some days, but the visit is not a success. He finds that he cannot articulate the strange new appetites of which he has become conscious. He is scolded by the younger girls for ignoring their music making and absconding to his room. Listening to a discussion of the comparative merits of the local beauties, he blurts out that he takes greater pleasure in looking on Llynidwal lake than on any female face. 'Does the lake' Emily muttered tartly 'return your tender sentiments?'

It is difficult to be sure whether the verses report an actual abortive adolescent flirtation, and if so, which of many cousins was the prototype of Emily. However the verses are likely to be an accurate recall of Clough's ambivalence about the other sex in the years just after the onset of puberty. As 'Edmund' puts it:

How ill our boyhood understands
Incipient manhood's keen demands!
(P, 385)

The year 1836 was an important one in Clough's life, and because of his loneliness it is particularly well documented: he wrote many letters to his ex-schoolfriends now at Oxford and Cambridge and he made many detailed entries in his diaries. At the beginning of the year, at the suggestion of Lake, he decided to sit, in the following November, the scholarship examination for entry to Balliol College in Oxford. He was undeterred by the contrary urging of his Cambridge friends Simpkinson, Gell and Burbidge. The Balliol scholarship was regarded as the blue riband of schoolboy academic achievement. When Stanley had won it in 1834, Arnold had given the school a half holiday. In *Tom Brown's Schooldays* there is no better way for a senior scholar to impress upon a new boy the importance of football than to say 'I'd sooner win two School-house matches running than get the Balliol scholarship any day' (Hughes 1857: 123). A particular attraction of Balliol for Clough was that it already contained what he described as 'a High Arnold set' of scholars (B, 31).

In preparation for the examination Clough worked desperately hard, especially on Roman history (M, 34, 36). But he continued to find time for the magazine. The third issue, which appeared in January, carried a new poem of his, *The Song of the Hyperborean Maidens*. Six eight-line stanzas of bouncing anapaests, triggered by a passage in Herodotus that tells of two girls who travelled from the far north of Europe to bring gifts to a shrine on the island of Delos, the poem could pass for one written by Swinburne on a bad day.[6]

The prospect of going to Oxford aroused Clough's interest in religious, political and social issues outside the school. In letters he speculated on candidates for the Oxford divinity professorship, worried about the forthcoming general election, and commended the Report of the Poor-Law Commissioners, which he described as 'very amusing and instructive' (M, 37). His political leanings were towards the Whigs, and he welcomed Lord John Russell's Irish Tithe Bill (M, 39).

To judge by his diary, however, the internal affairs of the School-house were still his main preoccupation. He rebuked himself from time to time for weakness in the repression of fisticuffs and drunkenness. A new problem presented himself in the sixth form: William Conybeare, son of the geologist W. D. Conybeare, the discover of the ichthyosaurus. The young Conybeare, Clough told his friends, was coarse and rude and had become the worst bully in the school (B, 36; M, 48).

At the end of term examinations, Clough won the Latin verse prize, and was placed second in the competition for Latin prose and Greek verse. He wrote to his mother to tell her this, and to explain to her why he was competing for the Balliol scholarship.

> I shall not be very sorry to go to Oxford now, for I find Stanley and Lake like it very much, and I daresay Dr. Arnold will be a Bishop before very long. I only hope it may not be just yet. I must however do my very best to go there as I wish, namely with a Balliol scholarship, and that not only for the honour's sake – although the honour is the greatest part of it – but for the £30 per annum, which with an exhibition will, I trust, all but pay my way at Oxford, as Balliol is £20 or £30 cheaper than any other college, I understand. (M, 44)

After paying more than 50 guineas a year to Rugby, the elder Cloughs must have been very attracted by the prospect of their son becoming virtually self-supporting at Oxford.

The Easter vacation was a joyous time, when friends from the Oxbridge diaspora looked in on the old school for a few days on their way home. Burbidge, Lake, Gell and Simpson were reunited with Clough for a week of walking and talking; recalling it immediately afterwards Clough told Simpkinson that he was almost *too* happy. 'I really think that after the summer when my Father and mother and sister are come over I shall have too much happiness, and I am almost afraid of looking forward to that time, lest I should get to expect it too fondly and so be disappointed' (M, 45).

Meanwhile, the Arnolds provided a surrogate family. In March Clough had dined in their house, and stayed four hours, talking to Mrs Arnold about America. The youngest daughters were of the party, Susanna aged six and Frances aged three. 'Talked to Susy and made her love me, I hope' he wrote in his diary. In May he wrote to Simpkinson:

> I love Arnold, and Mrs Arnold, and the children, very much . . . It was but yesterday when I was thinking about these things, and just after Arnold had been very kind to me and asked me to dinner to meet Mrs Stanley (St's mother) and I had shaken hands with his sister, though no more, and I had talked to Lady Munro, who is indeed worthy of her husband and her boy, and Mrs Arnold had been almost too good to me, and I had been playing with little Susey, one of whose special favourites I am, and indeed I am sure I never could love Rugby more and feel more happy in this present situation than I did then. (M, 46)

Throughout his life, Clough was good with children: but in the contrast between the concentration on young Susey and the brief handshake with Miss Stanley perhaps one can detect the unease in the presence of young ladies that so afflicted 'Edmund'.

By now Clough was losing his enthusiasm for the magazine. After the first issue had sold well at Rugby, Oxford, Cambridge, London and Edinburgh, subsequent issues failed to cover their costs. As he prepared to send off copy for the fourth issue Clough proposed that the magazine should be brought to an end with a single volume covering the issues of 1835–6. He gave notice that in any case he did not wish to edit it beyond one further issue (M, 41).

Clough contributed three poems to the magazine in 1836. In a valedictory to a friend leaving for India he laments that they will no longer even share the same night sky – but they will, of course, still have one God. *The Old Man of Athens* exhibits classical erudition in laboured 15-syllable lines. The third poem is an apostrophe to Poesy, comparing her to the moon and exalting her above science and art as the lesser lights of the planet. This highly romantic piece – owing more to Keats and Shelley than to Wordsworth – is the most successful of the three, but the poet obviously felt he could not present it with a straight face, and gave it the ironic title 'The exordium of a very long poem' (P, 474–8).

An Apology, written probably in May, and clearly meant as a farewell to the magazine, resorts to the blocked writer's device of writing about writer's block (P, 482–4). Despite the welcome arrival of a long-delayed spring, the poet has lost all inspiration.

> I have not lost my finger's use
>   I have not lost my pen and ink
> And oft with musings most abstruse
>   Of Lady Maga do I think,
> Least, least of all forget I thee
>   Thou gentle power of poesy
> Yet am I mute as moulting bird
>   I cannot write a single word.

The next half-dozen stanzas describe, often with happy touches, the overdue advent of spring 'like truant child with guilty face and dried-up tears'. Each stanza ends, like the first, with the affirmation of inability to write a single word. Then:

> A pretty thing indeed it says
>   The last line of this eighth long stanza!
> In these utilitarian days
>   Poetic fiction ne'er will answer; –
> That tells, O honesty divine,
>   An open lie in each eighth line;
> Truly 'twere much to be preferred
>   That thou didst never write a word.

In the final stanza, the poet apologizes to Poesy and makes amends:

'Tis time indeed that truth was heard –
I'll write no more a single word.

That too, however, turned out to be false. In the event the magazine was continued, over Clough's objection, for a second volume which began in July 1836. He was to contribute nine more poems before he left the school, and he remained as the leading editor until the journal's final issue.

Summer 1836 brought the long-awaited return of the Clough family to England. Writing to his mother the previous March, Arthur had told her he suffered from periods of severe depression. 'I hope I am conquering these fits' he wrote 'and when you are come over and settled, I think they may cease altogether' (M, 43). He began the summer with the usual peregrination of aunts and uncles, but by mid-July he was in Liverpool, looking out lodgings for the family. In preparation for greeting his now much Americanized sister he read De Tocqueville's *Democracy in America*. He admired the work greatly: 'The man is so wise, and so good too, for a Frenchman' (M, 49).

The lodgings Arthur rented were found too cramped by the family when they moved in at the beginning of August. James Clough found it hard to adjust to the noise generated by the younger generation, and Annie found her younger brother George a source of constant irritation. But she found Arthur, after five years separation, quite adorable: 'a blooming youth of seventeen', as she later recalled 'with an abundance of dark soft hair, a fresh complexion, much colour, and shining eyes full of animation' (PPR, 12).

This summer was the last time the three Clough brothers were to be all together. In September the 19-year-old Charles sailed alone to America, and George, back at school, received a letter from his elder brother exhorting him to behave better at Christmas (M, 51; RD, 24/9/36). The parents and sister eventually found a house at 24 Hope Street, near the present site of the Roman Catholic cathedral: adequate, but a comedown from the Rodney Street mansion in which the children had been born (B, 48). Arthur himself seems to have been ill at ease in Liverpool, to judge by a short and mawkish poem written during the summer vacation. Entitled *An Incident* it complains of the commercialism of the city's crowded streets, redeemed only by the sight of a little boy hand-in-hand with his sister wearing a pinafore and carrying a basket of fruit and flowers.

Once back at Rugby for his final year Clough found the new sixth form much more to his liking than the previous one. The sixth form room was refurbished and refurnished with a grant from Arnold and the Trustees.

> We have our supper in the most gentlemanly fashion in the Room together, on a tray with plates and knives, and we buy very good cheeses occasionally for ourselves, and make a very sociable meal of it. (To Simpkinson, M, 52)

There was also to be a new sixth-form library, and Clough seems to have been in charge of the design and making the arrangements for a rota of librarians.

The return of his family seems to have had a good effect on Clough's health. Previously, his diary often mentioned indigestion and frequent headaches in addition to the usual adolescent infections such as measles (M, 40), and was full of complaints about the apothecary's bill. The autumn diaries of 1836, the most sober and complete of the series, contain many mentions of walking, cross-country running and especially of swimming in the Avon, where the Trustees had rented a mile of the river for the boys' bathing.

In her memoir of her brother Annie remarks, in a sentence echoed mockingly by Lytton Strachey, that Arthur suffered from a weakness in his ankles which prevented his attaining proficiency in games such as cricket and fives. Nonetheless, she tells us, 'his name is handed down in William Arnold's "Rules of Football" as the best goal-keeper on record'. William's elder brother Thomas also recalled his prowess.

> He wore neither jersey nor cap; in a white shirt, and with bare head, he would face the rush of the other side as they pressed the ball within the line of the goal-posts; and not seldom by desperate struggles he was the first to touch it down thus baulking the enemy of his expected try. (Veyriras 1964: 45)

Football at Rugby in Clough's day was somewhat different from the highly regulated game of skill that is Rugby Union today. There could be up to a hundred players a side, and no form of holding was barred in the scrum, with the exception of throttling and strangling which, the rules said sternly 'are totally opposed to the principle of the game'. Hacking was permitted provided hobnails and iron plates were not used. 'Rugby football' as the College historian admits 'was not then a game for tender hearted parents to look on with equanimity' (Rouse, 164).

Clough, however, as is clear from his diary, revelled in the game, and when leaving Rugby he recalled 'our broad fair Close with foot-ball's hundreds gay' (P, 505). On 3 October 1836 he records that he took part in a match 'in high and familiar spirits' . . . 'Touched the balls sufficiently well and had my hat crushed in a great scrimmage for it.' For each of the next two weeks he proudly recalls 'two goal keepings'. The great match of the year (as readers of *Tom Brown's Schooldays* will recall: Hughes 1857: 97–113) was the one in which the school house played against all the rest of the school. This might last as long as four days. In 1836 the game began on Saturday 12 November ('we kicked a goal and I nearly got a black eye') and ended on Monday 13 November ('the school house match played and finished by the "all below" kicking two goals; not without a little ill-will'). Clough lamented the drinking and singing of songs which followed the game ('a dozen fellows intoxicated last night which is indeed a disgrace'), and he sought consolation for the ill-will generated by the school-house's defeat by reading to himself the Sermon on the Mount.

At the same time, Clough kept in training by cross-country running. At the end of October he took part in a hare-and-hounds run of eight miles in unseasonable snow. When he repeated the course a week later, he arrived back too late for locking-up time, and went in great distress for fear of Arnold's anger. But when he saw Arnold on the following day he found – like Tom Brown in an exactly similar case – that the great man was extremely kind (Hughes 1857: 153–6).

November was not only the month of the school-house match: it was the month of the Balliol scholarship examination, held always near 25 November, the feast of the College's patron St Catherine. Clough went up to Oxford for nine days, and was taken under the wing of Stanley, who introduced him to one of the tutors, William George Ward, who was later to play a big part in his life.

The examination papers for the scholarship were written for several days in the College Hall, commonly unsupervised by any Fellow, and the proceedings on this occasion were unusually noisy and chaotic (K, xi). Clough kept his head and did himself justice: the assembled Fellows of Balliol, according to Stanley, were profoundly impressed when his English essay was read aloud to them. On Saturday 26 November he was able to write to his father:

> I have just come out from Balliol, of which College I am now a scholar. The examination concluded this morning about 12 o'clock and it has just been given out. I have got the Head one, which also includes an Exhibition, added to it to make it more valuable – as of themselves these scholarships are not worth much. (M, 53)

He stayed in Oxford until the following Wednesday in order to be matriculated into the University by the Vice-Chancellor on Tuesday 30 November.

On his return to Rugby Clough collapsed, and fell victim to headaches and feverish nights without sleep. As the sickroom was already full, he was taken into the Arnold's house. In the previous term he had become quite intimate with Mrs Arnold, often taking tea with her and noting meticulously in his diary her minor ailments and recoveries. When his convalescence was complete he was given an invitation to spend ten days at Fox How, the holiday house near Ambleside in the Lake District that the Arnolds had owned since 1832 (M, 54–7).

Before going to Fox How in the New Year, Clough spent Christmas week at home, and then went on family visits in Wales. If the behaviour of 'Edmund' of *Primitiae* is a safe guide, the winning of the scholarship had gone to Clough's head: he overcame his last year's shyness with his cousins at the price of becoming a coxcomb.

> Next year I went and spent a week,
> And certainly had learnt to speak . . .
> I talked in a superior tone
> Of things the girls had never known,
> Far wiser to have let alone;
> Things which the father knew in short
> By country-clerical report;
> I talked of much I thought I knew
> Used all my college wit anew,
> A little on my fancy drew;
> Religion, politics, O me!
> No subject could sufficient be.

This tactlessness, we are told, was the work of 'the busy argufying brain / of the prize schoolboy'. Unsurprisingly, the visit was not a success: 'Ill went the visit, ill the ball.'

> When I went away
> Alas, the farewells were not warm,
> The kissing was a weary form;
> Emilia was *distraite* and sad,
> And everything was bad and bad.
> (P, 386–8)

The visit to Fox How, however, was a great success, and Arthur reported glowingly to his family on the charm of his first sight of the Lake District and the thrill of walks with Arnold over Loughrigg fell. He was even introduced to William Wordsworth, a neighbour at Rydal Mount who, to his astonishment, lamented that in his published poems he had exaggerated the importance of flowers and fields, waterfalls and scenery (PPR, 324) .

Clough returned to Rugby for the remainder of the academic year. He was much happier during these final months in school, partly because Burbidge, having got into some scrape which led to his being rusticated from Cambridge, had returned to live under Arnold's supervision, in lodgings on the Dunchurch road. Clough found him most helpful in the production of the final numbers of the Rugby magazine. 'It is a greater blessing to me than I can well describe to have him here, and see every day at least once' he wrote to Simpkinson (M, 58).

The month of March was a propitious one. On the 6th Arnold announced in his morning lecture that Stanley had won the Ireland scholarship, the major award for classics at Oxford. This was celebrated throughout the school, and Clough wrote into his diary 'Hip Hip Hip Hurrah'. A few days later Wordsworth arrived to stay with the Arnolds, and Clough and Burbidge were invited to tea with him. Finally, Clough won the two school prizes that remained for him to win – the Latin essay and the Greek verse. The last one was shared with Richard Congreve, the future 'father of English positivism', who was due to go up to Wadham at the year's end.

The winter was long and the spring was cold, and this put a damper on the Easter reunion of the old Rugby set. Clough lamented the weather in a moralizing poem on the unsatisfactory nature of the vernal equinox:

> When gentle airs should rustle by
> And light clouds float along the sky
> And leaves should sprout and birds should sing
> And it should be, but is not, Spring.
>
> (P, 488)

Nonetheless Vaughan, Lake and Stanley came as usual, and Stanley brought the news that his father was to be the new Bishop of Norwich. Clough rejoiced that he was likely to be a staunch friend to the Whigs (M, 60).

The main task of the ten weeks after Easter was to prepare for the last school examination at the end of June. This was a competition, marked by external examiners from Oxford and Cambridge, for an exhibition to assist in funding Rugby scholars at university. Clough worked hard and was successful: but he did not let his cramming stand in the way of his final contributions to the magazine. One of the very last entries in his Rugby diary reads 'Sat up till 3 writing verses which is longer than I ever did before. The birds are singing and I hear the cuckoos and the doves. It is daylight and I feel quite sober but it will not do.'

The summer vacation in Liverpool was, in the words of Annie, a summer of financial distress. It was a difficult time for Liverpool merchants. Arthur's maternal uncle, Mr Crowder of Finch House in West Derby, was associated with James Clough in business ventures: earlier in the academic year Charles had sent from America disturbing news about the fortunes of the Crowders. Other friends of the Cloughs, the Buchanans, were rumoured to have been declared bankrupt. Among his family, Arthur had become used to keeping his new Whiggism under wraps; during this summer he was surprised to discover that the Liverpool poor (at least 'the respectable poor') actually preferred the Tories (M, 63).

After the vacation Clough returned to Rugby for the beginning of the half-year, for the seven weeks before the Oxford term began. It was in these last few weeks that the headmaster's sons, Matthew and Thomas Arnold, joined the school in the fifth form, having transferred from Winchester after several unhappy terms there (M, 63). Clough himself had become something of a school legend. William Hodson, a sixth former who was later to win fame in the cavalry during the Indian mutiny, greeted a new boy who arrived in October with these words: 'What a fool you were not to come a week earlier – because then you could have said one day that you had been at school with Tom Clough.'[7]

After Clough had departed for Oxford, Dr Arnold wrote the following testimonial to Clough's Jesus uncle Alfred, a regular attender at Rugby functions.

> I cannot resist my desire of congratulating you most heartily on the delightful close of your nephew's long career at Rugby, where he has passed eight years without a fault, so far as the School is concerned, where he has gone on ripening gradually in all excellence intellectual and spiritual, and from whence he has now gone to Oxford, not only full of honours, but carrying with him the respect and love of all whom he has left behind, and regarded by myself, I may truly say, with an affection and interest hardly less than I should feel for my own son. (M, 65)

Clough's last bequest to Rugby was a clutch of poems for the November issue of the magazine. The heaviest and weakest is *Rosabel's Dream*, 360 lines of would-be antique verse, packed with the small change of romantic vocabulary: 'damsels', 'what time', 'ladye', 'wassailry', 'chaunt', 'fays' and the like. The long narrative has no point except to raise the moral issue of whether one is responsible for what one does in dreams.

> 'Tis ill to choose, though but in dream
> What waking conscience dreads as sin;
> For who shall say no guiding beam
> Lit the dark labyrinth within,
> No whisper checked with mild controul
> The grosser instincts of the soul?
> (P, 498)

Despite the faery gossamer wrapping, the problem seems to have been a serious moral issue for Clough. One can only hope that he was reassured when, in the penultimate stanza of the poem, an angel tells fair Rosabelle:

Maiden, if when sleep hath bound thee
  Evil thoughts within awaken;
Evil spirits move around thee
  Fear not! Thou art not forsaken.
(P, 501)

Much more successful are two explicitly valedictory poems. Eighteen untitled eight-line stanzas take their start from the thought that 'slowly, strand by strand / the rope is parting that as yet hath bound / so many hearts to boyhood's lessening land'. The poet recalls the sights and sounds of Warwickshire excursions, piling up evocative place names and describing local scenes in affectionate and often felicitous detail. Clough here does for the Rugby countryside what Matthew Arnold, with a more practised hand, was to do for the Oxford countryside in *The Scholar Gipsy*.

Already Clough feels at a distance from his Rugby past:

'Tis Autumn here as there, sedately tinted
  With steady light the lazy clouds repose,
The moistened ground with tiny footsteps printed
  Tells of the flitting birds; and the late rose,
More deeply hued, more delicately scented,
  Across the naked trellis sadly throws
A dim faint light of Summer, – a serene
  Memento of the glories that have been.
(P, 507)

Clough had no illusions that a returning to one's old school could ever recreate the joys and miseries of boyhood. A week or two after leaving he was, he realized, already an old boy; whenever he returned to the school he would bore youngsters with reminiscences of the great days of the past. This universal phenomenon has not often been so well captured in verse as in *The Effusions of a School-Patriarch*. Only old Rugbeians will appreciate the name-dropping and the cryptic argot of all seven jovial stanzas of this poem, but its first verse needs no crib.

In the days when twenty fellows
  Drank out of one large mug
And pewter were the dishes,
  And a tin can was the jug; –
In the days when shoes and boots were
  Three times a week japanned,
And we sat on stools, not sofas –
  There were giants in the land.
(P, 502)

Notes

1 Details of the Clough's life in Charleston are taken from PPR, 1–9, and from the memoirs of Anne Jemima Clough.

2 *Mari Magno*, P, 378. The autobiographical nature of the Lawyer's First Tale is vouched for by Blanche Clough (PPR, 1, 10; P, 378); the location of the family of cousins as Beaumaris is clear from the detailed description on p. 387 which describes the house as looking across ten miles of water to Great Orme's head, flanked by the Carnedd mountains on the right and the open sea on the left.

3 See M. McCrum, *Thomas Arnold, Headmaster*, Oxford 1989, p. 124.

4 Thomas Hughes, *Tom Brown's Schooldays*, London 1857, p. 181.

5 A. P. Stanley, *The Life of Thomas Arnold D. D.*, London 1844; 1903, p. 171.

6 The comparison would not be welcomed by Swinburne, who once wrote

    There was a bad poet named Clough
    Whom his friends found it useless to puff
    For the public, if dull
    Has not quite such a skull
    As belongs to believers in Clough.

7 Katherine Chorley, *Arthur Hugh Clough: the Uncommitted Mind*, Oxford 1962, p. 33.

Chapter Two

Clough at Balliol

The Oxford to which Clough went up in 1837 was still a religious and almost monastic institution. It was a necessary condition for matriculation to subscribe to the Thirty-Nine Articles of the Church of England, so that not only Jews and atheists, but also Dissenters and Catholics were excluded from membership. Attempts to modify or abolish the obligation of subscription had been defeated in the University and in Parliament in 1835. Each member of the University attended daily morning and evening service in college chapel, according to the Church of England prayer book. The heads of the constituent colleges of the University, who collectively formed its governing executive ('Hebdomadal Board'), were all clergymen. So too were most of the college fellows who provided the basic teaching faculty of the University; these, as long as they retained their college posts, were obliged to be celibate, and if they wished to marry they resigned their fellowships and took up parochial or educational duties elsewhere. The fellows ate their main meals at High Table in the College Halls where the undergraduates dined, and they took their recreation together in a common room. The heads of house, who alone were allowed to be married, maintained, with their wives, separate establishments in dignified lodgings within the college walls. It was a consequence of the system that there was a much larger age gap between the university's governing group and the majority of its faculty than there was between the faculty and the students.

The chief executive officer of the University was the Vice-Chancellor. The heads of house took it in turns to hold this office in accordance with a rota of colleges. Neither the Vice-Chancellor nor the Hebdomadal Board, however, held absolute sway in the University. Their power was limited in two ways. The ultimate governing body of the University was Convocation, the assembly of all living masters of arts. Convocation included the teaching faculty, but they formed only a minority of those entitled to vote; on a contentious issue London lawyers and legislators might turn up, and also, in much greater number, clergymen from country livings. But the activities of both Convocation and Hebdomadal Board could be checked by the veto of two proctors, tribunes of the people chosen from among the college fellows to hold office for a year at a time.

The view from Balliol in the 1830s

An Oxford examinee in schools

In the first decades of the nineteenth century a series of reforms had raised academic standards throughout the University. Scholarships, hitherto often conferred through patronage, had been thrown open to competitive examination; fellowships began to be awarded on merit rather than by grace and favour. In order to obtain the degree of Bachelor of Arts undergraduates had to pass two examinations. The first was Responsions ('Little-Go') in which they were questioned orally in Greek and Latin and in logic and geometry. The second public examination, held in the fourth year after matriculation, contained written papers in religion, in *literae humaniores* (Greek and Latin literature and history, plus composition and logic) and, optionally, in the elements of mathematics and physics. The examinations were conducted on a University-wide basis and each year lists were published grading the candidates in classes. Colleges watched the performance of their undergraduates in these class-lists and also took pride when their members won prestigous prizes offered on the basis of other, optional, academic competitions.

Hand-in-hand with academic reform in Oxford had gone a degree of moral and religious reform. There was still room in many colleges for the aristocratic and well-to-do idlers, familiar from many a Victorian novel, who had no serious intention of obtaining degrees, and spent their time at Oxford in hunting, drinking, gambling, whoring and running up debts. But other colleges showed decreasing tolerance for the species, and devoted their main efforts to the encouragement of 'reading men' from less privileged families. Everywhere, it is fair to say, there was a growth in the seriousness of moral and religious attitudes. There was no agreement, however, where true seriousness in religion lay.

The college heads, for the most part, wished to preserve the established Church in the form in which it had emerged from the eighteenth century, in which many of them had been born. Their view of the nature of Christianity was very similar to that of the curates of Jane Austen, who were much of an age with them, and of Trollope's Archdeacon Grantly, who belonged to the generation just after them. They were hostile to Dissent and to Rome, and within the Church of England they were suspicious of any novel ideas without being particularly curious about its traditional doctrines. Christian morality, in their view, upheld decency and promoted benevolence, without demanding any great self-denial. Those who viewed Christianity in this light were High Churchmen – known by the younger generation as 'high and drys'.

When Clough arrived in Oxford the University was in a state of religious ferment. Several reforming currents were threatening the conservatism of the high and drys: the evangelical, the Anglo-Catholic and the liberal. The evangelical tradition laid stress on private Bible reading and on interio religious sentiment, the sense of sinfulness, the experience of conversion, and the conviction of personal salvation. The Anglo-Catholic movement, called

'Tractarian' because of the *Tracts for the Times* which had propagated its tenets from 1833, aimed to foster within the Church of England an emphasis on the mystical power of sacramental rites and symbols. It insisted on the necessity of a priesthood in succession to the apostles, to administer the sacraments validly and to give authoritative interpretation to the Bible.

The evangelical and Tractarian views of the priesthood are contrasted by Anthony Trollope in *Barchester Towers* when he describes the newspaper controversy between two clergymen, Mr Slope and Mr Arabin.

> Mr Slope declared that the main part of the consecration of a clergyman was the self-devotion of the inner man to the duties of the ministry. Mr Arabin contended that a man was not consecrated at all, had, indeed, no single attribute of a clergyman, unless he became so through the imposition of some bishop's hands, who had become a bishop through the imposition of other hands, and so on in a direct line to one of the apostles.

A young man coming to Oxford in the late 1830s did not necessarily have to side with either Slope or Arabin: there was a third option, the liberal current, which saw the essence of Christianity as being morality in conduct and motive, and which agreed with Slope in rejecting the apostolic succession doctrine of the Tractarians and with Arabin in despising the emotional and sanctimonious pretensions of the evangelicals.

Nationally the leader of the liberal Anglicans was Thomas Arnold whose 1833 manifesto had set out a blueprint for a broad and tolerant Church. In Oxford the liberal torch had been carried by his friend and one-time Oriel colleague, Renn Dickson Hampden, who in March 1834 was appointed Professor of Moral Philosophy. In the same year, supported by Arnold, he proposed a motion in Convocation to abolish subscription to the articles. It was defeated by 459 votes to 57. In 1836 the Whig government of Lord Melbourne appointed Hampden to hold the senior theological position in the University, the Regius Professorship of Divinity. Tractarians and evangelicals banded together with the high-and-dry faction to protest against this on the grounds that a series of lectures he had given in 1832 had been heretical. In March 1836 a vote of censure was prepared, depriving the Regius Professor of important prerogatives within the University.

* * *

It was the Hampden affair which brought young Arthur Clough, still a schoolboy at Rugby, face-to-face with the state of religious controversy in the Church of England. In March 1836 he wrote to his mother:

> There was to have been a Convocation of all the Graduate members of the University last Tuesday, and we should have had a whole holiday to allow the masters to go up and vote, but lo and behold, it was stopped suddenly by the Proctors, one of whom is Uncle Alfred's friend Henry Reynolds, the Jesus mathematician. It seems they can prevent all Masters of Arts from voting. So the Anti-Hampdenites are furious, and I know not what they will do. (M, 44)

All that the anti-Hampdenites had to do was to wait for a new pair of proctors to take office. Two months later the vote of no confidence in Hampden was carried by 474 to 94.

The leading spirits in promoting the censure had been the Tractarians. Arnold, outraged, published an anonymous article in the *Edinburgh Review*. He did not give it the title under which it became famous: 'The Oxford Malignants'. But he minced no words in his attack on the Tractarians.

> The attack on Dr Hampden bears upon it the character, not of error, but of *moral wickedness*. For such persecution, the plea of conscience is not admissible; it can only be a conscience so blinded by wilful neglect of the highest truth, or so corrupted by the habitual indulgence of evil passions, that it rather aggravates than excuses the guilt of those whom it misleads.

Naturally, the schoolboy Clough was on the same side as his headmaster. 'What glorious fellows those Proctors are for stopping that furious Convocation' he wrote, after the first attempt at censure (M, 42). But he regretted the publication of 'The Oxford Malignants': 'I am very sorry it was written' he wrote to Simpkinson 'and I wish it had, if written at all, been published with his name' (M, 47).

Clough knew that in Oxford he was entering a battlefield on which were ranged many enemies of his adored Arnold. The Tractarian movement owed its force in Oxford to three fellows of Oriel College: John Keble (whose 1833 sermon 'On the National Apostasy' was taken as marking the launch of the movement), Edward Bouverie Pusey (who had moved from Oriel to Christ Church as Professor of Hebrew) and John Henry Newman (the guiding spirit of the *Tracts for the Times*). By 1836 Newman, though junior in years and academic status, was undoubtedly the best known of the triumvirate.

When Clough came up to Oxford, aged 18, Newman was 37. He had succeeded Arnold as a Fellow of Oriel in 1822, and had held a tutorship there from 1826. He had been influential in securing, in 1828, the election as Provost of the College of Edward Hawkins, a friend and former colleague of Arnold's, of comparatively liberal persuasion. He succeeded Hawkins as Vicar of the University Church of St Mary's, but soon fell out with him on academic and theological issues. He resigned his Oriel tutorship in 1832, and made a continental tour as far as Sicily, where he wrote his most famous hymn *Lead, Kindly Light*. He continued as a Fellow of Oriel, and on his return to England he published a series of learned theological and historical works. He conducted theological seminars in the vestry of St Mary's on Tuesday evenings, and he preached regular Sunday afternoon sermons in St Mary's – sermons which made a much greater impact than the cycle of Sunday morning University sermons preached by officially appointed academic grandees.

The most famous description of Newman preaching was written in 1883 by Matthew Arnold, who listened to him in the early 1840s:

> Who could resist the charm of that spiritual apparition, gliding in the dim afternoon light through the aisles of St Mary's, rising into the pulpit, and then, in the most entrancing of voices, breaking the silence with words and thought which were a religious music – subtle, sweet, mournful. (Allot and Super 1986: 472)

In his project of making the Church of England return to the Catholic past, Newman always saw as his great opponent Thomas Arnold. In letters to his friends while on his continental tour, he said that the one thing which would convince him that the Church of England should be disestablished would be if the government were to make Arnold a bishop. When someone defended against him a particular interpretation of a passage in Scripture on the grounds that it was approved by Arnold, Newman riposted 'But is Arnold a Christian?' In 1837 he wrote to a friend 'What I fear is the *now* rising generation at Oxford, Arnold's youths. Much depends on how they turn out.'[1]

* * *

It was at this point that Clough, Arnold's pride and joy, came up to Balliol. Many people wondered how he would respond to the enchantment of the one man in England whose charisma was even greater than Arnold's. To find out they had to wait until he had been in residence for more than a term. On the first Sunday of term, 15 October, he wrote to his sister Annie:

> Behold I am in Oxford, safe and sound, capped and gowned, have attended Chapel twice, once with and once without surplice, have been

> to Hall (signifying dinner in Hall) also twice, to a wine party also, to call on the Master, and to the University Sermon this morning. So that by tomorrow evening, when I hope my books will be arrived and arranged on my shelves, and when, also I trust, I shall be furnished with a kettle and tea things (for as yet I have been dependent on the bountiful hospitalities of my friends) I shall be pretty completely settled. (M, 64)

After that, there was silence. No letters have survived from this first Michaelmas term; the weeks seem to have passed in a whirl, partly exciting, partly disconcerting. All we know about the term is the academic record, which, as might be expected, showed him as an earnest and hard-working student.

Balliol was at this time academically the most demanding of all the Oxford colleges. Since it had opened its scholarships to general competition in 1827 it had been able to attract the cream of applicants, and it had overtaken Oriel in the proportion of First Classes obtained in the final examination. Even among commoners Balliol had an unusual proportion of reading men with serious academic ambitions. The Master of the College from 1819 to 1854 was Richard Jenkyns, a high-and-dry Tory of the old school. Small, solemn and ponderous, he struck awe into undergraduates in his presence; when absent he was the subject of much mimicry and the butt of many an anecdote. Underneath his pompous exterior he had a kind heart, and he was loved as well as feared and mocked. He was no scholar himself, and published nothing beyond a few obituaries in the *Gentleman's Magazine*. But he encouraged learning in others, collecting around himself a talented and devoted group of tutors.

Clough's principal academic task in his first term was to compose three substantial essays to be submitted to the Master.[2] The first was entitled 'On the Effect of Dramatic Representation on the Taste and Morals of a People'. In this he argued, in Platonic fashion, that drama was a form of art much inferior to poetry, and repellent to pure and refined taste. Comedy, in particular, was only tolerable in a Christian community to the extent that it provided the poor with a distraction from drinking. In his second essay, on the effect on literature of the invention of printing, he inveighed both against the rhetorical frippery of ancient literature and the utilitarian materialism of modern philosophy. The third topic, Venice, gave less scope for moralizing. Jenkyns, who was in general suspicious of Arnold and his products, found nothing to object to in these essays, and in his end-of-term report he summed up Clough's work as 'good, but deficient in elegance and neatness of style'. In morals, however, he was described as 'excellent' and 'uniformly diligent'.

Besides submitting essays to the Master, Clough had to undergo internal college examinations at the hands of the tutors, called 'collections'. He was examined on the gospel of St Matthew, on one book of Thucydides, three of the *Iliad*, a play of Aristophanes and some early Greek history. In Latin he had been studying Virgil's *Eclogues*. None of this should have presented a serious challenge to him: it was largely a repetition of work he had done at Rugby in previous years.

The dons who examined Clough had the reputation of being the most effective tutorial team in Oxford. There were two classical tutors: Robert Scott and Archibald Tait. Scott, later Jenkyns' successor as Master, was a gentle scholar best known to posterity for the massive Greek lexicon that he produced in collaboration with Dean Liddell of Christ Church, the father of Lewis Carroll's Alice. Tait was less intellectual, but more vigorous: a shrewd and humorous Scotsman, a moderate low churchman who later became Archbishop of Canterbury. Benjamin Jowett, who was one of his pupils and who followed Scott to become the most famous of all Masters of Balliol, said of Tait 'He was one of the few by whom high preferment was never sought and to whom it did no harm.'

There was a third tutor who taught logic and mathematics: this was William George Ward. Ward was highly intelligent, with a passion for abstract logic that went hand-in-hand with a cavalier attitude to historical fact. Though only 25, he was already immensely portly – a clumsy, ill-dressed, Johnsonian figure, an eccentric about whom stories gathered ripely. Jowett once said of him 'You like him as you like a Newfoundland dog. He is such a large, jolly, shaggy creature.'

Ward, if he read it, must have disapproved of Clough's first Master's essay. He had a passion for theatre and opera; the actor Macready was one of his heroes, and on country walks he loved singing buffo arias of Mozart. He was himself a gifted entertainer, and one of the most popular items at his parties was a *ballet d'action* taking off Master Jenkyns, which would set his company into fits of laughter.

Beneath this jovial exterior lay a deeply insecure personality. Initially an admirer of Bentham and James Mill, Ward had fallen from a distance under the spell of Arnold. When ordained deacon he had subscribed to the Thirty-Nine Articles in the liberal sense in which Arnold understood them. When the brilliant Arthur Stanley came to Balliol from Rugby he was welcomed as a fellow Arnoldian. But Ward began to be dissatisfied with Arnold's system, and on an October day in 1836 he travelled to Rugby to present his objections in person, and so exhausted the busy headmaster with his questionings that he had to spend the next day in bed.

Ward was still suspicious of Newman: he had to be tricked into attending his first Sunday afternoon sermon at St Mary's. 'Why should I go and listen to such myths?' he asked. In 1837, however, he and Stanley began to attend Newman's Tuesday seminars in the vestry of St Mary's. The two of them used to sit in the front row, below the preacher's desk. Newman was propounding

W. G. Ward

J. H. Newman

A. H. Clough himself

Provost Hawkins

the thesis that the Church of England offered a middle position between the opposite excesses of Roman superstition and Protestant puritanism.

> [Ward] put the preacher somewhat out of countenance by his steadfast gaze, his play of features as some particular passage stirred him, his nudges of Stanley and whispered 'asides' to him ('What would Arnold say to that' etc. etc.).

Newman was so disconcerted that he rearranged the benches so that Ward and Stanley looked across at the congregation rather than facing the preacher.[3]

* * *

It was just when Ward was considering transferring his allegiance from Arnold to Newman, that Clough arrived in Balliol. He soon succeeded Stanley as Ward's closest associate. During the Christmas vacation he wrote to Simpkinson 'I like Oxford very much, and hope to live there very comfortably from next term forward. I am great friends with Brodie and still more so, I think, with Ward, whom I like very much' (M, 66).

Clough soon began to feel the attraction of Newman. He dated his letter to Simpkinson '*Newmanice* "The Feast" of the Epiphany'. 'Have you ever read Newman's Sermons?' he asked him. 'I hope you will soon if you have not, for they are very good and I should think especially useful for us' (M, 66). But he had not lost anything of his admiration for his old headmaster: 'Thank God for Arnold, and his kindness' he noted at this time (K, 4). He exulted in Arnold's success in securing the insertion of a religious examination into the curriculum of London University – a grand thing to achieve, he said, in that godless place. 'I do not know' he added in a letter to Gell 'how we shall get on in Oxford against those very opposite sort of enemies – the Newmanists – they are very savage and determined.' But he went on to add that they were good and pious men, and had done much good by attacking the tasteless and ungentlemanly manners of the evangelicals (M, 67).

On his return to Oxford for his second term, Lent 1838, Clough once again began to keep a diary. 'All the enjoyment and attention and be-praisement of this Place is too much as yet for me' he wrote on 2 Feburary (K, 3). The entries for the term are full of relentless self-examination, and contain a tally of tiny sins of speech and thought. These Balliol diaries, unlike the Rugby diaries, are free from denunciations of the wickedness of others. Indeed Clough is now astonishingly ready to make excuses for others while rejecting all palliation of his own misdeeds and mixed motives.

Amid the mass of introspection and self-reproach one can pick out the main features of his life at Balliol. He suffered from headaches and stomach troubles, which he was inclined to take as punishment for his sins. He consoled himself by reading Newman's sermon on bodily suffering (K, 10). In addition to the daily services in the college chapel he would, as at Rugby, spend hours in bible reading and private devotions in his room.

Clough was remembered by his contemporaries as having led a solitary and Spartan existence at Balliol. However, the diary makes clear that he led an active social life. He took regular walks with friends and during the month of February he attended no less than 15 wine parties. In the third week of term Arnold came up to preach at St Peter's in the East and there was a happy reunion of the Rugby set. New friends, outside the Rugby circle, included Benjamin Jowett from St Paul's.

Stanley, Lake and Ward were the three men closest to Clough at this time. Stanley and Lake were anxious to make this new Rugbeian at home. Stanley, however, was not long for Balliol: he had been warned that despite his double first in Schools he was unlikely to be elected to a fellowship there because of his reputation as a heretical Arnoldian. Clough was grateful to Lake, but also rebukes himself for his own irritation and 'pettishness' with regard to him. The person who took much the greatest part of his time was Ward.

The many hours spent with Ward were not tutorials: the tutorial system in the 1830s was rather different from that familiar to recent Oxford generations. Tutors imparted instruction not primarily to single pupils or to small groups, but in lectures to as many as 20 pupils at a time. Thus, Clough notes in his diary his attendance (or failures of attendance) at lectures of his classical tutors Tait and Scott. One-to-one sessions of instruction were known, but these were imparted by a 'coach' to his 'cub', and a coach was not provided as part of the normal college instruction, but had to be hired as an extra, perhaps in preparation for a university prize examination.

Clough's sessions with Ward were personal and theological rather than academic. Ward sought to solve his own religious perplexities by bouncing ideas off his pupil and used his constant companionship to shield himself from depression. The diary entry for 8 February captures the mixture of theology and emotion in these encounters.

> Dined and tead with Ward. Conversed (i) about the Strength of 'Tradition', viz the Unity of opinion as expressed at the Nicene Council . . . (ii) The 'being alone' question (iii) the 'expression of affection' question. (K, 11)

Such meetings put a strain on Clough. 'I am afraid Ward is and will be a trial' he wrote. Though concerned about Ward's excessive emotional demands, Clough was genuinely fond of him, and felt a responsibility for his welfare. The entry for 22 February is typical of many:

> Up at 10.30. Did scarcely any Work. Went to Ward at 1.45, stayed till 2.15. Went to Congreve till 4.45. Dined with Ward. Ward here from 7.45 to 9.45. Very poorly & fanciful, poor man. What can I do? (K, 11)

At the end of February Oxford was thrown into theological turmoil when Newman and Keble published the letters and journals of an Oriel Tractarian who had died young, Richard Hurrell Froude. Froude's vehement denunciation of the leaders of the Protestant Reformation went well beyond Newman's exhortations to the Church of England to return to a primitive Catholic past. The outrage caused by the book left a monument that stands to this day in Oxford – the Martyrs' Memorial, erected by subscription shortly afterwards in honour of the reformers Cranmer, Latimer and Ridley. No less controversial than the polemic against the reformers were the intimate records of Froude's endeavours to mortify his flesh by penance and fasting. The *Edinburgh Review* mocked Keble and Newman for publishing 'contrite reminiscences of a desire for roasted goose, and of an undue indulgence in buttered toast'.[4]

Other readers, however, found the *Remains* edifying. Ward obtained the book immediately on publication, took it to Clough on 26 February and spent two hours reading it with him. He liked the book better, he said, than anything of the kind he had ever read. Clough himself noted it down as 'most instructive'. He began to show the influence of Froude's style in his own diary, and he tried to imitate some of his austerities. Henceforth, from time to time, he resolved to take up fasting. This resolution, like his frequent resolutions about the times of rising and retiring, was only very irregularly carried into action.

Ash Wednesday fell on the last day of February, and on the first Sunday of Lent Clough attended Newman's early communion and listened to his sermon on fasting. On the same day he invited the preacher to a tête-à-tête dinner in his rooms; he found himself too bashful, however, to make any impression on the great man. Newman left at 8.45 and in his diary did not even note the name of his host (K, 19).[5]

Clough strove hard to reconcile his new admiration for Newman with his continued devotion to Arnold. In place of the generic evangelical sense of sinfulness, he now accepted Newman's Catholic distinction between merely venial sins and those that put a person out of a state of grace. In his diary he thanked God that he should be blest through Newman with new wisdom and with new exercises of devotion. 'How strange that I should owe so much to Arnold and so much to him! How have I deserved this second enlightenment?' (K, 33).

The sin with which in his diary he most often reproached himself was that of pride. Ward's constant admiration, he feared, made him full of self-conceit, and in theological discussion with him he was, he felt, frequently arrogant.

Above all, he was too inclined to approach the Bible in a critical fashion, as an interpreter rather than as a humble learner seeking a practical lesson. At the same time as he was drawn to Tractarian practices of devotion, he began to have 'aweful feelings of practical Atheism'. He was indeed, as he often reproached himself, 'Dipsychos' – a man in two minds (K, 66).

The Easter vacation marked the high point of Clough's flirtation with Tractarianism. On Palm Sunday in St Mary's he was deeply moved by Newman's reading of the Passion according to St Matthew. He kept Holy Week as a spiritual retreat, studying daily the gospel accounts of the last days of the life of Jesus and copying long passages of the Greek testament into his diary. On the Monday he noted:

> [M]any persons of the most advanced piety and goodness are this week engaged in all sorts of self-denial, & mortification, fasting from food and sleep, amusement & society – Newman, for instance, whose errors as we believe them to be must not make me ever forget how far he is above me in goodness and piety, and wisdom too, tho' in certain points we with less power may by our advantages be nearer the truth, and though less wise have more wisdom. (K, 40)

The retreat was not a success – Clough kept breaking his resolutions on walks with friends, seriously overate on two occasions, and rebuked himself several times for his snobbishness, which he called his 'degraded dependency *in rebus gentlemanlicis*'. On Easter Eve he wrote 'It has been indeed a poor week compared with my hopes' and on Easter Monday 'I, who have kept no fast, must not now dare to keep feast.' Ward, apparently, had done better. 'I ought to be strengthened' Clough lamented 'by Ward's noble example' (K, 45–6).

'When I am talking to Ward' Clough once told a friend 'I feel like a bit of paper blown up the chimney by a draught' (Ward 1889: 110). Stanley, seeing the two men walking together, remarked 'There goes Ward mystifying poor Clough, and persuading him that he must either believe *nothing* or accept the whole of Church doctrine.' In fact, theological discussions between the two seem to have been conducted on terms of equality, and Clough was quick to point out fallacies in Ward's arguments. 'Ward' he later recalled 'was always trying to put me on the horns of a dilemma; but somehow I generally managed to get over the wall.'

Because Ward later became so prominent in the Oxford Movement biographers have assumed that he was constantly urging Clough in a Romeward direction. In fact at this time Clough was closer to Newman than Ward was. As late as July 1838 Ward could say only 'with me the current is decidedly setting towards Newmanism' (M, 81). Newman's own diary for 1838 makes no mention of Ward and the only recorded meeting between the two men in the entire year was on 4 March, when Ward came into Clough's room and found him entertaining Newman tête-à-tête. Newman himself regarded Ward's conversion to 'good principles' as having occurred a year later, in the spring of 1839. 'He is a very important accession' Newman then wrote to a friend. 'He is a man I know very little of, but whom I cannot help liking very much – in spite of his still professing himself a radical in politics' (Newman 1995; 1999, VII: 75).[6]

In the Trinity Term of 1838 Newman began a new set of Tuesday seminars in St Mary's vestry, entitled 'Lectures on the Scripture Proof of the Doctrines of the Church'. The series was eventually published as No. 85 of the *Tracts for the Times*, and it was to this Tract that Newman later attributed Ward's conversion to his system (Newman 1995; 1999, VII: 33). Clough, on the other hand, began to move in a different direction. He attended the first lecture of the series, and reported that Newman had stated the scriptural objections to a mystical view of the sacraments 'in a very fair and candid manner'. After this he attended the next four lectures, but in the course of the term he gradually detached himself from 'Newmania'. In the second week he wrote to Gell:

> One thing I suppose is clear – that one must leave the discussion of Newmanist matters all snug and quiet for after one's degree. And it is no harm but rather good to give oneself up a little to hearing Oxford people, and admiring their good points, which lie, I suppose, principally in all they hold in opposition to the Evangelical portion of society – the benefit and beauty and necessity of forms – the ugliness of feelings put on unnaturally soon and consequently kept up by artificial means, ever strained and never sober . . . I should be very sorry ever to be brought to believe their further views of matter acting on morals as a charm of sacramentalism, and the succession notion so closely connected with it. (M, 71)

Towards the end of term, on 2 June, Clough once again took a meal with Newman (Clough described it as 'dinner', Newman as 'tea-supper'), this time as one of a party at Oriel. Once again, the encounter left little mark. All Clough noted about it was that it kept him late for Chapel; for Newman the memorable feature of the day was that some of his guests had come 'partly by railroad – a new thing' (K, 69; Newman 1995; 1999, VII: 252). A few days later Clough wrote 'I incline to think that I ought to give up seeking much about the great Newman question: for I have little or no real earnestness' (K, 74). A sign of his frivolity was that he had been wasting time reading instalments of the latest novel, *Nicholas Nickleby* (K, 69).

The term was not entirely devoted to Ward and Newmanism. Clough could sum up his activities to Gell as 'reading for little-go, and paying off wine-party scores'. He frequently went skiffing on the river, and attended at least one boat-race. He was also active in two debating societies, the Union and the Decade. The Decade was the more select of the two societies. It had been founded by Lake shortly after his arrival in Balliol 'to discuss rather graver subjects than were common at the Union' (Lake 1901: 38). Its membership was predominantly liberal, including Stanley and Jowett, and the topics of debate were literary and political. To avoid canvassing, members were elected without their knowledge. Clough was asked to join in his first year, and remained a member until 1848.

On 28 May Clough decided to put off Little-Go. That a prize-winning Rugby scholar should feel inadequate to sit a simple examination on texts and topics on which he had worked for years was a sign that something had gone very wrong during this first Oxford year. Escaping at the end of term, Clough denounced Oxford's 'hot-house atmosphere which destroys all strength and healthiness of genuine feelings in me'.

Clough's diaries for the term peter out on 25 June: they make no mention of the coronation of Queen Victoria on 28 June. He spent the last days of June travelling, first to Rugby, then by train to Liverpool and by steamer to Ulverston, and thence, after a Sunday at the Arnolds' house at Fox How, on foot to the Patterdale Inn, near Ullswater. He was joined by Thomas Burbidge, who had recently published a book, *Poems Longer and Shorter*, which Clough admired. The verses, he thought, were more promising, though less polished, than Tennyson's first published poems. On the other hand he thought they were far too self-revelatory. It was surely wrong to write so as 'to expose peculiar circumstances of your own life or conduct or friends' – as Burbidge had done about a housemother at Rugby and about a 14-year-old Rugby schoolboy, Theodore Walrond, nicknamed 'Todo'. Walrond, who was in due course to become one of Clough's own closest friends, joined the two elder students at Patterdale, and the three spent several happy weeks in spite of heavy rain and fierce storms. Clough in a number of lively letters described their expeditions over crags and around tarns in the Ullswater fells (M, 72–4, 78–80). One such letter went to Ward, who found the enthusiasm it expressed about Burbidge too much for his possessive jealousy. 'It altogether seemed' he wrote in a whining letter 'that you were thinking of him all the time you wrote and not of me' (M, 81).

After his holiday in Patterdale Clough spent most of the rest of the summer with his family, partly in their new Liverpool residence in St James's Terrace, and partly touring in Wales, where they were briefly joined by Ward (M, 70; B, 69; Blanche Clough 1897, 1903: 30). On his way back to Oxford he spent a few days at Rugby, where Burbidge was continuing as a teacher and where Todo ('very brave and manly') had now become a prefect. Clough discussed Montaigne, and found that Burbidge shared his distaste for Newman's theory of the sacraments.

After returning to Oxford in October Clough passed Little-Go without difficulty. A much greater problem was how to relate to Ward. He noted in his diary Ward's increasing craving for expressions of affection: 'Must not indulge Ward in re "dear" etc.' 'Felt great disgust at his indelicacies', 'Ward has asked me to make unnatural demonstrations'. These 'unnatural demonstrations' are unlikely to be what Victorians called 'acts against nature'. Clough was troubled by Ward's demands not as temptations to unchastity, but as provocations to insincerity. He felt he could not honestly respond with the same intensity of feeling. For the rest of the term he tried to walk the tightrope between insincerity and cruelty (K, 84–5).

While at Rugby Clough had been prolific in verse. His juvenilia fill 56 pages of the standard edition of his poems – more than a tenth of his lifetime's output. His first year at Balliol, by contrast, had been barren. He did not altogether give up writing – he blamed himself sometimes for 'sitting up doing Verses' (e.g. K, 76) – but not a single line survives. Now, on the night before he plucked up courage to set Ward at a distance, he took up his pen again:

> Truth is a golden thread seen here & there
> In small bright specks upon the visible side
> Of our strange Being's party coloured web
> How rich the converse. 'Tis a vein of ore
> Emerging now & then on earths rude breast
> But flowing full below. Like Islands set
> At distant intervals on Ocean's face
> We see it on our course; but in the depths
> The mystic colonnade unbroken keeps
> Its faithful way invisible but sure.
> O if it be so, wherefore do we men
> Pass by so many marks, so little heeding?
> (P, 137)

When Clough came to publish his Balliol poetry, he omitted this verse, and one can see why. The first ten lines develop, in three parallel images, the theme that there is such a thing as objective truth, but that subjective visions of it are never more than partial. However, the poem's final moralizing couplet reverses the sense, and makes the poem broken-backed. Truth is now not a hidden treasure, but something which only negligence prevents from being manifest.

Most of the term, however, seems to have been lonely. Uncle Alfred had left his Jesus fellowship for a college living at Braunston. Stanley was no longer at Balliol, but was residing at University, a college which he made no secret of regarding as inferior to Balliol. Lake had just won a first in classics and was promoted to a fellowship in November. So too, astonishingly, was Jowett, still an undergraduate with a year to go before taking Schools. Clough must have been sorry to see these friends depart from the scholars' table.

On his way to spend Christmas in Liverpool he spent several days with Burbidge at Rugby. The visit to Burbidge caused another outburst from Ward, who had apparently tried to extract a promise from Clough to avoid him. Clough wrote to Ward from Liverpool to say that the two of them should see less of each other in the future, and that Ward should alter his manner to him. In a long letter full of self-pity, Ward did reluctantly offer to reform: he would try to show his affection less.

> Further I *release* you from your promise about seeing Burbidge, wishing merely instead an assurance that I shall always know beforehand, and that for this year you will make no engagement inconsistent with your power of staying at Oxford till Easter Friday and of seeing me as much as 3 or 4 weeks in the Long Vac. should I so wish. (M, 87)

Even at the moment of accepting that his emotions towards Clough needed to be contained, Ward was still obsessively jealous.

Returning to Oxford after a New Year's round of visits to Aunts in Chester and Wales, Clough paid his last respects to the Oxford Movement. On 7 February he and Ward dined and wined with Newman in the rooms of Frederic Oakeley, a Tractarian fellow of Balliol, now best remembered as the author of *O Come All Ye Faithful*. Two days later, again with Newman and Oakeley, he attended a select breakfast at Oriel hosted by another Tractarian poet.

In a letter to Gell, Clough explained his understanding of Newman's position. Newman did not deny the supremacy of reason, but he believed that unaided reason, on a balance of probabilities, must come to the conclusion that Christian salvation depended on forms and sacraments which could only be administered by priests appointed in succession to the Apostles. Those who rejected this channel of divine blessing were therefore guilty of very great sin.

Clough rejected Newman's sacramental doctrine on the basis of a careful study of the Epistles of St Paul. What he most disliked about Tractarianism, however, was its exclusivity. In his diary at this time he denounces 'The Impolicy and Sin of Athanasianism' by which he meant the thesis that human beings, if they hold the wrong doctrines, are damned in hell for ever, as proclaimed in the Athanasian Creed in the Prayer Book (K, xxv, 92–4).

An opportunity soon came for Clough to express his broader view of religious truth in poetic form. Each year the University set a topic for a verse competition: entries were to be submitted at the end of the Lent term, and the prizewinner would recite his work in the Sheldonian Theatre at the grand Commemoration in the summer. In 1838 the topic set was 'Salsette and

Elephanta' – two islands off the Indian coast famous for their temple caves. Clough started work on 1 March by reading, in a recently published French translation, a work on Indian language and philosophy by the German orientalist Friedrich von Schlegel.

Clough identified the temple of Salsette with Buddhism, and that of Elephanta with Hinduism. Neither religion is described in his poem with much sympathy: Hinduism is debased idolatry, and Buddhism fosters sloth. However the moral of the poem's 132 heroic couplets is that both religions are corrupted versions of a single original knowledge of Truth.

Methought beneath these storied roofs there lay
Dim recollections of a holier day,
Memorials apt to wake repentant tears
Like toys that tell us of our childish Years,
And strong that genial spirit to impart
The tender Conscience, and the loving heart.
But all is dark: through all the Echoing Caves
'Tis Sloth beguiles, or Superstition raves . . .

And yet, as wilful children, when they roam,
Turn oft their hesitating glances home,
As troubled Spirits rove at close of day
Round the loved precincts where they dare not stay,
So come with all thine idol-forms combined
Strange conscious hauntings of a purer Mind:
And from afar some rays of glory shine,
And faintly gleams primeval Truth divine.

(P, 139ff)

The verse, though fluent, is rarely moving and often embarrassing. It does not reach the standard of the best of Clough's Rugby work. The panel of judges (chaired by Keble, the Professor of Poetry) passed it over in favour of a poem by John Ruskin.

Easter was spent at Rugby with one of the housemasters, Bonamy Price, a mathematics teacher who was later to become a professor of economics at Oxford. Price was well versed in German biblical criticism, and Clough was anxious to dispel any impression that he had succumbed to Newmanism. In retrospect he described his time with the Prices as 'a great rest and renovation'. Some of it he spent observing their young children, who were, he told Gell, 'psychological studies' (B, 78). As if in prescient dialogue with Freud, he put his observations into verse.

Thou bidd'st me mark how swells with rage
   The childish cheek, the childish limb,
How strongly lust and passion wage
   Their strife in every petty whim;
Primeval strains from earliest age,
   Thou sayst, our glorious souls bedim;
Yet not, though true thy Wisdom says,
   Will I love less the childish days.

In five further stanzas the poet seeks to reconcile the Christian doctrine that humans are 'prone to evil from their very childhood' with the Wordsworthian vision that childhood innocence is a glory brought from a better world.

With sin innate, that still descends
   On Adam's children, one and all
Perchance innate remembrance blends
   Of Adam's joys before the fall.
(P, 137)

Whatever may be the truth of the matter, Clough insists, in the last line of each stanza, that childhood is something to be cherished.

While with the Prices Clough learnt that Arnold, invited to propose a candidate for the headship of the first secondary college of education in Van Diemen's Land (Tasmania), had put forward the name of Gell, who had just completed his Cambridge Tripos. Back in Oxford, he wrote to congratulate him and suggested that he might turn Tasmania into a Platonic Republic. He had just read the *Republic* and been captivated by it. 'If you have not hitherto studied this wondrous book, I recommend you to cast aside those heterodox and heretical authors, Calvin and Milton, and immediately commence upon it. Plato not being a Christian is quite orthodox.' But he warned Gell that Romanism was on the increase in Oxford: on his return from the antipodes he might find apostolic clergy installed as philosopher kings, with Newman as Archbishop of Canterbury and father confessor to the Queen. He urged him to install in his college in Tasmania 'a good Germanized Cambridge Scholar' as a bulwark against Newmanism (M, 91–2).

This second year in Oxford ended in celebration. At Commemoration on 12 June Wordsworth was given a Doctorate of Civil Law. Stanley read out his prize Latin essay and Ruskin recited his victorious 'Salsette and Elephanta'. Simpkinson and Arnold came for the great event, and there were 'boat races with much shouting and beer drinking'. Clough himself was unable to enjoy the festivities to the full because of a hangover from dinner the night before with his uncle Alfred (K, 116).

In the diaries for Trinity 1839, indeed, excessive drinking appears frequently in the catalogue of sins. A typical entry is that of 24 April 'Took too much wine at Fanshawe's. Isn't two glasses enough?' In compensation, Clough resolved on Ascension Day 'never to touch tea again for 3 weeks – except out at breakfast, and then no sugar'. As ever, he constantly urged himself to work harder: there were, he reminded himself, only 480 working days left before he had to take his degree (K, 107–16).

In July, after a week with the Arnolds in company with Simpkinson, Gell and Burbidge, and a week with his family in Liverpool, Clough redeemed a promise of the previous Christmas and spent a month with Ward. The two friends went through Derbyshire and Yorkshire to stay at Keswick and enjoy the beauties of Borrowdale. Later they travelled together to Edinburgh, returning via Durham and York to admire the Cathedrals. Ward long recalled this holiday: his son tells us:

> Clough, he used to say, *interpreted* scenery for him. Ward loved natural scenery almost as much as he loved music, though his eye was not accurate and he could not explain the features which struck him. When first he and Clough came in sight of Grasmere, coming suddenly upon a view of the lake from behind the hills, Ward was fairly overcome and burst into tears.[7]

As often in their relationship, it is Clough who appears the senior, and Ward the junior.

The hot Lancashire August was commemorated with a sonnet 'Whence com'st thou shady lane?' which describes the ripening of the fruit and the harvesting of the grain in the orchards and fields beside a lane that recalled childhood wanderings. The teeming earth is lovingly described in a sentimental sestet, but the best that Clough could say of Liverpool at the end of the vacation was that he had 'got very nearly fond of it'. He was envious of Simpkinson and Burbidge who were both touring the continent (M, 95).

In September he took two weeks' break in Wales with his brother Charles, who was visiting from America. 'We are going to walk, eat, and sleep exclusively for four or five days among the mountains, which is a sure means of gaining health and strength' he told Gell (M, 94). It was a worrying time. James Clough's financial affairs were in disorder and, for a second time, his business was threatened with bankruptcy. Arthur's two brothers, fortunately, were now independent. It became ever more important that he in his turn should do well in Schools so that he could secure a fellowship and obtain pupils, whose fees would enable him to contribute to the family's support (K, 3121; M, 95; Blanche Clough 1897, 1903: 20–1).

Something else was troubling Arthur. From the spring of 1838 he began to record in his diary a series of events, occurring once or twice a week, which he marked only by a large asterisk. From the prose which accompanies these asterisks it appears that he regarded the events as something sinful. From the contexts in which they appear it is clear that these were private events: we get many entries such as '* lying in bed' or '* after rowing', but none of '* in Hall' or '* with Ward'. That they were physical events, unlike the sins of thought about which the diaries are so tediously explicit, is suggested by the fact that during this last week in Liverpool, on the advice of his father, he held a consultation about the matter with the family's physician, Dr Bickersteth (K, 122).

Clough offered no key to his code, but the most plausible interpretation is that the asterisks refer to solitary masturbation. Other Victorian diarists used similar symbolic notation for the same purpose. If this is correct, then it throws light on other entries in the diaries before the series of asterisks commences. He refers to a 'wretched habit' which he brought with him from Rugby to Oxford, and an entry of 6 April 1839 reports 'I was as nearly as possible committing my worst sin this morning. I was not *quite* roused from sleep, but fully conscious.' Several other succeeding entries refer to the commission of his 'worst sin'. We do not know what regime Dr Bickersteth recommended, but the series of asterisks continued in the diaries well into 1842.

Back in Oxford, enchanting in an Indian summer, Clough made a cheerful enough start to his third year, in excellent health after his Welsh hiking. Every day before breakfast, he took a plunge at Parson's Pleasure bathing place. He noted carefully whenever he missed his dip: in the last two days of October his excuse was that he was unwell with cholera. He resolved to 'escape the vortex of Philosophism and Discussion, whereof Ward is the centre': and though he could not altogether avoid Ward, the resolution to avoid metaphysics seems to have been reasonably well kept. Two new arrivals among the Balliol scholars provided fresh, non-Tractarian companionship: John Duke Coleridge from Eton, the future Lord Chief Justice, and Frederick Temple from Blundells, a future Archbishop of Canterbury. Both were soon elected to the Decade and made two Tory members of that otherwise Whiggish body (K, xxxii).

The essays of Carlyle had now succeeded the sermons of Arnold and Newman as Clough's favourite reading, to be recommended to his Cambridge friends. He even thought of presenting a copy of these essays to Gell to speed him on his way to Tasmania, but he reflected that Carlyle was 'somewhat heathenish' and instead settled for the *Confessions* of St Augustine as a farewell gift (M, 96, B, 84, 94).

The main excitement of the term was the marriage of his 43-year-old Uncle Alfred of Braunston, to the 20-year-old Miss Lamb of Bragboro (B, 93). Clough attended as groomsman, walking 20 miles of the way to Braunston. 'I have never been at a wedding before and expected it to be very pleasant, but found it more so than I expected,' he wrote to Burbidge (M, 97). To his maiden Aunt Jemima at Chester he wrote a full account of the ceremony, with details of the bridesmaids' dresses and of the breakfast table arrangements. The wedding was not without drama. Clerical Uncle Charles from Mold was to perform the ceremony, but his train was delayed and he missed the party to meet him at Rugby. Finding his own way to Braunston, he fell into a cinder hole at the roadside, laming himself and bruising his ribs. He was barely able to officiate, but bride and groom were eventually despatched towards Hastings for their wedding tour. The senior bridesmaid was Dr Arnold's eldest daughter Jane, 'very gorgeous to behold' in a canary coloured dress (B, 97).

Undeterred by the fate of his uncle, Clough walked back all the way from Dunchurch to Oxford, 40 miles, of which 20 were in the dark. The road was poor and the day rainy. 'The consequence is' as he reported to Burbidge 'that I am tied to my room today by a strained ankle which I managed to get myself in feeling my way along the dark and dirty road. I believe part of my motive for attempting it was the desire to be as long out of Oxford as possible' (M, 97).

Once again Clough decided to compete for the English verse prize, this year's subject being 'The Judgement of Brutus'. Brutus was the stern Roman consul who condemned his two sons to death for conspiracy against the Roman Republic. Though the deadline for submission was not until April, Clough began work in December. The finished product was inferior to 'Salsette and Elephanta'. Annie found it rough, and the examiners once again passed it over.

At the end of term collections, on 9 December, Clough was complimented on a great improvement in his work, and his morals, as ever, were rated 'uniformly good and exemplary'. The vacation followed a now familiar pattern: a visit to Arnold on the way to Liverpool, visits to Aunts in Wales, Christmas at home with the family, New Year with the Chester aunts. He read Schiller and Goethe with Annie, and spent some time in 'dissipation' with her and with his brother George, attending balls at Chester and Denbigh. He helped entertain Uncle Alfred and his bride on their honeymoon visit to Liverpool. Altogether he did less work than he had hoped: less than four hours a day, and at the year's end he accused himself of 'mulish idleness, indolence, and easiness'.

This was a winter of many concerns. The Chartist movement for parliamentary reform was alarming the middle classes. There were rumours of plans to burn London and to lame horses in Sheffield. Clough was able to reassure Gell, four months mail away in Tasmania, that Liverpool appeared quite safe from Chartism. But he spent part of the vacation reading Carlyle's treatise on the topic (M, 99; B, 100).

New Year's Day 1840 was Clough's twenty-first birthday. He marked it with a dismal sonnet 'Here I have been these one and twenty years' which describes his life as pointless tacking and tossing upon a wavy world. The sestet ends:

Here am I brotherless mid many brothers
With faculties developed to no end
Heart emptied & faint purpose to amend
(K, 131)

The winter term was indeed depressing, cheered only by a visit from Dr Arnold and his son Matthew early in February. Celebrations for the wedding of Queen Victoria to Prince Albert were clouded by the drowning in Sandford lock of Currer, a Balliol rowing man. Clough's own health was poor, and he felt ill enough to allow himself a fire in his room; at the start of Lent he was confined to his sofa for two weeks with a gathering on his knee (K, 135–6). Lake had now followed Ward into Newmanism and for support against the Tractarian tide Clough had to depend on Rugby friends outside Balliol such as Congreve at Wadham and Stanley (now a deacon) at University. No letters could be expected for many months from Gell in Tasmania, and Burbidge was abroad guiding a pupil on the grand tour. Only Simpkinson was within reach: he had become a curate to the liberal protestant Julius Hare at Hurstmonceux. From his sickbed Clough wrote to him on 15 March 'I, with the cloud of degree right before me, cannot realize except very dimly, the irreparable nature of the leap in taking orders and going to a curacy' (M, 101).

During the Easter vacation the usual Rugby reunion with Arnold, the Prices, Simpkinson and Burbidge was enlivened by a session of mesmerizing. 'Mr Arthur Clough' reported the practitioner 'assured me that he knew nothing about Mesmerism, but was willing to try . . . I left my patient comfortably installed in an arm chair . . . Suddenly, I heard a great kicking, and going back, I found Mr Clough in a most excited state, seizing whatever was next him, and hurling cushions &c. about the room.' 'It made me feel very ill' Clough said when he came round (K, 138; Honan 1981: 65).[8]

Trinity term seems to have gone better than the Lent term: diary entries are sparse, which is commonly a good sign. Later, however, Clough recalled 'since the end of the Easter Vacation I have been a good deal out of health and perhaps more out of spirits' (M, 107). He was working on St Matthew and the Book of Common Prayer for divinity, on Horace's Odes for Latin, and on Herodotus and Aristotle in Greek. At the end of the term he received the usual compliments on his work, and after three weeks with Ward at Grasmere he settled down at home in Liverpool to make his final preparations for the examinations he was due to take in November.

The long vacation diary is little more than a record of the number of hours worked each day (the average had now gone up to five-and-a-half). His sister records that he found it very hard to work, even though he shut himself up away from his family, even missing church on Sundays. Only his brother George, who was about to migrate to America with Charles, seemed to be able to drive away his gloom; to his elder brother Clough felt the need later to apologize for rudeness 'I was anxious and not in very good health during the summer vacation and had a good many things on my mind' (M, 105). He escaped to Wales in September, but he did not pay the usual visits to his aunts, merely spending a week with his favourite uncle at Mold and saluting his cousins at Beaumaris. Indeed, a poem written at this time, attacking the Kantian notion that duty is the highest motive for action, suggests that he was getting bored with his extended family.

Duty – that's to say complying
  With whate'er's expected here
On your unknown cousins dying
  Straight be ready with the tear;
Upon etiquette relying,
Unto usage naught denying,
Lend your waist
To be embraced,
  Blush not even, never fear;
Claims of kith and kin connection,
  Claims of manners honour still,
Ready money of affection
  Pay, whoever drew the bill.
(P, 27)

More typical of these early years than this bitter verse were two other poems. 'Sweet streamlet basin' is a wish for purification from adult guilt and for a return to childhood bliss (P, 24). 'When soft September' is a slight but graceful piece in praise of the scenery of Snowdonia, written, he told Burbidge, with a pencil on a slate while resting on a bridge near Llanrwst (P, 12, 573).

On his return to Liverpool Clough became convinced that he was not sufficiently prepared for his final examinations and wrote to Ward for advice. A week after returning to Oxford he wrote 'Putting off seems absolutely necessary.' The pattern of Little-Go had repeated itself. Having now completed the normal three years of residence in Balliol, he moved into lodgings five minutes walk away on the ground floor of a College scout's house in 99 Holywell. The house – now Grove Cottage in St Cross Road – was convenient for Holywell baths, where he took his daily dip when the river was too cold. He moved out of college, so his family believed, partly to save money and partly to enjoy solitude in preparation for his examinations. But during the term he attended 23 wine parties, and he was active in the Union, where he attended a debate on Chartism, and in the Decade, where he proposed a motion condemning the reading of novels.

A freshman who came up from Rugby that year, George Bradley, recalled a wine party given by Clough himself in November. Conversation centred on Wordsworth and Coleridge, and one of the guests, a bulky Scotsman, became very animated, and talked 'with such vehemence and gesticulation that my wine-glass was sent flying' (Knight 1888: 49f). The Scotsman was John Campbell Shairp from Glasgow, a Balliol exhibitioner who would later became Principal of St Andrews. Shairp, though three years junior to Clough, was henceforth a firm friend and counsellor.

The time secured by the postponement of Schools was devoted to Aristotle and Aeschylus and the entire set of Sophocles' plays. There were also the examples in Whateley's *Elements of Logic* to be painfully worked through. On 17 November Clough wrote an unrhymed verse in the pattern of a sonnet, which was later to be the centrepiece of a sequence that he published under the Wordsworthian title *Blank misgivings of a creature moving about in Worlds not realised.*

> O kind protecting Darkness! as a child
> Flies back to bury in his mother's lap
> His shame and his confusion, so to thee,
> O Mother Night, come I. Within the folds
> Of thy dark robe hide thou me close, for I
> Have played the liar with external things
> So long so heedlessly – that all I see
> Even these white glimmering curtains, those bright stars
> Which to the rest shine comfort down, for me
> Smiling those smiles which I may not reply
> Or frowning frowns of fierce triumphant malice
> As angry claimants or assured expectants
> Of that I promised and may not perform
> Look me in the face. Oh hide me, Mother Night!
>
> (K, 147; P, 31)

His fear of disappointing those who were relying on his academic success here assumes cosmic proportions.

However, not all was gloom in November. It was the month of the Balliol scholarship examinations, and on the day before writing his poem he wrote to tell Annie 'Our scholarship examinations are just beginning – who are to get them, no one can guess at all. There are 2 candidates from Rugby, one of them Dr Arnold's son and he of the two has the best chance.' On 27 November he noted the result in his diary 'Riddle & Mat. Arnold Scholars' – and he underlined jubilantly the name 'Mat. Arnold' (K, 148).

Clough did not return home for the winter vacation, but stayed working in

Oxford except for four days over Christmas at Braunston and Rugby. He moved into college when a room became vacant there and the winter was so cold that he allowed himself a fire. On his birthday, 1 January, it was his only pleasure: his diary reads 'Not up till past 9, after 10 hours in bed; fire all day; have seen no one at all; walked alone; 3–5 dined alone – & luxuriated with fire 5 to 8.' Being in college once more meant that he saw much of Ward, dining with him when the Hall dinner was suspended in mid-vacation.[9]

At the beginning of the Lent term Dr Arnold paid a visit to Oxford, and took Clough to dine with him in the Common Room at Oriel (K, 156). Arnold was not in good spirits. He strongly disapproved of Clough's decision to postpone his examination, and he did not like what he saw in Oxford. As Clough wrote, reporting the visit to Simpkinson (whose Rector, Hare, was preparing a written defence of Luther) 'You have no idea how fast things here are going Rome-wards' (M, 106). Oxford was being flooded with tomes of Catholic theology, including 15 folio volumes of Thomas Aquinas (M, 108).

The Romeward movement reached its climax on 27 February when an anonymous pamphlet appeared, number 90 in the series of *Tracts for the Times*. This, as Clough described it later in a letter to Gell, endeavoured to show 'that with the exception of that on the Pope, a Roman catholic may conscientiously sign the 39 Articles; at any rate that as to Purgatory, Pardons, Masses, Saint-worship etc. the Articles condemn merely the existing unauthorized teaching of Rome, not even the Tridentine doctrines nor those held by the better and truer Romanists' (M, 108).

Ward was highly excited by the Tract and thrust it on his colleague Tait with the words 'Here is something worth reading!' But Tait, along with others who saw the Articles as a bulwark defending a Protestant Church of England against Romish superstition, took great offence. As Senior Tutor of Balliol, and with three tutors from other colleges, he published an open letter of protest on 8 March. 'The Tract' the letter said 'appears to us to have a tendency to mitigate beyond what charity requires, and to the prejudice of the pure truth of the Gospel, the very serious differences which separate the Church of Rome from our own.' The tutors deplored the anonymity of the publication and called for the author to make himself known.

Newman came forward to acknowledge authorship of the Tract. The Hebdomadal Board resolved that the principles of interpretation in Tract 90 were inconsistent with the statutes of the University. The Bishop of Oxford pronounced the Tract dangerous in its tendencies. Newman, whose theory of church government exalted episcopal authority, could do little but acquiesce. 'I fear I am clean dished' he wrote to his sister. He agreed to terminate the whole series of Tracts.

Oddly, Clough in his diaries made no mention of the Tract's condemnation, though it was posted on the buttery hatch of every college ('after the manner of discommoned pastrycooks' Newman complained). His resolution to avoid theological discussion must have been sorely tried during a two-hour conversation with Ward on the day after the Tract's publication. He seems, in fact, to have taken less interest in Newman's theology than in a book for children by Newman's sister, *The Fairy Bower*, which he recommended to Annie (K, 156; B, 112). But his principal concern during this Lent term was with his own health. At the beginning of the year he had consulted the celebrated Oxford physician Tuckwell, and he followed out a series of his prescriptions: rhubarb, medicinal drops, castor oil and the use of a mysterious contraption called a Misopot (K, 154–62).

Whatever the nature of Clough's complaint, it did not prevent – indeed perhaps it called for – a strenuous regime of regular walking. Many entries in the diaries reveal him as a fast and energetic hiker. On the day after the publication of Tract 90, for instance, he walked alone from Oxford to Headington, Shotover, Bullingdon and back, taking three hours for a nine-mile journey. Later in the year he undertook a solitary seven-mile hike to Horspath and back twice in one day, spending only four-and-a-quarter hours on the road (K, 160, 182).

One of these walks was the subject of the term's only poem. Four times in a cold and miserable January Clough walked up the road to Abingdon past Bagley wood up to the top of Hinksey Hill. His destination was the spot now treasured by the Oxford Preservation Society as allowing the finest view of Oxford's 'dreaming spires'. The poem, begun *in situ*, took some weeks to complete, and was eventually published as the ninth (and weakest) of the 'Blank Misgivings' sequence. It begins:

Once more the wonted road I tread,
Once more dark heavens above my head
Upon the windy down I stand
My station whence the circling land
Lies mapped and pictured wide below; –
Such as it was, alas again,
Long dreary banks, and breadth of plain
By hedge or tree unbroken; – lo
A few dark woods that do but show
How vain that hope, and with the sense
Of one perpetual impotence,
Relieving not, meseems enhance
The sovereign dullness of the expanse.

Yet marks where human hand hath been
Bare house, unsheltered village, space

Of ploughed but hedgeless land between
From Nature vindicate the place
(Such aspect as methinks may be
In some half-settled colony),
A wide and yet disheartening view,
A cold, repulsive world.

(P, 31–3)[10]

Clough's spring visit to Rugby was early this year: he got leave (no doubt because of his health) to miss the end of term, and spent a few days with Bonamy Price, who was writing an article against Newman and Tract 90. At the Prices he found Burbidge, and listened to him as he preached his first Rugby sermon. He walked back to Oxford in time to sit his last college collections, being complimented once more on good work and uniformly exemplary morality.

For two weeks of the vacation Clough lodged in Margaret Street, in London, in order to take extra tuition from a science tutor, Robert Lowe. He did not enjoy this first visit to London, 'The Great Bablyon', and he wrote a disdainful sonnet 'To the Great Metropolis'.

Traffic, to speak from knowledge but begun,
I saw, and travelling much, and fashion – Yea,
And if that Competition and Display
Make a great Capital, then thou art one,
One, it may be, unrivalled neath the sun.
But sovereign symbol of the Great and Good,
True Royalty and genuine Statesmanhood,
Nobleness, Learning, Piety was none.

Cocking a snook at Wordsworth, he concluded that the city he had seen was 'Anything but a mighty Nation's heart' (P, 157).

Clough returned to Oxford on 21 April, with just three hot weeks left before the postponed examinations. These were due to begin with the first written paper on 10 May and were to conclude with an oral examination on 19 May. He worked feverishly and slept badly, and he decided to compete only in the classics papers, withdrawing from the optional examinations in mathematics and science.

Clough's walks now took a new and surprising turn. During March and April he paid frequent visits to Woodeaton, a distance of three miles north of Oxford. Woodeaton was the last place he visited before leaving for London and the first on his return to Oxford. In the four weeks before and during the examination he went to the region around Woodeaton and Elsfield, alone and on foot, no less than ten times. These included visits to the area on two out of the four days of written papers, and on the day of the *viva voce*.

That these walks were more than his usual constitutional is suggested by several things. The diary entry for 5 April (the day before leaving for London) reads 'Woodeaton and τα συσανικα'. The Greek expression means 'Susan's matter', and Clough often used Greek in his diary to conceal a topic of embarrassment. This unknown Susan appears also in a cryptic entry of the previous 8 February 'Spoke to Susan but weakly and to no purpose'. Flirtation between an undergraduate and a simple country girl was to become a favourite theme of Clough's later verse. If his descriptions are based on first-hand experience, then the reference to 'Susan's matter' may refer to a temporary infatuation, which would explain the frenetic expeditions to Woodeaton.

This can be no more than conjecture. The parish records of Woodeaton record the christening there of a shoemaker's daughter, Susanna Neale, who would have been 15 or 16 in 1841. It has been suggested that Clough's assignment may have been with a prostitute: nine such bearing the name of 'Susan' are listed in the proctors' registers for this period.[11] No doubt the wealthy bloods of Christ Church provided thriving custom for prostitutes who avoided proctorial interference by plying their trade in country lanes outside the city boundary. But in the case of an impoverished Balliol reading man with an over-active conscience, an innocent, if injudicious, flirtation seems more plausible.

Before the class lists of the examination were published, Clough left Oxford for a walking tour in the Cherwell valley. While he was staying with the family of Uncle Alfred a letter was brought to him to tell him that he had been awarded a second class. He at once went to Rugby to break the news to Dr Arnold. Young Tom Arnold recalled him standing in the middle of the school yard and saying 'with face partly flushed and partly pale "I have failed".'

Many different explanations have been given of Clough's disappointing Schools result. His friends blamed the examiners. 'They had' said his tutor Tait 'not only a first-rate scholar but a man of original genius before them, and were too stupid to discover it' (K, xli). Clough himself did not question the fairness of the verdict. Before the result was known he wrote to his sister 'I did the papers much worse than I expected'. Without false modesty, he reckoned that they were not a quarter as good as his reading should have enabled him to produce (M, 110). A fellow-student who attended the oral examination recalled him standing tongue-tied on one foot.

Though Clough did not ever blame the Oxford examiners, he was later to blame the Oxford curriculum. 'I had been pretty well sated of distinctions and competitions at school', he wrote in 1852 'I would gladly have dispensed with anything more of success in this kind. What I wanted was to sit down to happy, unimpeded prosecution of some new subject or subjects; surely there was more in the domain of knowledge than that Latin and Greek which I had been wandering about in for the last ten years' (PPR, 406).

Certainly, the Oxford system did not serve geniuses well: in failing to obtain a first Clough had been preceded by John Henry Newman and was to be succeeded by Matthew Arnold. There is no denying the mismatch between Clough's brilliant performance at Rugby and his dismal performance at Oxford. Some have blamed Arnold for forcing him too hard at school; Ward, with more justice, reproached himself with distracting him from his university studies. But surely the principal explanation of the failure must rest with Clough's own faults of character and temperament, in particular his perfectionism and procrastination. To do him justice, he never pretended otherwise, and he admitted that he would probably have done better if he had taken Schools at the normal time (M, 109). But may, perhaps, a small part of the blame rest with the last-minute distractions of the mysterious Susan?

Having hiked 50 miles, Clough returned to Oxford (via Woodeaton), to keep a vacation term so as to retain his scholarship, and to recruit pupils to teach during the summer, so that he would not have to call on his family for financial support. He brought himself up to date on the state of theological controversy since Tract 90. In the Balliol senior common room the debate raged with a remarkable combination of *odium theologicum* and personal affection. Tait had led the move to censure the Tract; Ward had written two pamphlets in its defence. In the second, 90 dense pages entitled 'A few words more in defence of Tract 90', he defended Newman's honesty, but did not deny that the natural sense of some of the articles was Protestant. He cited the twelfth article, which declared that good works, which are the fruits of faith and follow after justification, cannot put away our sins. This, he said 'is as plain as words can make it on the evangelical side. Of course I think its natural meaning may be explained away, for I subscribe it myself in a non-natural sense' (Ward 1889: 173).[12]

Tait suggested to the Master of Balliol that this kind of thing made Ward unfit to hold a tutorship. The ageing Jenkyns found it difficult to perservere through the closely reasoned pages of the pamphlet, but Tait pointed out specific passages referring to 'the present degradation' of the Church of England and 'the darkness of Protestant error'. Jenkyns was much shocked. 'He is a most dangerous man: what *heresy* may he not insinuate under the form of a syllogism.' He was greatly relieved when Ward, after chapel one day in June, came up to him and said 'Master, I am come to resign into your hands my two lecturerships'.[13]

But Clough was in no doubt that Ward had been constructively dismissed. 'Did I tell you' he wrote to Annie on 13 June 'that Ward, my friend and George's, has been turned out of his tutorship for ultra-Newmanism?' (M, 110).

Clough had hoped to take pupils to Westmoreland in the vacation. In the event he had only one pupil, passed on to him by Burbidge: Theodore Walrond, the holiday companion of 1838, who was now head boy of Rugby, and was working for the November Balliol scholarship examination. The two spent six weeks together at Grasmere, 'endeavouring' as Clough reported to Gell 'to produce from our two past idlenesses one industry to bring him to Balliol as a Scholar or at any rate to keep him from [his family's] office at Glasgow' (M, 112). Clough reported their daily schedule to Burbidge in doggerel:

Until four in the day
We are reading away
And then after four
It would be a bore
For at mealtimes I'm talking
As also when walking
To myself or Todo
So that time will no do . . .
Grasmere and Rydal
We can walk too, though idle
But for them I must trouble you
To refer to W. W.
Who you know very well
Of your own pretty sell'
Has wrot all can be wroot and said all can be said
Of Grasmere lake foot, or of Grasmere lake-head
(P, 158)

Once again Clough found that the tutor–pupil relationship presented emotional complications; but this time he experienced them from the tutor's side. 'I am now all along resting on the fancy of affection in Walrond' he wrote on 6 August 'whereas I have no reason to believe he cares for me, nor yet could be justified in expressing to him that I care for him.' Fortunately, the two were not thrown entirely on each others' company. Frequently they visited the Arnold household at Fox How, and there they often met Simpkinson and his family, who had a house nearby. Mrs Arnold was as kind as ever and old Rugby friends renewed their links. Clough got to know George Cotton, a Rugby master then courting Jane Arnold, to whom he became engaged later in the year (K, 169; M, 113).

At Fox How news had just reached Clough that his father's business had failed once more. He felt obliged to return home, and started southward on 18 August, walking 16 miles to Milnthorpe, doubling back 11 miles to Bowness on 19 August to pick up a portmanteau he had left behind, and then walking a further ten miles on 20 August to Lancaster to complete the journey to Liverpool by train (K, 175).

On arriving at Liverpool, he noted, he found 'Mother & Annie sad enough; the rest cheerful'. Brothers Charles and George were now independent, and their father, James Butler, was gifted, or afflicted, with a Micawber-like optimism. Two pieces of good news greeted him. First, Arnold wrote from Fox How to say that he had been appointed to the Regius Professorship of History in Oxford – a dignified, non-residential post, conferred as one of the last acts of the now defunct Whig government. Second, an ill wind at Rugby provided an unexpected chance to earn some money. Typhoid fever was feared at Rugby, and a number of wealthy Liverpool families who had sons at the school kept them at home and engaged Clough to tutor them until the scare was over (K, 175). He collected eight pupils, who between them paid £18 a week. 'I am at present earning at the rate of £1000 per annum' he boasted to Gell on September 11 – 'but of this' he added 'I have only had one week and do not expect more than another' (B, 125; M, 112). But in the end the boys stayed on for seven weeks, the last departing only on 8 October (M, 114; K, 179).

The teaching was hard work, and once he noted in his diary that he had broken down in class; but looking back on these weeks, he found that he 'preferred boy-teaching to man-teaching'. He found time to read Harriet Martineau's newly published novel about Toussaint l'Ouverture, *The Hour and the Man*. (Gell, to whom he recommended the book, found its moral tone shocking (B, 129). He took walks to Seaforth, Mossley Hill and Old Swan, all still rural destinations; but in Liverpool, he complained to Gell, there were no walks to be got at except by wading through a couple of miles of town (K, 176–7; M, 114). However, he was able to take weekend breaks in Wales. On Saturday 18 September, for instance, he taught his pupils until 3 p.m. and then took a steamer to Rhyl. On Sunday he walked to St Asaph for service in the Cathedral and then over the Clwyd mountains ('gorse-and-heath-tinted, windy, beautiful') to dine with his aunts who lived at Rhualissa near Mold. He slept the night at Queensferry and rose at 6.30, travelling on foot, by train, and by ferry, to meet up with his pupils in Liverpool at 10 (B, 125).

It was immediately after this breathless escape that he wrote his first poem about love, 'Thought may well be ever ranging'. While opinions may change, love 'must once for all be given, or must not at all be given'. The poem stresses that it is important not to trust life-long bliss to a momentary caprice, but equally important not to mistake dutiful affection for real love. Finally:

Loving – if the answering breast
Seem not to be thus possessed,
Still in hoping have a care;
If it do, beware, beware!

But if in yourself you find it,
Above all things – mind it, mind it!
(P, 27)

It is not clear why Clough felt the need to give himself this warning. Perhaps at Mold – where, he told his diary, he had been 'foolish' – he had encountered one of his female cousins – he mentions a 'Dora' – and wondered whether his feelings had gone beyond mere family duty. A week later, indeed, he referred back in his diary, in a Latin code, to his 'Rhualissa enslavement'. Rhualissa, it seems, was the place to which the Vicar of Beaumaris had retired with his daughters (K, 178).

This interpretation of the cryptic remarks in the diary would accord quite well with the penultimate encounter between the hero and his cousin Emily in the semi-autobiographical *Primitiae*:

One visit brief I made again
In autumn next but one, and then
All better found. With Mary Gwen
I talked, a schoolgirl just about
To leave this winter and come out.
Patty and Lydia were away,
And a strange sort of distance lay
Between me and Emilia.
She sought me less, and I was shy.
And yet this time I think that I
Did subtly feel, more saw, more knew
The beauty into which she grew
(P, 389)

Returning to Oxford in mid-October, Clough moved into new lodgings in Holywell, refusing Ward's offer of the use of his dressing room in Balliol. He had only a single pupil to teach but he could live on the savings from his summer 'academy' in Liverpool. He began reading Emerson's essays, which were to have a great influence on him; but his principal task was to prepare himself to compete for a Balliol fellowship in November.

Clough kept an eye on the newly arrived Matthew Arnold ('going out with the Harriers' he reported to Gell in shocked tones) and gave a lavish breakfast to introduce him to his Balliol friends, including Temple, Jowett and Lake. He took care of Theodore Walrond when he came up to sit for the scholarship on 19 November. During his own examinations (five days of written papers from 23–7 November) he spent afternoons on the river, with Todo and Matthew and Matthew's brother Tom who had come up to University College.

After the last of the written papers Clough was told by Ward that he was one of three front-runners for the fellowship, the others being Robert Lingen of Trinity and E. K. Karslake of Christ Church. He went in great excitement to the house of Mrs Greenhill, a niece of Dr Arnold, and gave the good news to his Rugby friends and to Arnold's daughter Jane, who was staying there. But once again his hopes were disappointed. Lingen, later to be Permanent Secretary to the Treasury, seems to have been the unanimous first choice of the electors. Clough himself was, he believed, the second choice of Tait, Ward, Lake and perhaps Oakeley; but four fellows voted for Karslake and the matter was put beyond doubt by the Master's casting vote. Among those who voted against Clough was Jowett, who later regretted his vote as a disastrous mistake. From University Stanley wrote to Simpkinson:

> It seemed so great a misfortune that I cannot help venting my lamentations over it. But there is this great comfort. Some of his papers were done so splendidly as fully to show that the spring of genius has not dried up within him, and therefore I hope he will get in at Oriel. (K, xlvi)

An Oriel fellowship was indeed at least as good as a fellowship at Balliol, and even some Balliol men regarded it as the highest distinction in Oxford. But the Oriel examinations were not until Eastertide, so Clough still had another term of cramming ahead.

*   *   *

Dr Arnold came to Oxford at the end of Michaelmas term to give history lectures as Regius Professor. His inaugural lecture in December drew an enormous audience unparallelled since the Middle Ages. Clough joined the family for the hours before the lecture, including the half-hour wait for the arrival of the Vice-Chancellor, who had mistaken the date. After the ovation, the family went over to Balliol to inspect Matthew's rooms and to call on the Master, who was laid up with gout (Honan 1981: 55).[14]

Clough's Christmas vacation was divided between Rugby, Oxford and Wales. Some scruple now worried him about taking communion: he wrote about it to Ward and Arnold and on Christmas Day he 'missed Communion openly' to the distress of his sister. Early in January he gave instruction to some of his pupils of the summer. He read a great deal of Kant, and spent time teaching Latin and German to Annie. Once back in Oxford, he looked back on this period as one of great dissipation.

Lenten term, though enlivened by the visits of the Arnold family as the History lectures continued, was once again a time of stress. Early in February Arthur wrote home complaining of poor health, and his father wrote back 'I do beg that you will not be injuring your health by over exertions and extra work [to assist with the family finances] as nothing on earth can compensate for *loss of health*.' At Liverpool there was now real financial distress. A large sum had to be borrowed from Uncle Charles, George had to be packed off to live with Uncle Alfred, and the family were grateful for small gifts, such as an anonymous envelope containing £10. James Clough felt he could not show his face at public events, and sent Charles to deputize for him at the St David's Day dance in the Town Hall to celebrate the birth of the heir to the throne (M, 115).

Pressure was now at its most extreme on Arthur to make himself independent, and contribute to the family fortunes, by winning a fellowship. There was a return of the spiritual turmoil that had marked his first year at Balliol. He began to see night-time visions, and to crave for some way of blotting out all his past sins. No doubt it was his father's bankrupcty that made him describe this, in a Platonic expression, as 'χρεών άποκοπη', 'cancelling of debts'. The thought of a total forgiveness was something that he alternately greedily welcomed and disowned as a delusion. Surely, at the very least, confession would be a necessary condition for such forgiveness: and to whom should he confess? He toyed with the idea of writing a full account of his sins to Burbidge or Arnold; he even seems to have consulted Newman. He was constantly 'floored' while teaching, and considered giving up his pupils altogether. To help him get through a difficult tutorial he called up fond images of Walrond, but Todo was no longer the only object of his affection. A younger man, whose name is uncertain and who appears in the diary only under the cryptic abbreviation 'B . . . y', he described as 'refilling his empty heart'.[15] His diary for the term peters out into incoherent expressions of hopelessness (K, 188–98).

As ever, an end-of-term visit to Rugby set him back on his feet, and he was able to return to Oxford to sit the Oriel examination in much better spirits. As he moved into the college to write his papers he wrote in his diary 'I have as yet, thank God, no connexions here at any rate'. His brother George came up and kept him company during the four days of the examination. On 1 April his diary contains the laconic entry 'Orielensis factus. Breakfast with Shairp.' Shairp himself left a fuller account of the breakfast, to which he had also invited another of the fellowship candidates.

> The party consisted of about a dozen. We had no notion that anything about the examination would be known so soon, and were all sitting quietly, having just finished breakfast, but not yet risen from the table. The door opened wide; entered a fellow of another college, and drawing himself up to his full height, he addressed the other candidate. 'I am sorry to say you have *not* got it.' Then 'Clough, you have' and stepping forward into the middle of the room, held out his hand, with 'Allow me to congratulate you'. (PPR, 23)

Notes

1 Maisie Ward, *Young Mr Newman*, London 1948, pp. 225, 312.
2 These and other undergraduate essays of Clough are preserved in the Bodleian library, MS Eng. Misc d.513–15. They are listed and studied in E. B. Greenberger, *Arthur Hugh Clough: the Growth of a Poet's Mind*, Harvard University Press 1970.
3 Wilfrid Ward, *William George Ward and the Oxford Movement*, London 1889, p. 83.
4 Maisie Ward, *Young Mr Newman*, p. 331.
5 J. H. Newman, *Letters and Diaries*, VI, ed. G. Tracey, Oxford 1995; 1999, p. 204.
6 Ibid., VII, p. 75.
7 Wilfrid Ward, *William George Ward and the Oxford Movement*, p. 106.
8 Park Honan, *Matthew Arnold: A Life*, London 1981, p. 65.
9 Diary entries show that in January Clough felt it necessary to define within precise limits his relationship with a third-year commoner called Tylden (K, 154).
10 Mr Philip Stewart, who is responsible for identifying the location described in the poem, remarks that it is instructive to compare this poem with Arnold's *The Scholar Gipsy* and *Thyrsis*. 'It is interesting to reflect' he writes 'that if Boars Hill – "cold" "dull" "dreary" and even "repulsive" – had been made known by Clough's poem instead of Arnold's, it might not have been transformed by romantic readers into a fashionable suburb and the "Hill of Poets",' *The Boars Hill Newsletter*, 1996, p. 66. Gell, to whom the poem was sent in Tasmania, complained that it was unfair to the colonies (B, 122).
11 See Rupert Christiansen, *The Voice of Victorian Sex: Arthur Hugh Clough*, London 2001, p. 24.
12 Wilfrid Ward, *William George Ward and the Oxford Movement*, p. 173.
13 Ibid., pp. 175, 437.
14 Park Honan, *Matthew Arnold*, p. 55.
15 When I edited Clough's Oxford diaries in 1990 I suggested that this might be a Balliol commoner named Thomas Battersby. I now think it more likely that the code refers to George Bradley, the future Dean of Westminster, who came up to University College from Rugby in 1841 and later wrote a textbook of Latin Prose Composition which tormented schoolboys of many generations, including my own.

Chapter Three
Fellow of Oriel

On his election to Oriel Clough was congratulated by relieved family and friends, and he paid a brief celebratory visit to Liverpool on 4–7 April (K, 201). 'Just 27 years before' wrote Dr Arnold 'on 31 March 1815, I was elected Fellow of Oriel, and I wish that your Election may bring you as much pleasure and as much good as I think I derived from mine.' Uncle Alfred wrote from Braunston to congratulate not Clough, but Oriel. 'You could not have introduced into your society' he wrote to Provost Hawkins 'a more amiable young man. During his Father's absence in foreign countries I have watched over his earlier years and have never known him guilty even of a boyish fault.' He had worried that his nephew, now as earlier, might not have done himself justice in the examination. 'I trust, however' he told Hawkins 'that he may now regain his former health and spirits and do credit to your selection (M, 116).

Clough's diary shows that his spirits did indeed improve during Trinity term, though he continued to reproach himself with various faults. 'I seem to know nothing' he wrote at the end of his first week at Oriel 'except that I am wholly wrong within – a hundred carats of positiveness and false enjoyments.' However, he threw himself into teaching. Though he was not yet a tutor, he now had no difficulty in collecting private pupils. During the term he made £80 by teaching in addition to the stipend that went with his fellowship; when term ended he was able to send home £66, his first contribution to the family finances.

It was some while before he felt fully at home in Oriel. Towards the end of term Arthur wrote to Annie 'I am becoming fairly resigned to Oriel High Table and Common Room, though I do not like them nearly as well as the Balliol Bachelor's Table.' And to Gell in Tasmania he wrote 'I am very sorry to leave Balliol, which I confess to liking better I fear than Rugby itself, and never expect to find equalled by Oriel' (M, 117). The term's only poem is a Swiftian piece, possibly targeted against the Oriel fellowship, describing how facial expressions conceal people's minds just as their clothes conceal their bodies. The poet however claims to be able to give an explanation:

Of every class of fixed or moving eye
The passing smile, the pouted smile unmoving
The twitchings and the lines about the mouth

because he has within himself:

A Papal Index Purgatorius
Of all the follies that in human shape
Walk and grimace it through the World.
(K, 206; P, 160)

Another poem addresses an attempt by a materialist writer to reduce poetry to physiology. In part the poem runs:

Is it true that poetical power,
The gift of heaven, the dower,
Of Apollo and the Nine,
The inborn sense, 'the vision and the faculty divine'
All we glorify and bless
In our rapturous exaltation,
All invention and creation,
Exuberance of fancy and sublime imagination,
All a poet's fame is built on,
The fame of Shakespeare, Milton,
Of Wordsworth, Byron, Shelley,
Is in reason's grave precision,
Nothing more, nothing less,
Than a peculiar conformation,
Constitution, and condition
Of the brain and of the belly?

The poem is a poor effort, full of idle repetition and forced rhyme, and it ends in a shuffle:

If it is so, let it be so,
And we will all agree so;
But the plot has counterplot,
It may be, and yet be not.
(P, 43)

Surprisingly, Clough thought sufficiently well of this verse not only to include it in the anthology *Ambarvalia* but to make it the concluding poem. To the biographer the interest of this pair of 1842 poems is that they are the first poems written since Rugby that are not mere expressions of self-torment.

During 1841–2 Matthew Arnold, at Balliol, was receiving tutorials from Tait and from Lingen, who had beaten Clough to the fellowship. He was acquiring a reputation as a dandy and an idler. At the end of his first term the Master described him as 'Respectable but desultory in habits of reading – & not sufficiently attentive to the rules of the College'. Later his studies improved but his termly evaluation never rose above 'Amiable and respectable, but far from regular'.[1]

Towards the end of the summer term the Arnold family suffered two grievous blows. Matthew's eldest sister, Jane, was betrothed to one of the Rugby masters, George Cotton. In mid-May the engagement was broken off, Cotton having revealed that he had an alcoholic mother. Dr Arnold was deeply distressed, and relations between him and his daughter came under strain; he suffered a 'furious attack' of ill-health. In Oxford, Clough and Ward discussed the news in hushed tones on 17 May. There followed a period in which Arnold was unusually quiet and gentle, and then, on 12 June, after having preached his end-of-term sermon and given a farewell supper to the boys of school house, he suffered agonizing chest pains and died, a few hours after, of a heart attack.

In a letter to Clough Arthur Stanley described his edifying death. To his son Tom, Arnold said 'My son, thank God for me – Thank God for having sent me this pain. I never had pain before, and I feel it is good for me, and I am *so* thankful.' 'The almost royal majesty of his death' Stanley wrote 'seems to affix the last seal which could be given to his character as being one of the greatest and holiest men whom this generation has produced' (M, 119).

Matthew was at Fox How and was brought the news of his father's death by Lake. He returned to Rugby to choose a place for his father's tomb. The family now moved permanently to Fox How, previously just a vacation residence. Lake and Stanley went thither to comfort them. Clough, on hearing the news, went neither to Rugby nor to Fox How, but set off on a solitary walking tour, first in Derbyshire and then in Wales. From 13 June to 15 July his diary is simply a sombre list of place names.

Once or twice he encountered friends. Shairp who was with a reading party at Tan-y-bwlch, tells us

> Clough, then wandering through the Welsh mountains, one morning looked in on us. I took a walk with him, and he at once led me up Moel Wyn, the highest mountain within reach. Two things I remember that day – one, that he spoke a good deal (for him) of Dr Arnold, whose death had happened only a few weeks before; another, that a storm came down upon the mountain when we were half-way up. In the midst of it

> we lay for some time close above a small mountain tarn, and watched the storm wind working on the face of the lake, tearing and torturing the water into most fantastic, almost ghostly shapes, the like of which I never saw before or since. (PPR, 23)

Clough refused a request from Stanley to write a memoir of Arnold. He did, however, write to the Rugby Trustees a letter of support for his old Tutor, Tait, who was a candidate to succeed Arnold as headmaster.

This summer was one of the worst troughs in Clough's life. Arnold's death brought a feeling of emotional bankruptcy to match his father's commercial bankruptcy. A poem of farewell to friends, which later found its place in the 'Blank Misgivings' sequence, expresses the mood in which he set off on his solitary tour:

> I owe all much, much more than I can pay;
> Therefore it is I go; how could I stay
> Where every look commits me to fresh debt
> And to pay little I must borrow yet?
> Enough of this already, now away!
> With silent woods and hills untenanted
> Let me go commune.
>
> (P, 29)

The solitary hiking and scrambling in Wales, however, effected a kind of purgation. From the low point of mid-July Clough's spirits began to rise and his emotions achieved an equilibrium never previously attained. Among his first Oriel pupils was an Irish Rugbeian, the son of General Sir Octavius Carey, commander of the Cork district, who had engaged him to give extra tuition during the long vacation. Clough crossed to Ireland on 17 July and stayed until early September, bringing another pupil to share the tutorials. His diary records many days of bathing, botanical exploration, balls, field days and yachting excursions; on one occasion he swam two miles across Cork Harbour. He found himself at ease in the Carey household at Cobh and after the tour wrote cheerfully to Gell:

> We saw all the world military there, captains and colonels and Knights in Arms, which last title might be given to some of the infant Careys (the family consisting of a dozen, besides one son in Afghanistan) for it seems they all go into the Army, excepting the genius under my tutorage and even he says that if he does not get a good degree he shall give up all thoughts of the Church and get a commission. (M, 122)

Clough obviously enjoyed teaching Carey, and back in Oxford often took walks with him and, occasionally, exercise on horseback. But despite the extra tuition, the young man took a fourth class in Schools in November, and, true to his word, applied for a commission and set off for India.

On 4 September Clough returned from Ireland by the packet to Milford Haven, and went, via Liverpool, to Leicester, where he acted as godfather to a young brother of Burbidge who was christened Arthur Arnold. Thence swiftly back to Wales for two more energetic weeks of hiking in Snowdonia, this time spent partly in company with Constantine Prichard, the Balliol scholar who by winning a double First at the first Schools examination after his own failure had restored the reputation of the college and the self-esteem of its High Table (K, 213–4).

The first week in October was spent in Liverpool, to say good-bye to James and George Clough who were setting out once more for America in the hope of restoring the family's fortunes. It was to be his last meeting with his younger brother. Arthur took walks with Annie and they discussed Byron's table-talk and the novels of Fenimore Cooper. He also visited the new Irvingite chapel, and a 'nunnery' (K, 215).

Michaelmas term 1842 passed happily enough. Ward, now on the other side of the High, was kept most of the time at a distance; Tom Arnold came up to University College, to be tutored by Stanley, and Theodore Walrond took up his scholarship at Balliol. Clough saw much of both of them: his once tense relationships with Walrond were now relaxed, and Prichard, Temple and Shairp also provided plenty of uncomplicated friendship.

Clough could now dine at more than one High Table. On 19 October he went to Balliol to meet Tait on his first visit since becoming Headmaster of Rugby. 'He is said to flog more than Arnold did' he reported to Gell 'and to be very strict'. Lake had succeeded Tait as tutor at Balliol, and was ordained at the end of the term. Clough quite often took walks with him, and on 11 December the two of them called on Newman, now in retirement at the nearby village of Littlemore (K, 219).

In memory of Arnold Stanley was collecting subscriptions for scholarships to Rugby or Oxford (to be held in the first instance by his sons) and for a monument in the college chapel. Clough had no spare cash to contribute, but he agreed to write a series of entries to a dictionary of classical biography being edited by W. Smith, and paid his fees into the memorial fund. Altogether he contributed some 77 biographies, specializing on Spartan kings, and his diary in this term is full of names from the beginning of the alphabet: Agesilaus, Aristeas, Aristides, Aristodemus, Aristocrates, Aristonymus, Astyochus.

Having celebrated Christmas Day in Westminster Abbey, and visited Simpkinson at Hurstmonceux, Arthur spent the first weeks of January 1843 with his family in Liverpool and Wales. A new Collegiate Institute had recently been founded in Liverpool, and young William Conybeare of Trinity Cambridge, with whom Clough had so often crossed swords at Rugby, was installed as the first principal. Clough paid several calls on Conybeare and his newly married wife, and on 6 January attended the inauguration of the Institute, where for the first time he met W. E. Gladstone, now 'the rising hope of those stern unbending Tories' (M, 124; K, 223).

1843 was a good year for Clough. He found teaching congenial, and he had now gathered a large circle of friends. Walrond was the closest of these, but he also saw much of Jowett, Prichard and Temple, all Balliol friends, and also Congreve of Wadham, a companion on horseback rides. He no longer inserted into his diary daily passages of self-rebuke and self-encouragement. The last self-reproach is the entry 'Sum turpissima bestia' ('I am a filthy beast') after a walk with Bradley and Carey on 26 October 1842. The only resolution in 1843 was one taken on 11 February 'not to talk to Ward'. Like Clough's other resolutions, it was swiftly broken: only a week later the two took a four hour walk together to Besselsleigh (K, 216, 224).

By the Easter term Clough had established with Walrond and the two Arnold brothers that round of easy-going Arcadian companionship commemorated by Matthew in *The Scholar Gipsy* and in *Thyrsis*. Thus, in the week beginning 14 May we are told on Monday 'Mat & Tom up Charwel: at Walrond's to tea'; on Tueday 'Mat and Walrond up Charwel. here to tea', on Friday 'With Walrond to the Fox [on Boar's Hill] & at tea. Tom & Mat. Visio beatifica' – though we are not told who or what provided the beatific vision (K, 229). The walk that Matthew remembered most fondly – he boasted that he could follow the path blindfold – went through North and South Hinksey, where they were on first-name terms with the landlady of the Cross Keys, along what is now the Oxfordshire Circular Walk, uphill past Chilswell farm, to an eminence on Boar's Hill with a view to the south over the Downs and to the north over 'that sweet city with her dreaming spires' (*Thyrsis*, 1–20).[2]

For a while the fire of theological controversy had died down in Oxford. Arnold was dead and Newman, at Littlemore, was, in his own words, on his deathbed as regards as the Anglican Church. In Newman's absence no single leader emerged for the Tractarian party: Pusey headed the Anglo-Catholic mainstream, while Ward was the most prominent of the Romeward faction. But in May there was a new outbreak of *odium theologicum*.

While the head of the Clough family, Uncle Richard, was paying a visit to Oxford, Arthur took him to Christ Church to hear Pusey preach the University Sermon, on the nature of the Eucharist. In the course of the sermon the preacher spoke of 'a substantial bodily presence' of Christ on the altar, and of 'a continual sacrifice in the eucharist for remission of sins'. The sermon was denounced to the Vice-Chancellor, and a court of six doctors pronounced that it contained 6 opinions at variance with the doctrines of the Church of England'. Pusey was prohibited from preaching for two years.[3]

Clough noted in his diary on 7 June 'Pusey's row'. But he gave greater prominence to the upsetting of a punt. Writing to his sister Annie he reported 'yesterday when I was bathing the man I was with dropped his watch in the river, and that took me there again in the evening though to no purpose'. We learn from his diary that the owner of the watch was Matthew Arnold (B, 145; K, 230).

Matthew, though still receiving equivocal reports at Balliol, was awarded the Newdigate prize for a rather tepid poem on Cromwell. The University never heard the poem recited. Arnold was due to deliver it at Commemoration on 28 June 1843, but he was unable to do so because the Sheldonian theatre was in turmoil. There were noisy protests against the award of an honorary degree to the American ambassador, who happened to be a Unitarian, and proceedings had to be abandoned.[4]

In the summer vacation Clough made his first continental tour, described in a letter to Gell in October.

> I left England the 1st of July with T. Walrond, went to Havre, Paris, Lyons, Marseilles, Genoa, Leghorn, where Burbidge met us, he having, as I hope he has informed you, spent the spring at Siena with pupils. With him we went to Pisa, and Florence, and from Florence made excursions to the Monasteries of Vallombrosa, Camaldoli and Laverna. I was then ill for about a week at Florence and then left Walrond and Burbidge and started for England. I went by Bologna, Parma, and Piacenza to Milan – saw the Cathedral, the most beautiful building I ever beheld, as also the Leonardo da Vinci, which is I almost think the most beautiful painting. Then I crossed the Simplon, went up the Rhone, over the Grimsel Pass and one or two others in the Bernese Oberland, so to Thun and Berne, and thence by Basle and the Rhine home. (M, 125)

Clough's solitary convalescent journey through Italy after his illness was to have a tragic mirror image in 1861, when with his wife he travelled the same route from Milan to his death in Florence. But once back in England he seemed possessed of unbounded health. He soon became tired of 'being continually lionized about galleries and the like', he told Gell, and much preferred 'walking through the beauty of a country'.

August and September brought plenty of opportunity for country walking, when he took his first reading party – of Balliol, not Oriel, students – to Grasmere. Reading parties were to become a familiar nineteenth-century institution, but they were still fairly new things, quite distinct from the individual vacation coaching that had long been on offer. Half holiday and half seminar, a reading party was an indication both of Oxford's increased academic seriousness (the study of texts was not for term-time only) and of the Victorian insistence on providing a healthy body to house a healthy mind (the hiking and swimming were no less important than the reading and talking).[5]

Clough's Grasmere party was described by one of its members, J. C. Shairp:

> He lived in a small lodging immediately to the west of Grasmere church; we in a farm-house on the lake. During these weeks I read the Greek tragedians with him, and did Latin prose. His manner of translating, especially the Greek choruses, was quite peculiar; a quaint archaic style of language, keeping rigidly to the Greek order of the words, and so bringing out their expression better, more forcibly and poetically, than any other translations I had heard. When work was done we used to walk in the afternoon with him all over that delightful country. His 'eye to country' was wonderful. He knew the whole lie of the different dales relatively to each other; every tarn, beck and bend in them. (PPR, 24)

The longest of the party's expeditions was a two-day walk – on Sunday from Grasmere over the Borrowdale Fells and Honister Crag to Buttermere, where they arrived by starlight and spent the night at the inn, and on Monday over Scarth Gap and the Black Sail pass to the head of Wastwater, then to the top of Scafell, and down over Bowfell and under the Langdale pikes back to Grasmere. On another day there was a race from Grasmere to the summit of Fairfield, a rise of some 2,500 ft. Clough, running with long strides and bent almost horizontal to the slope, was the second of the six competitors to reach the top. 'Few men' Shairp reports 'so stout as he then was, could have matched him up a mountain' (PPR, 25).

Extra pleasure was provided by the proximity of the Arnold family at Fox How. The family were adjusting to life without the Doctor. 'Mrs A was very cheerful' Clough reported 'more so a good deal than I expected to find her'. For most of September Arthur Stanley was staying at Fox How, working on Arnold's official biography. Jane Arnold had to bear a double grief, since she had not yet recovered from the breaking of her engagement to George Cotton. She and Matthew retraced a walk they had taken with their father ten years earlier: from Wythburn, at the foot of Thirlmere, over the Armboth Fells to Watendlath above Borrowdale. From meditation on this walk grew Arnold's poem 'On Resignation: to Fausta'[6] (Allot & Super 1986: 511).

The poem contains some of Arnold's finest lines, far superior to anything he, or Clough, had hitherto produced. The message nature teaches, it tells us, is 'not joy, but peace'. The poem evokes – if often to reject – a number of themes from Wordsworth: no lakeland poet, indeed no lakeland walker, could escape that influence.

Fausta, the mute turf we tread
The solemn hills around us spread
The stream which falls incessantly
The strange-scrawl'd rocks, the lonely sky
If I might lend their life a voice
Seem to bear rather than rejoice.

Central to *Resignation* as eventually published in 1849 is the definition of the god-like role of the poet, set above the ordinary run in a lofty isolation. Matthew himself does not claim such a role – he could hardly do so on the basis of two prize poems – but he reveals the ideal he sets out for himself at the beginning of his poetic vocation. 'To thee and to me', he tells his sister, Fate begrudges 'the poet's rapt security'. The poem holds out to poor Jane scant consolation for the transience of love: 'time's busy touch / while it mends little, troubles much'. The seriousness and solemnity of the poem offer a sharp contrast to the figure that Arnold at this time cut in Oxford – the idle, undisciplined, waistcoat-flashing, over-scented *flâneur*.

After the Grasmere reading party Clough spent a week or two in Liverpool reading John Stuart Mill's recently published *Logic* ('very well written and "stringent" if not sound') and also giving some thought to his future career. Should he stay in Oxford, or should he take flight? It seems that Provost Hawkins had in mind to offer him a tutorship at Oriel (provided 'that he was untainted with the principles of the Tract party', M, 166). But to become a tutor it was necessary to take an MA, and that would involve subscription to the Thirty-Nine Articles. In a letter to Gell at the end of the Long Vacation he expresses, for the first time, disquiet about doing so. Three years earlier Matthew Arnold, when subscribing the Articles on matriculation, had expressed to a neighbour his great aversion to some of them 'especially that which expresses an approval of the Athanasian Creed, and that which denounces the Pope of Rome'.[7] Clough's objection, he wrote to Gell, was not so much to particular articles as to the whole idea of subscription.

> I have a very large amount of objection or rather repugnance to sign 'ex animo' the 39 articles, which it would be singular and unnatural not to do if I staid in Oxford, as without one's MA degree one of course stands quite still, and has no resource for employment except private pupils and private reading. It is not so much from any definite objection to this or that point as general dislike to Subscription and strong feeling of its being . . . a bondage, and a very heavy one, and one that may cramp one and cripple one for life. (M, 124)

Gell wrote back, encouraging him to sign. 'You must sign something unless you mean to have nothing to do with anybody. Where will you find a more sensible set of clerical regulations?' (B, 152) Long before this letter reached him, Clough had overcome his scruples and signed 'whether or not in a justifiable sense' (M, 128).

From the beginning of the academic year 1843–4 until Easter 1848 Clough was a tutor at Oriel. He seems to have been popular: one of his pupils described him as 'a most excellent tutor, and exceedingly beloved by the undergraduates' (PPR, 34). Some thought he was a little too easy-going. 'There was no Oxford tutor' Stanley wrote in his obituary in *The Times* 'with whom the frolicsome youth of the rising generation felt so entirely at home'. Foremost among the frolicsome youth was no doubt Matt.

The tutorship gave Clough financial security. It paid £300 in addition to the emoluments of the fellowship, which might be £285 in a typical year. In addition he received fees for special coaching, and for conducting reading parties. After leaving his tutorship, he would never again be as prosperous: but at this time much of his income had to be passed on to his family. Brother George, whom he had seen off from Liverpool in October 1842, fell victim to malaria and died on 5 November 1843 and was buried in the graveyard of St Michael's church in Charleston. His father James had sailed to Boston to join him, and learnt of his death only on arrival. Arthur provided funds to send Charles to America to join his father in his desolation. He also composed an epitaph for George, commencing 'Of all thy kindred, at thy dying day, / Were none to speed thee on thy solemn way'. It was the only poem he wrote in 1842 (B, 147–8; P, 161).

Clough's charity did not end at home. During 1843–4 he worked as a volunteer at the offices of the Oxford Mendicity Society in the slums of St Ebbe's. His job was to distribute meal-tickets and help administer a hostel and soup-kitchen. In the long spring drought of 1844, he wrote:

> They used to come by twenties and one night I remember eighty. Yet even now the hay harvest is so scanty that many who usually have work are thrown out. Sometimes we have very nice people. There was a little boy under thirteen tonight, from Stratford, who was a rather interesting case. They get a pint and a half of broth and a piece of bread for supper, and (at present, only) a small piece of bread for breakfast. (M, 127)

Clough began to question the dominant theories of laissez-faire on which capitalist economics were based. At the Decade debating club he spoke in support of Lord Ashley's campaign to limit working hours for women and children to ten hours a day. Tom Arnold, newly recruited to the Decade, recalled Clough's speech. 'He combated the doctrines of laissez faire and the omnipotence and sufficiency of the action of supply and demand, then hardly disputed in England, with an insight marvellous in one who had so little experience of industrial life, and at the same time with a strict and conscientious moderation'.[8] Against him, the economist Price argued that the manufacturers could not be expected to pay a labourer twelve hours' pay for ten hours' work. To this objection, he responded in a letter:

> I do not mean that if a labourer has at present his proper proportion for 12 hours work he should have the same sum for ten; but I do believe that he has not his proper proportion, that capital tyrannizes over labour, and that government is bound to interfere to prevent such bullying . . . It is manifestly absurd that to allow me to get my stockings ½d a pair cheaper, the operative stocking worker should be forced to go barefoot. (M, 127)

He was delighted when Gladstone, at the Board of Trade, introduced a Railway Act which regulated fares and schedules and provided for the eventual nationalization of the railway companies (M, 128–30). The United States, he believed, had developed a more humane system of capitalism, at least in respect of the education and culture of the working classes. He offered his highest praise to *The Lowell Offering*, a journal published by two female mill-hands in Massachusetts. It was, he thought, 'quite as good as the Rugby Magazine' (M, 130).

The academic year ended with a more than usually solemn Encaenia. Clough, whose muse had been dormant for some time, produced three sonnets. One, only mildly satirical, commemorates the degree by Diploma given to the King of Saxony. Two others, more intriguing, are adressed to 'Leonina'. In elegantly teasing verses Leonina is described as 'singling upon the Isis' margent green / From meaner flowers the frail forget me not'; later as dozing amid white, pink and blue bonnets in the ladies' gallery while tedious Latin proses and verses were read by prizewinners; and finally, at the ball, 'to partner academical and slow / teaching upon the light Slavonic toe / polkas that were not, only should have been'.

'Leonina' no doubt means a lady visitor who is to be lionized (i.e. escorted admiringly through the ceremonies). Clough, when he sent the sonnets to Burbidge, did not reveal her identity, and the only suggestion offered by his biographers is that she was Miss Lockhart, granddaughter of Walter Scott and daughter of his biographer, J. G. Lockhart.[9] Whoever she was, the tripping tone of these polished sonnets does not suggest any serious love affair, and Clough told his sister that the verses were directed to a lady who was ideal rather than real (B, 155).

In the same month of June Arthur Stanley's life of Dr Arnold was published; the first printing, of 1,000 copies, sold out in a few weeks. Another book published in the same month was much more controversial. Ward brought out a dense tome entitled *The ideal of a Christian Church considered in comparison with existing practice*. The argument of the book was that the Church of England, in moral discipline and saintliness, fell far short of the Christian ideal. The way to reform it was to bring it closer to the principles and doctrines of the Church of Rome and to renounce the schismatic errors of the sixteenth-century reformers. The work was so outspoken as to cause embarrassment even to Newman. 'It won't do' he said, shaking his head, to one of his companions at Littlemore. But as the book was published just before the long vacation, there was a period of silence before the inevitable uproar.

Clough travelled northward for the summer, to meet pupils in the Lakes. In spite of his early passion for walking in Wales, he never took a reading party there. To Anne, who was staying at Min-y-Don, he wrote 'I am very fond of lakes and not very partial to the sea. There is no part of Wales equal to this except the immediate districts of Snowdon and Cader Idris.' This year there was no real reading party, just a threesome consisting of himself, Theodore Walrond and Matthew Arnold who was due to take Schools in November. On the way Clough spent a night at Fox How. Mrs Arnold, he reported 'was cheerful as usual though a little anxious at the approach of Matt's examination; he is certainly not the most industrious of students' (M, 133).

From Fox How Clough walked with Tom and William Arnold and their sisters to High Raise (a 2,800 foot eminence in the area of the *Resignation* walk). There he left the Arnold party, and walked over Helvellyn to the inn at Patterdale where he had stayed in 1838 with Walrond and Burbidge. ('Striding Edge I could walk along blindfold' he boasted, M, 131.) The inn was chosen because it was isolated and far from social temptations. The theory was that after breakfast at 8 the three would work from 9.30 to 1.30, bathe and dine between 1.30 and 3, and then resume work until 6 p.m., after which they were free to walk as long as they liked, ending the day with tea. But the pupils gave their tutor a difficult time. Todo turned up late, and Matt every so often went off to fish. Even when he was present and correct, it was hard to keep him up to four hours work a day. 'When Matt. is here' Clough wrote 'I am painfully coerced to my work by the assurance that should I relax in the least my yoke fellow would at once come to a dead stop' (M, 133–4). Matt took time off on 1 August to write a sonnet on Shakespeare: 'Others abide our presence: thou art free'. In the succeeding century, few of the many schoolboys who were forced to learn this solemn poem by heart can have realized that it was written by a truant undergraduate.

After five weeks with his pupils Clough went to Liverpool to greet his father who had just landed from America after having been diverted by storms to the Hebrides. He found him 'much shaken by grief and very ill in health'. James was tormented by gout, and his son Charles took over the Liverpool office while he was nursed by his wife and daughter. Arthur went off to make some money in Yorkshire by tutoring a pair of aristocratic pupils at Escrick Park. In a letter to his father (it was to be his last) he described the family as 'more amiable than intellectual'. Lady Wenlock was cultured, he said, and a member of Gladstone's circle, but Lord Wenlock, though a good-natured farmer and horse-breeder, was at bottom 'rather a goose' (B, 164). To his mother Arthur reported that though the domain was spacious, and 'no hauteur was displayed' by the family, the place was but a prison house. 'But for the filthy lucre, a week would be too much' (M, 135).

In Liverpool the family physician, Bickersteth, continued to make reassuring noises, but Mr Clough sank fast. He died on 19 October. Arthur's brief epitaph is tender to an ineffectual life.

> Thy busy toil thy soul had ne'er engrossed,
> And when thy griefs had purified thee most,
> Its chain, that kept thee painfully below,
> With a most gentle hand God loosed and let thee go.
>
> (P, 162)

Because of his father's funeral Arthur was unable to return to Oxford for the beginning of term. When he got there on 1 November his first visit was to take cocoa with Matt and Todo in Balliol: he quickly picked up the gossip about Ward's *Ideal* (M, 135). Master Jenkyns had been deeply shocked by the book. 'We are to sue for pardon at the feet of Rome humbly' he read, horrified. 'Humbly?' he snorted, and told Ward he must give up his chaplaincy at Balliol. At Communion on the feast of SS Simon and Jude (28 October) Ward was due to read the epistle and Jenkyns the gospel. An eye-witness records:

> Directly the Master saw Mr Ward advancing to the Epistle side of the table he shot forth from his place and rushed to the Gospel side, and just as Mr Ward was beginning. commenced in his loudest tones: 'The Epistle is read in the first chapter of St Jude'. Mr Ward made no further attempt to continue, and the Master, now thoroughly aroused, read *at him* across the communion table . . . 'For there are certain men crept in unawares' (pause, and look at Mr Ward) 'who were of old ordained unto this condemnation' (pause and look) 'ungodly men' (pause and look) – and a little later still more slowly and bitterly he read 'they speak evil of dignities!'[10]

Clough and his friends were amused by the story, but they thought Jenkyns was in the wrong. Ward found it prudent to leave Oxford for the time being (M, 136).

In December the University authorities announced three propositions to be put to Convocation in the following February. The first stated that six passages from the book were inconsistent with the Thirty-Nine Articles and with Ward having signed them in good faith, and the second deprived him of his degrees. The third proposed a general test by which those who signed the Articles in the future must accept them in the sense in which they had been originally uttered and in which the University now imposed them. Clough told his friends that he intended to vote against all three.

> The matter is clearly judicial and ecclesiastical; the Convocation is not a court of justice nor an ecclesiastical body. What right have our MA's to say whether statements x, y, z agree or not with the Articles, or say in what sense the University, which imposes the subscription simply as a Church of England body, understands the articles? If the Church does not settle it, the University has no business to do so. (M, 143)

In the vacation Clough protested also to Provost Hawkins, who was a member of the Board that had proposed the votes of censure. Hawkins urged Clough, if he could not vote against his 'misguided friend', at least to vote for the proposed new test (M, 145).

Very few in Oxford liked Ward's book. Apart from the younger Newman-ists, the only people anywhere who had a good word for it were, oddly enough, the philosophers Auguste Comte and John Stuart Mill. But Clough was in good company in objecting to the intolerance of the condemnation. Liberals on this issue made common cause with Tractarians: they too would fall victims to any attempt to enforce the Articles in the sense of the sixteenth century. The proposal for a new test had to be dropped.

The other two motions, however, were presented to Convocation as planned, along with a third proposal, to condemn Tract 90 and thus associate Newman with the degradation of Ward. On 13 February 1,500 Masters of Arts travelled to the Sheldonian Theatre, despite a bitter east wind which was later believed to have killed at least ten of them. The throng included Clough and his Oxford friends but also others, such as Gladstone, who had travelled from London to cast a vote.

Proceedings in Convocation were officially in Latin. Permission to speak in English was given to Ward alone, and this had the desired effect of shortening the debate. The passages from the *Ideal* were censured by a vote of 777 to 391 and Ward was deprived of his degrees by 569 to 511. The fellows of Balliol without exception voted against both motions; so too did Gladstone. Then came the proposal to condemn Tract 90. Above the shouts of 'placet' and 'non' from the throng was heard the voice of the Senior Proctor '*Nobis Procuratoribus non placet*.' It was the last time the Proctor's veto was used in Convocation.

The Vice-Chancellor hurried out into the snow: he was greeted by hisses and snowballs from the undergraduates. Ward, on the other hand, was cheered, but, ungainly as ever, slipped on the snow, his papers flying. He was escorted to his rooms by Tait, who had come from Rugby to vote in favour of the censure. Fellows of other colleges marvelled at the way in which the Balliol Senior Common was able to preserve friendships across theological divides. But such friendships were soon put to a further test.

No sooner had Ward been condemned than he made public that during the previous December he had become secretly engaged to the sister of one of his Christ Church contemporaries, Frances Mary Wingfield, whom he had come to know as a fellow devotee at Oakeley's services in his London church. Clough, half incredulous, reported the news to his sister just before it became public. '[I]t will do much more to quiet the storm of his Romanizing doctrine' he told her 'than half a dozen votes of the Oxford convocation' (M, 145). Ward confirmed the news and offered his resignation as a Fellow of Balliol. This, Clough told Gell, was a much greater degradation in the eyes of romantic Puseyites than the proceedings in the Sheldonian. Many thought it was hypocritical for a priest who had written so strongly in favour of clerical celibacy to choose matrimony for himself. Oxford hummed with sneers against 'Hildebrand the married man'. But Clough defended Ward's integrity.

> Assuredly, though he violently condemns the English Church for putting the married and ummarried states on an equality, he never said that even a large number of men were called to the latter, or would do otherwise than wrong in seeking it. The charge of humbug therefore I reject. (M, 147)

Newman and Stanley also backed Ward, and among his old Balliol colleagues from different ends of the ecclesiastical spectrum Oakeley and Scott joined in congratulating him. In some quarters the news brought positive relief. A Balliol scout, on being introduced to the new Mrs Ward, said 'O, ma'am, I'm so glad you've taken Mr Ward away. You don't know – he was leading the poor Master such a life of it'[11] (Ward, 325). Clough himself must have been relieved by news which signalled the final end of any emotional threat from his old tutor.

* * *

Clough's own thoughts were beginning to turn in the direction of love and marriage. A five-stanza poem written later in the year begins thus:

When panting sighs the bosom fill
And hands by chance united thrill
At once with one delicious pain
The pulses and the nerves of twain;
When eyes that erst could meet with ease
Do seek, yet seeking shyly shun
Ecstatic conscious unison, –
The sure beginnings, say, be these,
Prelusive to the strain of love
Which angels sing in heaven above?

Or is it but the vulgar tune
Which all that breathe beneath the moon
So accurately learn – so soon?
With variations duly blent,
Yet that same song to all intent
Set for the finer instrument
It is, and it would sound the same
In beasts, were not the bestial frame,
Less subtly organised, to blame;
And but that soul and spirit add
To pleasures, even base and bad,
A zest the soulless never had.

(P, 7)

This poem raises about sexual attraction the same question as the earlier 'Is it true, ye gods' raised about poetry. Do we have here something heavenly or something purely animal? The poem pursues that inquiry through 90 lines. How does one distinguish passion, admiration and reason? A wonderful feeling may make the heart rejoice, but then 'A small expostulating voice / falls in: Of this thou wilt not take /Thy one irrevocable choice?' Later on, there may arise another love, by comparison with which the present love will seem weak and beggarly. Surely, what should come first of all is esteem, then mental and moral sympathy; later, maybe, these sentiments will be transmuted and glorified by a beauteous halo. But will even that be decisive?

Yet, is that halo of the soul?
Or is it, as may sure be said,
Phosphoric exhalation bred
Of vapour, steaming from the bed
Of Fancy's brook or Passion's river?
So when, as will be bye and bye,

The stream is waterless and dry
This halo and its hues will die

In the version of the poem which Clough published four years later, the conclusion is ambiguous. The poet undoubtedly feels the impact of an intuition that is far superior to the dry grind of logic: 'a dream of glory most exceeding'. The feeling of that impact was something wonderful: but was it Love? 'Alas, I cannot say' (P, 8).

In its earliest version, however, the poem ends by putting the opposite argument, against the wisdom of holding back in hopes of some later, higher love.

Why, when I might dismissing doubt
Be warm within doors, starve without?
And were it not in truth too late
At twenty six or twenty eight
To problemize and speculate.
So if no higher love appear
Than this that hath been pictured here
Let sober Earnest banish fear
And fancies sentimental-gloomy
Of love to come that shall undo me –
Come this and I will take it to me
(P, 568)

The breathless energy of the poem's best parts suggest that it is more than an exercise in speculative psychology.

As was his custom, Clough sent his draft to Burbidge, and at the end of the poem placed some verses asking for advice about the dilemma it expresses. In the covering letter, of 2 November 1844, he says: 'You will duly observe, I trust, that this is wholly and solely a *loquitur quidam* composition. I, you will remember, am only twenty five, so that if I should marry within the year of course I shall not fall within the scope of the piece.' But he soon felt that this remark was imprudent as well as disingenuous, so he added a PS.

> You will please not show these even to Simpkinson. I think I had rather not, as I do acknowledge a *certain* sympathy and understanding with the quidam who loquitur in them. (B, 136)

Both internal and external evidence suggest that the poem was based on experience. It suggests that Clough himself had fallen in love, and was anxious to assure himself whether it was a passing fancy or something that might lead on to marriage. If this surmise is correct, then who was the object of his passion?

The poem was composed, Clough told Burbidge, on the coach from Braunston, while he was travelling back to Oxford from his father's funeral in Liverpool. It is surely unlikely that Arthur had suddenly fallen in love during the weeks he had spent in the bosom of his family around his father's deathbed. Before that, he had spent several weeks cooped up in the household of Lord Wenlock at Escrick Park, which as we have seen he described to his mother as a prison. In writing to his father, however, he exempted from his general condemnation of the family the Wenlocks' daughter, Miss Lawley. She was, he reported, rather reserved and silent – but this, he went on to add, was 'perhaps in fear of such aspirations as Aunt Mat. bethought herself of suggesting' (B, 164). Presumably Aunt Matilda had suggested to Arthur that his vacation job gave him an opportunity of paying court to a young noblewoman. It is unlikely that Arthur took her matchmaking seriously, but no doubt it is just possible that it was Miss Lawley who filled his bosom with panting sighs. If so, he was quickly doomed to disappointment. In November 1845 he reported to Annie 'I hear today from Lawley that his sister is to be married to a Mr Wortley, a brother of Lord Wharncliffe' (B, 203).

Other than Escrick, the only place to look for a possible sweetheart is the neighbourhood of Grasmere, where the early summer was spent. The only venue for meeting young ladies there was the Arnold household at Fox How. Possibly, therefore, it was a member, or friend, of the Arnold family who was the source of the sentiments that Clough leaked to Burbidge. But an evaluation of this conjecture must await further evidence, to be provided later.

Whatever the target of the poem, Clough continued to work on it, sending Burbidge in November a further 130 lines stressing the difficulty of distinguishing 'the hymn of heavenly love' from the animal 'vulgar tone'. The verses develop two ideas that were important to him: that marriage is a partnership of co-workers, and that in human relationships the intellectual and the sensual cannot be divorced.

> The loyalty of human kind
> No soil or sustenance can find
> In what it sees but with the Mind
> From Mind material things do win
> The appearance Love rejoices in
> But Matter must be, to begin.
> Material forms – or in the eyes
> Or brain – must feed it or it dies.
> So faith and loyalty, likewise.
>
> (P, 570)

When Clough came to publish the poem he was no doubt well-advised to delete these stumbling verses: he said that he was ill at ease with the 'Tennysonian triplets'. But he was to return to their themes many times in later life.

The winter vacation of 1844–5 provided many opportunities for reflection on love, marriage and family. At Braunston he stood godfather to a young cousin: he wrote home describing the infant's breast-feeding. While staying with the Prices at Rugby he reported himself as falling in love with the six-year-old Edith Price. During the yellow fog and sunless skies that ushered in the New Year at Liverpool, he was glad to learn that the insurance policies on his father's life would leave his mother fairly comfortable. 'In the summer' he told Burbidge 'I mean to take my Mother and Sister if possible to the Lakes; taking pupils myself of course to pay the piper' (M, 143).

Of his pupils of the previous summer, Walrond was now working hard and was predicted to get a first in mathematics. Matthew Arnold, however, when he took Schools in November had, as predicted, obtained only a second class. 'A worthy addition to our select band' Clough remarked ruefully, adding later that Wordsworth at Rydal, himself a second classman, had 'taken Matt under his special protection' (M, 146). In February Matt went to Rugby to teach there in place of a Master, Grenfell, who had fallen ill. To Clough's surprise he 'performed very satisfactorily and with great benefit to himself'. Besides teaching, the newly industrious Matt devoured a prodigious number of texts in preparation for the Oriel examination. In April he proved the strongest of the candidates: he was elected a Fellow, along with Henry Coleridge, son of the judge and a future Jesuit.

The Arnold family were of course delighted that Matt had followed in his father's footsteps. Clough visited Fox How at the end of March, after a journey to Westmoreland on which, he reported, he had conveyed two ladies and 23 packages. Once again, he found Mrs Arnold 'remarkably well and cheerful', though he remarked 'the party seemed strangely small, all the boys being away, as even the little Walter is now at school'. Harriet Martineau, who believed she had been cured of a life-threatening disease by mesmerism, had been proselytizing on its behalf in the Lake district. In January her favoured practitioner, Elizabeth Wynyard, had tried her skills on Jane Arnold at Fox How. An admirer of Harriet, Crabb Robinson, was present and sent a report to Wordsworth. 'Nothing at all decisive happened' Wordsworth reported, 'except that when the organ of veneration was touched the sleeper assumed an attitude of devotion more beautiful than anything he, Mr Robinson, ever beheld' (L, 64).

In July Clough carried out his plan of taking his mother and sister to the Lake District with a reading party. After a brief visit to Min-y-don early in July, he travelled north with this family so as to have some time alone before the students arrived. They went over to Fox How: it was Annie's first encounter with the Arnolds. 'They seem very nice friendly people' she wrote 'very sociable and easy to get acquainted with. Matt is very merry and facetious, Tom quiet, Miss Arnold rather a decided sort of person. Mary very pleasant and amiable, as also Susan. Fanny a merry, wild, child' (Blanche Clough 1897, 1903: 66; M, 161).

From Grasmere Clough went with Tom Arnold and his younger brother Edward (a last minute substitute for the ever unreliable Matt, B, 188) to Calder Park near Glasgow, the home of the Walrond family. 'In this house' he told Burbidge 'the most pleasing humanities are the three little boys – very jolly little fellows – but I like the whole family very fairly, and they are extremely kind and hospitable. The hours are disgracefully late and they dance and play to excess . . . Their gaieties perpetual must be very pernicious' (M, 150–4).

From Calder Park there was a general exodus to Argyll and the Highlands ('a great relaxation'). On Monday 22 August the party went by steamer up Loch Fyne, crossed the Mull of Kintyre by the canal, and then took another steamer past the southern Hebridean islands to 'the great Fiord of Loch Linnhe which narrows gradually and at the headland of Ardgower is transmuted into the inland lake, a salt Winandermere, Loch Eil'. After a night at Fort William most of the party ascended Ben Nevis, but Clough, because his leg was giving trouble again, went by pony seven miles up Glen Nevis 'really the most beautiful glen I ever saw'. The first layer of experience was being laid which would find its expression in Clough's first major poem, *The Bothie*.

He continued to meditate on the ambivalence and transience of love. A brief poem written in late August ('Ah, what is love?') describes it as a 'fire, of earthly fuel fed' which aims to rise to heaven – but warns 'Go look in little space / White ash on blackened earth will be / sole record of its place.' At best a poet's love was 'a star upon a turbid tide / reflected from above' (P, 4).

The final excursion of the party was to visit Edinburgh and see Holyrood, Calton Hill and all the famous sights. They dined and slept at Houston, near Hopetoun, the family home of John Campbell Shairp. Clough told Burbidge:

> I liked the place and people very much. It is a tall perpendicular house – four stories and attics – small peep-hole windows in thick stone walls – all manner of useless rooms on all manner of unequally disposed levels – a stone staircase from bottom to top –wainscotted partition walls and old folks by the dozen looking down on you there from.

He noted with approval that though the family were not rich they did not seem to have any wish to seem what they were not. 'Only I think five sisters' he concluded 'are too many when all are grown up.' Clough was still shy of nubile young ladies and was more at ease in the company of children (M, 152).

September 11 was the twenty-fifth anniversary of the wedding of Mr and Mrs Walrond. Clough composed 15 four-line stanzas in honour of the occasion. The poem is built around a single conceit: that it is strange that whereas a wedding day is a golden occasion ('the golden bliss of woo'd and won, and wed') 25 years of happy marriage should count only as a silver wedding.

> Ah, golden then, but silver now! In sooth,
> The years that pale the cheek, that dim the eyes
> And silver o'er the golden hair of youth
> Less prized can make its only priceless prize

Indeed, if a golden wedding is still 25 years ahead, the actual marriage day in the past must be counted mere base metal. The solution to the paradox is that the joys of the wedding were indeed golden, 'but golden of the fairy gold of dreams'.

> It needed cares and tears
> And deeds together done, and trials past
> And all the subtlest alchemy of years
> To change to genuine substance here at last . . .
>
> Come years as many yet, and as they go,
> In human life's great crucible shall they
> Transmute, so potent are the spells they know,
> Into pure gold the silver of to-day.
>
> (P, 21)

In celebration, the Walrond family and their guests went on the following day to see a performance by the great dancer Maria Taglioni, who had created *La Sylphide* in 1832, and was now nearing the end of her career. One of the Walrond sisters made Clough throw a bouquet at the ballerina's feet. He found the experience disturbing, as he wrote to Burbidge before breakfast the day after:

> May I never be carried again to the ballet! It is really strange that matrons and maidens delicately nurtured, not to speak of daughter-delighting-in-papas, should patronize such sights.

Taglioni was, he confessed in the decent obscurity of a learned language, most skilful at showing off her calves (*callida surarum ostentatrix*) (M, 152). But later when he described his Scottish holiday to Gell he felt it tactful to leave out all mention of the ballet.

Clough left the Walronds on 12 September being, on his own account, 'in a state bordering on distraction'. He sailed from Glasgow to Liverpool and found 'the action of the swell of the Atlantic on Scotch hospitality' probably medicinal but certainly disagreeable. He spent a week in Liverpool, reading Disraeli's *Sybil*. The story was flimsy, he thought, and the thoughts either obvious or extravagant. However, the plot – a patrician younger son falling in love with a Chartist girl – clearly stayed in his mind.

When Arthur arrived in Liverpool he found his brother Charles installed with his recently engaged fiancée, his cousin, Margaret Marshall Clough, an heiress who had lived since the death of her parents with her maiden aunts in Wales. The first reference to this alliance in Arthur's correspondence suggests that he viewed it as an arranged match. In the previous June, after a no doubt suitably enthusiastic letter to Margaret, he had written to his sister Annie 'I am very glad that Charles is contented. It is much the best for his prospects that he should be so. Within a year I hope all will be right' (B, 155). If in June the union had been proposed for dynastic and financial reasons, by September it had developed into something highly romantic. 'These super-connubial anteconnubialities are unpleasant' Arthur told Burbidge 'for an indifferent spectator: otherwise I am well content.' Rather than be an observer of his brother's courtship, he preferred reading fashionable books with his sister. During this summer Arthur and Annie read together Manoni's *I promessi sposi* and the life of Blanco White, an erratic ex-Dominican who had once been a colleague of Newman's at Oriel.

While in Liverpool Arthur sent to his Aunt Matilda at Ellesmere a suitably sanitized account of his three weeks' vacation in Scotland. He agreed with her that the elevation of the mountains and the beauty of the heather made Scotland superior even to the Lake country. Arthur thought his aunt would be particularly interested to learn the number of girls he had met. 'There were also three Miss Walronds, fixtures, five Miss Sharps, a Miss Lockhart, and other casualties' he told her: 'Music and dancing enough for ten prodigal sons – escortings, almost daily, of lady equestrians &c&c – but in these things you know I take little interest.' All the girly whirling in Scotland seems to have induced in Arthur a temporary bout of misogyny. The young couple-to-be, he told his aunt, were dully loving. 'It is happy that Charles is taken down town daily by his business, otherwise it would be an infliction upon an unconcerned person like myself.' It was to be hoped, indeed, that even after he was married Charles would find some suitable job. 'Matrimony may be very well as sauce and garnish, but business is the bread and staff of life. Bread without butter may be dry, but is not unwholesome, butter without bread would disorder the stomach of a pig' (B, 193).

When the vacation ended, Clough travelled to Birmingham to consult a surgeon, Hodgson, about his leg. The consultation was reassuring. 'He says that these injuries of the muscles always take an immense time – and he *recommends* a little walking which is a great blessing (M, 157). In better spirits, while travelling on the Birmingham to Oxford coach Clough wrote a poem taking a more balanced view of the pros and cons of 'escortings of equestrian ladies'.

With graceful seat and skilful hand,
   Upon the fiery steed
Prompt at a moment to command,
   As fittest, or concede,

O Lady! happy he whose will
   Shall manliest homage pay
To that which yielding ever, still
   Shall in its yielding sway:

Yea, happy he, whose willing soul
   In perfect love combined
With thine shall form one perfect whole
   One happy heart and mind!

And as the harp thy fingers wake
   To sounds melodious, he
To thy soul's touch shall music make
   And his enstrengthen thee.

Then shall to Waltzes unexiled,
   And Polkas not unheard
To strains capricious, wayward, wild
   Be other sounds preferred.

(P, 15, 575)

After these five stanzas, the poet interrupted himself with 'Ah, moralizing premature'. The poem peters out into muffled murmurings of praise for a life of unrecognized meekness. Once arrived in Oxford, Clough sent the poem to Burbidge; but he soon became dissatisfied with it. However, it was the first rather than the second part of the poem that he rewrote. Feeling that the switch of metaphor in stanzas three and four, from horse to harp, was too abrupt, he interpolated three new stanzas.

Fair, fair on fleeting steed to see,
   Boon Nature's child, nor less
In gorgeous rooms, serene and free
   Midst etiquette and dress!

Thrice happy who, amidst the form
   And folly that must be,
Existence fresh, and true, and warm,
   Shall, Lady, own in thee!

Such dreams, in gay saloon, of days
   That shall be, 'midst the dance
And music, while I hear and gaze,
   My silent soul entrance.

Even in this version, the poem, despite its agreeable fluency, is not quite successful. We are left in too much doubt who, in a happy marriage, is the rider, and who the horse; who is the harpist and who the harp. Clough himself was never totally happy with it: his best hope, when he sent the final version to Burbidge, was that it would no longer keep him awake at nights. 'I trust I shall now no more be rid by that terrible night mare, the Dam of Pegasus' (B, 169).

However, the poem undeniably piques the curiosity of the biographer. Was the Lady to whom the poem is addressed one of the nine whom Arthur listed in his communiqué to Aunt Matilda, and did he really 'dream of days that shall be' which would make her one happy heart and mind with himself? Or was he being simply truthful when he told his Aunt that he took little interest in these things?[12]

* * *

On his return for the new term Clough found the Oxford movement in crisis. While in Glasgow he had read in *The Times* a letter from Ward announcing his intention of becoming a Roman Catholic, and at Liverpool he learnt that he and his wife had been confirmed by Bishop Wiseman at Oscott. A week after he returned to Oriel, he heard Newman's announcement of the resignation of his fellowship. On 9 November Newman was received into the Roman Catholic Church by an Italian Passionist missionary, and at the end of the month he too went to Oscott. On 20 October Clough went with Stanley to Rose Hill, the suburb where Ward had now set up house with his bride. 'He seems remarkably happy and not at all altered by his removal' he reported to Burbidge (M, 158).

One of Clough's most anthologized poems is entitled *Qua Cursum Ventus*. It begins:

As ships, becalmed at eve, that lay
 With canvas drooping, side by side
Two towers of sail at dawn of day
 Are scarce, long leagues apart, descried;

When fell the night, upsprung the breeze
 And all the darkling hours they plied,
Nor dreamt but each the self-same seas
 By each was cleaving, side by side:

E'en so – but why the tale reveal
 Of those whom, year by year unchanged,
Brief absence joined anew, to feel,
 Astounded, soul from soul estranged?

(P, 34)

The poem – which in four further stanzas expresses the hope that the ships will eventually be united in a common port – has traditionally been regarded as Clough's farewell to Ward on his conversion: a poetic equivalent, perhaps, of Newman's valedictory sermon *The Parting of Friends*. But the verses do not fit the occasion. Ward and Clough had known for years that their thoughts were not running side by side, and Clough was anything but astounded to discover Ward a Roman Catholic. Moreover, the first draft of the poem is to be found written not in Clough's 1845 notebook, but in one of 1847. We must look elsewhere for a suitable recipient.

As Clough had predicted, not many senior academics followed Ward and Newman, other than Oakeley, the former chaplain of Balliol. But in the University devout Anglicans held their breath and trembled for the Church of England. As Stanley put it:

> To anyone who had been accustomed to look upon Arnold and Newman as *the* two great men of the Church of England, the death of one and the secession of the other could not but look ominous, like the rattle of departing chariots that was heard on the eve of the downfall of the Temple of Jerusalem. (Prothero and Bradley 1893: I, 332–3).

Notes

1 Park Honan, *Matthew Arnold: A Life*, London 1981, p. 52.
2 The 'signal-elm' that marked the spot has long since disappeared and it is a matter of local controversy where exactly Arnold and Clough terminated their walks.
3 M. C. Brock and M. C. Curthoys, *The History of the University of Oxford*, VI, Oxford 1997, pp. 248–9.
4 Nicholas Murray, *A Life of Matthew Arnold*, London 1996, p. 49.
5 Several different people, including Benjamin Jowett, claim to have invented the reading party. For a description of some twentieth-century reading parties, see A. Kenny, *A Life in Oxford*, London 1997.
6 M. Allott & R. H. Super, *The Oxford Authors: Matthew Arnold*, Oxford 1986, p. 511.
7 Murray, *A Life of Matthew Arnold*, p. 37.
8 E. B. Greenberger, *Arthur Hugh Clough: The Growth of a Poet's Mind*, Harvard University Press 1970, p. 71.
9 Paul Veyriras, (*Arthur Hugh Clough (1819–1861)*, Paris 1964, p. 192), describes this conjecture as 'a peu près certain' but he offers no evidence for it. No doubt he had in mind Clough's letter of 31 August 1835 describing, in Scotland, a song recital by 'la bella Lockhartina, with whom we all fell in love in general and Shairp in particular'. This, again, does not suggest any particular attachment on his own part.
10 Wilfrid Ward, *William George Ward and the Oxford Movement*, London 1889, p. 325.
11 Ibid.
12 Another love poem of this period, 'Oh ask not what is love', was described to Burbidge as a *jeu d'esprit*, and on this occasion the disavowal of serious intent rings true (P, 12, 574).

Chapter Four

Farewell to Oxford

In 1838 Ward had reported to Clough a prophetic remark of Henry Halford Vaughan, a colleague of Newman's at Oxford and a future University Reformer. 'There is no mean' Vaughan pronounced 'between Newmanism on the one side and extremes far beyond anything of Arnold's on the other' (M, 81). Thomas Arnold, however, believed it was a mistake to regard Newman and himself as opposite poles. 'You think' he wrote to Hawkins in December 1840

> that Newman is one extreme and I another and I am well aware that in common estimation we should be held – and thus in Church matters the mean would seem to be somewhere between Newman's views and mine. Whereas the truth is that in our view of the importance of the Church Newman and I are pretty well agreed, and therefore I stand as widely aloof as he can do from the language of 'Religion being an affair between God and a man's own conscience.[1]

This was precisely the language which was beginning to attract Clough. Like Newman and Ward, he was considering seceding from Oxford on religious grounds; but his doubts about the Church of England had quite different roots. He was still a regular churchgoer, but the frame of mind in which he attended church was every year less dogmatic. The prospect of taking orders, which at Rugby had seemed his predestined future, receded ever further into the background (M, 136).

We have seen how Clough had to stifle scruples in 1843 in order to sign the Thirty-Nine Articles. In a letter to Gell in November 1844 he did his best to justify his suspension of inquiry.

> I can feel faith in what is being carried out by my generation and I am content to be an operative – to dress intellectual leather, cut it out to pattern and stitch and cobble it into boots and shoes for the benefit of the work which is being guided by wiser heads . . . If I begin to think about God, there arise a thousand questions, and whether the 39 articles

> answer them at all or whether I should not answer them in the most diametrically opposite purport is a matter of great doubt . . . Without the least denying Christianity I feel little that I can call its power. Believing myself to be in my unconscious creed in some shape or other an adherent to its doctrines I keep within its pale: still whether the Spirit of the Age, whose lacquey and flunkey I submit to be, will prove to be this kind or that kind I can't the least say. Sometimes I have doubts whether it won't turn out to be no Christianity at all. (M, 141)

It is not suprising that this horrified Gell. Blind allegiance to the Zeitgeist is surely as much an abnegation of rational inquiry as any subscription to church formulae. Who are the 'wiser heads' whom Clough is happy to serve as an intellectual under-labourer? The style of the letter makes it obvious that prominent among them is Carlyle.

His growing enthusiasm for Carlyle was shared by the Arnold brothers. Tom Arnold's daughter, Mrs Humphrey Ward, recalled that during their years together in Oxford Clough, Matthew and Tom 'discovered George Sand, Emerson and Carlyle, and orthodox Christianity no longer seemed to them the sure refuge that it had always been to the strong teacher who trained them as boys'. Matthew seems to have sloughed off Christianity silently, without any personal anguish; but Tom underwent a severe crisis of faith. He later described it in the third person:

> The spring of [1845] was unusually cold; and the blasts of the North East wind shook the large oriel window of his room, and made him shiver with cold as he crouched over the fire. A universal doubt shook every prop and pillar on which his moral being had hitherto reposed. Something was continually whispering 'What if all thy Religion, all thy aspiring hope, all thy trust in God, be a mere delusion? The more thou searchest into the mystery of thy being, findest thou not that iron relentless laws govern thee, and every impulse and thought of thee, no less than the full stones beneath thy feet? What art thou more than a material arrangement, the elements of which might at any moment, by any accident, be dispersed, and thou, without any to care for or pity thee throughout the wide universe, sink into the universal night. Prate not any more of thy God and thy Providence; thou art here *alone*.'[2]

This vision was shared, at one time or another, by all three of the triumvirate. Matthew in one of his *Marguerite* poems gave famous expression to the solitariness ('we mortal millions live alone') and Clough in several poems addressed the clash between materialism and spiritual values. 'Is it true ye gods' confronted materialism with poetry, 'When panting sighs' confronted materialism with love. Now at the end of 1845, while staying with Tom Arnold in his lodgings in London, Clough wrote a poem more powerful than either, 'The New Sinai' which confronted materialism with religion (M, 244). Oddly, he seems not to have shown the poem to Tom himself, even though it addressed directly his major concerns. 'He would have worshipped it' brother Matt believed 'like the children of Israel' (L, 77).

The theme of the poem is that the scientific scepticism of the age is a stage in the fuller revelation of God. The poet describes how mankind in its infancy had chased idols and false gods. Moses, in the dark cloud on Sinai, had brought the revelation of the one True God who spoke out of thunder.

God spake it out, 'I, God, am One';
  The unheeding ages ran
And baby-thoughts again, again
  Have dogged the growing man;
And as of old from Sinai's top
  God said that God is One,
By Science strict so speaks He now
  To tell us there is None!
Earth goes by chemic forces; Heaven's
  A Mécanique Céleste
And heart and mind of human kind
  A watch-work as the rest!

Is this a Voice, as was the Voice
  Whose speaking told abroad
When thunder pealed, and mountain reeled,
  The ancient Truth of God?
Ah, not the Voice, 'tis but the cloud,
  The outer darkness dense
Where image none, nor e'er was seen
  Similitude of sense
'Tis but the cloudy darkness dense,
  That wrapt the Mount around;
When in amaze the people stays
  To hear the Coming Sound.

Some chosen prophet-soul the while
  Shall dare, sublimely meek,
Within the shroud of blackest cloud
  The Deity to seek:
'Mid atheistic systems dark

And darker hearts' despair,
That soul has heard perchance His word,
And on the dusky air
His skirts, as passed He by, to see
Hath strained on their behalf,
Who on the plain, with dance amain,
Adore the Golden Calf.

'Tis but the cloudy darkness dense;
Though blank the tale it tells,
No God, no Truth! yet He, in sooth,
Is there – within it dwells;
Within the sceptic darkness deep
He dwells that none may see
Till idol forms and idol thoughts
Have passed and ceased to be.
(P, 18–19)

The poem goes on to draw the moral that one should neither relapse, like the Puseyites, into the infantile idolatry of the Golden Calf, nor accept the current atheism of science as the last word from the mystic mountain. Mankind should neither reject science, nor embrace superstition, but wait in faith for God to complete his plan of revelation.

The poem presents a more coherent form of the interim Christianity which Clough had held out to Gell as the justification for remaining an Oxford Anglican. But he continued to be uncomfortable, and once more contemplated resigning his tutorship. He speculated that he might find the irreligious university of London an environment more congenial to Christian belief. In Oxford, he complained 'what religion I have I cannot distinguish from the amalgamations it is liable to' (M, 141).

In Liverpool in the summer of 1845, when reading the life of Blanco White, he felt a pull towards Unitarianism. James Martineau, Harriet's brother, was the preacher in the Liverpool Unitarian church. When he met him Clough was sufficiently impressed to compare him with Dr Arnold. '[H]e talked simply, courteously, and ably, and has a forehead with a good deal of that rough hewn mountainous strength which one used to look at when at lesson in the library at Rugby, not without trembling' (M, 155, 168). Arthur's mother was alarmed by this, but she took comfort in the fact that though he sometimes attended Unitarian services he never actually joined the church.

Sir Robert Peel's government was proposing to set up in Ireland a group of non-denominational colleges at Belfast, Cork and Galway. Clough applied to be considered for a professorship, and collected a resplendent set of testimonials, from his old tutors Tait and Scott, from Bonamy Price at Rugby, from Stanley at University and Jowett at Balliol, and from Provost Hawkins at Oriel. Hawkins was willing to oblige, observing only 'I take it for granted that you are a serious member of the Church of England.' Clough did not demur. However, the scheme for setting up non-denominational colleges was delayed, and his professorship application came to nothing (M, 165).

* * *

Once again, Clough put his religious misgivings on hold. Instead, he focused his attention on the social and political problems of the day. In 1846 there appeared a new weekly periodical, *The Balance*, under the editorship of the Quaker Joseph John Gurney, modelled on the *Spectator* but with more liberal and philanthropic views. According to Clough it was 'Arnoldite out of Evangelical' and its aim was to 'become a sort of Sunday newspaper for all sorts of people, gentle and simple, noblemen and serving man, and working man'. One of the sponsors was Bonamy Price, who encouraged Clough not only to subscribe to it but also to write for it. During its short life of 20 issues, he contributed six articles in the form of letters.

The first article, published in the issue of 23 January, is concerned with the Corn Laws, the burning political issue of the day. The failure of the harvest in 1845, bringing with it the threat of famine, had led the conservative Prime Minister Sir Robert Peel to introduce a measure abolishing all duties on the import of corn. Attacked by the agricultural interest in his own party, and failing to carry his cabinet with him, he resigned early in December, but returned to office later in the month since Lord John Russell had been unable to form a Whig government. In January he introduced a Corn Law and Customs Bill proposing the total repeal of the corn duties.

Clough saw the repeal of the Corn Laws as portending a fundamental change in the nature of English society: a change which would have both good and bad consequences. 'It may be, though this is a question, that labour will have to remove from the field to the mill, and such transfers are pretty sure to be attended with hardship; but the money which the country saves will ere long be a benefit to all. To the nation at large, and in the long run, the change will be economically a blessing; that is, in the matter of pounds, shillings and pence. We shall stand better in the columns of the national account book. The new system will, by increasing change, make us richer; but will it make us better?'[3]

The economic advantages, Clough argues, must be weighed against the social strains that they will bring in their train. The invention which rendered obsolete the spinning wheel has introduced many changes in moral habits. The young girl who once learnt the use of the spinning wheel by her mother's side in a lonely Yorkshire hamlet now finds herself an immigrant serving in the army of a mill in some huge central Manchester. We cannot simply rely on the grace of God to take care of her in her new position: careful planning is needed to ensure her welfare. 'Social changes of some kind assuredly there will be; nor will they . . . be unmixedly either good or evil. It is but prudence to think beforehand what they will be on either side, and seek to be prepared to avail ourselves of the good and provide against the evil.'

The succeeding essays seek to show what kind of social arrangements will be appropriate when the centre of national economic power passes from the landowners to the manufacturers. Clough accepted that the manufacturers had now become 'the real rulers of England' but he believed that they should not be absolute rulers, governed by no laws other than the 'law' of supply and demand. He attacked unremittingly the thesis that unfettered competition was the way to maximize wealth and that no question arose about the fairness or unfairness of the distribution of wealth. The rules of trade, he urged, require the continual interference of higher principles, such as that of equity.

> The whole system is a mere expedient, the best, indeed, we can lay our hands on; it serves in nine cases, but in the tenth it fails; an instrument demanding perpetual superintendence; a sort of ruthless inanimate steam-engine, which must have its driver always with it to keep it from doing mischief untold.

If some system other than capitalism could be devised which was more exactly and unerringly just in the rewarding of labour, it would be the duty and interest of the nation to adopt it even if it were less productive (PPR, 31).

There were those who argued that the present system was self-correcting. No radical reform was needed: the way to redress the hardships capitalism involved was to stimulate production by ever greater demand. On this view, extravagance was a virtue, not a vice. 'We find men continually acting on the belief that it is their duty to be large consumers; to use the expensive where the cheap would do, to employ labour to frivolous purposes for the good of trade.' This, Clough argued in his February *Balance* letter 'Expensive living', promoted wasteful consumption: rich men bought horses that they never rode, rich ladies bought dresses and wore them only once.

An abrupt termination of such fruitless consumption would be neither possible nor desirable: it would throw an immense number of labourers out of work. But gradual reforms were possible. First of all, the money now spent on pointless extravagance should be diverted to capital investment. Capital was needed by manufacturers for new mills, by farmers for improvements, by mining companies, canal companies and railway companies. Another more profitable way of spending one's surplus income was to support emigration.

> What you have hitherto expended in buying what you confess you were as well or even better without – that same sum spend now in assisting emigration. Far more good will you do by sending one labourer to Canada or Australia, than by supporting twenty at home as idle footmen, or useless shop-boys. (PPR, 31)

But voluntary changes in the expenditure patterns of the 'enjoying classes' would be insufficient, in Clough's eyes, to prevent the ruthless engine of capitalism from causing ruin. There must be regulation both by chambers of commerce 'endowed with powers far transcending any now thought of' and by agencies of central government.

Clough artfully introduced his argument for central regulation by pointing out the benefits it would bring to entrepreneurs. Suppose a builder has erected too many houses: under the present system the price might fall indefinitely, and no existing authority could set a limit to the builder's loss. As a safeguard, we need a body with power to regulate prices as well as wages. But Clough is willing to go further in the direction of a command economy.

> The state, I should hold, has a right as perfect to compel shoemakers to make shoes, as it has to exact their respective services from soldiers in the army, sailors in the navy, or judges on the bench. I pay the price because it is part of a system which, on the whole, is the most efficient means for making men work in their trades and getting them their honest return. (PPR, 31)

Clough was not a socialist, though he was sometimes labelled such by his contemporaries: he did not advocate the abolition of private property. He was arguing rather for a controlled capitalism, and the degree of regulation he proposed is now commonplace in many liberal democracies. What is remarkable about his ideas is that they were propounded two years before Mill's *Political Economy*, 11 years before Marx's *Grundrisse* and 53 years before Veblen coined the phrase 'conspicuous consumption'.[4]

The long exchange of chatty, news-packed letters with Gell, Simpkinson and Burbidge came to an end at the beginning of 1846. There is no clear reason for this loss of intimacy. Gell remained in Van Diemens land until 1849, when he came home 'the same as ever, but a little crusted with Episcopalianisms' (M, 245). Simpkinson continued as an assistant master at Harrow until 1855. Burbidge continued to collaborate on the joint volume of poems he had suggested in 1845 (M, 160) which appeared in 1848 as *Ambarvalia*. In the same year he married an Italian wife, whom Clough found to be 'a very nice, simple, lively and affectionate little body' (M, 245). Whatever it was that led Clough at this period to distance himself from his friends, it is surely one of this trio, and not W. G. Ward, who is the most likely addressee of the poem 'As ships becalmed at eve' which he published in *The Balance* under the title 'Differing to agree'.[5]

Among Clough's male friends, the torch was taken up by J. C. Shairp and Tom Arnold, but their correspondence was not voluminous. It was not until the end of 1847 that Clough's most famous exchange of letters began with Matthew Arnold. In the meantime, we depend on the letters to Annie for any close glimpse of his life. The two were drawn together by the loss of father and younger brother, and the marriage of their elder brother on 3 February, followed by his departure with his bride Margaret for a matrimonial Grand Tour.

Annie was a highly intelligent and energetic woman who was to prove a pioneer in the field of feminine education, ending her life as the founding principal of Newnham College. While Arthur was still at Rugby, she had taken an interest in the Liverpool charity school for Welsh pupils that her father had founded in his days of prosperity. She assisted in local day and Sunday school teaching: during vacations Arthur sometimes assisted her and found it difficult to cope with the ignorance of the pupils. From 1840 Annie included in her rigorous daily schedule (Up $5^1/_4$ Devotions etc $6^1/_2$ Euclid and Kant 8 Bible 9.30 &c) several hours of schoolteaching. From 1841 she kept a small school of her own on a regular basis. Now, after the death of her father, she wondered whether she and her mother should move from Liverpool. Arthur urged her to stay: her school work might be discouraging from time to time, but it was bound in the long run to be of great benefit. No decision to move should be taken until his fellowship ended in June 1849 'and whatever you can do in the interval must of course be done not with much hope of staying to see the fruit of it, but still with a good deal of confidence that it will bear fruit' (M, 170).

Annie loved and admired her brother: she undertook courses of serious reading with him in every vacation, and she was willing to allow him to correct the spelling and syntax of her correspondence. She observed with keen attention the progress of his religious opinions, and to a considerable extent followed them herself – hesitantly at first, but later with growing confidence. To cheer her up during the period of bereavement, Arthur sketched plans for them to make a tour to Switzerland and the Italian lakes in the ensuing summer, possibly in company with Walrond and his sister. Simultaneously he was assembling a group of pupils for a reading party. Charmed by his Scottish visit of the previous year, he had decided to move the venue from the Lakes to Scotland, at Castleton Braemar (M, 170; B, 223, 225).

In April there was an engagement in the Arnold family: Mary, the fourth child and second daughter, now aged 21, was betrothed to an assistant physician at St Bartholomew's Hospital named Aldred Twining. Arthur wrote to Annie shortly afterwards:

> Jane Arnold I think is probably superior to Mary – though less attractive. But I have always found it difficult to make much of either of them – the boys of course come in between. (B, 223)

The occasion led him to reflect, in a postscript, on the obstacles which Victorian convention placed upon the quest for a suitable partner:

> Concerning marriage – it is true, my child; – but to fall in love without knowledge is foolery – to obtain knowledge without time and opportunity and something like an intimate acquaintance is for the most part impossible – and to obtain time, opportunity etc. is just the thing which somehow or other has never duly befallen me, at least in the cases where I could have wished it most. Then again there comes the question of reconciling marriage with one's work, which for me is a problem of considerable difficulty. It is not everyone who would like to be an helpmate in the business I am likely to have.
>
> However, my child, remember in conclusion that I am but just of age for the holy state in question. According, that is, to the laws of prudence, as laid down by Papas and Mamas. (M, 170–1)

Arthur and Annie set off for their continental tour from Oxford on 25 June, the day after Commemoration. They spent a couple of days in London, visiting Westminster Abbey, listening to Parliamentary debates and admiring a Turner exhibition. Crossing by the Ostend packet, they joined a steamer at Cologne and cruised down the Rhine to Mannheim. Travelling by railway and diligence, they reached Lucerne on 1 July, duly admired the Lion and the bridges, and met up with the newly married George Cotton (Jane Arnold's former fiancé). On the following day they took a carriage into Italy and spent the next two weeks amid the Italian Lakes. Before returning northward they paid a brief visit to Milan to see the Duomo which Arthur had admired so greatly on his earlier tour with Walrond. They had planned to rendezvous on the Swiss border with brother Charles and his bride, but it is not clear whether they ever did so.[6] Retracing their way northward, by Rhine steamer and train, they spent two days in Antwerp with an archdeacon and his family and were back in Liverpool on the last day of July.

Arthur left at once by Glasgow steamer, to prepare for his reading party which assembled at Castleton Braemar at the end of the first week in August. After two solid days of rain the weather improved, and Arthur wrote to Annie:

> Our house is very comfortable and affords us two sitting rooms one of which is conceded to my special use. The other has a nice lookout up the Glen of Clunie, a little stream which dashes through the granite just

> beside us and gives us a pool to bathe in. But the country in general is not what I require for full delight. The hills are round and somewhat tame, though beautifully clad with heather. (M, 171)

There were five students in the party: two were from Oriel, John Deacon and J. S. Winder, two were from Christ Church, H. W. Fisher and George Warde Hunt, plus a shadowy figure named Jelf. Several of these were later canvassed as possible originals of the characters in *The Bothie*, Clough's long narrative poem about a Scottish reading party. A careful log was kept of their expeditions (sometimes 18 miles in a day) and of their entertainments. For instance:

> Thursday [27 August] Braemar Sports – Running $^{3}/_{4}$ mile – running up Craig Coyash – Throwing the hammer – putting the stone – tossing the tree. Hammer 88 ft 10. Dinner $4^{1}/_{2}$ – 9 Dance 9–4. (K, 235)

This was recalled in the opening lines of *The Bothie*:

> It was the afternoon; and the sports were all but over.
> Long had the stone been put, tree cast, and thrown the hammer;
> Up the perpendicular hill, Sir Hector so called it,
> Eight stout shepherds and gillies had run, two wondrous quickly;
> Run too the course on the level had been; the leaping was over:
> Last in the show of dress, a novelty recently added,
> Noble ladies their prizes adjudged for costume that was perfect,
> Turning the clansmen about, who stood with upraised elbows;
> Bowing their eye-glassed brows, and fingering kilt and sporran.
> It was four of the clock, and the sports were all but over,
> Therefore the Oxford party went off to adorn for the dinner.
> (P, 44)

On 10 September Arthur wrote to Annie, then holidaying in the Lake District 'Tonight we all go to a party at General Duff's, to see Highland dancing – rather stupid I fear, but a civility, and perhaps there may be some agreeable people.' This was a little ungracious to the General, who had been supplying the party with gifts of grouse and venison. This occasion too provided material for *The Bothie*, but with the venue transposed:

> At the farm on the lochside of Rannoch in parlour and kitchen
> Hark! there is music – yea flowing of music, of milk, and of whiskey,
> Dancing and drinking, the young and the old, the spectators and actors
> Never not actors the young, and the old not always spectators:
> Lo, I see piping and dancing. (P, 66)

Amid the excursions and festivities, from time to time a note in the diary reveals Clough's abiding social and economic concerns.

> Thursday [24 September] farmer (?) from Charleston Aboyne. rents £2 per acre, farm labourers hired by 6 months at £6 or £8 & feed either in kitchen or store of meal per week & 2 pts of milk per day . . . Many farmers never touch meat. (K, 237)

The party broke up on the last day of September, and Clough spent a week on a solitary expedition, partly retracing the route of the previous year and ending once more at Glasgow. This was, as he explained to Annie before setting out 'a little rambling to make up for the somewhat poor scenery of this Valley of Dee' (M, 172).

Clough was not looking forward to returning to his work in Oxford: college tuition, he had come to think, was an inefficient method of teaching. He wrote to Hawkins at the end of September, suggesting that his tutorship should become a half-time post, shared with another. This would give him more time for reading, since once he ended his fellowship he would have to take a job which would leave little leisure. He had, he said, given up any intention of taking orders. A frosty response from the Provost put an end to the proposal for dividing the tutorship (M, 173–4).

In November Clough wrote from Oxford a letter to Annie which is our first indication that he was seriously thinking of marriage, and that he had chosen a partner whom he had set himself to win. In a letter that does not survive Annie had expressed a worry that she and her brother were drifting apart. Arthur assured her that any separation was temporary and unimportant. But he went on to say 'If I should succeed and marry, that of course would in itself be a separation in some respects still greater.' Even so, there would remain a substantial union between brother and sister. He went on:

> As for her whom I hope someday to see your sister it is very true that it won't be in a moment that you will quite understand each other – but there is no fear in the end. She is very slow to advance – and I almost think that the visit to Ambleside, pleasant as it was, was *too* much an advance. If you can, let all advances come from her, and don't be afraid, that they will. – Shall I tell you, for example, I would, were I you, call her by her name as little as possible. I doubt whether she is quite up to it, except from Mother. When you write to her, it would come best at the end of a bit from Mother. (M, 175)

A courtship has clearly reached a serious stage when sister and mother are involved. But who was Clough courting?

This letter is no less mysterious than a more famous one written by Matthew Arnold to Clough on 29 September 1848 from a hotel in Switzerland. 'Tomorrow I repass the Gemmi and get to Thun: linger one day at the Hotel Bellevue for the sake of the blue eyes of one of its inmates: and then proceed.' Scholars have exercised effort and ingenuity in trying to identify the owner of these blue eyes, because their owner is the subject of Arnold's *Marguerite* poems. Less energy has been expended in tracking down the woman whom Arthur hoped to make Annie's sister: but several scholars have done their best.

In 1966 James Bertram suggested that Clough's beloved was Agnes Walrond, the eldest of Todo's sisters, whom Clough had found attractive (if too devoted to gaiety) during his summer visit to Calder Park in 1845.[7] B. K. Biswas in 1972 suggested instead that it was an unnamed Scottish girl, with whom Clough would have fallen in love during the summer of 1846. Biswas points out that the theme of love for a highland lassie, cutting across class barriers, is a frequent one in Clough's verse. It appears in *The Bothie*, where the hero Philip falls in love with a crofter's daughter and takes her off to New Zealand. More to the point, the theme appears in the fourth poem of the semi-autobiographical *Mari Magno* series, when a 25-year-old Oxford tutor, relaxing at a Highland inn after the departure of his reading party, seduces, and later plans to marry, one of the servant girls in the hotel. 'Is it possible' Biswas asks 'that the extraordinarily shy girl referred to in his letter of November to Anne was the "Highland Girl"?'[8]

I accept that there is an autobiographical element in 'The Lawyer's Second Tale', and I agree with Biswas that Clough's attachment to his hoped for bride 'ripened if it was not actually formed' between May and November of 1846. But the suggestion that the woman referred to in the November letter is a Scottish servant girl rests on a misreading of the November letter. The woman who objected to Annie's use of her Christian name was surely not shy but starchy. The one solid piece of information that we have about Clough's intended is that Annie met her at Ambleside during the summer of 1846. This rules out not only a Highland lassie, but also Agnes Walrond, who spent the summer either abroad or in Calder Park.

Annie spent September at Broadlands, the Ambleside home of the Claudes, a French Protestant family from Liverpool. It is, I suppose, just possible that Clough had fallen in love with Mary Claude, the most nubile of the daughters of that family. It would be an extraordinary coincidence if it were so, because two years later in 1848 Matthew Arnold was teased by his family for having a 'romantic passion for the Cruel Invisible, Mary Claude', and some scholars have built on this the theory that Mary Claude was none other than his mysterious Marguerite.[9] But there is no possible reason why Annie should have had the difficulty in relating to Mary Claude which the November letter shows she had in relating to Arthur's intended. Annie knew the Claude family well from Liverpool and was their guest in their Lakeland house.

There is a far more probable candidate for identification as the prickly lady on whom Arthur had placed his hopes. In an unpublished letter of 26 September, sent from Castleton Braemar to Annie at Broadlands, he wrote 'You will of course see the Arnolds who must be at home now. I should think you might as well go and call on them yourself, but at any rate you will see them at church or elsewhere. Give my kind remembrances to Mrs Arnold and my love to Tom and Edward' (B, 233). The mysterious woman who in Ambleside rebuffed Annie's advances as a future sister-in-law was, in all likelihood, the Arnold's elder daughter Jane, whom Arthur had known and admired for more than ten years.[10]

Jane had by now had time to recover from her jilting by George Cotton: it would not be improper for Clough to imagine her as a possible wife.[11] The letter of May in which he complained to Annie that it was difficult to get to know a woman well enough to decide to marry her was the same letter in which he complained that because of the omnipresence of Matt and Tom Arnold he had never become properly acquainted with their sisters. In the same letter, reflecting on the marriage of the younger sister Mary, he declared that Jane was her superior. It would be difficult, he told Annie, to find someone likely to be a helpmate in the austere career he foresaw for himself. In both her letters to her brother and in her later life – devoting herself, as she did from 1854, to bringing up the four orphaned children of her dead brother – Jane Arnold showed herself the kind of person who would not be overwhelmed by the demands of a conscience even as hyperactive as Clough's.

It can, of course, be no more than a conjecture that Jane Arnold was the mysterious lady whom Clough in 1846 hoped to marry. We do know, however, that the lady was someone whom Annie met at Ambleside in that summer, and other than her hosts at Broadland Jane is the only woman we know Annie met. We know also that when Annie had met Jane earlier at Fox How she had found her difficult ('decided' was the way she put it), just as she had now been rebuffed by the mysterious lady.

Supporting evidence in favour of the conjecture can be derived from *Mari Magno* – not from the fourth of the tales, but from the second, 'The clergyman's first tale'. In this tale the hero and heroine are Edmund and Emma. The first encounter described between them is a family game in the garden of a house in the northern hills on a summer night. Edmund is 20 and Emma is 17. (Clough was two-and-a-half years older than Jane Arnold). The two of them join in the game.

A game it was of running and of noise;
He as a boy, with other girls and boys
(Her sisters and her brothers), took the fun;
And when her turn, she marked not, came to run,
'Emma' he called, – then knew that he was wrong,
Knew that her name to him did not belong.
Half was the colour mounted on her face,
Her tardy movement had an adult grace.
Her look and manner proved his feeling true, –
A child no more, her womanhood she knew;

Already Emma at 17 is sensitive to the unauthorized use of her Christian name, just as the mysterious lady was when Annie presumed to use it in 1846. Some verses a few lines further in the poem, which record a second visit when Edward was 22 years old, suggest that Emma's home was in fact Fox How.

Beside the wishing-gate which so they name,
Mid northern hills to me this fancy came,
A wish I formed, my wish I thus expressed:
Would I could wish my wishes all to rest,
And know to wish the wish that were the best.
(P, 397)

These verses echo an entry in Clough's diary when he, too, was 22. On 3 August 1841 he records that he went to Ambleside and Fox How and was very foolish. He then writes down eight lines of verse, of which the last two run thus:

Would I could wish my wishes all away
And learn to wish the wishes that I ought
(K, 173)

When Clough sent these verses to Burbidge he described them as 'a wishing gate conceit'. It is difficult to resist the conclusion that Emma of the wishing gate is Jane of Fox How.

Edmund, in *Mari Magno*, eventually, and improbably, marries Emma. But the concluding message of the poem is a severe one, delivered in Edmund's concluding words.

I sought not, truly would to seek disdain,
A kind, soft pillow for a wearying pain,
Fatigues and cares to lighten, to relieve;

But love is fellow-service, I believe.
No, truly, no it was not to obtain,
Though that alone were happiness, were gain,
A tender breast to fall upon and weep,
A heart, the secrets of my heart to keep;
To share my hopes, and in my griefs to grieve;
Yet love is fellow-service, I believe.

(P, 403)

Once again, the poem of Clough's last days echoes his earlier thoughts. The bride acquired by Edmund is just the bride whom Clough was seeking in 1846 when he wrote 'it is not everyone who would like to be an helpmate in the business I am likely to have' (M, 170).

If Clough ever did propose to Jane Arnold, he must have been rejected; and the affair has left no trace other than the poem in *Mari Magno*. When, in August 1850, Jane married the Quaker William Foster, the episode may, like the brief betrothal to Cotton, have been air-brushed out of the record.[12] Such was the Victorian custom concerning broken engagements and failed attachments. But perhaps matters never went as far as a formal proposal. Possibly Clough's method of wooing, whatever it was, was found too flirtatious by the austere Miss Arnold.

Clough's rejection by his intended, whether or not she was Jane Arnold, must of course have been, at least for a time, a great disappointment to him. W. M. Thackeray, when he first met him in 1848, described him as manifestly crossed in love. Perhaps it is this grief which is reflected in a poem in a notebook dated 1847.

My wind is turned to bitter north
  That was so soft a south before;
My sky, that shone so sunny bright,
  With foggy gloom is clouded o'er
My gay green leaves are yellow-black
  Upon the dank autumnal floor;
For love, departed once, comes back
  No more again, no more.

(P, 25)

* * *

For some years to come we hear no more talk of a possible marriage for Clough. The terrible Irish famine of 1847 turned his mind back to social and economic questions. He took care to secure accurate information about the famine from Dr Arnold's old colleague Richard Whately, now Archbishop of Dublin. Almost three million people, Whately replied, depended on a potato harvest which had failed. 'In England the poor man's resource would be to buy with his wages some other kind of food. But most of the poor Irish have hardly any real wages, but rent a patch of potato ground as a set off against work done' (M, 176).

The effects of the famine were worsened by the laissez-faire doctrine according to which any attempt to provide relief would in the long run worsen the situation. Clough joined an Oxford Retrenchment Association which sought to induce members of the University to restrain unnecessary expenditure during the period of distress. He wrote and published a pamphlet in support of the Association's aims.

> Let not the sky which in Ireland looks upon famishment and fever see us here in Oxford in the midst of health and strength and over-eating, over-drinking, and over-enjoying. Let us not scoff at eternal justice with our champagne and our claret, our breakfasts and suppers, our club dinners and desserts, wasteful even to the worst taste, luxurious even to unwholesomeness – or yet again by our silly and fantastic frippery or dandyism, in the hazardous elaboration of which the hundred who fail are sneered at, and the one who succeeds is smiled at. (PPR, 1, 275–9)

Clough rehearses undergraduate objections to reducing expenditure and giving alms: their money is not their own, but their parents'; to cut down spending would take the bread out of the mouths of the Oxford traders and workforce; if any saving is possible, debts must be paid before alms are given; simplest and boldest 'The money is mine, and I will not have the good of it; I have got it, and I will spend; the Irish have not and they must do without.'

The pamphlet answers each of the objections in turn, repeating the arguments against wasteful consumption that had appeared in *The Balance* in the previous year. But he went further in his criticism of the unrestricted right to private property. The question 'May I not do what I like with my own?' was a dangerous one to ask. 'The property is not your own: scarcely your own at any time; during times of calamity in no wise, except to do good with and distribute.' Every man's wealth came from his own or his ancestor's work, and ultimately from the earth which forms our real wealth and subsistence. Giving to the starving was a matter of justice, not of generosity.

> Let it be fairly felt that what we call bounty and charity is not, as we fain would persuade ourselves, a matter of gratuitous uncalled-for condescension – as of God to men, or men to meaner animals, as of children feeding the robins or ladies watering their flowers, but on the contrary a

> supplementary but integral part of fair dealing; the payment of a debt of honour . . . As a matter of pure justice and not of generosity, England is bound to share her last crust with Ireland, and the rich men to fare as the poor. (PPR, 282–3)

The pamphlet was widely read and brought a variety of reactions. A stranger wrote thanking the author and repenting of his own extravagance. Bonamy Price wrote a lengthy letter in defence of private property: it was very dangerous to say that the poor had rights against the rich. In the short term, it was likely to encourage the disaffected to violence; in the long term any diminution of property rights would damage national prosperity (B, 252, 254, 257).

* * *

The year 1847 brought to a head the crisis in Clough's religious beliefs. He was impressed by the writings of the Tübingen school of criticism, especially of J. C. Baur and of D. F. Strauss, which questioned the historicity of the Gospels. Baur attributed the New Testament synthesis to the second century AD, regarding it as a late attempt at reconciliation between Judaism and universalism in primitive Christianity. Strauss's *Life of Jesus*, translated by George Eliot in 1846, rejected all the miraculous and supernatural elements in the Gospels, and regarded the presentation of Christ by the evangelists as the produce of a collective myth.

Clough shared his religious doubts with Tom Arnold and with his sister Annie. He told Tom that he regarded the arguments of the Tübingen school as unanswerable, and to Annie he wrote that the only thinker who helped him to continue in Christian belief was Coleridge. But he added:

> My own feeling certainly does not go along with Coleridge's in attributing any special virtue to the facts of the Gospel History: they have happened and have produced what we know – have transformed the civilization of Greece and Rome, and the barbarism of Gaul and Germany into Christendom. But I cannot feel sure that a man may not have all that is important in Christianity even if he does not so much as know that Jesus of Nazareth existed . . . Trust in God's Justice and Love, and belief in his Commands as written in our Conscience, stand unshaken, though Matthew, Mark, Luke and John, or even St Paul, were to fall. (M, 182)

This reaction to George Eliot's version of the *Leben Jesu* was expressed in an intricate verse, *Epi-Strauss-ion*, which is one of the most successful of Clough's early metrical experiments.[13]

Matthew and Mark and Luke and holy John
Evanished all and gone!
Yea, he that erst, his dusky curtains quitting,
Through Eastern pictured panes his level beams transmitting
With gorgeous portraits blent,
On them his glories intercepted spent,
Southwestering now, through windows plainly glassed,
On the inside face his radiance keen hath cast,
And in the lustre lost, invisible and gone,
Are, say you, Matthew Mark and Luke and holy John?/
Lost is it? lost to be recovered never?
However,
The place of worship the meantime with light
Is, if less richly, more sincerely bright,
And in blue skies the Orb is manifest to sight.

(P, 163)

The poem operates at several levels. The title *Epi-Strauss-ion* is modelled on two Greek words: *epitaphion* or epitaph and *epithalamion* or epithalamium. The poem is both an epitaph for the evanished evangelists, and an epithalamium for the wedding of divine wisdom and human scholarship. The allusion is to Psalm 19, which compares the divine law to the sun God has set in the sky:

> Which is as a bridegroom coming out of his chamber, and rejoiceth as a strong man to run a race. His going forth is from the end of the heaven, and his circuit unto the ends of it; and there is nothing hid from the heat thereof.

The central image is plain. The morning sun shines through the stained glass images in the chancel, the afternoon sun, shining through the plain windows of the nave, illuminates the church more brightly but less gorgeously as it deadens the images in the coloured glass. Just so, the legendary gospels are more colourful but less illuminating than the austere message of contemporary criticism. But the new learning enables the worshippers not only to see the world more clearly, but to have a less fractured vision of the source of light in God himself.

For Clough the progressive divine revelation is parallel to the circuit of the sun from rising to setting: first, through the primitive glory of the evangelical legends, now through the more austere maturity of modern critical thought. But, as in the Psalms, the heavens still show forth the glory of God. As in *The New Sinai* we are encouraged to wait for some yet unforeseen synthesis to mediate between the naïve Gospel message and the sophistication of criticism.

Clough's doubts about historical Christianity were combined with a profound theistic piety. Thomas Arnold was now living in Mount Street in London, working as a clerk at the Colonial Office, after having obtained a first-class degree and made a false start in barrister's chambers. During a Whitsun break, Clough stayed with him overnight, and Tom recalled:

> In the evening before bed-time the conversation had turned on the subject of prayer; and it had been argued that a man's life, indeed, ought to be a perpetual prayer breathed upward to Divinity, but that in view of the dangers of unreality and self-delusion with which *vocal* prayers were beset it was questionable how far their use was of advantage to the soul. Clough slept ill, and in the morning, before departing, gave to his host a sheet of paper. (P, 574)

The paper contained the first draft of the poem *Qui Laborat, Orat*, which begins:

O only source of all our light and life
  Whom as our truth, our strength, we see and feel,
But whom the hours of mortal moral strife
  Alone aright reveal!

The next three verses develop the theme that even the most abstract thoughts about God fall blasphemously short of the reality. Then come the crucial stanzas:

O not unowned, Thou shalt unnamed forgive,
  In worldly walks the prayerless heart prepare,
And if in work its life it seem to live
  Shalt make that work be prayer.

Nor times shall lack, when, while the work it plies,
  Unsummoned powers the blinding film shall part,
And scarce by happy tears made dim, the eyes
  In recognition start.

(P, 14)

The poem has been admired by both devout and sceptical readers.

* * *

Tom Arnold and Clough also shared less solemn moments. In May Clough reported to Annie that 'the adorable Swede, Jenny Lind, has enchanted all the world'. Tom was swept off his feet by the soprano's appearance in Bellini's *La Sonnambula*. 'The mere sight of her is enough to drive from one's mind forever all ideals but that of the pure guileless Northern maiden, in whom stormy passion is replaced by infinite supersensual Love.' He rushed to buy two tickets in the pit at the bargain price of half a guinea, and saved one for Clough. Sadly, the tickets had to be returned as the diva was indisposed (B, 250). The two men, in any case, could not agree about her attractiveness. Tom thought her superhumanly beautiful; Clough, who had seen her only in a lithograph, described her face as 'not very beautiful, but very pleasant and true-loving' (M, 181).

For more than a year, Tom had harboured thoughts of emigrating to New Zealand (M, 268). 'Those are indeed happy who can still hope for England' he wrote to Clough during this spring 'who can find, in identifying themselves with our political or social institutions, a congenial atmosphere; and a suitable machinery for accomplishing at last all that they dream of. Of such sanguine spirits, alas! I am not one.' He remained in England only in response to family pressure: he wanted, he said, to give a fair trial to his Colonial Office job and then he would set off abroad.

Tom's brother Matt, by contrast, was just about to become secretary to a Whig grandee. He had visited Paris early in 1847, and caused a flutter when he returned to Oriel in February with long hair and a new swagger. He was stage-struck, not by a Swedish singer, but by a French actress. 'Matt is full of Parisianism', Clough told Shairp 'theatres in general, and Rachel in special. His carriage shows him in fancy parading the rue de Rivoli; – and his hair is guiltless of English scissors: he breakfasts at twelve, and never dines in Hall, and in the week or 8 days rather (for 2 Sundays must be included) he has been to Chapel *once*' (M, 179).

Clearly, Matt was not long for Oriel; but his friends were surprised when he accepted the offer of post of private secretary in the Berkeley Square establishment of Lord Lansdowne, the Lord President of the Council (M, 181). Tom and Clough disliked the appointment. 'My situation with [Lord Lansdowne]' Matt later explained ' gave me, besides many other advantages, comparative leisure for reading at a time of my life when such leisure was of the greatest value to me.' The job, which he held for four years, was, indeed, a suitable sinecure for a young man with ambitions as a poet.

Clough began the long vacation of 1847 by renting a cottage in Westmoreland with his mother and his sister (who joined them after another stay with the Claudes). 'The Arnolds will be there' he told her 'We shall, I think, be at the right kind of distance from them' (B, 253). At the end of June he went on to Scotland to take his last reading party, this time to Drumnadrochet on Loch

Ness. George Ward Hunt accompanied him, as in the previous year; so too, for short periods, did Deacon and Jelf. The new members of this party were John Blackett, a Fellow of Merton, later MP for Newcastle-on-Tyne, George Scott, later archdeacon of Dublin, and the future novelist, G. A. Lawrence, a Rugbeian now at Balliol.

As before, Clough kept a careful log from 1 July to 19 September, recording hikes, deer hunts and steamer expeditions, and including an elegant sketch map of the region. There were short daily walks to nearby beauty spots, and Sunday expeditions which might be as long as 13 miles. From time to time he was visited by senior friends. Tom Arnold, Todo Walrond and J. C. Shairp were there for a few days in July, and Simpkinson spent a night in late August. The Arnold–Walrond–Shairp party was described by one of its members, George Scott's brother Edward:

> We turned up in the small hours of the morning, and did not even know which was the inn. I remember, in the twilight, Arnold climbed in by an open window, and returned with a book which proved to be [George Sand's] *Consuelo*. Assuredly a book from Oxford. Meanwhile Walrond, always practical, had gone upstairs and invaded a bedroom. The occupant started and remonstrated, but Walrond nevertheless had secured his prize, and returned triumphant with a sock on which was marked the name Scott. This was taken as an indication that my brother and Lloyd had arrived . . . Putting together these sufficient tokens, we felt justified in rousing the household, and accepting what beds we could get. We stayed three days. (K, lvii)

Clough noted in his diary the arrival of this party at 2.30 a.m. on 18 July. Next day he visited Foyers with Tom Arnold and his companions, and liked it so much that he went back a couple of days later after their departure. He wrote to Annie on 25 July:

> Foyers is by the highest of the Scotch waterfalls, and [there] is a pleasant, quiet, sabbatic country inn, overlooking the whole lake, with our highest hills, Mealfourvonie just over the water, and with the Foyers river less than a mile off.
>
> This Sunday excursion will last me out the week, I think, and at the end of the week I shall have the satisfaction of saying 'Half over' – not that I am as yet in any degree tired either of my pupils as companions or of their books and lectures. (M, 183)

The inn Arthur described to Annie figures in *The Bothie*, where one of the characters tells tales about another found in the morning in the kitchen of the inn:

> Watching the porridge being made, pronouncing them smoked for certain
> Watching the porridge being made, and asking the lassie that made them
> What was the Gaelic for girl, and what was the Gaelic for pretty.
>
> (P, 62)

At the beginning of September Clough went with Hunt and Blackett to the Fort William area, where he stayed at the Glenfinnan Inn on Loch Shiel. The Oxford trio joined the deerstalking party of a minor royalty, and Clough went into Greek to log his meeting with 'Fitzclarence and the bigshots'. The diary records 'The Feast and the Carouse. The Song & the Dance. even unto 5 AM', followed on the next day by 'cool reflection and bitter' (K, 242). Shairp later described the event in more detail:

> The Queen had gone to Loch Laggan, and the ships that escorted her to Fort William were lying at the head of Loch Linnhe. McDonald of Glen Aladale had invited all the officers of those ships to have a day's deer-stalking on his property of Loch Shiel, and to have a ball at the Glenfinnan Inn, after their days sport. Clough came in for the ball. It was a strange gathering – the English sailors, officers, a few Highland lairds, Highland farmers and shepherds, with their wives and daughters, were all met together at the ball, Clough and one of his reading party were invited to join the dance, and they danced Highland reels, and went through all the festivities like natives. (PPR, 1, 30)

The dance stayed in Clough's memory. In his 1847 notebook there is a poem beginning 'Farewell my Highland lassie!' in which the poet promises that wherever he may be, he will call to mind 'the laughings and the whispers and the pipings and the dance'.

> I shall see thy soft brown eyes dilate to wakening woman thought,
> And whiter still the white cheek grow to which the blush was brought;
> And oh! with mine commixing I thy breath of life shall feel,
> And clasp the shyly passive hands in joyous Highland reel;
> I shall hear, and see, and feel and in sequence sadly true
> Shall repeat the bitter-sweet of the lingering last adieu.

In the second stanza the poet dreams of living, in the braes of Lochaber, a laborious homely life with 'thee the cheery wife', but on waking he recalls that the encounter closed with a chaste kiss on the brow and a Greek benediction of farewell. That ended the brief poem as Clough later published it: but in the notebook more than a hundred further verses, in several reworkings, explore two different possibilities. One possibility is to relieve pent-up passion with 'oblivious hasty love'; the other is to form, in despite of differences of class and status, a permanent union, with a 'life-long kiss the lips upon, not only on the brow'.

> Thrice blessed, oh, the life wherewith, new blood of strength and health
> Thy pure and democratic lips endue the child of wealth
> Oh blessed hundredfold, to hold enfranchised by thy kiss
> The charter, and the freeman's fee of unfactitious bliss:
> Of the lies of breeding, birth, and rank confession made, the grace
> Of absolution plenary to gain in thy embrace.
>
> (P, 589)

Clough was no doubt well-advised, on critical as well as tactical grounds, to omit lines like these from the versions of the poem published in his lifetime. But they are the first poetical enunciation of themes that he was to explore, in verse that was less clumsy and more assured, in *The Bothie* in the following year.

It is not clear from Clough's diary when the reading party ended, but by 18 September he was back in Glasgow, with the Walrond family at Calder Park. The last two weeks of September were spent in solitary wandering in Argyllshire. Arnold and Shairp had visited Loch Ericht on their way to Drumnadrochet, and had rhapsodized about its solitary beauty. On 23 September Clough spent the night at an Inn they recommended, called 'Tighnalyne', at the west end of Loch Rannoch. He walked up the west side of Loch Ericht, and stopped at a heather-thatched forester's hut, where Arnold and Shairp had slept. Shairp, in his memoir of Clough, describes what happened next.

> He found one of the children lying sick of a fever, the father I think from home, and the mother without any medicines or other aid for her child. He immediately set off and walked to Fort William, about two days' journey from the place, but the nearest place where medicines and other supplies were to be had . . . He had four days' walk, over a rough country, to bring medicines to this little child and the people did not even know his name. (PPR, 1, 29)

The itineraries in Clough's diary confirm the story. The forester's bothie was called Dallungart, and he reached it on Friday 24 September. He then walked ten miles over hills to Laggan where he spend the night. Next day he walked to the Bridge of Roy, a hike of nearly 25 miles. On the Sunday he walked the ten miles into Fort William and back. Finally, he reached Dallungart by a shorter route from Loch Lagan by Loch Pattack, and slept there on the Monday night (K, 243).

The brief entries in the diary do not give away the purpose of this strenuous journey. Indeed, other than place names, there are just three intriguing entries in the diary for this period, all of them macaronic. On 19 September we read 'versificatio'; on 23 September 'cockneyus quidam', and on 25 September 'Bridge of Roy, avec une trampe' (K, 242–3).

I have no suggestion to identify the cockney, but the versification surely refers to the composition of 'Farewell, my Highland lassie' which in the earliest versions begins with a lament at the departure of his reading-party companions. The word 'tramp' had not at this time acquired its slang meaning of 'promiscuous woman', but meant simply a vagrant pedlar or beggar. But the lady who was a tramp was surely the subject of a short poem, never published until 1974, with the title 'Homo sum, Nihil Humani'. The first two stanzas run:

> She had a coarse and common grace
> As ever beggar showed
> It was a coarse but living face
> I kissed upon the road.
>
> And why have aught to do with her,
> And what could be the good?
> I kissed her, O my questioner,
> Because I knew I could.
>
> (P, 164)

The poem should be considered in conjunction with another erotic poem belonging to this summer vacation of 1847. One of them, with a Greek title meaning *On Latmos*, consists of a 110 irregular, breathless, pentameters. It begins:

> On the mountain, in the woodland
> In the shaded secret dell,
> I have seen thee, I have met thee!
> In the soft ambrosial hours of night
> In darkness silent sweet
> I beheld thee, I was with thee
> I was thine and thou wert mine!

The poem is a rendering of the myth of Endymion, a handsome young mortal with whom the moon goddess Selene fell in love. According to the legend, he now sleeps eternally in a cave on Mount Latmos, in Asia Minor, visited from time to time by his lover. The overwhelming of an initially reluctant male by an overpowering female force makes a striking contrast with the evocation of imperious masculine brutality in the previous poem.

Endymion's final surrender to sacrilegious bliss is thus described:

By her orb she moveth slow,
Graceful-slow, serenely firm,
Maiden-Goddess! while her robe
The adoring planets kiss.

'Twas the vapour of the perfume
Of the presence that should be,
That enwraps me!
That enwraps us,
O my Goddess, O my Queen!
And I turn
At thy feet to fall before thee; And thou wilt not:
At thy feet to kneel and reach and kiss thy finger-tips;
And thou wilt not:
And I feel thine arms that stay me,
And I feel –
O mine own, mine own, mine own,
I am thine, and thou art mine.

(P, 40–1)

A final, very different, erotic poem, *Natura Naturans*, was written on the railway journey back to Liverpool at the beginning of October. It celebrates a tiny bat's squeak of sexuality between two passengers in the same railway carriage, otherwise totally unknown to each other.

Beside me, – in the car, she sat,
  She spake not, no, nor looked to me:
From her to me, from me to her,
  What passed so subtly, stealthily?
As rose to rose that by it blows
  Its interchanged aroma flings;
Or wake to sound of one sweet note
  The virtues of disparted strings.

Beside me, nought but this! – but this,
  That influent as within me dwelt
Her life, mine too within her breast,
  Her brain, her every limb she felt;
We sat; while o'er and in us, more
  And more, a power unknown prevailed,

Inhaling, and inhaled, – and still,
'Twas one, inhaling or inhaled.

Beside me, nought but this; – and passed;
I passed; and know not to this day
If gold or jet her girlish hair,
If black, or brown, or lucid-grey
Her eye's young glance: the fickle chance
That joined us, yet may join again
But I no face again could greet
As hers, whose life was in my then.

Each of the two felt the power which even in stones and earths 'By blind elections felt, in forms / organic breeds to myriad births'. Tiny spots of lichen on granite, a lily growing to pendent head, the tallest cedars: all these express the same power. So too does the insect and animal kingdom:

Flashed flickering forth fantastic flies,
Big bees their burly bodies swung,
Rooks roused with civic din the elms,
And lark its wild reveille rung;
In Libyan dell the light gazelle,
The leopard lithe in Indian glade,
And dolphin, brightening tropic seas,
In us were living, leapt and played.

The elemental force that underlies all plant and animal development finds its culmination in human sexuality.

Such sweet preluding sense of old
Led on in Eden's sinless place
The hour when bodies human first
Combined the primal prime embrace
Such genial heat the blissful seat
In man and woman owned unblamed
When, naked both, its garden paths
They walked unconscious, unashamed;

Ere, clouded yet in mistiest dawn,
Above the horizon dusk and dun,
One mountain crest with light had tipped
That Orb that is the Spirit's Sun;

Ere dreamed young flowers in vernal showers
   Of fruit to rise the flower above
Or ever yet to young Desire
   Was told the mystic name of Love.
(P, 36–8)

These verses, with their evolutionary framework and their frank exaltation of transient sexuality are astonishingly different from our conventional expectations of a Victorian writer. They also manifest a technical skill that show that Clough had at last come of age as a poet.

The erotic force of the verses of this long vacation cannot fail to suggest that underlying them was some personal experience of passion. The last of the semi-autobiographical poems in *Mari Magno* tells of an affair between a tutor, resting at the end of a reading party, and a waiting-maid in a Highland inn.

A College fellow, who has sent away
The pupils he has taught for many a day,
And comes for fishing and for solitude,
Perhaps a little pensive in his mood,
An aspiration and a thought have failed,
Where he had hoped, another has prevailed,
But to the joys of hill and stream alive,
And in his boyhood yet, at twenty-five.
(P, 426)

Clough was in fact now 28; but it was his first reading party since his disappointment about the mysterious lady he had hoped to marry. In the story, the college fellow flirts for half a week with the maid, but then resolves to flee because of 'the horror of seduction, such he felt / the miseries of the woman that ensue'. The girl offers him an assignation: her friend 'whispered clear the how, the when, the where / e'en for tonight'. He tries to run away but finds his clothes are still at the wash. By the time they return, it is dark and to leave would mean a 16-mile night march in a dreary drizzle – and then she looks so lovely in her blue jacket and linsey petticoat!

Worn with the mental conflicts of the day
He sat and slept three solid hours away.
So with her thickest conclave of still air
Deep night descends, and how, and when and where
In council meet, and plying swift their charms
Convey the sweet companion to his arms

He remains in the inn for a week, fishing by day and making love by night. He then escorts the girl by sea to Glasgow, giving her tutorials on astronomy in her cabin, and comforting her during a terrifying storm beside the coast of Mull. He then takes lodgings with the girl's uncle, a grocer named Macfarlane. He decides to marry the girl, give up his £300-a-year stipend as a College Fellow, and earn a living by taking pupils. But first he has to return home for the three weeks of the College Audit, which he cannot fail to attend since he is Junior Bursar.

There is no need at this point to follow the poem further, and learn how the hero loses his bride, who is sent to South Australia, and how the two, years later, are reunited in very different circumstances. The immediate question is: how far do the events in 'The Lawyer's Second Tale' correspond to actual experiences of Clough at the time of his Scottish reading parties?

At one extreme, it is clear that the sea voyage to Glasgow, the renting of lodgings and the promise of marriage are completely fictional. Clough's diaries show that after each reading party he returned to Glasgow by road and inland steamer, and visited only Calder Hall, the Walrond home. At the other extreme, it seems quite probable that he did fall briefly in love with a Scottish serving maid and had some kind of affair with her. The 'Highland inn among the Western Hills' of the poem is most likely the Glenfinnan Inn at Fort William, where he stayed for nearly two weeks in September, including five days after the departure of the last of his pupils. Whether the affair went as far as seduction it is impossible to say. On the one hand, in the later drama *Dipsychus* the poet represents the semi-autobiographical hero as being still sexually inexperienced in Venice in 1850; on the other hand, the emotion with which he was eventually to recall this episode on his deathbed suggests that it was something more than a mild flirtation.[14]

Michaelmas term of 1847 was Clough's last at Oriel. Tom Arnold, in quest of a freer and less artificial society, had now resolved to put into effect his project of emigrating to New Zealand (B, 261). He, like Clough, had recently been disappointed in love, having failed to win the hand of Archbishop Whateley's daughter Henrietta. But his trip was not simply a piece of romantic idealism. His father, in 1839, had invested in the New Zealand Company, and the family possessed there more than 200 acres of land.

Tom paid a farewell visit to Oxford in November. He took a Sunday breakfast with Clough and Stanley. The group was joined after church by Walrond and young Edward Arnold, and in the afternoon by Matt from London, at last – Clough observed – beginning to grow out of his childish fondness for bad language. Tom's friends collected books for farewell presents: a mixed bag, Tennyson, Spinoza, Carlyle and Keble's *Christian Year*.

Tom's ship, the *John Wicliffe*, was due to leave Wapping docks on Sunday 20 November. Clough went up to London on Friday for a weekend of farewell theatre-going with Tom and Matt at the Princess's theatre and the Lyceum. On Sunday they boarded the vessel and inspected the cabin. 'After a little delay we got into Tom's Cabin' young Edward Arnold reported to his mother, horrified by its tiny size. 'Clough indeed says that it is a good-sized one for an emigrant ship & that Tom is very lucky. I did not like to laugh at what was so serious a matter to Tom, but my firm conviction was that *I* could not live out a voyage of 5 months there' (L, 72). Tom worried that his evangelical fellow-passengers would be shocked by the heretical texts he was taking with him: Rousseau and Emerson for instance. His friends joked that it was probably the first time that Spinoza and Hegel had ever crossed the equator.

The days in London had given Clough a taste for theatre-going, and he returned in December to see *Much Ado* at the Haymarket and *Tipperary* at the Adelphi (K, 245). On the same visit, he offered the publisher Chapman the collection of poems by Burbidge and himself that was in the following year to see the light under the title *Ambarvalia* (M, 190). He had now begun to send his poems for criticism to Matt, as he had previously done to Burbidge. The first one, published as 'The Questioning Spirit', preached, in complex syntax and elaborate imagery, the theme that selfless duty is the only form of human life which does not deceive itself, since it does not expect reward either in this life or the next. Matt admired the workmanship, but grimaced at the message. 'Goly what a !!!Shite's!!! oracle! But profoundly true. – Besides its trueness to its purpose, or constituting this, the feeling is deep in the Poem, & simultaneously runs clear' (L, 75).

Matt was lent Clough's notebooks, and during December he read many more of the *Ambarvalia* poems. On the whole, he thought, 'they would stand very grandly' and he praised the 'great precision and force you have attained in these inward ways'. However, he objected to a number of the poems of the *Blank Misgivings* series. He claimed that Clough had not fully appreciated Shakespeare's remark that 'if imagination would apprehend some joy it comprehends some bringer of that joy'. It is indeed a fair criticism to say that many of Clough's earlier poems express guilt and remorse without making clear the object of those passions. Matt also thought that the collection was overloaded with apostrophes to duty. But he admired 'The New Sinai'. Stanley, he predicted, would have it by heart the day it appeared.

Clough returned to Oxford in a discontented state. Oriel was lonely without Matt, and Tom's motives for emigration were a bitter reminder of his own religious, political and sexual frustration. This finds extraordinary expression in an unpublished manuscript preserved in the Bodleian library. It is a parody of parts of the Vulgate text of the Apocalypse. Its satiric impact is powerful, and even today anyone accustomed to the Vulgate as a sacred liturgical text is bound to read it with a sense of shock. In the translation which follows,

I have tried to render quotations and echoes from the Vulgate into quotations and echoes from the Authorized Version.

> And the spirit said to me, These things are dreams.
>
> And it said, I am the Spirit, that is I am nothing; I have no Body, that is substance.
>
> And it said unto me, See, this is my sister Pandemia who has body and flesh and limbs and substance. Come take her and lie with her. For with me no man can lie. And the spirit and the Virgin said Come.
>
> And I stood in the desert, in Babylon, in the streets of the ways of Babylon, and I opened my arms and I bared my loins, and I cried and said, Come holy Pandemia, behold thy servant, be it done according to thy will.
>
> And here stood before my face a woman slender and tall, of about thirty years of age. And she said unto me
>
> I am Pandemia whom thou seekest.
>
> Lo, I am not spirit, I have body and flesh and limbs and substance. Blessed are those that lie with me.
>
> And she said, I am the life and the way and the truth . . .
>
> And in the evening I lifted up my face and I looked and I saw a woman dressed in white clothings, and she came to me and held up my hand and said, I am thy fellow servant, the servant of the Most High who is the creator of all things whatsoever there are.
>
> Come, let us serve together, you and I, and let us help one another.
>
> And I looked into her face and I said
>
> Art thou not that Pandemia whom I called upon and who spake unto me?
>
> And she said, I am thy fellow servant, the servant of the Most High. Let us serve together you and I. Come
>
> And the Spirit and the Virgin said, Come. This is a great mystery. Blessed are they that have ears to hear, and hear.

Clough certainly meant this piece to be shocking, as is shown by the title itself 'Addenda to the Apocalypse'. This recalls the verses that conclude the book of Revelation 'I testify unto every man that heareth the words of the prophecy of this book, if any man shall add unto these things, God shall add unto him the plagues that are written in this book'. The text's most blasphemous feature is placing in the mouth of Pandemia, Plato's earthly Aphrodite that offers herself to all comers, words that the Bible gives to Christ. And yet, at the end, the carnal Pandemia seems to give place to a heavenly Aphrodite, identified with the Virgin of the Apocalypse, whose motto is the one that Clough forever repeats in soberer contexts: love is fellow service. But who, if anyone, was the piece written for? And who, if anyone, ever read it? Clough's widow preserved it for us on a fine piece of marbled paper; but whether she understood it must remain doubtful. She headed it, chastely, 'Latin Prose'.

The incongruity of Clough's position as an Oriel tutor was highlighted in December by a casual remark of Provost Hawkins about the Thirty-Nine Articles. Clough was seriously worried: he sent a letter which he took the trouble to draft in his diary in code. In clear, the letter read:

> You spoke of a Tutor as a Teacher of the 39 Articles. For such an office I fear I can hardly consider myself qualified. I can only offer you the ordinary negative acquiesence of a layman. (M, 191)

He explained that his current lectures were entirely classical and mathematical, but admitted that his religious position was not perhaps consistent with a tutorship, and placed his office in the Provost's hands.

Hawkins, despite his long and frustrating experience of tutors who liked to find a way around the Thirty-Nine Articles, was remarkably patient. He offered Clough the chance of moving to a lay fellowship, and he agreed that, since Oriel had four tutors, it was possible to dispense one of them from carrying out the statutory duty of teaching the Articles. He agreed that subscription did not bind one to hold the same opinions for ever. 'But if he seeks an office to which Subscription is the necessary passport, he is surely pledged to resign the office if at any time his opinions shall become changed' (M, 193).

Over the Christmas vacation and into the beginning of the Lent term Clough put forward ever more slippery defences of his position: could he not retain his privileges until the Vice-Chancellor, as he was entitled to do, requested a renewal of his subscription? Hawkins was polite, but unconvinced.

> I *should by no means wish to hurry anyone into Dissent*. But when his mind was decidedly made up, *upon the best evidence he could procure*, then I think he ought not to wait for the V.C.'s inquiry, but act upon his own convictions. (M, 195)

At this point, Clough gave in. On 23 January 1848 he resigned his tutorship. He wished to retain his fellowship until it ended in June 1849, but in any case he intended to spend his final year abroad (M, 196). Hawkins encouraged him to retain his tutorship until Easter, and to take counsel before taking any further step. 'I am very sorry to see whereabouts you stand. I am afraid of unrestrained speculation leading to scepticism – a very unhappy state and one for which God did not design us. In truth you were not born for *speculation*. I am not saying a word against full and fair enquiry. But we are sent into this world not so much to speculate as to serve God and serve man' (M, 198).

Hawkins' letters from this period remained in Clough's mind, and sentiments from them are often echoed in his later poetry – sometimes seriously presented, sometimes with ironic intent. But the news of his resignation was told, in his first letter to Tom Arnold on 31 January, in a jaunty tone.

> I feel greatly rejoiced to think that this is my last term of bondage in Egypt, though I shall, I suppose quit the fleshpots for a wilderness, with small hope of manna, quails, or water from the rock. The Fellowship however lasts for a year after next June: and I don't think the Provost will meddle with my tenure of it, though I have let him know that I have wholly put aside adherence to 39 articles. (M, 199)

Clough was not, however, altogether proud of his dealings with the Provost. 'I am not quite sure, my dear Tom', he wrote 'how far you would think me honest in my correspondence with him – and you being away I don't know who to ask.' Tom was clearly seen as a more reliable source of moral advice than his loud-mouthed brother Matt, who was, indeed, at this time regarded by some of his friends as no more than 'a Puppy' (M, 198). But consultation via correspondence with the antipodes was impossibly slow – more so, as Clough underpaid the postage and his letter was returned, to be redespatched on 25 February. By then, the most burning news was that 'the French have begun a new revolution' (M, 199).

The deposition of King Louis Philippe by the Paris mob in February 1848 was only the first of a series of revolutions throughout Europe. On 20 March, returning to Oxford from another theatre-going weekend with Matthew Arnold, Clough noted in his diary reports of the resignation of the Austrian statesman Metternich, to be followed by jerky notes of major events as the revolutionary tide swept on.

> These were the days (18th 19th) of the Prussian revolution: the Declarations, the Concourse in the Palace Square, the Charge of Dragoons, whose colonel was insulted: the Barricades and To Arms, the Neufchatel rifles . . . The King's night-missive the New Ministry: the Funeral; the Amnesty & Liberation of Poles. The new Cockade. (K, 245)

Clough was anxious to travel and see for himself the momentous events on the Continent. But an important engagement detained him in England for the Easter Vacation. He had long been a reader and admirer of Emerson, as of Carlyle. (By 1846 he was sufficiently familiar with their works to complain that a Unitarian sermon had been 'a mere rechauffé of Carlyle and Emerson, dished up in Brummagem ware' M, 168.) In 1847 Emerson visited Liverpool to give a series of lectures. Annie attended the lectures and was introduced to the lecturer by a friend, Samuel Bulley, who at a party afterwards read out passages from Arthur's Retrenchment pamphlet. On 26 November Clough wrote inviting Emerson to visit Oxford. 'Amongst the juniors there are many that have read and studied your books, and not a few that have largely learnt from them, and would gladly welcome their author' (M, 187).

Emerson was not able to accept the invitation until the end of the Lent term. He arrived in Oxford on 30 March, and was introduced by Clough to Stanley and other friends in various colleges. 'Everybody liked him' Clough reported to Tom Arnold,

> and as the orthodox mostly had never heard of him, they did not suspect him. He is the quietest, plainest unobtrusivest man possible – will talk but will rarely *discourse* to more than a single person – and wholly declines 'roaring'. He is very Yankee to look at, lank and sallow and not quite without the twang; but his look and voice are pleasing nevertheless and give you the impression of perfect intellectual cultivation as completely as would any great scientific man in England . . . Some people thought him very like Newman. But his manner is much simpler. (M, 215)

Clough took Emerson to London on 1 April and introduced him to Matthew Arnold and the publisher Chapman. The two discussed Swedenborg and the *Bhagavadgītā*, and quickly became friends. At the end of April they travelled separately to Paris, where they continued to see each other almost daily.

Notes

1 The letter is preserved in Mary Arnold's diary, in Wooster College.
2 Bernard Bergonzi, *A Victorian Wanderer: the Life of Thomas Arnold the Younger*, Oxford 2003, pp. 34–6.
3 E. B. Greenberger, *Arthur Hugh Clough: the Growth of a Poet's Mind*, Harvard University Press 1970, p. 75.
4 Ibid., 79–81.
5 See above, p. 92.
6 A diary entry for 18 July, the day before Arthur and Annie crossed the frontier at Splugen, notes a meeting with Mr and Mrs Taylor *cum fratre*: but whether the frater is Clough's brother or a Taylor brother does not emerge.
7 *New Zealand Letters of Thomas Arnold the Younger*, ed. Jim Bertram, London and Wellington 1939, pp. 222–3. See p. 87 above.
8 R. K. Biswas, *Arthur Hugh Clough: Towards a Reconsideration*, Oxford 1972, p. 185.
9 See especially Park Honan *Matthew Arnold: A Life*, London 1981, pp. 151–67, and the other scholars he quotes on p. 451.
10 See above pp. 53, 75–6, 85–6.
11 See above, pp. 102, 104.
12 See A. P. Stanley, *The Life of Thomas Arnold D. D.*, London 1844; 1903, p. 666.
13 The poem is analysed in detail in my *God and Two Poets*, London 1988, p. 76.
14 See below, p. 202.

Chapter Five
Revolutions and Hexameters

Clough stayed in Oxford for the Oriel fellowship elections – the last he ever took part in – and on 1 May had the satisfaction of bringing Emerson and Carlyle together. He also introduced Emerson to F. T. Palgrave, an old Balliol and Decade friend, later to be famous as the compiler of the *Golden Treasury* anthology, who had just returned from a visit to Paris in company with Arthur Stanley and Benjamin Jowett. The next day he crossed to Boulogne himself and reached Paris on 3 May, where he took a room on the Rue Mont Thabor at 12 francs a week. With a group of Emerson's disciples he visited both the palace of Versailles and the site in Paris where in February the mob had burnt the royal throne (M, 203). On 10 May Emerson himself arrived, and the two of them went to Racine's *Phèdre* to assess the acting of Rachel, the admired of Matthew Arnold. Clough found himself disappointed, both in the play and the actress, and wrote to tell Matt so.

Arnold at this time shared Clough's enthusiasm for the February revolution, and wrote him a sonnet, *To a Republican Friend,* beginning 'God knows it, I am with you'. He praised Clough for despising the short-sighted sophistry of the comfortable, and striving to relieve the sufferings of the homeless and unfed. The poem ended:

> If these are yours, if this is what you are,
> Then I am yours, and what you feel I share.
> (OA, 51)

After the February insurrection a provisional government of seven members had been formed, including the poet Lamartine. Elections in April had confirmed the Republic, but disappointed the working-class elements among the revolutionaries. A new provisional government included as well as the moderate Lamartine the radical Ledru-Rollin. 'I don't expect much good will come of this present Assembly' Clough told Annie. 'It is extremely shopkeeperish and merchantish in its feelings, and won't set to work at the organization of labour at all, at all . . . The Socialist people are in the dumps' (M, 204). He feared that the bourgeoisie, to distract the working class from labour reform, wanted war – war against Austria to support liberal nationalists in Italy, and war against Russia for the liberation of Poland.

During his time in Paris Clough wrote regularly to Arthur Stanley. Lamartine's dominance had now peaked, he told him on 14 May. The working-class boys of 17 and 18 who had been enrolled in a Garde Mobile were being infected with bourgeois loyalty. He preferred watching workers from the St Antoine quarter, in blouse and red bonnet, arguing with well-dressed multitudes in the Rue de Rivoli.

> I do little else than potter about under the Tuileries chestnuts and here and there about bridges, pour savourer la republique. I contemplate with infinite thankfulness the blue blouses, garnished with red, of the garde mobile; and emit a perpetual incense of devout rejoicing for the purified state of the Tuileries, into which I find it impossible, meantime, to gain admittance. I growl occasionally at the sight of aristocratic equipages which begin to peep out again, and trust that the National Assembly will in its wisdom forbid the use of livery servants. (M, 207)

But two days later he wrote excitedly to Annie:

> Yesterday was a day of great peril and disorder – an Emeute. The Chamber was invaded and turned out by a mob – and the hall occupied by them for two hours. At last the Natl. Guard turned them out. A new government had been named by the mob, and some of the chiefs went off to the Hotel de Ville, a mile up the Seine, to set it going. However the Natl. Guard followed and put it down. La Martine came with Ledru-Rollin and rode along the quays to finish the work, with dragoons and cannon. I was at his side for a quarter of a mile and saw him, of course, distinctly. There was no firing and scarce any fighting. The whole thing is put down, for the present, and I am glad it is, on the whole. The cry was 'Vive la Pologne', but the object was to get rid of the Assembly and set up a more democratic set of people. (M, 205)

To Stanley on 19 May he gave a rather different description of the suppression of the rising. Liberty, Equality and Fraternity, he said, had been driven back by shopkeeping bayonets. 'Well-to-do-ism shakes her Egyptian scourge to the tune of Ye are idle, ye are idle; the tale of bricks will be doubled and Moses and Aaron of Socialism can at the best only pray for plagues.' How sad that the blouses of the garde mobile were now discarded for a green epauletted uniform! 'Bring forth, ye millionaires, the three-month hidden carriages . . . ride forth, ye cavalier escorted amazons, in unfearing flirtation, to your Bois de Boulogne: the world begins once more to move on its axis and draw on its kid gloves' (M, 207).

On the following Sunday, 21 May, Clough was woken by drums at 4 a.m. and rose at 6 to watch the Fête de la Republique in the Place de la Concorde. Members of national and regional assemblies processed, and deputations of the oppressed of Poland, Italy, Germany and Ireland joined in the procession. A float carried girls classically dressed in white with oak-wreaths in their hair and tricolours streaming from their left shoulders, 'pretty en masse, but individually not by any means remarkable either for face or figure'. A tricolour balloon was sent up, and there were endless cannon salutes. The gunfire gave him a headache, and he retired early. He spent the evening with Emerson, talking, according to his diary, about sex (*de sexualibus*). Next day he wrote to Annie, who had been expressing Malthusian fears of overpopulation.

> About increase of population – you are right, I suppose. It is no wonder that the more wretched a population becomes, the more rapidly it should increase. To live together as man and wife is sometimes the only enjoyment people can get without immediate ready money payment or certainty of getting into debt for it. I suppose the thing wanted in society is to raise the lower classes either in material comforts or morality or both to that state where they will of themselves feel the duty and find the inclination to refrain – as the upper classes, for the most part, do, at present. (M, 209)

Clough stayed in Paris for five weeks conversing with Emerson, visiting tourist attractions, and attending the theatre almost every other day (K, 249). He attended the Club des Femmes, much disrupted by male intruders. 'A more grievous spectacle of the un-politesse of Frenchman I never saw, but I believe it has been a good deal worse. Occupying the seats reserved for women – laughing and shouting – greedily seizing and creating double-entendres etc.' Clough admired the patience and strength of the chairwoman, a Madame Niboyer. It was, he thought, useful for French males to see a woman face up to them not for purposes of flirtation. The topic of discussion was a proposed Divorce bill which allowed dissolution of marriage, after three years, on grounds of incompatibility of temper, provided the man was over 25 and the woman between 21 and 45 (M, 212–13).

Clough had left Paris before the infamous 'June Days' (23–6 June) in which a proletarian rising was suppressed and 10,000 workers killed – a greater loss of life than in any of the insurrections of the Revolution of 1789. He took the news with surprising nonchalance. 'I confess I regard it' he told Tom Arnold 'in the same light as a great battle – with, on the whole, *less* horror and certainly more meaning than most great battles that one reads of.' Later, in the second Canto of Clough's epistolary novel *Amours de Voyage*, the hero Claude tells us that he

> Never predicted Parisian millenniums, never beheld a
> New Jerusalem coming down dressed like a bride out of heaven
> Right on the Place de la Concorde
>
> (P, 104)

Matthew Arnold's enthusiasm for the Revolution cooled rather faster. He teased Clough by addressing letters to him as 'Citizen Clough, Oriel Lyceum, Oxford'. As a sequel to *To a Republican Friend,* he wrote a second sonnet, beginning:

> Yet, when I muse on what life is, I seem
> Rather to patience prompted, than that proud
> Prospect of hope which France proclaims so loud –
> France, famed in all great arts, in none supreme
>
> (OA, 52)

Liberty and equality could not be achieved by human endeavour, the poem argued, and must wait for the day when all mortals stood in fellowship face to face with God. 'Matt was at one time really heated to a very fervid enthusiasm' Clough told Tom in July 'but he has become sadly cynical again of late. However, I think the poetism goes on favourably' (M, 215).

Clough returned to England to hear a set of lectures given by Emerson between 6 and 13 June. The topic was 'The mind and manners of the Nineteenth Century'. Clough's brief note on the final lecture was 'Politics and Socialism: anti-Social analysis & acknowledgement of individual right. Socialism.' 'I liked his lectures' Clough told Tom Arnold 'better than either his conversation or his appearance . . . He is much less Emersonian than his Essays. There is no dogmatism or arbitrariness or positiveness about him.' But though he disliked controversy he was, Clough reported, unequivocally Pagan (M, 216).

Emerson sailed back to Boston from Liverpool on 16 July on the steamer *Europa.* Before departing he stayed a few days with the Cloughs and some other Liverpool admirers. On the deck of the steamer, about to depart, Arthur said 'what shall we do without you? Think where we are: Carlyle has led us all out into the desert, and he has left us there.' Emerson replied by placing his hand on Clough's head, announcing that he was to be bishop of all England, and show the wanderers in the desert the way to the Promised Land. Later, Emerson recalled that Clough's intellectuality 'seemed so little English that I wrote home to my friends that I had found in London the best American'.

Whatever – if anything – Emerson meant by his farewell gesture, his departure left Clough in an exalted state. On the pages of his diary after the note of the sailing of the *Europa* ('Explicit Liber Emersonianus') he began a meditation on life, work and death which suggests he believed himself to have had a mystical experience. His pen sped over the paper, filling it with pseudo-biblical rhetoric, writing and crossing out, rewriting and interpolating. Pages upon pages pour out, bombastic and bathetic by turns, varying from manic to suicidal. Among the more lucid passages are the following:

> Truly indeed I believe that Moses & Isaiah & David, Paul & John & their Master, & with these moreover many that shall come from the east & west, Zoroasht it may be and Socrates, Confutzee and Zeno, Mahomet and the teacher of Peru spake in old time as they were moved of the Holy Ghost . . .
>
> A Presence I acknowledge, I am conscious of a Power, whose name is Panacea – whose visits indeed are seldom & I know not where to bespeak them; but who itself is Prescription & Recovery & of whom though invisible I feel is about my path & about my bed & spieth out all my ways.

But at other times he will compare himself to the deluded Joanna Southcote, who believed that she was pregnant with the Messiah. He is simply, he tells himself on one occasion 'feeding on fantastic memories of angelic visitation that came to thee of green tea wholly unsexual' (K, 252–4).

At the same time, however, Clough was working on the first draft of an impressive verse drama about the Christian doctrine of the Fall of Mankind. He sent a portion of it in draft to Matthew Arnold, who did not like it. 'I confess that productions like your Adam and Eve are not suited to me at present' he wrote on 20 July. Discouraged by this, Clough wrote to Tom Arnold 'I don't much intend writing any more verse, but have a notion for Essays.' If he resigned his fellowship, which he intended to do in October, he had to find some way of earning his bread. He was attracted by an offer, passed on by Matt, of travelling on the continent as tutor to Byron's grandson Ralph King, the son of Lord Lovelace. 'They are ultra-liberal people' he told Tom 'otherwise I would not venture' (M, 217).

In spite of Clough's abdication of poetry in his letter to Tom, the germ of his most substantial poetic work was already beginning to sprout in his mind. His diary came down to earth on 15 August while he was staying near Windermere with Wordsworth's friend, the manufacturer and essayist William Rathbone Greg. Amid sober entries about the rent of houses for reading parties, and about misprints in an edition of Keats, there occur the following lines.

The Games & Dinner (? & Dance)
The Tour
The bothie of Topernafuosich.
Oh if your high born girls only knew the charm the attraction . . .
Or high kilted perhaps – interposed the in anger
Or high kilted perhaps, as once at Dundee I saw them
Petticoats to the knee or indeed a trifle over
Shewing their thighs were more white than the clothes they trod in their washtub.

Any reader of *The Bothie* can recognize here lines which were taken into the finished poem with little alteration.

The Bothie itself was composed at amazing speed. Clough went home to Liverpool from the Lakes on 7 September, having looked in on a reading party in Patterdale conducted by H. W. Fisher, one of his own pupils from the Drumnadrochet party. He wrote to Fisher on 15 September 'Liverpool is a dismal place, & the Sun & Moon which shine so brightly on it also conjure up visions of places more worthy of such adornment,' and recalled the pre-breakfast dips of the previous years, and the time of bathing between logic and dinner (B, 308).

While in Liverpool he read aloud to his mother and sister Longfellow's recently published *Evangeline*. He was fascinated by its hexameter metre:

This is the forest primeval. The murmuring pines and the hemlocks
Bearded with moss, and in garments green, indistinct in the twilight,
Stand like the Druids of eld, with voices sad and prophetic,
Stand like harpers hoar, with beards that rest on their bosoms.

Ever since his earliest days as a tutor he had been pondering on the best way of rendering into English the metres of classical poets. In 1847 he had published an article in a learned journal on the problems set by Latin lyrical metres. He had begun to experiment in the translation of the hexameters of Homer. Here, in Longfellow, was a poet who was using hexameters not just for translation but as a metre for original composition. The great danger of this – as *Evangeline*, Clough believed, illustrated – was of monotonous regularity (Scott IV 1976: 7). Stirred by the challenge of Longfellow, and full of nostalgia for his Scottish reading parties, he set himself to compose a poem of 2,000 hexameters without falling into this trap.

During the three weeks he spent at home he wrote furiously. The family had now moved to 51 Vine Street, towards the eastern edge of the rapidly expanding city. Early morning walks into the Liverpool suburbs took the place of the Scottish daybreak swims of the previous year. Their atmosphere is captured in a prolonged simile near the end of the poem.

But as the light of day enters some populous city,
Shaming away, ere it come, by the chilly daystreak signal,
High and low, the misusers of night, shaming out the gas lamps, –
All the great empty streets are flooded with broadening clearness,
Which, withal, by inscrutable simultaneous access
Permeates far and pierces, to very cellars lying in
Narrow high back-lane, and court and alley of alleys:
He that goes forth to his walk, while speeding to the suburb,
Sees sights only peaceful and pure; as, labourers settling
Slowly to work, in their limbs the lingering sweetness of slumber;
Humble market-carts, coming-in, bringing-in, not only
Flower, fruit, farm-store, but sounds and sights of the country
Dwelling yet on the sense of the dreamy drivers; soon after
Half-awake servant-maids unfastening drowsy shutters
Up at the windows, or down, letting-in the air by the doorway;
School-boys, school-girls soon, with slate, portfolio, satchel,
Hampered as they haste, those running, these others maidenly tripping;
Early clerk anon turning out to stroll, or it may be
Meeting his sweetheart – waiting behind the garden gate there;
Merchant on his grass-plat haply, bare-headed; and now by this time
Little child bringing breakfast to 'father' that sits on the timber
There by the scaffolding; see, she waits for the can beside him;
Mean-time above purer air, untarnished of new-lit fires:
So that the whole great wicked artificial civilized fabric, –
All its unfinished houses, lots for sale, and railway outworks, –
Seems reaccepted, resumed to Primal Nature and Beauty.

(P, 90)

By the middle of October the poem had gone through a couple of drafts and been handed over to Francis Macpherson, the Oxford printer who had published the Retrenchment pamphlet. On 23 October Arthur wrote to Annie that his 'little book' would be out in ten days. In fact the poem appeared, after further substantial revision, in the middle of November, a little over two months since the reading of *Evangeline*.

Writing and revising *The Bothie* had not been Clough's only occupation during these months. He was still a fellow of Oriel and his fellowship had a year to run. In July he told Tom Arnold that he was thinking of giving it up, and in October he decided to carry out his resolution. He did so against the advice of all his friends, except the Arnolds. In Oxford Stanley and Jowett argued strongly against resignation. Shairp, from Rugby, urged 'Let me say unless you feel *strongly* that it would be a lightening to your spirit to resign, let Jowett's remonstrances have their weight' (M, 219).

Only a year since, Shairp had been asking Clough's advice whether he should proceed to orders in spite of some doctrinal misgivings. Now the roles were reversed and Shairp was the counsellor. In correspondence with Clough he was to remain, for years to come, the voice of Christian conscience.

> Let me urge you most strongly not to take your name off the books, nor to cut Oxford entirely. And this not at all from the hopes of future professorships or other worldly goods in some prospective Oxford rediviva. But . . . above all that you may not be cut off from the future of Christianity.
>
> Though Christianity has passed through many systems both political and dogmatical now outworn, there is nothing in it specially congenial with divine right of feudalisms – monarchies, aristocracies – nor with bygone creeds, confessions, priesthoods. These are certainly of the past, but though they die, Christianity may live. (M, 218)

Clough held to his resolve. Back in Oriel on 8 October he offered his resignation to Hawkins: 'I can have nothing whatever to do with a subscription to the xxxix articles – and deeply repent of ever having submitted to one. I cannot consent to receive any further pecuniary benefit in consideration of such conformity'. On 17 October he signed a Latin act of resignation. The Provost, kindly as ever, delayed the official announcement in case there were second thoughts, even at this late stage.

Clough retired to his old lodgings in 99 Holywell. Hawkins visited him there and urged him to undertake a serious study of the arguments in favour of orthodox Christianity, and particularly of the authenticity of the Pauline epistles. He followed up this advice with a lengthy reading list, composed mainly of eighteenth-century texts. Despite Clough's chilly response, he continued, well into 1849, to keep open the possibility of a resumption of the fellowship (M, 223, 226, 233, 236).

Clough was relieved to find that his action made little difference to his friendships. In Oxford, he told Tom 'people don't cut me at all; I dine at some high tables and generally I am treated as a citizen.' At Rugby he was able to stay with Walrond, now a housemaster. He was in Walrond's house, along with Matthew Arnold and the newly married Burbidge, when *The Bothie* appeared (M, 224). The poem took everyone in Oxford by surprise. Those who knew of his Oriel resignation expected some solemn statement of his reasons; instead there appeared this lively novel in verse, on the surface a very light-hearted piece of work.

The Bothie consists of nine books, of an average length of just over 200 lines. The poem is set in the context of an Oxford reading party in Scotland, and features of the tutor and his pupils bear a strong resemblance to Clough and his young friends. The overall line of the story is simple: the student hero leaves the group for a solitary tour of the Highlands and falls in love several times. Finally he settles his love on a crofter's daughter, marries her, and emigrates with her to New Zealand. But the narrative takes many twists, and the poem operates at several levels.

The first book tells of a banquet after a day of Highland games, and it establishes the characters by describing them dressing for dinner. The tutor's name is Adam: a grave clergyman, soberly dressed in old fashioned clothes. Foremost among the undergraduates is Hope, an Earl's nephew, simple and elegant in dress. Lindsay, a great smoker and a master of slang, wears a fancy waistcoat. Most extravagant of all is Airlie ('May-fairly') who keeps all waiting while he dons his:

> Waistcoat blue, coral-buttoned, the white tie finely adjusted,
> Coral moreover the studs on a shirt as of crochet of women

The three other undergraduates take little time to dress because they have rushed in from a bathing pool: Arthur Audley (modest and athletic, 'the bather of bathers par excellence'), Hobbes (clumsy and corpulent, unwisely sporting a kilt) and finally Philip Hewson ('poet and radical'), who is to be the hero of the story.

The dinner is described in lively detail, from the small decanters of sherry ('not overchoice') through the venison, mutton and grouse course, to the final black bottles of well-mixed toddy. After dinner the host, the old soldier Sir Hector, gives a grammar-defying speech, leaping like a circus rider from one to another of six concurrent sentences. He is followed by the Marquis of Ayr, a lifelong deerstalker, full of game and mess-room recollections. Finally it is the turn of the Oxford guests to reply to a toast; the shy Adam delegates the duty to Philip Hewson, to the consternation of his less radical companions. Philip, however, makes a civil speech on the theme that the historic battles between Scots and English are now a thing of the past. He is widely cheered – until he slips in a final innuendo against the preservation of game. Among the guests the Oxford men, a Liberal MP, and some members of the royal entourage are shocked: but luckily the Scottish hosts fail to grasp the drift, and Sir Hector beats on the table in applause. But as he leaves, Hewson has his arm caught by a thin, shabbily dressed Scotsman who says 'Young man, if ye pass through the Braes o' Lochaber, / See by the loch-side ye come to the Bothie of Toper-na-fuosich'. Hewson and Audley and the tutor return home by eleven; the others stay 'till the round sun lighted them bedward'.

In the second book, over a long and lazy breakfast, the young men talk, as young men will, about women. While Lindsay smokes in the garden, and the others drink tea and coffee, Hewson, eloquent on mere water, sings the praise of peasant beauty.

Oh, if our high-born girls knew only the grace, the attraction,
Labour, and labour alone, can add to the beauty of women.
(P, 50)

His own first experience of sexual attraction, he confesses, was when on a holiday his eye fell on a bonnetless maiden uprooting potatoes with a three-pronged fork. Only then did he begin to understand 'all the fuss about girls, the giggling, and toying, and coying' – though

Still, as before (and as now) balls, dances and evening parties,
Shooting with bows, going shopping together, and hearing them singing,
Dangling beside them, and turning the leaves on the dreary piano,
Offering unneeded arms, performing dull farces of escort,
Seemed like a sort of unnatural up-in-the-air balloon-work.

Women are most beautiful when they are performing some useful household task – 'needful, graceful therefore, as washing, cooking, and scouring'.

At this point Lindsay breaks in scornfully. Hewson, he says, likes watching girls digging or treading in washtubs only because it gives him a chance to see their thighs. The tutor is embarrassed, and the courteous Audley diverts the conversation, suggesting that Hewson's ideas about beauty in women resemble E. W. Pugin's architectural thesis that beauty consists in the fitness of form to function. Hobbes leaps up from the sofa, and runs with this conceit, devising a *Treatise on the Laws of Architectural Beauty in Application to Women*. Women, like churches, should be classified as Early English, Decorated, Debased or Flamboyant. With a wink, perhaps, at Lindsay, he suggests that to a reverend eye the most moving female form is the one corresponding to the Norman style, that is 'the scullіony stumpy columnar'.

By now, the tutor has recovered his composure. He delivers a sententious homily to Hewson on the importance of placing goodness above attractiveness: the attractiveness of poverty may well turn out to be as delusive as the cosmetics of rank and fashion. Nowhere in creation is equality to be found: star is not equal to star, and herb is not equal to herb. There is a glory of daisies, and there is a glory of carnations: the carnation should not refuse the gardener's tender care because a field-daisy cannot share it. The daisy itself would tell the carnation 'Up, grow, bloom and forget me; be beautiful even to proudness.'

Education and manners, accomplishments and refinements,
Waltz, peradventure, and polka, the knowledge of music and drawing,
All these things are Nature's, to Nature dear and precious.
We all have something to do, man, woman alike, I own it;

We all have something to do, and in my judgement should do it
In our station.

Hewson picks up the phrase from the prayer-book:

Doing our duty in that state of life to which God has called us
Seems to me always to mean, when the little rich boys say it,
Standing in velvet frock by mamma's brocaded flounces,
Eyeing the gold-fastened book and the chain and the watch at her bosom,
Seem to me always to mean, Eat, drink, and never mind others
(P, 55)

The tutor agrees with the condemnation of luxurious living – but by now the others have become bored. Hewson's thesis is surely, at this point, confused, mingling together aesthetic and moral considerations. While praising toil as the source of beauty, he denounces it as a curse imposed by the rich on the poor. His first erotic experience, on seeing the potato-digger, embodies this very confusion.

But a new thing was in me; and longing delicious possessed me,
Longing to take her and lift her, and put her away from her slaving.
Was it embracing or aiding was most in my mind? hard question!
(P, 50)

At this point, the reading party has lasted four weeks: there are seven more weeks before it is to come to an end. Audley, Lindsay and Hope decide to take three weeks holiday to explore the Highlands and visit other Oxford groups – located, as it happens in Castleton Braemar and at Drumnadrochet, the scenes of Clough's 1846 and 1847 reading parties. Airlie, Hobbes and Hewson, who are closer to their final examinations, are supposed to continue their studies throughout. To the tutor's vexation, Hewson decides to go off with the travellers. 'Weary of reading am I, and weary of walks prescribed us' he wants to wander free over the heather.

The stay-at-homes, during the next three weeks follow a strict timetable:

Reading nine hours a day with the tutor Hobbes and Airlie;
One between bathing and breakfast, and six before it was dinner
(Breakfast at eight, at four, after bathing again, the dinner)
Finally, two after walking and tea, from nine to eleven.
(P, 57)

It is a regime stricter than Clough had ever managed to impose on his own reading parties.

All the wanderers outstay their leave, but Audley and Lindsay return just in time to join the evening bathe, on the third day after their scheduled return. Hope, they report, has stayed on with his uncle the Earl for a week's shooting at the castle of Balloch. Hewson has been left in a farmer's house on Loch Rannoch, helping with laundry, peat-gathering and reaping. The returned wanderers report on their travels, listing the lochs they have seen and the peaks they have climbed:

> How they had walked, and eaten, and drunken, and slept in kitchens,
> Slept upon floors of kitchens, and tasted the real Glen-livat,
> Walked up perpendicular hills, and also down them,
> Hither and thither had been, and this and that had witnessed,
> Left not a thing to be done and had not a copper remaining.

Egged on by Hewson, they had violated game laws and roamed as of right in many a forbidden glen. They had visited the other reading parties, and taken a suitably superior view of their idleness and anti-social behaviour. During three days of rain they had sheltered in a farm by the lochside of Rannoch, and there Hewson had been 'smitten by golden-haired Katie, the youngest and comeliest daughter', with whom he had danced until daylight. Lindsay reported:

> How the whole next afternoon he was with her away in the shearing
> And the next morning ensuing was found in the ingle beside her
> Kneeling, picking the peats from her apron, – blowing together,
> Both, between laughing, with lips distended, to kindle the embers;
> Lips were so near to lips, one living cheek to another. –
> Though, it was true, he was shy, very shy
>
> (P, 63)

When Audley and Lindsay left, Hewson had stayed on, claiming to be lame in the leg. Lindsay clearly disbelieved this, but Audley defended the claim as true. Lindsay, he protested, had flirted with an elder sister more in a single evening than Hewson had flirted with Katie in the entire stay. The tutor decides he should go to Rannoch himself to find out the truth, but on the following day Hope returns from his shooting, and reports that when he passed through Rannoch he found Hewson no longer there.

Nothing more is heard of him for another week, but at the beginning of the poem's fourth book a letter from Hewson arrives for Adam. Philip admits that he had been deeply taken by Katie, but he had now kissed her good-bye. He had – as, in real life crises, Clough had often done – set off on a fierce, furious, solitary walk. As he was leaving Rannoch a strange girl passing by had given him a glance which convinced him he had been living in fairy-land. While sleeping rough in the mountains he had constant dreams of city prostitutes, which caused him great remorse. Not, he wrote, that Katie was likely to end up as a prostitute, but once maiden modesty has been broken through, who knows what may happen next?

> O, who saws through the trunk, though he leave the tree up in the forest
> When the next wind casts it down – is not *his* the hand that smote it.

The tutor replies in a sententious letter that is both reassuring and warning. No great harm has been done, and Hewson and Katie will be the wiser for the experience. Women are, as Hewson says and Adam agrees, 'passive, patient, receptive, yea, even of wrong and misdoing'. But Katie's yielding was due not just to her sex but to her social status. 'To the prestige of the richer the lowly are prone to be yielding / think that in dealing with them they are raised to a different region / where old laws and morals are modified'. The lesson to be learnt was that he should, in future, look within his own station for what he sought (P, 70).

While the tutor has been composing the letter, his pupils have gone off to Rannoch to see Katie for themselves. They find her none the worse for wear, and very content to dance with Airlie of the fancy waistcoat, even though she still wears a favour of Hewson's. The Tutor adds this information in a post-script; but before he can post the letter Hope brings news from his aunt that Hewson is now at Balloch castle, shooting and dancing with her daughter, the Lady Maria.

As September draws on the fifth book takes up the tale: the longer nights force a revision of the daily schedule for the five pupils who have returned to the tutor. The morning dip continues to be obligatory no matter what the weather:

> So they bathed, they read, they roamed in glen and forest;
> Far amid blackest pines to the waterfall they shadow
> Far up the long, long glen to the loch and the loch beyond it,
> Deep under huge red cliffs, a secret: and oft by the starlight,
> Or the aurora perchance, racing home for the eight o clock mutton.

Another letter to Adam from Hewson arrives, this time from Balloch. The 'grace and imperial sweetness' of the Lady Maria has almost convinced him of the truth of the tutor's parable of the daisy and the carnation. His concern for the poor and weary has evaporated.

Were it not well that the stem should be naked of leaf and of tendril,
Poverty stricken, the barest, the dismallest stick of the garden;
Flowerless, leafless, unlovely, for ninety-and-nine long summers,
So in the hundredth, at last, were bloom for one day at the summit
So but that fleeting flower were lovely as Lady Maria.

(P, 72)

We accept that soldiers should kill and die in war for the sake of honour; why not accept equally that workmen should toil and suffer in labour for the sake of beauty? He finds himself saying, he tells Adam:

Dig in thy deep dark prison, O miner! and finding be thankful;
Though unpolished by thee, unto thee unseen in perfection,
While thou art eating black bread in the poisonous air of thy cavern,
Far away glitter the gem on the peerless neck of a Princess

(P, 73)

God, who has created beasts of prey like the lion, has perhaps made men, as he made animals, in order to live off each other. Back in Oxford, Philip says, the tutor will find him altogether altered.

I yield to the laws and arrangements
Yield to the ancient existent decrees: who am I to resist them?
Yes, you will find me altered in mind, I think, as in manners,
Anxious too to atone for six weeks' loss of your logic.

(P, 74)

Hewson's conversion to conventional wisdom is too exaggerated to last, and on his homeward way south from Balloch he at last discovers who is to be the love of his life. The horse of his coach casts a shoe, and the man called in to repair it is a disabled smith called David Mackaye, the smallholder of the Bothie of Toper-na-fuosich. He is, it turns out, the man who accosted him at the banquet after the highland games.

When the coach reaches its destination, Hewson walks back to the Bothie, and meets there David's daughters, Elspie and Bella. Elspie, he discovers, is the girl whose passing glance had woken him out of his fairy dream of Katie; now she cures him of his infatuation for the Lady Maria. He writes to Adam, who now, in October, has dismissed his pupils:

The needle
Which in the shaken compass flew hither and thither, at last, long
Quivering, poises to north. I think so. But I am cautious;
More, far more than I was in the old silly days when I left you.

His new-found caution makes him beg Adam to come and inspect the Bothie and its inhabitants. Adam agrees, and spends ten days in a nearby hostelry, talking with father and daughter. One evening at dusk Philip and Elspie have a long conversation in the dusk, which constitutes the seventh, and now best-known, book of the poem. Elspie begins by rebuking Philip for the time he wasted on the humdrum charms of Katie; Philip confesses that it was Elspie's glance that had guided his thoughts during his days of wandering. Without mentioning the Lady Maria, he comes at once to the point.

> Elspie, why should I speak it? You cannot believe it and should not:
> Why should I say that I love, which I all but said to another?
> Yet should I dare, should I say, O Elspie, you only I love; you
> First and sole in my life that has been and surely that shall be;
> Could – O could you believe it, O Elspie, believe it and spurn not!
> Is it – possible – possible – Elspie?
>
> (P, 79)

Elspie continues with her knitting. But she does tell Philip the ideal of marriage she conceived while watching a stone bridge being built over the nearby burn.

> I keep saying in my mind – this long time slowly with trouble
> I have been building myself up, up, and toilfully raising,
> Just like as if the bridge were to do it itself without masons,
> Painfully getting myself upraised one stone on another,
> All one side I mean; and now I see on the other
> Just such another fabric uprising, better and stronger,
> Close to me, coming to join me: and then I sometimes fancy, –
> Sometimes I find myself dreaming at nights about arches and bridges –
> Sometimes I dream of a great invisible hand coming down, and
> Dropping the great keystone in the middle: there in my dreaming,
> There I feel the great key stone coming in, and through it
> Feel the other part – all the other stones of the archway
> Joined into mine with a queer happy sense of completeness, tingling
> All the way up from the other side's basement stones in the water,
> Through the very grains of mine.
>
> (P, 79)

At this point Elspie breaks off in confusion, and gives up her knitting. When Philip takes her hand she does not withdraw it. 'See the great key stone coming down from the heaven of heavens' he sighs; he falls at her feet and buries his face in her apron. She urges caution, and on the following day, having avoided him until the evening she rebukes him for his impetuosity.

Freudian critics have given a phallic interpretation to the vault's keystone; but that is a misinterpretation of the point of the simile. It is not describing sex but marriage, conceived, as so often in Clough's writing, as a union between partners allied in service to a goal. When Clough wanted lively images to describe sexual vigour, he was quite capable of producing them. One such occurs in the course of Elspie's rebuke to Philip.

> You are too strong, you see, Mr Philip! You are like the sea there,
> Which *will* come, through the straights and all between the mountains,
> Forcing its great strong tide into every nook and inlet,
> Getting far in, up the quiet stream of sweet inland water,
> Sucking it up, and stopping it, turning it, driving it backward,
> Quite preventing its own quiet running.

In her dreams, she tells him, she is the burnie, trying to get along through the tyrannous brine, but confined and squeezed in the coils of the great salt tide. Philip withdraws, abashed; but then Elspie begins to feel in herself an answering flow of passion.

> Felt she in myriad springs, her sources, far in the mountains,
> Stirring, collecting, rising, upheaving, forth-out-flowing,
> Talking and joining, right welcome, that delicate rill in the valley,
> Filling it, making it strong, and still descending, seeking,
> With a blind forefeeling descending, evermore seeking,
> With a delicious forefeeling, the great still sea before it;
> There deep into it, far, to carry and lose in its bosom,
> Waters that still from their sources exhaustless are fain to be added.
> (P, 82)

Book seven ends with the couple's first embrace.

The next book begins by asking: is a marriage possible between lovers of such different wealth, education and status? 'Should *he*, *he* have a wife beneath him?' Elspie wonders 'Herself be / an inferior there where only equality can be?' She seeks Adam's advice – all the more important because Philip's mother and father are dead. He convinces her that the match is not impossible. Philip had indeed been wild and flighty, but this time he was serious. She will make him a good companion, intelligent as she is and well-educated as she has been. Her father, it transpires, has been a schoolmaster in his time as well as a smith. Encouraged by Adam, Elspie accepts Philip's offer of marriage – though there is a moment, when he refuses to leave his books behind for her to read during the winter, when she nearly sends him about his business.

She makes her terms:

> Philip, she said, I will not be a lady,
> It is a weakness perhaps and a foolishness; still it is so
> I could not bear to be served and waited upon by footmen,
> No, not even by women.

On the morrow Philip asks David Mackie for his daughter's hand. David is not hostile, but insists on delay. Philip must return to his books; he may write, and he may return, but a year must elapse before any decision is taken.

The ninth and final book – after a further exchange between Adam and Hewson on the topic of the 'state to which God calls us' – tells, briskly, the story of that year.

> Philip returned to his books, but returned to his Highlands after;
> Got a first, tis said; a winsome bride, tis certain.
> There while courtship was ending, nor yet the wedding appointed,
> Under her father he learnt to handle the hoe and the hatchet.
> (P, 90)

Three of last year's reading party, along with the tutor, come to visit him: Audley, Hope and Lindsay, who has narrowly escaped failure in Schools. They found Philip 'delving at Highland soil, and railing at Highland landlords' – partly, this time, just to tease Lindsay.

> Then in the bright October, the gorgeous bright October
> When the brackens are changed, and heather blooms are faded
> And amid russet of heather and fern green trees are bonnie,
> Then, when shearing had ended and barley-stooks were garnered,
> David gave Philip to wife his daughter, his darling Elspie;
> Elspie, the quiet, the brave, was wedded to Philip the poet.
> (P, 91)

The couple depart for New Zealand, loaded with wedding presents: a medicine chest and tool-box from Adam, a saddle from Hope and a plough from Audley, a Bible and an iron bedstead from Hobbes, and a necklace for Elspie from Airlie.

The final postcript to the poem tells us that in New Zealand Philip hewed and dug and built a home, and Elspie bore him several children:

> There hath he farmstead and land, and fields of corn and flax fields
> And the Antipodes too have a Bothie of Toper-na-fuosich.

The poem can be read as a novel: its title might be 'The sentimental education of Philip Hewson'. Philip's encounters with the three women of the poem turn him from an impractical romantic idealist into an idealist who knows the costs of love and the limits of the practical. While he is neglecting the study of Aristotle's ethics he is learning by experience the doctrine of the mean. Katie is too lightweight, Maria too artificial: only Elspie is serious and steady. In social terms Katie is too far below, Maria too far above him in status. Elspie, the schoolmaster's daughter, is close enough in gifts and character to make him a suitable helpmate: but it is only in New Zealand that the couple will not be parted by barriers of class.

In the novel Elspie is the dominant character: more steady and sensible than the immature volatile Philip, less weighed down by convention than the sententious clerical Adam. She is in her own person the contradiction of the view (shared initially by both Adam and Philip) that women are by nature weak, yielding creatures. Her first words to Adam are a well-merited rebuke, and it is she who sets the pace of the Philip's wooing. She makes clear that her view of marriage is a partnership of absolute equals – that is why they must go to New Zealand where she can be Philip's social as well as personal equal. Husband and wife should share intellectual interests: but this does not mean that they must share the same household functions. Philip is not to waste his time in the laundry, as he did with Katie: he must be taught to use the hatchet and the hoe.

Considered as a novel, *The Bothie* has many merits. Every paragraph is rich in concrete detail. The main characters are sharply defined and clearly differentiated. Lindsay, Audley and Hobbes speak with different voices and move with different motions. Hope and Airlie are more shadowy, but their clothes and manners are lovingly described. Only Lady Maria totally fails to establish an identity: perhaps we are meant to conclude that she does not have one to establish.

To create the appropriate undergraduate milieu, Clough makes skilful use of slang. The text is peppered with juvenile words of approval ('topping', 'clipping', 'stunner') and disapproval ('shady', 'hairy', 'seedy'). Classical authors are known by nicknames ('Thicksides' and 'Tottle'), and there are private terms for local features ('matutine' for the morning bath, 'the town hall' for a too-public bathing place). At this distance of time it is not possible to tell which expressions were current Oxford jargon, which were coinages of actual reading parties, and which were inventions of the poet. But anyone who has attended a reading party, in the twentieth century no less than the nineteenth, can attest that the poem catches to perfection the atmosphere of such a group.

To read *The Bothie* simply as a novel, however, would be to miss many of its riches. It is not just a poem about a don, it is a donnish poem, full of allusions to classical texts, and full of experiments with classical forms. Most of these, when first published, would be immediately obvious to readers who had graduated from the Oxford course in Greek and Latin; nowadays many of them need considerable elucidation for the average reader.[1] I will draw attention only to some very general features of the poem.

The poem is written in hexameter, the metre that Homer used for the *Iliad* and *Odyssey*, and that Virgil used for the *Aeneid*. A classical hexameter is a line of six feet, and the basic foot is the dactyl (–˘˘); but in any foot except the fifth a dactyl may be replaced by a spondee (– –), and in the sixth foot it must be so replaced. A couple of lines may illustrate how Clough adapts this to English.

Only a / Liberal / member, a/way at the / end of the / table

Ye un/happy/ statu/ ettes, ye /miserable / trinkets

There are two important differences between Clough's hexameters and his classical sources. In Latin and Greek the type of foot is defined by the length ('quantity') of the syllables occuring in it – quantity being the feature that distinguishes, for example, the 'a' in 'gaze' from the 'a' in 'gas'. In English verse, on the other hand, a foot is defined by the position of the stress or accent: 'noun', for instance, carries the stress in 'pronounce' (˘–) but not in 'pronoun' (–˘). In Clough's hexameters the feet are defined by stress, which may, on occasion, clash with quantity. A second difference, which is related to the first, is that in the first four feet and the sixth foot Clough commonly offers a trochee (–˘) where classical metre would demand a spondee (– –). Even after making allowance for these differences, Clough warned his readers in an introductory note 'to expect every kind of irregularity in these modern hexameters'. This disconcerted some of his first readers, pedantic classicists; but the flexibility of his verses enabled him to capture with remarkable fluency the rhythms of casual speech.

In addition to hexameter metre, Clough employs a number of other Homeric devices. Homer likes to define a character with a characteristic epithet, frequently repeated ('white-armed Hera', 'Nestor of sweet speech'). Clough gives his undergraduates similar attributes ('the cheery, cigar-loving Lindsay', 'Arthur, the glory of headers'). Indeed, the cigar-puffing Lindsay is from time to time given the actual epithet Homer reserves for Zeus, 'the cloud-compeller'. Homer adorns his text with lengthy, self-standing similes, and so does Clough, but within Homeric form he inserts Victorian matter; as when Hewson describes his initial failure to appreciate the merits of Elspie:

I was as one that sleeps on the railway; one who, dreaming
Hears thro' his dream the name of his home shouted out; hears and hears not –

Faint, and louder again, and less loud, dying in distance;
Dimly conscious, with something of inward debate and choice – and
Sense of claim and reality present, anon relapses
Nevertheless, and continues the dream and the fancy, while forward
Swiftly, remorseless, the car presses on, he knows not whither.

Like Homer, Clough from time to time invokes the Muses. They are, after all, faster to deliver news than Royal Mail or even the telegraph.

O Muse, that encompassest Earth like the ambient ether,
Swifter than steamer or railway or magical missive electric
Belting like Ariel the sphere with the star-like trail of thy travel,
thou with thy Poet, to mortals mere post-office second-hand knowledge
Leaving, wilt seek in the moorland of Rannoch the wandering hero.
(P, 65)

The use of Homeric metres and devices suggests that the poem aspires to be an epic; but of course it can be no more than mock-epic, since a reading party, even followed by a wedding and an emigration, hardly provides the grandeur of topic that classical epic demands. In fact on the title page Clough describes his poem not as an epic, but as a pastoral. Its model is not to be the *Iliad* or the *Aeneid*, but elegiac poems of shepherds and shepherdesses such as Theocritus wrote in Greek and Virgil in Latin. Each book is given as an epigraph or headline a Latin quotation, usually from Virgil's *Eclogues*. The scene of the poem is, after all, Arcadian, and Hewson's love for Katie and Elspie recalls a shepherd's love for his Amaryllis – though in the poem the only woman actually called 'Amaryllis' is Lady Maria, in a mocking letter from Hobbes recalling Hewson to his democratic principles.

Every book is packed with allusions to themes from the pastoral poets of Greece and Rome, which would be easily picked up by the members of an Oxford reading party. It is a pleasant irony that a poem whose hero is desperate to escape from the 'cares of classes and classics' should itself be cast in such a classical mould. But after all, Hewson, once reformed by Elspie, works hard at his books during their engagement year and ends his Oxford career with a first-class degree.

For the biographer, the poem presents a number of intriguing questions. Where was the reading party held? Where was the Bothie? Who are the originals of the characters? What does the poem, as a whole, tell us of Clough's state of mind in the closing months of 1848?

We are given only the vaguest indications of the locality of the reading party. The poem itself suggests that this is deliberate. The fullest piece of scenic description is 30 lines about a stream whose pent-up water falls to make a basin, eighteen feet by ten, in which the undergraduates take their daily dip (P, 58). But the stream is introduced thus:

> There is a stream, I name not its name, lest inquisitive tourist
> Hunt it, and make it a lion, and get it at last into guide-books
> (P, 57)

Wherever it is located, the reading-party of the Bothie is not at either of the sites of Clough's actual reading parties: Castleton Braemar and Drumnadrochet are both mentioned as places visited by the undergraduates during their absence on holiday. Most likely Clough did not have a particular location in mind, but used features of several places to build up the party's background scenery.

Toper-na-fuosich, on the other hand, is usually regarded as a definite place. We are told that the name refers to a forester's cottage on the west shore of Loch Ericht, six miles from its head, where Tom Arnold, Shairp and Clough had all stayed in September 1847.[2] But this cannot be right. To Tom Arnold Clough wrote on 6 November 1848 'It is *not* the Bothie on Loch Ericht. The name of that is Dallungart. The map's Toper-na-fuosich is unknown to the natives there.' This puts beyond doubt that the place where the three friends severally stayed is not the location of the Bothie. Dallungart is further south than the Toper-na-Fuosich marked on eighteenth-century and early nineteenth-century maps, and from what Clough says to Tom it seems that the original Toper-na-Fuosich no longer existed, or was only a ruin, by 1847. No doubt he chose the name, picked up from the old maps, precisely because it was not attached to any existing Bothie.

Several features of the poem make clear that the Bothie of the poem was not the hut of the 1847 visit to Loch Ericht. The owner of that hut was a forester: David Mackaye, though jack of all trades, has never been a forester, and is currently a small farmer, raising potatoes, barley and oats. Loch Ericht is a freshwater loch, then as now far from any road, and Dallungart was far from other habitations. The Bothie looks down to a road and a salt sea loch, with a distant view of the ocean and steamers, amid a cluster of cottages upon a mountainside (P, 75). The way to reach it is to go through Glencoe and ask at the ferry. Glencoe, on the sea-loch Leven, is many miles to the west of Ericht. No doubt it is a great mistake to look for a specific location with all the features of *The Bothie*'s bothie.

Something similar is true of the characters in the poem. From the day of its publication, people have claimed themselves, or their friends and relations, as the authentic originals; the most favoured candidates, naturally, were those who had attended one or other of Clough's reading parties. But Tom Arnold was probably correct when he told Clough's widow, in 1897 'I feel sure that he took good care not to allow any one character to be paralleled by any one living individual.'[3]

Arnold was, however, willing to offer partial identifications. Airlie, he thought, resembled Frank Lawley, who had attended the 1845 Grasmere party (a keen gambler, who later became an MP and would have been governor of South Australia had he not been detected in speculating with public funds). On the other hand, since Lawley was the most aristocratic of Clough's pupils, he might well lurk behind the character of Hope. Family tradition has always identified the handsome, athletic, and tactful Arthur Audley with the barrister H. W. Fisher, founder of an Oxford dynasty, whose son was warden of New College and whose granddaughter was principal of St Hilda's. The corpulent Hobbes has been identified by many with G. Warde Hunt, the future Chancellor of the Exchequer and First Lord of the Admiralty – the identification even found a mention in his *Times* obituary. No one seems to have been keen to claim identity with the cigar-smoking Lindsay with his racy slang and his Irish jokes.

The two most important male characters are of course Adam and Philip. It is easy to take it for granted that Adam is a self-portrait: but Clough took pains to give the tutor characteristics different from his own. Adam is in orders, for instance, and he is nearer 40 than 30, and from time to time he gives solemn utterance to sentiments which Clough himself had long mocked in private. Tom Arnold was better inspired when he said that it was the character of Philip that was a portrait of Clough's own essential personality. The fact that Philip emigrates to New Zealand has led many to regard him as modelled rather on Arnold himself, who had emigrated, without an Elspie, in the previous year, carrying with him a set of presents from his friends very like Philip and Elspie's wedding gifts. Tom was indeed at this very time writing to Clough about the difficulties of making a household in the bush in the absence of a wife (B, 306). Moreover, Philip's rapid ideological swings mirror a characteristic that was to dominate the life of Tom Arnold. In the years to come he converted from agnosticism to Roman Catholicism and then back to Anglicanism, in each case placing his livelihood in jeopardy. But many features of Philip's history – the endeavour to find a solution for the age's social and sexual problems, the attempt to achieve sober self-knowledge as a mean between exaltation and depression, the painful struggle to balance ideal with realization – replicate the inner life of Clough himself.

In the autumn of 1848 Clough did seriously consider migration to New Zealand. Tom Arnold, quickly tiring on his primitive estate of hoeing and hewing, was encouraged by the authorities to believe that he might become principal of a college newly to be founded at Nelson. At once he wrote to Clough to inquire whether he would consider a professorship there. Clough replied 'The thing is not *quite* impossible, my dear Tom. That is to say, I am not prepared to go out and *settle* in New Zealand, in any capacity, but I have a great fancy to go out for 3 years or so' (M, 223).

The feature of Clough's meditations which is almost totally absent from *The Bothie* is religion. It is seriously touched on only once in the final book when Adam once again urges Philip to work in his station in life. 'There is a great Field-Marshal, my friend, who arrays our battalions; / Let us to Providence trust, and abide and work in our stations'. Philip replies:

> I am sorry to say your Providence puzzles me sadly;
> Children of circumstance are we to be? You answer, On no wise!
> Where does Circumstance end, and Providence where begins it?

Is it true that we are fighting a war under the orders of a great Field Marshal above?

> If there is battle, 'tis battle by night: I stand in the darkness,
> Here in the melee of men, Ionian and Dorian on both sides,
> Signal and password known: which is friend and which is foeman?

The allusion is to the story of the night-battle of Epipolae in the seventh book of Thucydides' History. It was a commonplace image for theological controversy, put to its most famous use in Matthew Arnold's *Dover Beach*:

> We are here as on a darkling plain
> Swept with confused alarms of struggle and flight,
> Where ignorant armies clash by night.
> (OA, 136)

Despite its avoidance of religious controversy, *The Bothie* gave offence to the devout. Hawkins wrote 'I have been reading your poem *The Bothie* and cannot but say that what I was told of it was true, that there are parts of it rather indelicate; and I very much regretted to find also that there were frequent allusions to Scripture, or rather parodies of Scripture, which you should not have put forth' (M, 247). Some other dons condemned it as 'indecent and profane, immoral and communistic' (M, 240).

In general, however, the poem was well received. Clough sent a copy to W. M. Thackeray, who had not long completed *Vanity Fair*. Thackeray was charmed, and in a letter of thanks said 'I must tell you that I was very much pleased indeed by your sending me the book, and don't mind owning that I took a great liking to you.' Arthur Stanley, on reading the poem, described its hexameters as the best in any modern language. Charles Kingsley wrote hoping that the poem would receive wide circulation outside Oxford. 'Its very local and "slang" allusions, so far from unfitting it for the public, are a very good instance of "the universal best manifested in the particular"'. He went on to write a long review of exuberant commendation, singling out for praise the creation of Elspie. 'We know no recent fiction of a female character so genial, so original, and yet so natural' (M, 228–9; L, 127).

When the poem crossed the Atlantic (first in gift copies, then in a pirated edition) Emerson described it as a high gift from angels, and warned Tennyson to look out for his laurels. Longfellow too, flattered by the emulation of *Evangeline*, gave the poem generous praise. The only sour note in literary circles was sounded by Matthew Arnold. He visited Oxford at the end of November 1848, and found that the book was selling well, and was being highly praised by Clough's successor at Oriel, W. Y. Sellar. Grumpily, he reported this to Clough. 'Hearing Sellar and the rest of that clique' he wrote 'who know neither life nor themselves rave about your poem gave me a strong almost bitter feeling with respect to them, the age, the poem, even you'. But he grudgingly admitted that his own family greatly admired the poem's humour and pathos (L, 126–7).

One final embarrassment awaited Clough. The name which gave the poem its title was, as we have seen, drawn from an old map. Clough asked a boatman on Loch Ericht what the name meant, and understood that it was ' the bairds' well'. He took this to mean 'the bairns' well', though more likely he was told 'the bearded well' – but in any case, as he learned later, the phrase was a Gaelic circumlocution for the female genitals. Clough was thus, as he reported to Tom, unwittingly responsible for publishing an obscenity throughout the drawing rooms and boudoirs of the world. 'It is too ludicrous not to tell some one, but too apallingly awkward to tell anyone on this side the globe.' Even when writing to New Zealand, he felt able to explain the title's true meaning only by employing a Latin paraphrase from Horace. All future editions of the poem were given the title 'The Bothie of Tober-na-Vuolich' – a safely meaningless manufactured name.

Notes

1 This has been provided, with meticulous erudition, in the edition of the poem by Patrick Scott (*Victorian Texts I: Amours de Voyage by Arthur Hugh Clough*, St Lucia, Queensland, 1976).

2 Ibid., p. 27.

3 Katherine Chorley, *Arthur Hugh Clough: the Uncommitted Mind*, Oxford 1962, p. 69.

Chapter Six

1849: Annus Mirabilis

During the winter of 1848–9 Clough had no fixed abode. From his Holywell lodgings he went to stay with Walrond at Rugby. In January he went to stay in London with Frederick Temple, now working in the Education Office and living in Tom Arnold's old lodgings at 24 Margaret Street. Early in February he explored a new circle of liberal and Unitarian friends in Manchester ('not so handsomely streeted as Liverpool' he told Annie 'but there are far pleasanter suburbs' M, 238). While there he at last had an opportunity to see Jenny Lind at close quarters: he liked her face, now, better than her voice (M, 243). In mid-February his resignation of his Oriel fellowship was at last formally accepted by the governing body. The rest of February and most of March was spent with the family in Vine Street in Liverpool.

There was no time to write verse: the pressing task was to find a means of subsistence (M, 245). The proposal to escort young King to Rome fell through, perhaps because many of the towns on the Grand Tour were still politically unstable. However, an opportunity opened out nearer home. University College in Gower Street had been set up in 1826 as a non-sectarian institution of higher education; in 1836 it had been incorporated with the Anglican King's College in a new University of London. The students of University College in its early days had lived in lodgings or with families: it was now proposed to set up a hall in which they were to live together under a discipline like that of Oxbridge colleges. On 20 July 1848 the foundation stone was laid on a site in Gordon Square: the inaugural speaker was F. W. Newman, brother of John Henry, who had detached himself from orthodox Christianity and gone from a Balliol fellowship to non-sectarian professorships in Manchester and London. The major contributors to the new project – mostly Unitarians – were anxious to safeguard the non-denominational character of the institution. The principal, they laid down, must not be a minister of any denomination, and should preferably not be a Unitarian. They offered the principalship to Newman, and he accepted, but resigned very shortly afterwards. In November, Clough was invited to apply for the post in his stead.

Clough was immediately tempted by the offer, in particular because the job was calculated to demand no more than two hours work a day (M, 224).

Negotiations continued until the middle of January. Clough was willing to dine in Hall and have continual intercourse with the young men; and he was happy to teach Aristotle and Plato. He was, however, reluctant to conduct morning prayers. Moral and religious sentiment, he explained to the trustees, should be spontaneous rather than compulsory. It was eventually proposed that a Unitarian minister should come in to take prayers, and that Clough would attend 'like a member of a family at domestic worship'. He had no objection in principle, he said, to attending non-Anglican services: he had worshipped with Presbyterians in Scotland and with Unitarians in Liverpool. The Trustees need not fear that he would proselytize in any way: 'I do not account myself to have made up my own mind, and should be shy of meddling with those of other people.' Was it his view, then, the Trustees asked, that religious convictions and sentiments were simply a matter of taste? By no means: all that he had meant was the his own 'religious sentiments had not as yet formed themselves into very explicit dogmatical results' (M, 231).

In fact, since leaving Oriel Clough's opinions had been moving fast and he had arrived at a point more distant from Anglican Christianity than any of his Unitarian interviewers had reached. In a letter to Annie of November he had urged her to separate belief in religion from belief in an afterlife. It is far nobler, he said:

> to teach people to do what is good because it is good simply, than for the sake of any future reward. It is, I dare say, difficult to keep up an equal religious feeling – at present, but it is not impossible and is necessary. Besides, if *we* die and come to nothing, it does not therefore follow that Life and goodness will cease to be in Earth and Heaven. If we give over dancing, it doesn't therefore follow that the dance ceases itself, or the Music. (M, 227)

To his future employers, he said nothing so explicit. But he did warn them that his distinctive religious views 'may very possibly prove in the end to be essentially different from those commonly entertained by Unitarians' (M, 231). True to their non-sectarian principles, the Trustees swallowed this, and appointed Clough to the principalship in the third week of January. Clough wrote to Tom Arnold to decline the New Zealand post. University Hall was not to open until October, however, and so there was time again for travel – and for poetry.

Clough was not the only fellow of an Oxford College to resign his fellowship during this academic year. James Antony Froude, the younger brother of the Tractarian Hurrell Froude, made a more noisy exit. He had become a fellow of Exeter College in 1842 after an undergraduate career at Oriel, and had taken deacon's orders, but felt himself unsuited for the priesthood. He expressed his doubts and frustrations in a semi-autobiographical novel, *The Nemesis of Faith*, which was published early in 1849. The sub-Rector of the College thought the book so scandalous that he burnt it in the quadrangle. Froude, having departed from Exeter, renewed an earlier friendship with Clough and became, for a while, one of his most regular correspondents.

F. T. Palgrave, who had shared Clough's interest in the Paris revolution of 1848, was another faithful friend to him after his self-imposed exile from Oxford. Now working for the education committee of the Privy Council, he strove, unlike Froude, to act as a brake on his gradual abandonment of traditional Christian orthodoxy. So too did Constantine Prichard, who wrote from a sickbed urging him not to commit to any distinct rejection of Christianity. 'If a person *can* bring himself to believe that St Paul's Epistles are forgeries – and the Gospels also – I must confess myself unable to deal with him' (P, 250).

In January 1849 Chapman and Hall published *Ambarvalia*, a 64-page selection of Clough's Oxford poems along with a larger treasury of Burbidge's. The project had been first mooted in 1845 and the manuscript had been with the publisher since December 1847 (M, 160, 190). Most of the poems have been mentioned in earlier chapters at the time of their composition. Clough had been revising all of them, but substantial changes and deletions were made only to the erotic ones ('Ah what is love', 'When panting sighs', 'The silver wedding', 'Farewell my Highland lassie').

The title of the collection puzzled even some classically educated Victorians. The *ambarvalia* was a ceremonial religious procession to purify the boundaries of ancient Rome. The poets saw their task as the purification of contemporary civilization. There are two different kinds of music in human affairs, Clough explained in a poem which alluded to the anthology's title. One is the music to which the great throng dances, music which is loud and bold and coarse – but actually a mere product of imagination. The other is a softer tune, not easy to discern, and easily forgotten: it is the poet's task to make men catch its gentle sound (P, 570).

Critics did not take as favourable a view of this collection as they had of *The Bothie*. Robert and Elizabeth Browning, for instance, thought the pastoral poem was worth twenty of *Ambarvalia*. Within that book itself, some reviewers even preferred the poems of the now deservedly forgotten Burbidge. But a number of readers thought otherwise. A reviewer in the Catholic *Rambler* urged his readers to peruse the poems repeatedly, since a first reading did no sort of justice to the poet's talent. He was, however, horrified by the content of some of the verses. When the 'The New Sinai' compares traditional Christianity to the worship of the golden calf, the reviewer remarks, 'it quite baffles comprehension how a thinker, in many respects so humble and so profound as Mr Clough, can be blind to the strange, the absolutely incredible audacity of such a mode of thinking'. And 'Natura Naturans', he complains, shamelessly records thoughts and feelings 'to which, were a good Catholic so unhappy as to give consent, he would be off at once to his confessor in anguish of soul'.[1]

In February Clough's two volumes were joined in the bookshops by Matthew Arnold's first published collection of verse, *The Strayed Reveller and other Poems, by* A. The two poets were sometimes reviewed together. An anonymous writer in the Guardian thought that both owed a debt to Tennyson. Clough had more of Tennyson's 'deep insight into things as they really are', A. had more of his 'pictorial power'. The reviewer, who did not like *The Bothie*, found great promise in every line of Clough's *Ambarvalia* poems. Dismiss Burbidge, he advised his readers, and bind up A with Clough. 'If Mr Clough is a mountain stream, "A" is a sparkling fountain'. A, he thought, was more likely to be popular; but Clough's poems 'shed a light around, deep and wide, on human nature' (Thorpe 1982, 79–84).

On first reading *Ambarvalia*, Arnold quoted his own dictum 'not deep the poet sees, but wide'. He made three complaints about the poems: they were not natural, they did not attain beauty, and they did not give pleasure. Clough's attempt to get to the bottom of things was fatal, he thought, to the sensuousness of poetry; it merely excited curiosity and reflexion. To Tom he wrote that Clough 'had no vocation for literature'. Clough was kinder to Arnold than Arnold was to Clough. His message to Tom Arnold was 'At last our own Matt's book. read mine first, my child, if our volumes go forth together. Otherwise you won't read mine, *Ambarvalia* at any rate, at all' (L, 130, 136; M, 244).

No doubt it is a good thing for a man to have friends who do not feel obliged to give his books favourable reviews. But Arnold's comments seem to be based on a narrowly sensuous idea of poetic beauty. Even by this standard it is hard to deny the beauty of many of Clough's descriptions of Scottish woods and waterfalls. One must give a highly specialized interpretation to 'natural' if one is to regard *The Strayed Reveller's* mannered treatments of classical themes as more natural than the contemporary realism of *The Bothie*. But Arnold was always a hard man to please. In the same letters he denounced Keats and Browning and said that young writers should read nothing in English except Milton and parts of Wordsworth (L, 128).

As we have seen, Clough had often shown his poems to Arnold before publication; Arnold rarely reciprocated. The one poem in *The Strayed Reveller* on which he sought Clough's opinion was 'Resignation, to Fausta'. 'I must hear some day' he wrote shortly after publication 'how you feel about Resignation. Tell me freely if you do not like it.' Someone who did not like the poem was J. A. Froude. 'I don't see what business he has' Froude wrote to Clough in March 'to parade his calmness and lecture us on resignation when he has never known what a storm is and doesn't know what he has to resign himself to' (M, 251). Clough's own response took the form of a poem 'Resignation to Faustus' – but this had to wait a while.

In April 1849 Clough at last realized his ambition of visiting Rome. During the revolutionary year of 1848 the Pope, Pius IX, had been hailed by many as a liberal churchman and a possible head of a united Italy. Edward Scott, an Oriel pupil of Clough's, had visited Rome in March of that year, and had written him a letter describing the crowd's incessant shouts of 'Viva il Papa', 'Viva Pio Nono' (B, 287). The Pope set up a Parliament and in September appointed a reforming Prime Minister, Pellegrino Rossi; but he was unwilling to accede to popular demand to make war on Austria. After two months in office Rossi was assassinated and a threatening mob surrounded the Quirinal Palace. The Pope was forced to dismiss his Swiss Guards and on 24 November fled in disguise to Gaeta, in the Kingdom of Naples. In the following February a Constituent Assembly in Rome declared that the Pope had forfeited temporal power. A Republic was proclaimed; the Piedmontese patriot Giuseppe Mazzini was declared a Roman citizen and arrived in March to be the effective dictator of the city. In the following month he was joined by Giuseppe Garibaldi with a small band of irregular soldiers.

Clough arrived in Rome at about the same time as Garibaldi. He had been excited by the revolution and in March sought travel advice from the experienced Congreve at Wadham: no, he was told, one did not need to know Italian in Rome; the landlord and staff of the Hotel d'Angleterre spoke French (B, 359). He left London on 4 April and travelled across France, spending two days in Paris, and visiting Lyons and Avignon. On 11 April he took ship at Marseilles and sailed to Genoa, where he spent a day ashore visiting the Doria palace and inspecting the damage done during the recent insurrection. He returned on shipboard to sail via Livorno to Civita Vecchia. The ship was held up by a storm, and for a night and a day lay tossing in Livorno roads with a shipful of seasick passengers (PPR, 142).

It was not until noon on Monday 16 April that the ship reached Civita Vecchia, and it was not until 11 o'clock that night that Clough arrived in Rome. He found rooms in the Hotel d'Angleterre, deserted by its normal English clientele in alarm at the revolution. He spent the next two days on the obligatory tourist trail – St Peter's, S. Pietro in Montorio, the Forum, the Pantheon, St Mary Major, St John Lateran.[2] He described his first impressions in a letter to his mother:

> St Peter's disappoints me: the stone of which it is made is a poor plastery material. And indeed Rome in general might be called a *rubbishy* place; the Roman antiquities *in general* seem to me only interesting as antiquities – not for any beauty. (PPR, 141)

The weather, he admitted, had 'not been very brilliant' – but only the Arch of Titus, he thought, had any beauty in its own right. The views over the countryside from San Pietro in Montoro and from the Lateran were, however, superb.

When, later, Clough wrote his epistolary novel in verse, *Amours de Voyage*, he placed these sentiments, with only slight changes to clothe them in hexameters, in the mouth of the hero, the puppyish Oxford don, Claude.

> Rome disappoints me much – St Peter's perhaps in especial;
> Only the Arch of Titus and the view from the Lateran please me:
> This, however, perhaps is the weather, which truly is horrid . . .
> Rome disappoints me much; I hardly as yet understand but
> *Rubbishy* seems the word that most exactly would suit it.
> All the foolish destructions and all the sillier savings,
> All the incongruous things of past incompatible ages,
> Seem to be treasured up here to make fools of present and future.
> (P, 94–5)

In a postscript, Arthur warned his mother not to believe everything she read in *The Times*, which seemed almost to be in the pay of the Austrian government. 'At any rate the story of the proposed sale of the Belvedere Apollo to the Americans is simply a joke, I am told, as another story which went about here, that the Pantheon was sold to the English for a Protestant Chapel.' These stories too appear in *Amours de Voyage*. The Trevellyns, the family of the heroine to whom Claude has begun to pay attention, are worried about him because he says he attends daily service in the Pantheon. They explain to a friend:

> This was a temple, you know, and now is a Catholic church; and
> Though it is said that Mazzini has sold it for Protestant service
> Yet I suppose the change can hardly as yet be effected.
> (P, 102)

Again, Claude tells his friend Eustace to be careful what he believes in *The Times*:

> Although it was slightly in error
> When it proclaimed as a fact the Apollo was sold to a Yankee,
> You may believe when it tells you the French are at Civita Vecchia
> (P, 104)

A problem for the tourist during these revolutionary days was that many of the Vatican Galleries were closed. Clough found this a great nuisance, and soon after his arrival went to the top to complain: he demanded an audience with Mazzini, and received a reply of exquisite courtesy.

> Mr Mazzini will be happy to see Mr Clough here, at the Government's Palace, tomorrow or any day after tomorrow between 3 o'clock and five, if convenient to Mr Clough. It is through absolute impossibility that Mr Mazzini does not offer to visit Mr Clough at his own residence: his time is entirely taken up by public business.[3]

Clough took up the invitation on the afternoon of Sunday 22 April; he was kept waiting for half an hour in an anteroom, he complained later, while the dictator gave audience to a French envoy.

Mazzini, whose English was fluent, rewarded his patience with a full and candid conversation. He admitted that it was likely that the great powers would intervene, and that the Republic would be brought down. 'Still he is convinced' Clough wrote to a friend 'that the separation of the temporal and spiritual power is a thing to be, and that to restore the Pope as before will merely breed perpetual disquiet.' In the meantime he asked Clough to contradict the false rumours in *The Times*: any English resident, he said, would bear witness to the tranquillity of the city. He was repressing any violence against the 'Blacks' or clericals, and though he was distributing some Church land to peasants, he was ensuring that enough would remain to support all ecclesiastical institutions. 'The religious customs seem to thrive still' Clough reported; 'they kissed away yesterday at St Peter's toe as fast as they could have done in its best days' (PPR, 1, 144). Despite Mazzini's courtesy, it was not until 28 May that Clough received a permit from the Ministry of Public Works to visit the closed galleries. 'Once having seen a couple of lines from Mazzini, how the officials skipped about for me' he told Tom Arnold (M, 257).

Clough had now moved into private lodgings with a Sig. Pfyffer at 74 Via della Croce, the least fashionable of the streets which lead into the Piazza di Spagna. He paid six scudi a month for a large room which doubled as bed and sitting-room. The family was half Swiss, he told his mother, and accustomed to English inmates, so the house was cleanly and there was no problem with fleas (M, 258).

Gradually Clough came to admire the beauty of Rome, but he never lost sight of its squalor. The contrast and combination of the two was the theme of the poem that he now wrote in reponse to Arnold's poem for his sister: *Resignation to Faustus*.

> O land of Empire, art and love!
>   What is it that you show me?
> A sky for Gods to tread above,
>   A floor for pigs below me!
> O in all place and shape and kind
>   Beyond all thought and thinking
> The graceful with the gross combined
>   The stately with the stinking!

The graceful portico of the Pantheon was home to filthy dossers; dogs lifted their legs against its massive gates; the patterned pavement was strewn with filthy husks; its statues of angels were covered in spittle.

> Must babied hags perform with rags
>   That napkin-evolution?
> Though priest from prayer stop short to spit
>   Beside the altar solemn
> Must therefore boys turn up to ——
>   By this Corinthian column?
>
> (P, 669)

Verses such as these, even when modified for publication ('Yet, boy, that nuisance why commit / On this Corinthian column') seem at first to have little connection with Arnold's poem. But then the mood of the poem changes, and the message becomes clearer. The mixture of sordid and sublime is not something peculiar to Mediterranean countries, nor is it uniquely a feature of cities: it is a universal feature of Nature. The most beautiful woodland flowers draw the juices that fill their petals from sour and fetid mixtures underground. The final lines of the poem urge the appropriate response of resignation. When we walk on fells and in forests (as we do in Arnold's poem) we do not mind getting our boots dirty: why should we be any more disturbed by urban filth?

> O Nature, if indeed thy will
> Thou ownest it, it is not ill!
> And e'en as oft on heathy hill
> Or moorland black, and ferny fells,
> Beside thy brooks and in thy dells,
> Was welcomed erst the kindly stain
> Of thy true earth e'en so again
> With resignation fair and meet
> The dirt and refuse of thy street
> My philosophic foot shall greet
> So leave but perfect to my eye
> Thy columns set against thy sky!
>
> (P, 193)

No doubt Clough was teasing when he wrote to Arnold 'Now you shall have some sweet pretty verses in *your* style' – but the poem is indeed a response to *Resignation: to Fausta*. That poem had argued that one could not look to nature for consolation: the best it could offer was Stoic tranquillity. Clough, in response, urges jovial acceptance rather than chill detachment. Nature teaches us, not to reject, but to welcome, both the sordid and the sublime as bound inescapably together.

The Fausta of Arnold's poem was his sister Jane, and both poems acquire a new level of meaning if, as I have argued, Clough had hoped, in vain, to marry Jane. This would, among other things, explain why Matt was, unusually, anxious to have Clough's response to this particular poem. We do not know why the hopes of marriage failed: but could it be that the austere and upright Jane regarded Clough's wooing as too crude? The theme that 'Resignation to Faustus' applies to Rome is one that other poems apply to marriage: spiritual and intellectual love between spouses cannot be divorced from its earthy and corporeal basis. It is no accident that 'Resignation' recalls 'Natura Naturans'. When Clough found the woman he was eventually to marry, and she discovered that poem, she nearly broke off the engagement.[4]

During April and May Clough's diary records an almost uninterrupted series of visits to the churches and palaces of Rome. But his life was not that of a normal tourist. Two days before Clough's interview with Mazzini the Pope had issued from Gaeta a denunciation of the Republic. 'Rome has been turned into a forest of wild animals – and apostates and heretics and communists and socialists and haters of the faith flock in and teach their diseased errors and pervert minds'.[5] He appealed to the great powers to restore him to his throne.

France, under a constitution approved in November 1848, was now ruled by Prince Napoleon Bonaparte as elected executive President. Anxious to take control in central Italy and restore the Pope before the Austrians did so, he despatched an expeditionary force under General Oudinot, which landed at Civita Vecchia on 23 April. The French met no initial opposition, but when they reached the walls of Rome they were checked by Garibaldi's irregulars, firing from the walls and carrying out sorties into the Campagna. The Roman Republicans claimed to have killed and wounded 500 and taken 600 prisoners (whom they returned unharmed). While the guns were still firing, Clough started a letter to his sister:

> I went up to the Pincian Hill and saw the smoke and heard the occasional big cannon and the sharp succession of skirmisher's volleys, bang, bang, bang, away beyond St Peter's.

He doubted whether Rome could hold out. The French withdrawal was likely to be temporary, and pro-Papal Neapolitan troops were advancing from the south on the suburban towns of Velletri, Marino and Albano.

Once again, the prose of correspondence was turned into verse in *Amours de Voyage*. Claude's first intimation of battle is that in the Caffe Nuovo in the Via Condotti he cannot get milk for his coffee. He walks uphill to see the battle for himself.

Twelve o'clock, on the Pincian Hill, with lots of English,
Germans, Americans, French – the Frenchmen, too, are protected –
So we stand in the sun, but afraid of a probable shower;
So we stand and stare, and see, to the left of St Peter's,
Smoke, from the cannon, white – but that is at intervals only, –
Black, from a burning house, we suppose, by the Cavalleggieri;
And we believe we discern some lines of men descending
Down through the vineyard-slopes, and catch a bayonet gleaming.
Every ten minutes, however – in this there is no misconception –
Comes a great white puff from behind Michel Angelo's dome, and
After a space the report of a real big gun, – not the Frenchman's? –
That must be doing some work. And so we watch and conjecture . . .
Half past one, or two. The report of small arms frequent,
Sharp and savage indeed; that cannot all be for nothing:
So we watch and wonder; but guessing is tiresome, very.
Weary of wondering, watching, and guessing, and gossiping idly,
Down I go, and pass through the quiet streets with the knots of
National Guards patrolling, and flags hanging out at the windows,
English, American, Danish – and after offering to help an
Irish family moving en masse to the Maison Serny,
After endeavouring idly to minister balm to the trembling
Quinquagenarian fears of two lone British spinsters,
Go to make sure of my dinner before the enemy enter.
But by this there are signs of stragglers returning; and voices
Talk, though you don't believe it, of guns and prisoners taken;
And on the walls you read the first bulletin of the morning. –
This is all that I saw, and all I know of the battle.

(P, 107)

Claude, one feels, was too honest to have been a good war correspondent. In real life Clough wrote to reassure his mother. The warfare reported in the English papers 'would seem very small to you if you saw it as I am doing'. He had hung out a British flag from his window, and the British attaché from Naples, backed by HMS *Bulldog*, had secured from Oudinot a guarantee that the English would be unmolested. There had been, however, one 'awkward thing', namely:

> the killing of four or perhaps five priests by the mob, about a week ago, soon after the news of the advance of the Neapolitan army. One cannot of course know the truth; some say that one of them had fired out of a window and killed a soldier; others, that they were found making off to the Neapolitans. (M, 254)

Claude, in *Amours de Voyage*, was an eye-witness to these events – well, almost.

> So, I have seen a man killed! An experience, that, among others!
> Yes, I suppose I have; although I could never be certain,
> And in a court of justice could never declare I had seen it,
> But a man was killed, I am told, in a place where I saw
> Something; a man was killed, I am told, and I saw something.

Claude narrates how, returning from St Peter's with his guidebook under his arm, he crossed the Ponte S. Angelo to find in the nearby piazza a seething crowd, with men dragging something in the middle of the throng.

> Ha! bare swords in the air, held up! There seem to be voices
> Pleading and hands putting back; official perhaps; but the swords are
> Many, and bare in the air. In the air? They descend; they are smiting,
> Hewing, chopping – At what? In the air once more upstretched! And
> Is it blood that's on them? Yes certainly blood! Of whom then?
> Over whom is the cry of this furor of exultation?
> While they are skipping and screaming and dancing their caps on the
> points of
> Swords and bayonets, I to the outskirts back, and ask a
> Mercantile-seeming-bystander. 'What is it?' and he, looking always
> That way, makes me answer 'A Priest, who was trying to fly to
> The Neapolitan army' and thus explains the proceeding . . .
> Three or four, or, it may be, five of these people were slaughtered.
> Some declare they had, one of them, fired on a sentinel; others
> Say they were only escaping; a Priest, it is currently stated,
> Stabbed a National Guard on the very Piazza Colonna:
> History, Rumour of Rumours, I leave it to thee to determine.
>
> (P, 109)

Claude, in the story, makes himself scarce, fearing that in his black clothes he might himself be mistaken for a priest. In real life, Clough, wandering the city with map in hand, was more than once in danger of being arrested as a spy; but when questioned he was able to talk himself out of trouble (PPR, 149).

Rome was now on a war footing, with the city gates closed and barricades across all the main streets. The French were repulsed again on 7 May, and the Neapolitans thrashed by Garibaldi on the 9th at Palestrina. On 16–17 May there was a truce. French commissioners entered the city and urged the Romans to send troops northward against the Austrians, who captured Bologna on the 20th. The Romans were prepared to welcome the Pope as head of the Church, but the French insisted on some restoration of temporal power. After a fortnight of inconclusive discussion they broke off negotiations.

'This, my dear Tom' Clough wrote to Arnold on 3 June 'is being written while guns are going off – there – there – there. For these blackguard French are attacking us again. May the Lord scatter and confound them.' The assault continued for 17 hours, raging round the Villa Pamfili at the western edge of the city. The battle was inconclusive, but the French now began a siege in earnest and the gunfire lasted for two weeks. The bombardment penetrated into the centre of the city and Clough saw grenades bursting in the air nearby. 'It is funny' he told Tom 'to see how much like any other city a besieged city looks. Unto this has come our grand Liberty, Equality and Fraternity revolution!' (M, 256).

Once again Clough was keen to reassure his mother. 'This is the 9th day of our siege, to call it so' he wrote on the 11th, 'the French construct their approaches, and the Romans fire, and once or twice have sallied out, to obstruct them; — one hears a small occasional cannonade, and once in three days an affair of musketry.' Within the city all was tranquil, he reported: promenaders, including ladies, appeared as normal in the Corso from six to ten. His worst problem was being 'startled out of sleep into headache' by a 3 a.m. cannonade (M, 258–9).

However, though Arthur did not tell his mother this, he began to worry that a new Fire of Rome might destroy the Vatican with all its treasures. 'I wish England could intervene if it were but for the monuments, which one way or another I fear are but too likely to receive irreparable damage, if not to be destroyed.' In letters to all his friends he was anxious to deny that there was any form of 'Terror' in the Republic: he does not seem to have known of the murder of ten monks in Trastevere. In general it was indeed true, as he said, that Mazzini's proclamations had been remarkably effective in repressing violence.

Clough had intended to go to Florence, and perhaps also to Naples, but the siege kept him in the city until July. His habit was to ascend the steps of the Ara Caeli – the staircase made famous by Gibbon – to survey the city and the battle points. On the night of 21 June the French effected a breach in the southwest corner of the city, near the Porta Portese on the bank of the Tiber. The soldiers opposing them panicked and fled, and the French were able to plant guns on the breach and fire upon the high points of the Republican defence, the batteries at S. Pietro in Montoro and the Porta S. Pancrazio. Bombs began to fall in the centre of the city, the Piazza Venezia, the Via del Gesu, and the Piazza S. Apostoli. In the Piazza Colonna at nine o'clock in the evening, Clough stood with a crowd watching the explosions like fireworks. When he went home he found his host's family watching from the loggia, where they stayed until 1 a.m.

Claude in *Amours de Voyage* risks a visit to the battle area. He is sitting, he writes to his friend, not in any of the beauty spots of Lazio,

> But on Montorio's height, looking down on the tile-clad streets,
> The cupolas, crosses and domes, the bushes and kitchen gardens
> Which, by the grace of the Tiber, proclaim themselves Rome of the
> Romans –
> But on Montorio's height, looking forth to the vapoury mountains,
> Cheating the prisoner Hope with illusions of vision and fancy, –
> But on Montorio's height, with these weary soldiers by me,
> Waiting till Oudinot enter, to reinstate Pope and Tourist.
> (P, 121)

We do not know whether Clough ventured as near the front line as did Claude. The Republican army, after the rout of the 21st, continued to defend the city bravely for a further week. Clough visited a hospital on the Quirinal, run by an Italian princess and an American woman, Margaret Fuller. He went there partly to be able to contradict a rumour that the Republican army was composed largely of foreign adventurers.

On the night of Friday 29 June for the first time cannon balls and grenades fell near the Piazza di Spagna area, and between 2 and 4 a.m. Clough and the Pfyffer family were obliged to descend to the lower floors. On the following day, after the S. Pancrazio battery had been taken, the Roman Assembly, against the advice of Mazzini, decided to capitulate. Garibaldi with his free corps and two Roman regiments left the city and marched northward on 2 July. The next day the French entered the city via the Ponte Sisto and the Porta del Popolo. At noon on the same day, Clough ascended the Capitol to watch the Assembly proclaim the new constitution on the Campidoglio. The constitution had a very short life: Oudinot declared martial law, and celebrated his victory with a Te Deum in an empty St Peter's. The American consul Cass negotiated a safe passage for Mazzini. The Pope did not return for another nine months.

Clough remained in the city two more weeks. 'It is a sight to make one gnash one's very wisdom teeth to go about this fallen Jerusalem, and behold the abomination of desolation standing where it ought not' he wrote to Palgrave. But he had to allow that the occupying French soldiers were behaving very well. He himself suffered nothing worse than being jostled by a soldier with a bayonet when he was out on the Corso after curfew (M, 267).

The ending of the siege meant that it was now possible to visit nearby towns and villages such as Albano, Arricia, Nemi and Castel Gandolfo, and the classical sights for which Claude longed when cooped up in Rome:

Tibur is beautiful, too, and the orchard slopes, and the Anio
Falling, falling, yet to the ancient lyrical cadence;
Tibur and Anio's tide; and cool from Lucretilis ever,
With the Digentian stream, and with the Bandusian fountain,
Folded in Sabine recesses, the valley and villa of Horace.

(P, 120)

Clough left the city finally on 17 July, and travelled southward. He spent part of August in Naples, and then journeyed home by short stages, stopping at Florence, Genoa, Turin and Geneva and sailing down the Rhine. He was back in London in good time to take up his duties when University College Hall opened in October.

* * *

This Italian sojourn of 1849 was fertile in poetry. Most important of the works from this period was a second novel in verse, *Amours de Voyage*. Unlike *The Bothie*, *Amours* is an epistolary novel, consisting mainly of letters written by Claude, a supercilious Oxford don on the Grand Tour, to his clerical friend Eustace in London. The poem went through many revisions before reaching publication, and there is nearly twice as much cancelled material as there are lines in the final poem.[6] In an early version there are a number of letters from Eustace. In the final version the only correspondents other than Claude are two sisters of a Cornish family met in Rome, Georgina and Mary Trevellyn. The poem is divided into five cantos, each containing a dozen or so hexameter letters, and each framed in a pair of stanzas in elegiac couplets expressing an authorial voice. The stanza that prefaces Canto I may stand as an example of the elegiac mode.

Over the great windy waters, and over the clear crested summits,
  Unto the sun and the sky, and unto the perfecter earth,
Come, let us go, to a land wherein gods of the old time wandered,
  Where every breath even now changes to ether divine.
Come, let us go; though withal a voice whisper, 'The world that we live in,
  Whithersoever we turn, still is the same narrow crib;
'Tis but to prove limitation, and measure a cord, that we travel;
  Let who would 'scape and be free go to his chamber and think;
'Tis but to change idle fancies for memories wilfully falser;
  'Tis but to go and have been' – Come, little bark! let us go.

(P, 94)

The poem, as we have seen, is rich in description of the siege of Rome; but it is less a battle narrative than a love story. The main lines of the plot are simple. Claude is initially contemptuous of the city of Rome and of the bluestocking Mary Trevellyn. By the end of the poem he has fallen in love both with Mary and with the Roman Republic, only to watch them both pass away. The poem puzzled some contemporaries, but has delighted twentieth-century readers, because of the character of its anti-hero and the downbeat ending of its story.

The first Canto sets the scene. Early letters from Claude express his initial disgust with Rome and in particular with the art and architecture of the Catholic Baroque. St Ignatius and the Jesuits are denounced for this decadence. But even Luther does not escape blame – it was after all his reformation that provoked the counter-reformation. Better to have let renaissance Rome go smoothly on its way to cultured paganism!

The Trevellyn family, on the contrary, find Rome delightful. Papa and Mamma are installed in the Piazza di Spagna with 77 travelling trunks, three nubile daughters, Mary, Susan and Georgina, and an unspecified number of younger children. George Vernon, a mustachioed friend of Claude's, is engaged to Georgina, but is willing to pay attentions to all three of the young ladies. Claude, however, looks down on the Trevellyns:

> Middle-class people these, bankers very likely, not wholly
> Pure of the taint of the shop; will at table d'hote and restaurant
> Have their shilling's worth, their penny's pennyworth even:
> Neither man's aristocracy this, nor God's, God knoweth!
>
> (P, 98)

He condescends, however, to accept their hospitality and admiration. 'Is it not fitting that wealth should tender this homage to culture?' Gradually he becomes more at ease, and is happy to discuss the Oxford Movement with Mrs Trevellyn. He finds himself sleepwalking into an affair with her daughter Mary – a dangerous situation, like that of Theseus in the labyrinth or Odysseus on Circe's magical island.

> I have come into the precinct, the labyrinth closes around me,
> Path into path rounding slyly; I pace slowly on and the fancy,
> Struggling awhile to sustain the long sequences, weary, bewildered,
> Fain must collapse in despair; I yield, I am lost and know nothing;
> Yet in my bosom unbroken remaineth the clew; I shall use it.
> Lo with the rope on my loins I descend through the fissure; I sink, yet
> Inly secure in the strength of invisible arms up above me;
> Still, wheresoever I swing, wherever to shore or to shelf, or

Floor of cavern untrodden, shell-sprinkled, enchanting, I know I
Yet shall one time feel the strong cord tight about me –
Feel it, relentless, upbear me from spots I would rest in; and though the
Rope sway wildly, I faint, crags wound me, from crag unto crag re-
Bounding, or, wide in the void, I die ten deaths, ere the end I
Yet shall plant firm foot on the broad lofty spaces I quit, shall
Feel underneath the great massy strengths of abstraction,
Look yet abroad from the height o'er the sea whose salt wave I have
    tasted.

(P, 102)

Potholing, whether for sporting or scientific purposes, did not become popular until the end of the century. Clough here describes it in anticipation with wonderful metrical skill.

Claude's meaning is that he is willing to let himself indulge in lovemaking in the confidence that his abstract intelligence will pull him back before he falls into serious commitment. The remaining stages of the poem deal out the punishment of this hubris. At the end of Canto I we read the first of Mary Trevellyn's lines, written in response to a query about her new acquaintance:

I do not like him much, though I do not dislike being with him
He is what people call, I suppose, a superior man, and
Certainly seems so to me; but I think he is frightfully selfish.

(P, 102)

Up to this point the poem has hardly mentioned the political and military situation. The second and longest canto is largely devoted to this: the arrival of the French, the Republican victory in the battle of 30 April, the murder of the priest near the Ponte S. Angelo. Claude is stirred by Republican ardour – the 'Marseillaise' rings in his ears, and he dreams of a sword at his side and a battle-horse underneath him. But in waking moments he puts away the thought of dying for the cause, attractive though it is. 'Sweet it may be and decorous, perhaps, for the country to die; but, / on the whole we conclude the Romans won't do it, and I shan't.' But may he not be called on to risk his life to defend the honour of his new friends the Trevellyns?

Am I prepared to lay down my life for the British female?
Really, who knows? One has bowed and talked, till, little by little,
All the natural heat has escaped of the chivalrous spirit.
Oh, one conformed, of course; but one doesn't die for good manners,
Stab, or shoot, or be shot, by way of graceful attention.
No, if it should be at all, it should be on the barricades there;

> Should I incarnadine ever this inky pacifical finger,
> Sooner far should it be for this vapour of Italy's freedom,
> Sooner far by the side of the d——d and dirty plebeians.
> Ah, for the child in the street I could strike; for the full-blown lady –
> Somehow, Eustace, alas! I have not felt the vocation.
>
> (P, 105)

On the day of the battle, however, Claude behaves with sufficient gallantry for Georgina Trevellyn to report 'Mary allows she was wrong about Mr Claude *being selfish*; / He was *most* useful and kind on the terrible thirtieth of April'.

By this time Claude is beginning to take Mary with real, if condescending, seriousness. In the tenth letter of the Canto he writes:

> It is a pleasure, indeed, to converse with this girl. Oh, rare gift,
> Rare felicity, this! She can talk in a rational way, can
> Speak upon subjects that really are matters of mind and of thinking,
> Yet in perfection retain her simplicity; never, one moment,
> Never, however you urge it, however you tempt her, consents to
> Step from ideas and fancies and loving sensations to those vain
> Conscious understandings that vex the minds of man-kind.
> No, though she talk, it is music; her fingers desert not the keys; 'tis
> Song, though you hear in the song the articulate vocables sounded
> Syllabled single and sweetly the words of melodious meaning.
> I am in love, you say; I do not think so exactly.
>
> (P, 111)

But as letter succeeds letter it becomes clear that Claude is indeed in love, but is somehow impotent to express it. The family cannot even tell whether it is Mary or Susan who attracts him. Georgina Trevellyn finds his behaviour baffling, and complains that Mary ('who might bring him to in a moment') will neither help him nor dismiss him. Mary, for her part, resents Georgina's attempts to throw them together.

Claude begins to worry – with some justification – that Mary finds him repulsive.

> My manner offends; my ways are wholly repugnant;
> Every word that I utter estranges, hurts, and repels her;
> Every moment of bliss that I gain, in her exquisite presence,
> Slowly, surely, withdraws her, removes her, and severs her from me.

The Trevellyns decide to leave Rome to escape from the republican terrors. They plan to travel by carriage to Siena and Florence, while George Vernon remains behind, eventually to rejoin the family at Leghorn in preparation for his marriage with Georgina. Claude is invited to assist Papa Trevellyn in escorting the ladies to Florence. He accepts the invitation – but then:

> Only the day before, the foolish family Vernon
> Made some uneasy remarks, as we walked to our lodging together,
> As to intentions, forsooth, and so forth. I was astounded,
> Horrified, quite; and obtaining just then, as it happened an offer
> (No common favour) of seeing the great Ludovisi collection,
> Why, I made this a pretence, and wrote that they must excuse me.
> (P, 122)

He could not bear, he tells Eustace 'to conduct a permitted flirtation / under those vulgar eyes, the observed of such observers'.

Mary, travelling towards Florence, is brought by Claude's non-appearance to realize that she finds him attractive as well as repulsive. In a letter to her former governess, Miss Roper, who has been left behind in Rome to nurse a sick brother, she admits that when Claude talks of ideas he can be unaffected, expansive and easy – but perhaps he is simply a cold intellectual being.

> When does he make advances? – He thinks that women should woo him;
> Yet, if a girl should do so, would be but alarmed and disgusted.
> She that should love him must look for small love in return, – like the ivy
> On the stone wall, must expect but a rigid and niggard support, and
> E'en to get that must go searching all round with her humble embraces.
> (P, 115)

While the city is closed by the siege, Claude gives himself over to contemplation on the themes of knowledge, love and marriage. Does he really love Mary? Surely it was simply accident that brought them together in juxtaposition?

> Juxtaposition, in fine; and what is juxtaposition?
> Look you, we travel along in the railway-carriage or steamer,
> And *pour passer le temps*, till the tedious journey be ended,
> Lay aside paper or book, to talk with the girl that is next one;
> And *pour passer le temps*, with the terminus all but in prospect,
> Talk of eternal ties and marriages made in heaven.
> (P, 117)

Such talk, of course, is insincere: but, asks Claude, could it ever be sincere? Could a man really want to bind himself to a wife for ever and ever?

But for his funeral train which the bridegroom sees in the distance,
Would he so joyfully, think you, fall in with the marriage-procession?
But for that final discharge, would he dare to enlist in that service?
But for that certain release, ever sign to that perilous contract?
But for that exit secure, ever bend to that treacherous doorway?
(P, 117)

But is that the way the bride sees it? Well, perhaps women don't think at all about it. But if they reflected deeply on the meaning of life, death and marriage they would surely not be at all pleased. Religious traditions have taught that after death a human being is absorbed in contemplation of divinity; idealist philosophers have gone further and claimed that death is followed by total assumption into an Absolute. On this view, marriage can be nothing but a second-class destiny for a man. But any woman:

Hardly would tender her hand to the wooer that candidly told her
That she is but for a space, an *ad-interim* solace and pleasure –
That in the end she shall yield to a perfect and absolute something,
Which I then for myself shall behold and not another.

Can an intellectual, then, only win his beloved by cheating her? 'Will you have us your slaves to lie to you, flatter and – leave you?' (P, 118).

Meanwhile, in Florence, Vernon and Georgina marry and set off for their honeymoon. Mary Trevellyn writes to Miss Roper, asking, hesitantly, that Claude be told that Vernon's interference took place without her knowledge, and that she would prefer things to be as if it had never happened. Miss Roper passes on the message, and Claude at once decides to follow the family, however difficult it may be to escape the siege.

Canto IV is a chapter of missed rendezvous. When Claude reaches Florence he finds the Trevellyns have left five days earlier for Milan. He rushes on after them. ('Why, what else should I do? Stay here and look at the pictures, / Statues and churches? Alack, I am sick of the statues and pictures'). The Trevellyns leave Milan for Como three days earlier than expected, but Mary is distressed by the haste. As she informs Miss Roper (by now safely in Florence):

I thought, if he came all the way to Milan, he really
Ought not to be disappointed; and so I wrote three lines to
Say I had heard he was coming, desirous of joining our party; –
If so, then I said, we had started for Como, and meant to
Cross the St Gothard, and stay, we believed, at Lucerne for the summer.
(P, 126)

Claude never receives Mary's letter because it is lost by the *cameriere*, but he does learn that the family have left for Como. But at Como he cannot discover which route they have taken – to Switzerland, or the Tyrol, or to Turin. In a journey that recapitulates Clough's 1845 tour with his sister, Claude dashes to the Splügen pass, and to the Stelvio, and to Porlezza, but finds no trace of the Trevellyns' names in any inn's visitors' book. Returning to Como, he notices that beside their names in the book is added in a feminine hand 'By the boat to Bellaggio'. Mary had, indeed, written this specially for him; but at the last minute the family's plans were altered and they went to Lugano. There, too, she writes a note in the visitor's book 'To Lucerne, across the St Gothard'. But at Bellagio Claude gives up, baffled and at last aware of the folly of his behaviour in Rome.

> There is a tide, at least in the *love* affairs of mortals
> Which, when taken at flood, leads on to the happiest fortune, –
> Leads to the marriage-morn and the orange-flowers and the altar,
> And the long lawful line of crowned joys to crowned joys succeeding, –
> Ah, it has ebbed with me! Ye gods, and when it was flowing,
> Pitiful fool that I was, to stand fiddle-faddling in that way!

Desperate with desire, Claude he decides to go back to Florence to get news of Mary from Miss Roper.

> But it is cruel to turn. The mountains seem to demand me, –
> Peak and valley from far to beckon and motion me onward.
> Somewhere amid their folds she passes whom fain I would follow;
> Somewhere among those heights she haply calls me to seek her.
> Ah, could I hear her call! could I catch the glimpse of her raiment!

In the fifth and final canto the lovers move further and further away from each other. Miss Roper is no longer at Florence; she and her brother have gone to Bagni di Lucca to escape the heat. Claude, in pursuit of a rumour, travels from Florence to Pisa and back, all in vain. Mary, meanwhile, writes ever more anxious letters to Miss Roper, complaining of her failure to keep Claude informed of the family's movements.

Claude now sits idly in Florence, moping, and trying to fix Mary's image in his mind 'to write the old perfect inscription / over and over again upon every page of remembrance'. He continues to write letters to Eustace, but neglects to post half of them. He hears of the capitulation of Rome and the death of Risorgimento heroes:

Rome is fallen; and fallen, or falling, heroical Venice,
I, meanwhile, for the loss of a single small chit of a girl sit
Moping and mourning here – for her, and myself much smaller.

He begins to doubt whether he ever really cared for Rome, or even for Mary.

Do whatever I will, I cannot call up her image;
For when I close my eyes, I see, very likely, St Peter's
Or the Pantheon façade, or Michel Angelo's figure,
Or at a wish, when I please, the Alban hills and the Forum
But that face, those eyes, – ah no, never anything like them;
Only, try as I will, a sort of featureless outline . . .
(P, 131)

Perhaps, in some way, at some time, he will be united with Mary in some Absolute; but it will not do to suppose it. He returns, briefly, to Rome, and finds it full of priests and soldiers; he has no heart any more for marbles or frescoes. From these months all he has gained is a little knowledge.

Knowledge is hard to seek, and harder yet to adhere to.
Knowledge is painful often; and yet, when we know we are happy.
Seek it, and leave mere Faith and Love to come with the chances.
As for Hope, – tomorrow I hope to be starting from Naples.
Rome will not do, I see, for many good reasons.
Eastward, then, I suppose, with the coming of winter, to Egypt.
(P, 132)

Those are Claude's last words in the poem. The final letter is one by Mary Trevellyn, in which she confesses to Miss Roper that often and often she has looked for the little lake-steamer to bring Claude to Lucerne. 'But it is only fancy, – I do not really expect it.' She resigns herself to journeying back to England with her family.

The concluding set of elegiacs provides an envoi. 'So, go forth to the world, to the good report and the evil? / Go little book! Thy tale, is it not evil and good?' The final lines tell the poem to proclaim its origin. 'I was writ in a Roman chamber, When from Janiculan heights thundered the cannon of France' (P, 133).

If we take this last couplet as literally true, then *Amours de Voyage* was completed in the last days of June, and is an example of whirlwind composition comparable to *The Bothie*. But the poem I have described is the poem finally published nine years later. It went through many stages of composition, some during and some after Clough's sojourn in Rome.[7] First, it seems, he wrote a number of self-standing descriptions of the sights of Rome and episodes of the siege. Next he conceived the idea of an epistolary novel, and incorporated these early direct-voice utterances into it in the form of letters. The love theme seems to have developed later than the war theme. Clough kept changing his mind about the number of correspondents to be involved: one version tells the story entirely in letters from Claude, then letters of the Trevellyn sisters are added, and then, in the longest version, half a dozen letters of Eustace, which were struck out again before publication.

Here is an example of a letter from Eustace, inserted in Canto III after Claude has revealed that he is in love with Mary.

> Marry, of course, my dear fellow; I rejoice in my heart at the prospect.
> Marry, of course, my dear boy. I know in my soul it will cure you,
> Force you, malgré vous-même, to abandon these follies that now can
> Spume on your idleness, tempt you. I'll come I declare to Rome, in
> Spite of the soldiers, in spite of the Sermons you cast in my teeth, in
> Spite of whatever may be to perform you that Sacred Office.
>
> (P, 637)

The long version was complete by the end of October, and Clough sent a copy to Rugby, inviting comments from Shairp and Walrond. He asked them not to show the manuscript to anyone else, and he does not seem to have shown the poem to Matthew Arnold until much later. Shairp did not like the poem: he thought it inferior to both *Ambarvalia* and *The Bothie*. 'The state of soul of which it is a projection I do not like . . . There is no hope, nor strength, nor belief in all these; everything crumbles to dust beneath a ceaseless self-introspection and criticism which is throughout the one only inspiration. The gaiety of manner where no gaiety is, becomes flippancy' (M, 275). Shairp begged Clough not to publish the poem, but he added a number of detailed suggestions for improvement – for example, 'not so many Well's and other monosyllables'.

It was not only devout Christians like Shairp, easily offended by swear words and impious allusions, who took against the poem. Emerson, too, when he read the poem years later in published instalments, passed a similarly severe judgement. He was outraged by the inconclusive conclusion. 'How can you waste such power on a broken dream? Why lead us up the tower to tumble down?' The poet, he felt, had broken faith with his readers by not giving them a happy ending. 'It is true a few persons compassionately tell me, that the piece is all right, and that they like this veracity of much preparation to no result' (M, 548).

Clough's response to Emerson was 'I always meant it to be so and began it with the full intention of its ending so.' To Shairp he pointed out that he had missed, in the poem, the development of Claude's character. 'Do you not, in the conception, find any final strength of mind in the unfortunate fool of a hero?' But he told Shairp that he had no immediate plans to publish the poem – he did not wish to offend his new employers at University Hall. But undoubtedly he felt also that the work was not yet sufficiently polished to be published.

With a century and a half of hindsight we can wonder whether the polishing that took place between 1849 and 1858 was altogether beneficial. Though *Amours* is more fluent in versification than *The Bothie*, it is weaker in dramatic structure. The ending is no longer a problem: twentieth- and twenty-first century readers find it easier to accept the downbeat conclusion of *Amours* than the conventional happy ending of *The Bothie*. The main problem is that so much of the poem is a monologue by a single character: this means that the possibilities offered by an epistolary novel are thrown away. In the final version of the poem Eustace, who in his cancelled letters speaks with a voice rather like Shairp's, is put to silence. George Vernon and Miss Roper are no more than dummies. More importantly, Mary Trevellyn is a mere cipher, who cannot in any way be compared to *The Bothie*'s Elspie. There are good dramatic reasons why the reader cannot obtain a lifelike image of her from the letters of Claude; but these would not be frustrated if she were given a clearer voice of her own. The vapid, matchmaking Georgina sometimes comes to life, but even she is more lively in the earlier version which includes her correspondence with her fiancé. A twenty-first century editor might well feel that he could put together a more satisfactory work by omitting some of the more metaphysical passages in the final version, and replacing them by some of the colloquial snatches that the poet jettisoned.

But for the biographer, once again, the question is: what does the poem tell us about Clough's own thoughts and hopes in 1849? It is a great mistake to regard Claude as nothing more than a mask or mouthpiece for his creator. When Shairp complained about the 'blasé disgust at men and things' in the poem, Clough replied 'Gott und Teufel, my friend, you don't suppose all that comes from myself! I assure you it is extremely *not* so!' (M, 276). To treat Claude's letters as autobiographical statements is to insult the poet's remarkable creative power. It was no small achievement to make the reader identify with, and by the end of the poem share the vexations and sorrows of, a character who is presented, initially at least, as a clearly odious person.

Claude has several characteristics which set him apart from Clough. He is superior to him in wealth and social status: he is, indeed, Clough's *bête noire*, the gentleman. The real Clough was more likely to hear than to make sneering remarks about those whose family are 'not wholly pure of the taint of the shop'. Claude comes to Rome simply as a tourist seeking escape from domestic monotony – not, as Clough did, in order once again to observe a revolution at first hand. Claude arrives with not the faintest thought of matrimony, and has no idea what he should look for in a wife; Clough, we know, had given years of thought to the matter.

Nonetheless, there are autobiographical elements in the poem which go beyond the eye-witness account of the siege and assault, and beyond the mastery of Rome's topography, that Clough acquired with such remarkable speed. The meditation on death in battle started life, as Patrick Scott has pointed out, as a self-standing poem in the voice of Clough rather than a letter from the hand of Claude. Does this mean that Clough himself weighed arguments for and against enlisting in the Republican army? If he did so, it is not surprising that he decided against. Young English intellectuals did not feel called on to fight for the Risorgimento in the way that they felt called to volunteer, nearly a century later, in the service of the Spanish Republic.

The main themes of *Amours de Voyage* are three: politics, art and love. They are the same three as are enunciated in the opening address to Rome in *Resignation, to Faustus*. 'O land of Empire, art and love!' To grasp Clough's message on each topic we need to attend not so much to what Claude tells us, as to what Claude is made to learn in the course of the story.

With respect to art, Claude and Clough start from the same point: uncritical admiration for Greco-Roman sculpture, and fastidious distaste for counter-reformation architecture. They learn to appraise and discriminate: the Quirinal horsemen surpass other classical statues, and St Peter's would be excellent if only Michelangelo's designs had been adhered to. Claude, in the final version of the poem, has little eye for painting, but Clough himself appreciated Baroque painting if not Baroque buildings. He spent long hours admiring the Sistine ceiling and he told Tom Arnold that an engraving of the Creation of Eve was one of the things that had made him come to Rome in the first place. In a cancelled passage of the poem, Claude tells Eustace 'I lie on my back and adore the Sistine frescos / Till the Custode returns the fifth time'. Clough much preferred Michelangelo to Raphael: the one was intellectual, and the other merely natural (M, 256). But the theme of *Amours* is not that intellectual art is superior to sensual art: it is that all art gives way to things more serious, notably love and politics. In pursuit of Mary, Claude has no taste for the pictures and statues of Florence, and once the Pope regains possession of the Vatican, Claude loses all enthusiasm for any marble or fresco (P, 124, 132).

What, then, of politics? Claude comes to Rome with no political interests; he has never been a radical like Clough. However, he soon takes sides with the Romans against the French, and glorifies Mazzini's Republic. But he comes to realize that his support is worthless, and his commitment to the cause is superficial. His last words on the topic, during the French occupation, are these:

> Politics, farewell, however! For what could I do? with inquiring,
> Talking, collating the journals, go fever my brain about things o'er
> Which I can have no control.
>
> (P, 132)

Here we do, I think, detect Clough's own mind. He had left Oriel as a radical, believing that justice demanded a fundamental reconstruction of the economic and social institutions of European states. He had now witnessed two revolutions at first hand. He had learnt two things, one about himself, and one about revolutions. He had discovered that he was unwilling to fight on the barricades, and without such willingness he felt a hypocrite in calling for revolution. In Claude's words 'I cannot / Fight, you know; and to talk I am wholly ashamed' (P, 115). Henceforth, Clough was willing to work within existing political institutions. He spent his reforming energies in areas where he could have an actual effect: universities and hospitals. Already, after his Parisian but before his Roman experience, he had written to Tom Arnold, for once allowing Matthew to be in the right.

> Something I think we rash young men may learn from the failure and discomfiture of our friends in the new Republic. The millennium, as Matt says, won't come this bout. I am myself much more inclined to be patient and to make allowance for existing necessities than I was. (M, 243)

The title theme of *Amours* is, of course, love, in particular the transience of love. On this topic a great gulf separates Claude and Clough. The issues that divide them can be summed up under three heads: contingency, commitment and concreteness.

Love, and happiness in love, the poem tells us, is a matter dependent completely on accident. It is juxtaposition in the Piazza di Spagna that brings Claude and Mary together; it is the mislaying of a letter in Como that parts them forever. There are no marriages made in heaven, or partners predestined from eternity. A lover must make up his own mind to woo: he must not expect a sign from heaven, or wait from day to day like Hamlet for an ever clearer call to action.

But though the occurrence of love is a contingent matter, there are laws that constrain its course. One is that success in love demands total commitment. The kind of love that Claude offers Mary – a superficial dalliance with the inmost self held back – is a love which deserves to fail. When entering into the affair, Claude compares himself to Theseus with his clew of thread in the labyrinth, and to a climber descending while belayed to 'the great massy strengths of abstraction'. When Claude lets go of himself and chases Mary through the Italian lakes, he is Theseus without a clew, and the heights of abstraction offer him no security. The Arnoldian detachment preached in *Resignation to Fausta* is no basis for marriage.

Above all, love is love not of an abstract ideal but of a concrete individual. The love of Claude and Mary fails because neither will come sufficiently close to the other to find out whether they are really suited to each other. Claude is held back by character, and Mary is held back by convention. Claude is too self-centred to see Mary as she is: no wonder his image of her fades to a blank featureless orb. Mary has a clearer vision of Claude then he has of her, but she believes – or at least believes that he believes – that in courtship a woman should not lead the advance. Claude himself tells us that his idea of a successful wooer is a man who is audacious, wilful and vehement, and takes his beloved by storm. Neither Mary nor Claude share Elspie's vision of marriage as an arch built equally from either side.

In all this, the lovers of *Amours* fall short of the ideal of marriage that Clough had been painfully working out for himself during his years at Oriel. The lessons that the fate of Claude is to teach us were lessons that Clough was giving to himself. His salaried appointment at University Hall, with its tied house, gave him for the first time a realistic prospect of marriage. He needed to be clear what he expected from the institution and what kind of person he wanted to share it. And if he found such a person, he must not delay, Hamlet-like, as he had delayed when conscience called on him to leave Oriel.

During his stay in Rome, scholars have speculated, he might have thought he had found a suitable partner. Margaret Fuller, a teacher and journalist from Massachussetts, had been Italian correspondent of the *New York Tribune* since 1847. She was a disciple of Emerson, and had been involved in the publication of many of his early works. She was also the author of the first substantial work of American feminism, *Woman in the Nineteenth Century*. She was in Rome during the siege, and, along with another visitor from Massachusetts, William Wetmore Story (later the author of a best-selling guide to Rome) she met Clough on Sunday 20 May, during the temporary lull in hostilities. His diary shows that he then met her again, usually without Story, every few days until 12 July, when she departed.

Did he fall in love with her? If so, any hopes of marriage were shattered when he discovered that she had been secretly married for nearly two years to one of the Italian officers in charge of Rome's defences. She was now the Marchesa Ossoli, but had been helping to run the Monte Cavallo hospital under her maiden name. Her marriage first became public knowledge at the end of 1849, when she had a son and left Italy for America.

It is impossible to know what passed between Clough and Fuller during that summer in Rome. Patrick Scott states the case thus:

> Clough saw a lot of Margaret Fuller during late May and early June. These meetings are easily understandable when one remembers their common respect for R. W. Emerson, and the lack of other company in the besieged Rome. There is no evidence, or at least no firm evidence, that, unwittingly, Margaret was Mary to Clough's Claude. Clough's journal entries for 19 and 21 June, 'M.F. impossibile' and 'Impossib. *bis*' might be taken to indicate that only then had Clough realised that his new friend was married: but equally they might mean that she was unable to keep an appointment.[8]

This is very well said. It is tempting to read 'Impossib. *bis*' as a cryptic lament that a marriage is impossible because it would be a second, bigamous, marriage. But the temptation should be resisted. In a letter to Clough after they had both moved elsewhere, Margaret expressed regret that 'I threw away the chance of knowing you in Rome'. This, too, admits of more than one explanation, but the least dramatic one is to be preferred (M, 282).

Along with politics, art and love, *Amours de Voyage* treats of religion; but the topic is not given prominence. Biblical language is used from time to time, in the jocular manner that so distressed Hawkins in *The Bothie*; but the name of God is hardly ever seriously invoked. Instead Claude talks of the Absolute, and identifies Christianity with 'aspirations from something most shameful here upon earth and / in our poor selves to something most perfect above in the heavens'. His preferred place of worship is a de-Christianized Pantheon, and his own religion seems, appropriately, to be pantheism.

> All that is Nature's is I, and I all things that are Nature's.
> Yes, as I walk, I behold in a luminous, large, intuition
> That I can be and become anything that I meet with or look at:
> I am the ox in the dray, the ass with the garden-stuff panniers;
> I am the dog in the doorway, the kitten that plays in the window,
> On sunny slab of the ruin the furtive and fugitive lizard,
> Swallow above me that twitters, and fly that is buzzing about me;
> Yea, and detect as I go, by a faint but faithful assurance,
> E'en from the stones of the street, as from rocks or trees of the forest,
> Something of kindred, a common, though latent vitality, greet me;
> And, to escape from our striving, mistakings, misgrowths, and perversions,
> Fain could demand to return to that perfect and primitive silence,
> Fain be enfolded and fixed, as of old, in their rigid embraces.
>
> (P, 119)

Claude's sentiments here no doubt owe much to Emerson's writings on nature, which in their turn were influenced by Spinoza and Hegel. But Claude's references to the Absolute – frequent in the printed text, and more abundant in cancelled passages – suggest that at this period Clough had also made more direct acquaintance with German Idealism. Tom Arnold had taken Hegel's works with him to New Zealand, and Jowett and Stanley had introduced his philosophy to their Oxford colleagues.

The great topic of discusssion in Oxford in 1849 was no longer Newmanism, as Mrs Trevellyn had thought, but the introduction of a University Professoriate to counterbalance college tutors. For many at the time 'Professor' was synonymous with 'German Idealist'. A squib opposing the creation of a professoriate addresses a chorus of Professors as

> Ye who scan
> The universe of Being and reveal
> How Werden, eldest born of Seyn and Nichts
> Gave birth to Daseyn, whence in succession
> The world of thought and substance.

and the chorus replies:

> Professors we
> From over the sea
> From the land where professors in plenty be
> And we thrive and we flourish, as well we may,
> In the land that produced one Kant with a K.
> And many Cants with a C.
> Where Hegel taught, to his profit and fame,
> That something and nothing were one and the same;
> The absolute difference never a jot being
> 'Twixt having and not having, being and not being
> But wisely declined to extend his notion
> To the finite relations of Thalers and Groschen[9]

It is not surprising that the fashionable Claude should speak this esoteric language: he can (in a cancelled passage) even speak of the Sistine Creation as being 'Man taking shape by the Act of the thought of the Absolute thinker'. But Clough, in his first-person religious poetry, eschews the language of Idealism, and even for the expression of the most unorthodox sentiments he prefers biblical language.

On one matter Clough and Claude saw eye to eye: they shared a hatred of Roman Catholicism. Neither his flirtation with Newmanism nor his rejection of the Thirty-Nine Articles had cured Clough of the staunch prejudices of an English Protestant. Early in the poem, Claude denounces the impact of the counter-reformation on Rome:

Alaric, Attila, Genseric; – why, they came, they killed, they
Ravaged and went on their way; but these vile tyrannous Spaniards,
These are here still, – how long, O ye Heavens, in the country of Dante?
These, that fanaticized Europe, which now can forget them, release not
This, their choicest of prey, this Italy; here you see them, –
Here, with emasculate pupils and gimcrack churches of Gesu,
Pseudo-learning and lies, confessional boxes and postures, –
Here, with metallic beliefs and regimental devotions, –
Here, overcrusting with slime, perverting, defacing, debasing
Michel Angelo's dome, that had hung the Pantheon in heaven,
Raphael's Joys and Graces, and thy clear stars, Galileo!

(P, 97)[10]

Both Claude and Clough hold in particular detestation Ignatius Loyola, the chief of the 'vile tyrannous Spaniards'. After the bombardment of 29 June Clough wrote to Palgrave 'A bomb I am happy to say has left its mark on the façade of the Gesù. I wish it had stirred up old Ignatius' (M, 264).

Clough's most carefully crafted attack on the Catholic system during this period was not anything in *Amours*, but a self-standing poem in irregular blank verse, finally entitled *Sa Majesté tres Chretienne*, which in its final form consisted entirely of an address by the French King Louis XV to his father confessor. In the first version, which Clough wrote in his Rome notebook, it is headed simply 'L.XV' and the confession is preceded by a monologue in which the king fondles a group of mistresses ('Would I had mouths as berries on a bush / for all of you at once to pick in kisses') which contains the lines:

We will all go you know at last to heaven,
Confess our naughty deeds, repent, receive
The wafer and the unction of the Church
And so – through Purgatory pass to heaven:
And Purgatory also is not long,
But much like penance upon Earth; ye say
The seven penitential psalms, repeat
Eight or nine prayers with holy meditations
And so, washed white, and clad in virgin robes
The good kind God receives us to himself.
You laugh, my pet ones. Ah, I mean it though,
Yes, and tomorrow, I will not forget
I'll bring with me the Catechism of Trent
And test you in your faith, my little ones.

(P, 671)

To his confessor, Louis is full of childish, self-pitying, self-justification. It is such a difficult life, being a King!

> I know I am not what I would I were.
> I would I were, as God intended me,
> A little quiet harmless acolyte
> Clothed in long serge and linen shoulder-piece
> Day after day
> To pace serenely through the sacred fane,
> Bearing the sacred things before the priest,
> Curtsey before that altar as we pass,
> And place our burden reverently on this.
> There – by his side to stand and minister,
> To swing the censer and to sound the bell
> Uphold the book, the patin change and cup –
> Ah me –
> And why does childhood ever change to man?
>
> (P, 195)

Only confession and absolution make life tolerable. Mother Church makes such hard demands of Christian Kings, even though France is her eldest daughter.

> To younger pets, the blind, the halt, the sick,
> The outcast child, the sinners of the street
> Her doors are open and her precinct free;
> The beggar finds a nest, the slave a home,
> Even thy altars, O my Mother Church –
> O *templa quam dilecta*. We the while,
> Poor Kings, must forth to action, as you say,
> Action, that slaves us, drives us, fretted, worn
> To pleasure, which anon enslaves us too.

Despite the Church's demands, the King thanks God that he is not 'a lonely Lutheran English heretic'.

> If I had so by God's despite been born,
> Alas, methinks I had but passed my life
> In sitting motionless beside the fire,
> Not daring to remove the once-placed chair
> Nor stir my foot for fear it should be sin.
> Thank God indeed,
> Thank God for his infallible certain creed.
>
> (P, 197)

But for kings God's commandments are not easy to read, and 'Ministers somehow have small faith in them'. It must be much easier to be a priest or a religious – or at least a lay brother.

> Would I were out in quiet Paraguay
> Mending the Jesuits' shoes!

The king concludes his confession not so much by repenting his sins as by disowning them. The final lines were added by Clough when he drew up a fair copy after returning to England.

> Depraved, that is, degraded am I – Sins
> Which yet I see not how I should have shunned,
> Have, in despite of all the means of grace,
> Submission perfect to the appointed creed,
> And absolution-plenary and prayers,
> Possessed me, held, and changed – yet after all
> Somehow I think my heart within is pure.
> (P, 198)

The kneeling monarch's final desperate whimper of self-delusion clinches the poet's message that the sacramental system is powerless to cure sin and produces only an illusion of righteousness.

While in Rome, Clough attended services conducted by the Anglican chaplain, Mr Hamilton, in a room outside the Porta del Popolo. But he had now for some time ceased to be a Christian believer. During August in Naples he gave poetic expression to his disbelief in the central Christian doctrine, the Resurrection of Christ. *Easter Day* passionately denies the Resurrection, using the very words in which it is proclaimed in the Gospels and by St Paul.

> Christ is not risen, no
> He lies and moulders low,
>   Christ is not risen.
>
> What though the stone were rolled away, and though
>   The grave found empty there –
>   If not there, then elsewhere;
> If not where Joseph laid him first, why then
>   Where other men
> Translaid Him after; in some humbler clay
>   Long ere today
> Corruption that sad perfect work hath done,

Which here she scarcely, lightly had begun.
  The foul engendered worm
Feeds on the flesh of the life-giving form
Of our most Holy and Anointed one.

He is not risen, no
He lies and moulders low;
  Christ is not risen.

Ashes to ashes, dust to dust;
As of the unjust, also of the just –
  Christ is not risen.

The poem sets out, in terms as concrete as possible, what is involved in denying the Resurrection. It states alternative accounts to explain the Gospel stories, and draws out the consequences of each. If Jesus did not rise, then his body has long since rotted. If the tomb was empty, as the Gospels says, that can mean only that Jesus' body had been moved elsewhere. The words of the burial service apply to Jesus, just as to any other human saint or sinner. Perhaps there were indeed appearances of Jesus to disciples after his death; but this need not mean a genuine rising from the dead. St Matthew tells us that even some of the original disciples doubted the story.

Or what if e'en, as runs the tale, the Ten
Saw, heard and touched, again and yet again?
What if at Emmaus' inn and by Capernaum's lake
  Came One the bread that brake
Came One that spake as never mortal spake,
And with them ate and drank and stood and walked about?
  Ah, 'some' did well to 'doubt'!
Ah, the true Christ, while these things came to pass,
Nor heard, nor spake, nor walked, nor dreamt, alas!

How then did the story of the Resurrection ever gain credence? Clough's recent experiences in Rome had offered him many examples of baseless rumours acquiring currency.

As circulates in some great city crowd
A rumour changeful, vague, importunate and loud
From no determined centre, or of fact
  Or authorship exact,
  Which no man can deny

Nor verify
So spread the wondrous fame;
He all the same
Lay senseless, mouldering low
He was not risen, no,
Christ was not risen

St Paul told the Corinthians that if Christ was not risen from the dead, then they too would not rise. 'If in this life only we have hope in Christ, we are of all men most miserable.' Clough accepts Paul's conclusion as a truth, not a *reductio ad absurdum*. Jesus on his way to Calvary told the sorrowing women that they should weep for themselves and for their children: days were coming when they would pray to the hills and mountains to fall upon them and cover them. Clough sees these words as coming true precisely because of the failure to rise again.

Is he not risen, and shall we not rise?
Oh, we unwise!
What did we dream, what wake we to discover?
Ye hills, fall on us, and ye mountains, cover!
In darkness and great gloom
Come ere we thought it is *our* day of doom
From the cursed world which is one tomb
Christ is not risen!

Eat, drink, and die, for we are men deceived,
Of all the creatures under heaven's wide cope
We are most hopeless who had once most hope
We are most wretched that had most believed
Christ is not risen!

Eat, drink, and play, and think that this is bliss!
There is no heaven but this!
There is no Hell;
Save Earth, which serves the purpose doubly well,
Seeing it visits still
With equallest apportionments of ill
Both good and bad alike, and brings to one same dust
The unjust and the just
With Christ, who is not risen.

(P, 201)

What, then, should we do? Service to the dead Christ must be replaced by service to the living in the workaday world. The women disciples must give up the hope of laying up treasure in heaven, and the apostles must abandon their ambition to be fishers of men.

> Yea, Daughters of Jersualem, depart
> Bind up as best ye may your own sad bleeding heart;
> Go to your homes, your living children tend,
> Your earthly spouses love;
> Set your affections *not* on things above
> Which moth and rust corrupt, which quickliest come to end . . .
>
> Ye men of Galilee!
> Why stand ye looking up to heaven, where Him ye ne'er may see,
> Neither ascending hence, nor hither returning again?
> Ye poor deluded youths, go home
> Mend the old nets ye left to roam
> Tie the split oar, patch the torn sail;
> It was indeed 'an idle tale'
> He was not risen.
>
> (P, 202)

Easter Day is one of the most powerful of Clough's poems on religion. It speaks to believers and unbelievers alike. It speaks to, and for, unbelievers because of its unqualified and unblinking denial of the Resurrection. It speaks to believers because it accepts the importance of what is denied, and accepts unflinchingly that one who abandons Christianity has much to lose. The poem's compelling power derives from the skill with which the poet uses the language of the New Testament to negate the New Testament's key message.

Some have thought that Clough protests too much: surely, to write the poem he must have retained at least a vestige of belief – perhaps he is even covertly exhorting to faith by painting a Christless world as unbearably bleak. Support for this view might be sought in the fact that Clough went on to write a poem entitled *Easter Day II*, which proclaims 'In the true Creed / He is yet risen indeed / Christ is yet risen'. But it is clear that the kind of resurrection affirmed in this second poem is not a literal one, but one compatible with Jesus being, and remaining, dead. The poem – much less powerful than *Easter Day* itself – is not a reaffirmation of traditional Christianity, but simply a softening of the pessimism that accompanied its denial.

Sit if ye will, sit down upon the ground,
Yet not to weep and wail, but calmly look around.
  Whate'er befell,
  Earth is not hell;
Now, too, as when it first began,
Life is yet Life and Man is Man.
For all that breathe beneath the heaven's high cope,
Joy with grief mixed, with despondence hope.

Hope conquers cowardice, joy grief:
Or at the least, faith unbelief.
  Though dead, not dead;
  Not gone, though fled;
  Not lost, not vanished
  In the great Gospel and true Creed,
  He is yet risen indeed;
    Christ is yet risen.

(P, 203)

Though much inferior as a poem to *Easter Day*, this sequel may well be a fairer reflection of Clough's own state of mind at this time. The best known of all his poems, 'Say not the Struggle', written not long after, breathes the same note of optimism triumphing over despair, but this time in a secular context. The poem was first drafted in Clough's Rome notebook, and was an attempt to console himself and his readers for the failure of the democratic cause in Rome and throughout Europe. In its initial form it ran as follows:

Say not the struggle naught availeth
  The labour and the blood are vain
The enemy faints not, nor faileth
  And as things have been things remain

If hopes were dupes, fears may be liars;
  Beyond that parting cloud hard by
Your comrades chase e'en now the fliers
  E'en now upraise the victor cry

For while these billows, vainly breaking
  Seem scarce one painful inch to gain
Far back through creeks its passage making
  The silent seas came flooding in

> Nor is't by eastward windows only
> When daylight comes, comes in the light;
> In front, the sun climbs slow, how slowly;
> Behind you, look, the field is bright.
> (P, 677)

In this form, the poem would never have achieved its later popularity. No sooner was it on the page than Clough began to polish it, cancelling, substituting, rewriting every other word. But the most significant of his changes was to the last line: 'But westward, look, the land is bright'. The contrast between the rising sun and the light from the west was a metaphor that Clough had used before, more dexterously, in *Epistraussion*; in its present context the meaning must be that since the revolutions had now failed throughout Europe, only America held out hope for democracy.

The change was made after Clough had returned to England. Perhaps it was triggered by a letter from Margaret Fuller, who had travelled to Florence when the Roman Republic collapsed. The letter recalled their days together. Clough had told her, she said, that marriage must have been an advantage for her, 'because the position of a unmarried woman in our time is not desirable'. On the contrary, she said, she had found the liberty of single life most precious.

> With Ossoli I liked when no one knew of our relation, and we passed our days together in the mountains, or walked beautiful nights amid the ruins of Rome. But for the child I should have wished to remain as we were, and feared we should lose much by entering on the jog-trot of domestic life. However, I do not find it so; we are of mutual solace and aid about the dish and spoon part, yet enjoy our free rambles as much as ever. (M, 281)

Fuller told Clough that she planned to return to America, with its 18 million people with their railroads, telegraphs and ridiculous phobias, 'but with ever-successful rush and bang'. A short time afterwards she sailed to New York with her husband and infant son. The ship on which they sailed was wrecked off the coasts of Long Island, and all passengers were drowned. Clough preserved as a relic a note he had received from her in Rome, thanking him for a gift of eau de Cologne to the patients in the hospital. When he became engaged in 1852 he sent the note to his fiancée with the words 'Take care of the enclosed, my dearest; and be tender to the memory of the good Margaret. I thought you would like to see her writing' (M, 262).

Whether or not 'Westward, look, the land is bright' was meant as a compliment to Margaret, without its final line the poem could not have been used for its most famous purpose, namely to plead, nearly a century later, for the involvement of the United States in the Second World War. In a radio speech in April 1941, Winston Churchill praised and encouraged the commitment of Franklin D. Roosevelt to the Allied cause. He ended the broadcast by quoting in their entirety Clough's last two stanzas. The poem, he told a friend at the time, had stayed in his mind ever since he had first heard it more than thirty years before (Jenkins, 652).[11]

Notes

1 Michael Thorpe, (ed.), *Clough, the Critical Heritage*, New York 1982, pp. 53, 97.
2 Clough's Roman diary is in Balliol College, MS.441; extracts are printed in Patrick Scott's edition of *Victorian Texts I: Amours de Voyage by Arthur Hugh Clough*, St Lucia, Queensland 1976, p.77).
3 Letter in possession of the author.
4 See below, p. 263.
5 Owen Chadwick, *A History of the Popes, 1830–1914*, Oxford 1998, p. 89.
6 The deleted lines are given in full in Patrick Scott's edition of the poem, *Victorian Texts I*, pp. 40–75.
7 Here I follow Patrick Scott's edition, *Victorian Texts I*, pp. 8–11.
8 Patrick Scott, *Victorian Texts I*, p. 7.
9 K. Lake (ed.), *Memorials of William Charles Lake*, London 1901, p. 78.
10 For the honour of Clough's scansion, the reader should note that in the nineteenth century English people put the stress (correctly) on the second syllable of 'Pantheon'.
11 Roy Jenkins, *Churchill*, London 2001, p. 652.

Chapter Seven
The London Years

From Italy Clough returned to England via Switzerland: it had long been his ambition to 'Stand in the shadow of Mont Blanc'. From Geneva he travelled up the valley of the Arve to Chamouni, and there he was inspired to write a ballade 'Les Vaches' – eight stanzas of uneven length – placed in the mouth of a cowgirl singing to her cows.

> The skies have sunk and hid the upper snow,
> Home, Rose, and home, Provence and La Palie
> The rainy clouds are filing fast below,
> And wet will be the path, and wet shall we.
> Home, Rose, and home, Provence and La Palie.
> (P, 207)

So runs the first verse, and in the remainder of the poem the girl meditates on her lover, absent for a year. Will he be faithful to her? Shall she be faithful to him? The poem is a pleasing trifle, in the *Lieder* tradition.

Clough was back in London by the end of August 1849. On the last day of the month he was entertained to dinner by Jane Brookfield, the model for Amelia in W. M. Thackeray's *Vanity Fair*. Mrs Brookfield found him a difficult guest: he simply sat at the foot of her sofa, and scrutinized her face, without saying anything. 'His eyes cut one through and through' she complained in a letter to Thackeray in Paris. In reply, Thackeray described his first meeting with her guest, in 1848. 'I took a very great liking and admiration for Clough. He is a real poet and a simple affectionate creature. Last year we went to Blenheim from Oxford and I liked him for sitting down in the Inn Yard and beginning to teach a child to read off a bit of Punch which was lying on the ground. Subsequently he sent me his poems which were rough but contained the real genuine solid[?] flare, I think.'[1]

The uncomfortable evening with Mrs Brookfield began a dismal period in Clough's life. His time as Principal of University Hall was brief and unhappy, marked by constant friction with the Hall's governing body. Before he had even accepted the post, he had been alerted to likely problems by his old friend Gell, who had now returned to England from running his college in Tasmania in order to marry the daughter of his former superior as Lieutenant Governor of Van Diemens Land, the famous explorer Sir John Franklin. Gell had cast an experienced eye over the statutes of the Hall and had warned that they left the principal with too little power and the governors with too much (B, 341). After only a few days in post, Clough wrote to Tom Arnold to complain that intolerance 'is not confined to the cloisters of Oxford or the pews of the Establishment, but comes up like the tender herb – partout'. In the end, he predicted 'I shall be kicked out for mine heresies' sake' (M, 273).

Initially, the Governors were pleased enough, and regarded Clough as a catch. One of them, Wordsworth's friend Henry Crabb Robinson, wrote in his diary at the beginning of October 'He is modest and amiable, as well as full of talent, and I have no doubt that we have made a very good choice in him.' Robinson thought Clough was wise not to talk about his own religious opinions; but after a while he found that the new Principal was silent on other topics too, and was generally criticized for taciturnity. As Clough's widow wrote of this period in her posthumous memoir 'he became compressed and reserved to a degree quite unusual with him, both before and afterwards. He shut himself up, and went through his life in silence' (PPR, 39).

In October 1849 A. C. Tait had resigned the headmastership of Rugby to become Dean of Carlisle. Speculation about his successor was rife. Jane Arnold, in a letter to Tom, listed the candidates ('mostly deplorable'): Lake, Cotton, Simpkinson, Goulburn and Gell. Gell, now a temporary curate at St Martin's in the Fields, was preferred by Clough and all the Arnold family, while Lake was the favourite of the Rugby masters, who thought Gell insufficiently scholarly. Matt wrote to Jane in protest:

> Lake is, like most people who have lived at Oxford all their lives without being born philosophers – a perfect child – if all does not go as he wishes it, he can neither keep his temper, nor conceal that he has lost it. He would be as unfit as possible, I think. (L, 161)

From Rugby, Shairp wrote to Clough 'If you had not been so erratic a bird we might have had you' (M, 277). In December the post was given to E. M. Goulburn, a former dean of Merton, who soon showed himself to have been a disastrous choice.

A brief Christmas vacation did nothing to raise Clough's spirits. 'London generally speaking is lonely' he told Shairp on the second day of the new year, 'A loneliness relieved by evening parties is not delightful' (M, 278). It is not surprising that Clough should miss the common room life of Oriel, even though he had often found it stifling when he was forced to be part of it. Moreover, leaving Oxford put a distance between Clough and friends in other colleges like Jowett, Stanley, Prichard and Congreve.

There is a passage in *Mari Magno* which biographers often take to be a description of Clough's life at this time.

> He has a life small happiness that gives,
> Who friendless in a London lodging lives,
> Dines in a dingy chop-house, and returns
> To a lone room, while all within him yearns
> For sympathy, and his whole nature burns
> With a fierce thirst for some one – is there none? –
> To expend his human tenderness upon.
>
> (P, 422)

But though Clough was lonely, his position was not at all as here described. His tied house was ample for entertainment, and he could eat his meals in company in Hall. Several of his old Oxford friends were now themselves in London or nearby. Frederick Temple and F. T. Palgrave were both at Kneller Hall at Twickenham, an experimental training college for teachers in the workhouses. He could entertain friends like these in Hall, where he quite enjoyed eating with the young men. In place of the old Oriel breakfasts with Matt and Tom Arnold, he began to take afternoon walks and dinner with Matt and his younger brother Edward (M, 273, 279).

It is possible that during 1849 there had been something of a cooling of relations between Matt and Clough after each had reacted so negatively to the other's published poetry. While in Rome Clough wrote only one letter to Matt, as compared with half a dozen to Palgrave. In September Arnold wrote to Clough from Thun, where in the previous year he had tarried for the sake of Marguerite's blue eyes. The letter begins 'It is long since I have communicated with you', and it continues in self-centred vein. There is no word about Clough's adventures in Rome, even though others of his friends had been worrying that he might get himself killed there (L, 156; M, 271). In the late summer the two poets were both in Switzerland, but made no attempt to join up with each other.

If there was any estrangement, it did not last long. In a letter to Tom Arnold in October 1849, Clough listed Matt, along with Emerson and Carlyle, as one of the profoundest thinkers of the age. He could hardly have known how he could pay a higher compliment. The compliment, however, might not have been appreciated by Matt, if he ever learnt of it. In the letter just quoted he described Carlyle as a 'moral desperado'.

Carlyle's radicalism was indeed beginning to take strange forms. At the end of 1849, now aged 54, he published the first of his *Latter Day Pamphlets*,

Thomas Carlyle

Lady Ashburton

'Occasional discourse on the Nigger question' in which he argued that the emancipation of slaves in the British Empire had been a terrible mistake. It had led to the moral ruin of the blacks who were now rotting away in sensuous idleness amid the wrecks of the plantations (Clubbe 1979: 485) On the other hand, Carlyle's savage denunciations of the contemporary ruling classes did not prevent him from accepting frequent invitations to the London and Hampshire establishments of Lady Harriet Baring, who in 1849 became, on the death of her father-in-law, Lady Ashburton. He attended a series of luxurious house-parties at the Ashburtons' Hampshire home, The Grange. He reconciled this with his conscience by making a terrible nuisance of himself whenever he was there.

Lady Ashburton had the reputation of being the most conspicuous woman in the society of the time. An earl's daughter, she did her best to conceal from herself that her husband's £60,000 a year was derived from banking. Philip Ziegler has written of her 'She was anxious to shine in the high aesthetic line, and turned the Grange into a menagerie where literary lions like Carlyle and Thackeray grazed among politicians and assorted grandees.' Visitors were impressed by the grandeur and splendour of the hospitality, managed by a groom of the chambers, a butler, an under-butler and a vast staff. Introduced by Carlyle, Clough became a member of this glittering socio-literary set, a cub among the elder lions.[2]

As well as a literary menagerie, The Grange was also a cauldron of Platonic loves. Carlyle's worship of Lady Ashburton ('the lamp of my dark path') drove his wife to distraction. With Thackeray came his friends the Brookfields, the husband a clerical school inspector and the wife, Jane, the long-term object of what Thackeray called his 'longing passion unfulfilled'. Sadly, Clough has left us no record of his impressions of either menages or menagerie. However, when, on his engagement, he wrote for his fiancée a year-by-year account of the main events of his life, among the items recalled from 1850 'The Grange' figured on equal terms with 'Italy' and with 'University Hall'.

When Clough was first appointed to University Hall his mother had suggested that she and Annie might move to London and live with him. The Principal's house consisted of eight rooms on two floors: four bedrooms, three sitting rooms and a kitchen: clearly there would have been room for the whole family (B, 363, 365). While he was in Rome, Arthur encouraged the idea: 'Mother would not have much cooking to do in London, for there would be the general kitchen to draw on like a bank.' By the spring of 1850, however, he had come down definitely against the proposal. 'Dull and dismal as Liverpool is' he told his mother 'still London is drearier to those who have no old acquaintance in it; and after 30 as I find, one is not very quick at forming new ones.' His prospects in Gordon Square were uncertain: he might leave, voluntarily or involuntarily, in a year or two, while if he stayed, he would probably marry. In either case, the female Cloughs would have to leave, and would find it difficult to rent a house in a respectable part of London. As for Annie, the devoted schoolmistress, 'she will be going into horrid places here as there: and she will have little or nothing else to do. Spite of fleas and noise and teetotums and all that, I think it is well enough that she confine herself on the whole to seeing the dirty children in the way she does at present' (M, 282–3). It is difficult to sort out in this letter how much is honest advice and how much is self-protection, but undoubtedly there is also a grain of snobbery. The people who would call, he told his mother, might be rather fine ladies, and it would take her some time to feel at ease with them. During his visits to the Ashburtons the author of *The Bothie* seems to have caught a certain infection.

Amid the general solitude and gloom, Clough continued to write poetry of high quality. An impressive product of the years 1849–51 is a series of poems based on the narratives of the Book of Genesis. A poetic drama, first published posthumously in 1869 with the title 'The Mystery of the Fall', was pieced together by Clough's widow from four manuscript notebooks and several eparate sheets. The modern standard edition prints it as an unfinished drama of 14 scenes with the title 'Adam and Eve'. This title is less suitable than Mrs Clough's, because powerful scenes in the sequence concern not just the first parents but also their children, the pious Abel and his murderer Cain. Indeed, it is quite possible that Clough had not one, but two, dramatic poems in mind when he wrote these verses.

The earliest poems in the sequence – which constitute scenes II–IV of the published version – were probably written as early as 1848. We see, first, Adam alone just after the Fall, trying to come to terms with the possibility that he has committed some disastrous, irretrievable act. Pangs of remorse alternate with calmer moments in which he dismisses such spasms as idle fits. First, he cries with limbs convulsed:

> Fool, fool; where am I? O my God! Fool, Fool!
> Why did we do't? Eve, Eve! where are you? quick!
> His tread is in the garden! Hither it comes!
> Hide us, O bushes, and ye thick trees hide!
> He comes on, on, on. Alack, and all these leaves,
> These petty, quivering and illusive blinds,
> Avail us nought; the light comes in and in,
> Displays us to ourselves; displays, ah, shame,
> Unto the inquisitive day our nakedness.
>
> (P, 169)

These lines are then dismissed as a passing, if terrible, possession, a curious new phenomenon. For a while, Adam sees himself as a mental alchemist, seeking the formula to transmute the drossy contents of his mind into something splendid and magnificent.

> Though tortured in the crucible I lie,
> Myself my own experiment, yet still
> I, or a something that is I indeed,
> A living, central, and more inmost I
> Within the scales of mere exterior me's
> I – seem eternal, O thou God, as Thou;
> Have knowledge of the Evil and the Good,
> Superior in a higher Good to both.

The Transcendental Ego haunted much of the philosophy of the nineteenth century, from Kant before its beginning to Wittgenstein after its end. But the alchemist Adam is closer to Faust than to Hegel:

> Really now, had I only time and space,
> And were not troubled with this wife of mine,
> And the necessity of meat and drink,
> I really do believe
> With time and space and proper quietude
> I could resolve this problem on my brain.
> But no, I scarce can stay one moment more
> To watch the curious seething process out.
> If I could only dare to let Eve see
> These operations, it is like enough
> Between us two we two could make it out.
> (P, 170)

We are all familiar with the scientist who is convinced that with a few years leisure and a sufficiently ample research grant he will be able to give a full and final explanation of the workings of the human mind in terms of his own discipline – whether it is biological genetics, or social Darwinism, or cognitive science, or whatever. It was a remarkable intuition of Clough's to see this kind of Luciferian ambition as the first fruits of original sin.

The focus of the next scene is the birth of Cain. Eve, with her newborn, finds Paradise returned. But Adam looks on the baby Cain with a pessimistic eye: he is beginning to believe in the possibility of inherited sinfulness.

> Hope not too greatly, neither fear for him,
> Feeling on thy breast his small compressing lips
> And glorying in the gift they draw from thee

Hope not too greatly in thyself and him.
And hear me, O young mother – I must speak.
This child is born of us, and therefore like us
Is born of us, and therefore is as we;
Is born of us, and therefore is not pure.
(P, 172)

By the beginning of the third scene Adam has convinced himself that the story of the Fall is just a feminine fantasy of Eve's.

Adam: What is it then you wish me to subscribe to?
That in a garden we were put by God,
Allowed to eat of all the trees but one,
Somehow – I don't know how – a serpent tempted,
And eat we did, and so were doomed to die;
Whereas before we were meant to live for ever.
Meantime, turned out –
Eve: You do not think then, Adam
We have been disobedient to God?
(P, 174)

Adam replies that he cannot conceive that God gave such a command as 'you shall not touch these apples here' – but if he did, then they did no wrong in eating them. Shocked, Eve says that if God said – God being God – 'You shall not' that is a commandment his creatures must obey. Adam replies defiantly:

My child, God does not speak to human minds
In that unmeaning arbitrary way;
God were not God, if so, and Good not Good.

He refuses to acknowledge that they have done anything wrong. Eve reminds him that when Cain was born he said 'He's born of us and therefore is not pure'. Adam responds that his remark was rash and foolish – 'a first baby is a strange surprise'. He is determined that the story of the Fall shall not be passed on to their children, and commands:

Put not, when days come on, your own strange whim
And misconstruction of my idle words
Into the tender brains of our poor young ones
(P, 176)

These three scenes add up to a self-contained treatment of the story of the Fall. The background assumption of the drama is that the Genesis narrative is true. The theme developed in its scenes appears to be that the effects of sin are successive layers of self-delusion, with the female less deluded than the male. This version of the drama may have been completed as early as July 1848, when Matthew Arnold wrote 'productions like your Adam and Eve are not suited to me at present' (L, 114, 116).

During the next year or so, Clough developed the poem in a different direction. He wrote a new scene to be placed in front of the original drama, a scene in which from the start Adam is anxious to demythologize the expulsion from Paradise. At the beginning of the poem Eve, pregnant with Cain, is oppressed with a sense of guilt; as the scene opens she has been rehearsing the story of the serpent and the forbidden fruit. Adam refuses to accept it; the whole story is a fantasy.

> What!
> Because I plucked an apple from a twig
> Be damned to death eternal! parted from Good,
> Enchained to Ill? No, by the God of Gods,
> No, by the living will within my breast,
> It cannot be and shall not; and if this,
> This guilt of your distracted fantasy,
> Be our experiment's sum, thank God for guilt,
> Which makes me free!
>
> But thou, poor wife, poor mother, shall I say?
> Big with the first maternity of Man
> Draw'st from thy teeming womb thick fancies fond,
> That with confusion mix thy delicate brain;
> Fondest of which, and cloudiest call the dream
> (Yes, my beloved, hear me, it is a dream)
> Of the serpent and the apple and the curse.
>
> (P, 166)

It had all begun with a dream of Eve's on the day when she first encountered death: a lamb had fallen from a rock and broken its neck. That night, a harmless snake gliding by their bed gave her a nightmare. Adam had tried to soothe her to sleep:

> In vain; for soon
> I felt thee gone, and opening widest eyes
> Beheld thee kneeling on the turf; hands now

Clenched and uplifted high; now vainly outspread
To hide a burning face and streaming eyes
And pale small lips that muttered faintly 'Death'.
And thou woulds't fain depart; thou saidst the place
Was for the likes of us too good.
(P, 166)

Eve's fantasy forced them to leave their comfortable home for a barren countryside and 'a residence sadly exposed to wind and rain'. But Adam admits that he too, has moments when he half-believes Eve's dream to be true.

Listen! I too when homeward, weary of toil,
Through the dark night I have wandered in rain and wind,
Bewildered, haply, scared, – I too have lost heart,
And deemed all space with angry power replete,
Angry, almighty; and panic-stricken have cried,
'What have I done? What wilt thou do to me?'
Or with the coward's 'No I did not, I will not',
Belied my own soul's self.
(P, 167)

But he urges himself to put away such childish dreams. But Eve cannot put aside the horror that haunts her in her pregnancy:

The questionings of ages yet to be,
The thinkings and cross-thinkings, self-contempts,
Self-horror; all despondencies, despairs,
Of multitudinous souls on souls to come
In me imprisoned, fight, complain and cry.
(P, 168)

A reader, taking this scene by itself, may give more credit to the male scepticism than to the female foreboding. But, as we have seen, the other scenes – that in this new version come later in the series – present the male as more adept than the female in the work of self-deception. The composite drama is a balanced whole in which the poet seeks to avoid taking sides with either interpretation.

Critics have complained that it is anachronistic to make Adam and Eve discuss the critical issues raised by the Tübingen school and the ethical problems that concerned philosophers like Kierkegaard. But of course to speak of 'anachronism' here is itself to treat Adam and Eve as historical characters belonging to a particular time and culture. What Clough does here with

Genesis is what he did with the Gospels in *Easter Day*. In each case he takes a key doctrine of orthodoxy – the Fall, the Resurrection – and examines it by spelling out the consequences of taking it as literally true or literally false.

According to many centuries of Christian theology, the sin of Adam and Eve not only brought death and grief into the world, but also gravely impaired human intellectual faculties. If that is the case, then not only within critical scepticism, but within dogmatic orthodoxy, the question arises: what, after the Fall, did our first parents think had happened? Could they with any clarity remember the events in Paradise? If so, could they interpret them correctly? Clough's poem takes these issues seriously. The dialogues in *Adam and Eve* may be absurd as actual conversations between primitive human beings, but what Clough is doing here is turning latent nonsense into patent nonsense. The nonsense he expresses may contain important messages about ourselves – in particular, about the perennial topics of self-knowledge and self-delusion.

* * *

In the years between 1849 and 1851 Clough wrote poems of various lengths in various metres about other characters in Genesis: Cain and Abel, Lamech, Isaac and Rebecca, and Jacob with his wives Rachel and Leah. Byron had written a famous poem about Cain: in Rome Clough started his own treatment of the topic. On the back of a manuscript of a piece of *Amours* he wrote a monologue for Cain holding the body of Abel. Cain's first emotion is surprise – nobody, after all, has ever seen a dead human being before; the first death in the Bible is that of the lamb killed in sacrifice by Abel himself.

What? fallen? so quickly down, so easily felled,
And so completely? Why, he does not move.
Will he not stir – will he not breathe again?
Still as a log, still as his own dead lamb.
Dead, is it then? O wonderful! O strange!
Dead! Dead! And we can slay each other then?
If we are wronged, why, we can right ourselves;
If we are plagued and pestered with a fool
That will not let us be, nor leave us room
To do our will and shape our path in peace,
We can be rid of him.

(P, 179)

To this scene, then or later, Clough added others to precede it. One is a monologue for Abel, a mother's boy, highly devout, who looks down on his brother and father as unspiritual and godless, and is very conscious of his standing as one of God's elect. Another is a monologue for Cain, riled by his brother's smugness, and anxious to perform some action to assert his own independence – 'to give proof I also am, as Adam is, a man'. Other scenes bring Cain before his parents after the murder, and lead (in alternative versions) to a final curse or a final forgiveness.

Clough did not make clear whether he intended to bring together the Adam and Eve scenes and the Cain and Abel scenes to make up, together, a single drama. Blanche Clough was, I believe, well inspired when she did so. The case for uniting them is not just that they were written during the same periods of composition. Rather, it is that the Cain and Abel episodes work out further the characters that are given to Adam and Eve in the earlier scenes. Adam blames Eve for causing Abel's death by encouraging him in superstitious practices like sacrifice. Eve exhorts Cain to repentance and prayer, but in response he asks her to curse him: he seeks not atonement but punishment. It is only when Cain comes to say goodbye to Adam that he hears about the Fall for the first time. Adam, having told the story, recommends that it should be forgotten.

> . . . whether a dream, and, if it were a dream,
> A transcript of an inward spiritual fact
> (As you suggest, and I allow might be)
> Not the less true because it was a dream
> I know not.
>
> (P, 182)

In a different version, Adam tries to comfort Cain by speaking of the healing touch of time. But Cain insists that to forget the past is not to undo the past. Nothing will bring back warmth into Abel's clay, or the gentleness of love into his face.

However Clough would have concluded the drama if he had brought it to conclusion, the dramatic impetus of the play as we have it comes to an end with Cain's departure into the wilderness:

> Welcome Fact, and Fact's best brother, Work;
> Welcome the conflict of the stubborn soil,
> To toil the livelong day, and at the end,
> Instead of rest, re-carve into my brow
> The dire memorial mark of what still is.
> Welcome this worship, which I feel is mine;
> Welcome this duty –
> – the solidarity of life
> And unity of individual soul.
>
> (P, 184)

Just as in *Paradise Lost* the most heroic figure is the wicked angel Lucifer, so here, one feels, of all the members of that unhappy family it is the murderer Cain with whom the poet most identifies.

The Bible traces out the posterity of Cain, and tells us that his great-great-great-grandson was called Lamech. The fourth chapter of Genesis tells us that Lamech married two wives, Adah and Zillah, and puts in his mouth a single, puzzling, line 'Hear my voice, ye wives of Lamech, hearken unto my speech: for I have slain a man to my wounding and a young man to my hurt.' Clough turned this into the chorus of a hundred-line piece of blank verse, 'The Song of Lamech'. The poem is in fact mainly concerned with the story of Cain, as told by Lamech to his wives. It may indeed be an earlier treatment than the dramatic version in *The Mystery of the Fall*; but whether earlier or later, it is a much softer and less powerful treatment of the myth. It has a gentle, lilting rhythm and builds up to a happy ending. Adam, in response to a dream, goes to seek out Cain, eastward of Eden in the Land of Nod.

And Adam laid upon the head of Cain
His hand, and Cain bowed down, and slept and died.
And a deep sleep on Adam also fell,
And in his slumber's deepest he beheld
Standing before the gate of Paradise
With Abel, hand in hand, our father Cain.

(P, 190)

Lamech's two wives are not fleshed out in the poem; but the bigamous patriarchs of the Old Testament had a fascination for Clough, still seeking a wife to satisfy both his sensuous and his moral needs. In *The Bothie* Philip's well-wishers utter the prayer 'Go, be the wife in thy house both Rachel and Leah to thee'. The poem 'Jacob's Wives', written at about the same time as 'The Song of Lamech', spells out this biblical allusion in an antiphonal characterization of the passionate Rachel and the matronly Leah. Jacob sits in the evening beside the door of his tent:

And Rachel spake and said, The nightfall comes;
Night, which all day I wait for, and for thee.

And Leah also spake, The day is done;
My lord with toil is weary, and would rest.

In six stanzas each wife presses on Jacob her claims for preference. Then, each wife under the veil of a pretended tolerance savages the other.

And Rachel said, But we will not complain,
Though all life long an alien unsought third
She trouble our companionship of love.

And Leah answered, No; complain we not,
Though year on year she loiter in the tent,
A fretful, vain, unprofitable wife.
(P, 212)

After another eight stanzas of balanced abuse between the wives, at the end of the poem honours are even.

And Rachel wept and ended, Ah my life!
Though Leah bear thee sons on sons, methought
The Child of love, late-born were worth them all.

And Leah ended, Father of my sons,
Come, thou shalt dream of Rachel if thou wilt,
So Leah fold thee in a wife's embrace.
(P, 214)

None of these biblical poems were published in Clough's lifetime. He wrote drafts and fair copies in notebooks which survive, mainly in the Bodleian library in Oxford. The notebooks bear titles, given by the Clough family, which indicate their principal contents, such as 'Adam and Eve notebooks I and II', '1849–50 (Lamech) Notebook'.

*   *   *

In the year 1850 two events marked an epoch in English poetry. On 23 April Wordsworth died. Matthew Arnold travelled to Fox How to attend the funeral, and was asked to write an elegy.

Goethe in Weimar sleeps, and Greece,
Long since, saw Byron's struggle cease.
But one such death remain'd to come;
The last poetic voice is dumb –
We stand to-day by Wordsworth's tomb

In May Matt submitted the dirge to Clough for his approval: it appeared in print in June.

On the first day of the same month Alfred Tennyson published *In Memoriam*, the poem which established him as the leading poet of the age. Shortly after, he married his sweetheart of 17 years. He was married from the house of an old Rugby friend of Matthew Arnold, who later in the year brought the two poets together. Tennyson had by now become Poet Laureate in Wordsworth's stead (L, 170–2).

In the Arnold family it was a year of change. In January Tom Arnold had moved from New Zealand to Hobart, where he had been appointed Inspector of Schools for Van Diemen's Land. Within a month he had met and fallen in love with Julia Sorrell, the daughter of the registrar of the supreme court: his proposal of marriage was accepted on 20 March. In April Jane became engaged to a Quaker philanthropist, William Edward Foster. Matt, who had no great liking for his prospective brother-in-law, invited Clough one day in May to make his acquaintance at breakfast in London. Finally, by the time the news of Tom's engagement reached England in July, Clough was able to report '[Matt] is himself deep in a flirtation with Miss Wightman, daughter of the Judge. It is thought it will come to something, for he has actually been to Church to meet her' (M, 286).

Matt and Clough arranged to spend a vacation together. Clough was to travel to Interlaken in July, and Matt was to join him in Switzerland after attending his sister's marriage. However, Matt's own love-making was not going well. Judge Wightman thought the salary of a mere secretary insufficient to support his daughter in appropriate style, and forbade any meeting of the two lovers. The Wightmans left for a continental tour, and Matt rushed after them incognito. When Jane was married on 15 August he failed to appear, and the bride had to be given away by her younger brother Edward. Matt also failed to keep his rendezvous with Clough. He continued his pursuit of Fanny Lucy Wightman like a latter-day Claude. He stayed in the Rhineland, consoling himself by reading Spinoza and writing poems with titles like 'Longing' and 'Separation'.

Clough, left solitary, went south to Venice. He was there on the feast of the Assumption, the day of Jane's wedding. He visited the public garden, and imagined a voice saying to him:

This rather stupid place to-day
It's true, is most extremely gay;
And rightly – the Assunzione
Was always a *gran' funzione*.
What numbers at the landing lying!
What lots of pretty girls, too, hieing
Hither and thither – coming, going,
And with what satisfaction showing,

To our male eyes unveiled and bare
Their dark exuberance of hair,
Black eyes, rich tints, and sundry graces
Of classic pure Italian faces! . . .
'Tis here, I see, the custom too
For damsels eager to be lovered
To go about with arms uncovered;
And doubtless there's a special charm
In looking at a well-shaped arm.
(P, 222–3)

These lines were later taken up into a dramatic drama, to which Clough gave the name *Dipsychus*. Just as in Rome he jotted down self-standing poems which later became integral parts of *Amours de Voyage*, so while in Venice he sketched a number of vignettes which were later incorporated in *Dipsychus*. Such was, for instance, a barcarolle about a trip on the Grand Canal which begins:

Afloat; we move. Delicious! Ah,
What else is like the gondola?
This level floor of liquid glass
Begins beneath it swift to pass.
It goes as though it went alone
By some impulsion of its own.
How light it moves, how softly! Ah
Were all things like the gondola
(P, 237)

From the entries in the Venice notebook we can trace Clough's tourist journeys. In the Academy he compares Titian's painting of the Assumption with a modern depiction of Byron's death at Missolonghi. He takes the *barchetta* to the Lido and thinks once again of Byron, riding upon the sands of Malmocco. He finds the Piazza San Marco overcrowded, but revels in the view from the bell-tower.

At a step, I crown the Campanile's top,
And view all mapped below: islands, lagoon,
An hundred steeples and a million roofs,
The fruitful champaign and the cloud-capt Alps
And the broad Adriatic.
(P, 275)

Most of these self-standing entries found their way eventually into the dramatic structure of *Dipsychus*; but some of the entries in the Venice notebook are already in the form of a dialogue between two characters, at this point named Mephisto and Faustulus. Most remarkable are a series of stories in iambic tetrameters, placed in the mouth of Mephisto, describing encounters with prostitutes. Here are two examples:

Tiring of cafes, quays and barks
I turned for shade into St Marks
I sat a while – studying mosaics
Which we unauthorised laics
Have leave to like – a girl slips by
And gives the signal with her eye
She takes the door; I follow out:
Curious, amused, but scarce in doubt
While street on street she winds about
Heedful at corners, but *du reste*
Assured and grandly self-possessed
Trips up a stairs at last, and lands me
Up with her petticoats, and hands me
Much as one might a *pot de chambre*
The vessel that relieves *le membre*
No would-be-pretty hesitation
Most business-like in her vocation
She but the brief half instant lingers
That strikes her bargain with five fingers.
(P, 692)

O yes, that was a rare adventure
I took the pains to make you enter;
You saw the lady well undrest,
And wishing her a good night's rest
Went off because (you said) twas Sunday
You'd probably return on Monday
(P, 690)

These notebook entries never found their way into printed versions of *Dipsychus*, whether in the nineteenth or twentieth century; at best they lurked in footnotes and appendices. But in the standard edition of 1974 the following was finally given an honoured place:

Here's many a lady still waylaying
And sundry gentlemen purveying.
And if twere only just to see
The room of an Italian fille,
Twere worth the trouble and the money.
You'd like to find – I found it funny –
The chamber *où vous faites vôtre affaire*
Stands nicely fitted up for prayer;
While dim you trace along one end
The Sacred Supper's length extend,
The calm Madonna o'er your head
Smiles, *con bambino* on the bed.
(P, 233)

Dipsychus is in very rudimentary form in the Venice notebooks, and the story of its development belongs to the next chapter. But many a stanza throws light on Clough's interests and observations during this August visit.

* * *

During the year of revolutions Venice had revolted from Austria, and had been declared a Republic. It was reconquered by the Austrians in the summer of 1849, shortly after the fall of Mazzini's Rome. The Venice notebooks contain a number of references to the Austrian occupation, and one vignette shows the Clough-like Faustulus insulted by a Croatian soldier. He has to resist the suggestion that he challenge the man to a duel. Mephisto teases:

Oh never mind, 'twont come to fighting –
Only some verbal small requiting;
Or give your card – we'll do't by writing.
He'll not stick to it. Soldiers too
Are cowards, just like me or you.
What! not a single word to throw at
This snarling dog of a d——d Croat?
(P, 255)

During this same visit to Italy Clough commemorated the heroes of the Risorgimento in a poem *Peschiera*, named after the fortress captured by the Piedmontese in 1848 and lost a year later to the Austrians under General Radetzky.

The tricolor a trampled rag
Lies, dirt and dust; the lines I track
By sentry-boxes yellow black
Lead up to no Italian flag.
I see the Croat soldier stand
Upon the grass of your redoubts;
The Eagle with his black wing flouts
The breadth and beauty of your land.

The poem's message is that the memory of Lombard gallantry in the defence of Peschiera will give pride and hope to those who now endure Austrian servitude. The poem, written in the metre of *In Memoriam*, was a tribute to Tennyson as well as to the Risorgimento. It ends with an echo of his poem's most famous couplet.

This voice did on my spirit fall
Peschiera, when thy bridge I crost,
''Tis better to have fought and lost
Than never to have fought at all.'
(P, 300)

Retracing his steps through Switzerland in September 1850 Clough consoled himself for the dreary prospect of London by drafting on his Geneva hotel bill a poem in rhyming pentameters celebrating the delight of the summer's escape from the city. Entitled 'July's Farewell' it addresses the countryside:

I come, I come, upon the heart's wings fly to you
Ye dreary lengths of brick and flag, good-bye to you,
Ambitious hopes and money's mean anxieties.
And worldly-wise decorum's false proprieties
And politics and news and fates of nations too,
And philanthropic sick investigations too,
And company and jests and feeble witticisms,
And talk of talk, and criticism of criticisms
I come, I come, ye banks and bowers, to hide in you,
And once again, ye loves and joys, confide in you . . .
(P, 302)

Life in London on his return was as frustrating as Clough expected. The Council of University Hall continually interfered with the domestic arrangements, and gave orders to the Principal's staff behind his back, and encouraged them to spy on the students. In an outraged letter at the end of October, heavily blotted and cancelled and probably never sent, Clough complained that he was treated no better than a housekeeper (B, 409). In February he was hauled before the Council and rebuked for being unwilling to expel a student 'because his bill for malt-liquor is large, and because he occasionally plays at cards'. Under the statutes – which Gell had warned him against – he was forced to acquiesce in the expulsion. He pointedly refused to offer the Council any advice on how to refill the vacancy or increase the number of students beyond the existing twelve (M, 288, 294).

There were, however, consolations in the winter of 1850–1. The Chair of English Literature and Language at University College became vacant when the Scottish divine Alexander Scott resigned to become the first principal of the Owens college for working men in Manchester. Clough applied for the chair, with testimonials from Frederick Temple and H. H. Vaughan the Oxford Professor of Modern History. He was appointed, and gave a series of lectures on English literature from Chaucer to Scott. His lecture notes have survived, and some have been published: for the most part they are judicious without being exciting. One of the most interesting, on Wordsworth, was delivered late in his professorship, probably in 1852: it analyses the interrelationships between the romantic poets.

> Out of Wordsworth and Byron came forth Shelley; nor is Keats (there is no such thing) an independent genius. We may remark also, how, as the brief career of Byron encloses within itself the yet briefer life of Shelley and Keats's briefest of all, so is Byron himself included in the larger arc of Scott and the yet larger arc of Wordsworth.

In general popularity, the young Wordsworth was displaced by Scott; Scott as a poet had to yield to Byron; but after Byron died young and Scott in premature age, Wordsworth again came into his own.

The lecture teaches us what elements in a poet Clough most valued. Wordsworth's special virtue, he said, was the infinite toil and labour that he expended on style, on the nice and exquisite felicities of poetic diction. He lacked the vigour and heartiness of Scott, and the sweep and fervour of Byron: but in the pursuit of permanent beauty of expression, in achieving harmony between thought and word, they were mere negligent schoolboys in comparison.

Poetry, like science, has its final precision; and there are expressions of poetic knowledge which can no more be rewritten than could the elements of geometry. There are pieces of poetic language which, try as men will, they will simply have to recur to, and confess that it has been done before them.

There is hardly anything in Byron or Scott, Clough says, that later generations will not think they can say over again quite as well: not so with the best of Wordsworth.

Clough admits, however, that Wordsworth wrote far too much. To find the rich spots of pure beauty, you have to traverse waste acres of dull verse that had better been prose. Moreover, Wordsworth was inclined to place feeling above fact. 'He is apt to wind up his short pieces with reflections upon the way in which, hereafter, he expects to reflect upon his present reflections.' His excessive emphasis on nature palls: Clough admits that he cannot heartily sympathize with repeated poems to the daisy. 'Blue sky and white cold, larks and linnets, daisies and celandines —these it appears are 'the proper subject of mankind'; not, as we used to think, the wrath of Achilles, the guilt and remorse of Macbeth, the love and despair of Othello.'

How does Wordsworth compare, from a moral point of view, with Scott and Byron? His frugal life at Grasmere was certainly more rational and dignified than Byron's hot career of wilfulness, or Scott's active but easy existence amid animal spirits. But 'to live in a quiet village, out of the road of all trouble and temptation, in a pure, elevated, high-moral sort of manner is, after all, no such very great a feat' (PPR, 315, 324). He has little to offer the man in the busy city street. The lecture is, of course, more interesting for what it tells us about Clough's own ambitions and discipline as a poet than as an overall critical judgement on Wordsworth.

In 1849 F. W. Newman, the Professor of Latin at University College whose resignation had made the University Hall post available for Clough, had published a book entitled *The Soul: its Sorrows and Aspirations*. Now, in 1850, Clough took the occasion of a review of this book to present the first public statement since leaving Oriel of his own religious position.

The review is written in a spirit of revulsion from the religious institutions Clough had rejected. He speaks of himself as a 'new convalescent' who finds it unpleasant to 'talk of his sick-room phenomena, to re-enter the diseased past, and dwell again among the details of pathology and morbid anatomy'. The object of his polemic, Clough insists, is not religion but 'devotionality'; 'The belief', he says 'that religion is, or in any way requires, devotionality, is, if not the most noxious, at least the most obstinate form of *ir*religion' (PPR, I, 299).

'Devotionality' appears to mean any prayerful relationship to God which takes the form of an imagined sense of closeness to a personal individual. 'Is it otherwise than superstitious for a Protestant devotee to recognise the sensuous presence of the Son, or for the Romish to believe in the visits of the Mother, who lived and died in Palestine eighteen centuries ago?' Such spiritual communion may, in abstract theory, be possible; but 'to expect it is perilous; to seek it pernicious; to make it our business here is simply suicidal'.

Clough goes on to attack the 'blind benevolence' fostered by Christianity. In Roman Catholic countries almsgiving leads to beggary and laziness; in England enlightened philanthropy peters out into exhortations to be resigned to one's poverty. He mocks those who claim to have discovered God as the designer of the universe ('Was it nobody, think you, that put salt in the sea for us?'). Prayer is important: but the best form of prayer is silence. If one cannot be content with silence it is best to stay with the prayerbook's daily service – the old Catholic forms have the prestige of antiquity and the superiority of taste over the new-fangled observances of the prayer meeting (PPR, 304).

The review is an embarrassing piece of work, bullying and bantering in turns, full of insensitive gibe and clumsy humour. Later in the year Clough redeemed himself by writing the finest of all his religious poems, *Hymnos Aumnos*. The sentiments of the poem are not very different from the review; but in style and sensitivity it is as much superior as the Book of Common Prayer is to an impromptu prayer-meeting. The first stanza begins with an invocation to the incomprehensible Godhead:

O Thou whose image in the shrine
Of human spirits dwells divine;
Which from that precinct once conveyed
To be to outer day displayed,
Doth vanish, part, and leave behind
Mere blank and void of empty mind,
Which wilful fancy seeks in vain
With casual shapes to fill again.

The poem starts from the assumption that the place to look for God is in the individual's inmost soul ('The Kingdom of God is within you'). Well and good; but attempts to give public expression to the God encountered in the soul yield only meaningless, self-contradictory utterances ('blank and void') or idle images with no contact with reality ('casual shapes').

After the second stanza of the poem has developed the theme of the impotence of human utterance to embody the divine, the third restates the manifesto of the Newman review that silence – inner as well as outer – is the only response to the ineffable.

O thou, in that mysterious shrine
Enthroned, as we must say, divine!
I will not frame one thought of what
Thou mayest either be or not.
I will not prate of 'thus' and 'so'
And be profane with 'yes' and 'no'.
Enough that in our soul and heart
Thou, whatso'er thou may'st be, art.

Clough's agnosticism, at this point, is radical. The *via negativa* is rejected as firmly as the *via positiva*. Not only can we not say of God what he is, we are equally impotent to say what he is not. The possibility, therefore, cannot be ruled out that one or other of the revelations claimed by others may after all be true.

> Unseen, secure in that high shrine
> Acknowledged present and divine
> I will not ask some upper air,
> Some future day, to place thee there;
> Nor say, nor yet deny, Such men
> Or women saw thee thus and then:
> They name was such, and there or here
> To him or her thou didst appear.

In the final stanza Clough pushes his agnosticism a stage further. Perhaps there is no way in which God dwells – even ineffably – as an object of the inner vision of the soul. Perhaps we could reconcile ourselves to the idea that God is not to be found at all by human minds. But even that does not take off all possibility of prayer.

> But only thou in that dim shrine,
> Unknown or known, remain, divine;
> There, or if not, at least in eyes
> That scan the fact that round them lies.
> The hand to sway, the judgement guide,
> In sight and sense, thyself divide:
> Be thou but there – in soul and heart,
> I will not ask to feel thou art.
>
> (P, 312)

The soul reconciled to the truth that there can be no analogue of seeing or feeling God, that nothing can be meaningfully said about him, can yet – if Clough is right – address him and pray to be illuminated by his power and be the instrument of this action. To this day there has been no more eloquent attempt to be faithful to a critical agnosticism and yet draw support from the consolations of theism.

For the rest of his life Clough retained, with regard to religion, this stance of an agnosticism that made room for prayer. There is nothing incoherent in such a position: an agnostic's prayer to a God whose existence he doubts is no more unreasonable than the act of a man adrift in the ocean, or stranded on a mountainside, who cries for help though he may never be heard or fires a signal which may never be seen. Perhaps it is a mistake to describe Clough's position as agnostic: he seems always to have retained a belief in some kind of divinity, but undoubtedly the God he worshipped was an unknown God. He also adopted a terrifyingly solitary conception of religion, which finds expression in a poem written at this time, entitled posthumously 'The Hidden Love':

> O let me love my love unto myself alone
> And know my knowledge to the world unknown;
> No witness to my vision call
> Beholding, unbeheld of all;
> And worship Thee, with Thee withdrawn apart,
> Who'er, Whate'er thou art,
> Within the closest veil of mine own most inmost heart.
>
> What is it then to me
> If others are inquisitive to see?
> Why should I quit my place to go and ask
> If other men are working at their task?
> Leave my own buried roots to go
> And see that other plants shall grow;
> And turn away from Thee, O Thou most Holy Light,
> To look if other orbs their orbits keep aright,
> Around their proper sun,
> Deserting Thee, and being undone:
>
> O let me love my love unto myself alone,
> And know my knowledge to the world unknown;
> And worship Thee, O hid One, O much sought
> As but man can or ought
> Within the abstracted'st shrine of my least breathed-on thought.
>
> (P, 240)

The soul's love of God, and knowledge of God, is no concern of others; it needs no witness to its vision of God, dim and secret as that vision is. Equally, the self is not to concern itself with the spiritual welfare of others: each human's course is as separate from each other human's as the orbit of one plant or planet is from its neighbour's. Clough could claim authority for his attitude from a passage in the sermon on the Mount which he quoted in a letter to Tom Arnold early in the year. 'Thou, when thou prayest, enter into thy closet, and when thou has shut thy door, pray to thy Father which is in secret' (Matt. 6, 6, M, 279).

On 31 August 1850 a Royal Commission was appointed by Lord John

Russell's government to inquire into the discipline, studies and revenue of Oxford University. Since Clough's last years at Oriel University reform had been a major concern of his Oxford friends, especially Jowett and Stanley. In 1848 Clough had written from Paris to Stanley proposing an Oxford revolution to match the French one. The aims of academic 'chartists' should be five: the abolition of subscription to the Thirty-Nine Articles; the reconstitution of college fellowships; a new Hebdomadal Board; the opening of matriculation to non-members of colleges; and a permanent commission of reform (M, 211). Now, in 1850, Stanley was made secretary of the Royal Commission, and at the end of the year Clough was able to put his proposals formally in evidence before it.

It took two years for the Commission to report, and two more years for its proposals to work their way through Parliament. But the University Reform Act of 1854 enacted almost everything that Clough wanted. In place of the old Hebdomadal Board, composed of heads of house, there was to be an elected Hebdomadal Board. The Vice-Chancellor was to be empowered to licence private halls in which non-college students could live. Antiquated fellowships were to be suppressed, and the funds used to support professorial chairs. The foremost of Clough's proposals, and the one which would have made most difference to his own Oxford career, namely the abolition of religious tests, was inserted into the Bill at the last minute on the motion of a Unitarian private member.

In some ways the reforms went further than Clough had demanded. The powers of Convocation – a chronically conservative body consisting of all MAs – were largely transferred to Congregation, the assemby of senior members actually studying or teaching in Oxford. Honours examinations, hitherto restricted to classics and law, had in 1850 been thrown open to new subjects such as history, law and natural science. Clough had long complained about the narrowness of the Oxford course and its tendency merely to repeat matter covered in school (PPR, 202). But he would have preferred to add to history 'the stronger aliment of Political Economy' (M, 248). It was only after his death, in 1872, that economics found a place on the syllabus – and then only in the pass school.[3]

Notes

1 Gordon N. Ray, *The Letters and Private Papers of William Makepeace Thackeray*, 4 vols, Oxford 1945–6, II, pp. 580–1.

2 Philip Ziegler, *The Sixth Great Power: Barings 1762–1929*, London 1992, p. 159.

3 M. C. Brock & M. C. Curthoys, *The History of the University of Oxford, VII, The Nineteenth Century*, Oxford 1997, pp. 331–62.

Chapter Eight
Dipsychus

1851, like the three previous years, was richly productive of verse. Clough filled half a dozen notebooks with drafts and fair copies of poems. Several poems express distaste for London. 'In the Great Metropolis' has as a refrain 'The devil take the hindmost, o!' – a rule, the poet says, learned at school, but applicable also in the church and at the bar, on 'change or at court. In 'Blessed are those who have not seen' the capital is compared to Sodom in a series of quatrains which ends with the hope 'that upon two million odd / transgressors in sad plenty / Mercy will of a gracious God / be shown – because of twenty' (P, 306; cf. Gen. 18, 23–33).

Naturally Clough did not exempt himself from his censure on the emptiness and folly of London life. One of the better poems of this period of dejection begins:

> Go, foolish thoughts, and join the throng
> Of myriads gone before;
> To flutter and flap and flit along
> The airy limbo shore
>
> Go, words of sport and words of wit,
> Sarcastic points and fine
> And words of wisdom wholly fit
> With folly's to combine
>
> Go, words of wisdom, words of sense,
> Which, while the heart belied,
> The tongue still uttered for pretence,
> The inner blank to hide.
>
> (P, 308)

At this time Clough was finding even his most profound intellectual inquiries pointless.

To spend uncounted years of pain,
Again, again, and yet again,
In working out in heart and brain
The problem of our being here . . .
Is this the object, end, and law
And purpose of our being here?
(P, 313)

Ever sensitive to variations of weather and season, he struck a more cheerful note in the spring. In a letter to Tom Arnold he included a poem 'On grass, on gravel, in the sun' celebrating the courting of a footman and a maid on a sunny April Sunday in Kensington Park. Once again he spelt out the message, familiar since 'Natura Naturans', of the harmony between nature's rhythms and human desires.

I read it in that arm she lays
  So soft on his; her mien
Her step, her very gown betrays
  What in her eyes were seen
That not in vain the young buds round
  The cawing birds above
The airs, the incense of the ground
  Are whispering, breathing, love

Ah years may come and years may bring
  The truth that is not bliss
But will they bring another thing
  That can compare with this?
(P, 315)

While this poem breathes Clough's own desire for success in love, others make clear that he was beginning to feel that life had passed him by. Now in his early thirties, he writes as if he was already an old man, and could only be a spectator of the loves of others. In 'Say, will it, when our hairs are grey' he expresses the fear that his intellectual achievements will end as 'feeble shapes of beggars grey / that, tottering on the public way / die out in doting, dim decay' (P, 314). His enjoyment of the exuberance of youth can only be vicarious, as he proclaims in 50 arthritic tetrameters.

Dance on, dance on, we see, we see
Youth goes alack, and with it glee
A boy the grown man ne'er can be;
Maternal thirty scarce shall find

The sweet sixteen long left behind;
Old folks must toil and scrape and strain
That boys and girls may once again
Be that for them they cannot be
But which it gives them joy to see.
(P, 316)

It is pleasant to think that within a year of writing these geriatric verses Clough was writing boyish lyrics to a new-found love. But for the moment the evening hours devoted to the writing of verse were the one thing that made life worth living during these dark days. In one poem he tells that he finds 'old friends dull and new friends dry, / dinners a bore and dancing worse / compared to the tagging of verse upon verse'. The notebooks of the period contain many passages describing the fascination and the difficulty of the poet's task of 'long hours of vext correction' spent in the endeavour 'to turn, to twist, reject, replace / And win the rebel rhymes to grace'.

If to write, rewrite, and write again,
Bite now the lip and now the pen,
Gnash in a fury the teeth, and tear
Innocent paper or it may be hair,
In endless chases to pursue
That swift escaping word that would do,
Inside and out turn a phrase, o'e and o'er,
Till all the little sense goes it had before,
If to be these things make one a poet,
I am one – Come and all the world may know it.
(P, 319)

Some of the finest verse Clough wrote at this time bore until his death the marks of the never-concluded struggle for perfection. *That children in their loveliness should die*, a suite of seven sonnets on the topic of death, survival and immortality, underwent many revisions, but continued to contain gaps which had to be filled by conjecture when the poems were posthumously published in 1869. The sequence is not easy to read: the thought is dense, and the syntax is complex. Nonetheless, once read, the sonnets haunt the reader. I quote the fifth of the series.

But if (as not by what the soul desired
Swayed in the judgement) wisest men have thought
And furnishing the evidence it sought
Man's heart have ever fervently required,

And story, for that reason deemed inspired
To every clime in every age hath taught
If in this human complex there be aught
Not lost in death as not in birth acquired
O then though cold the lips that did convey
Rich freights of meaning, dead each living sphere
Where thought abode and fancy loved to play
Thou, yet we think, somewhere somehow still art
The where and how doth not desire to hear.
(P, 326)

Not just to polish the expression, but to fix the thought itself, was a superhuman task: how sift out the sober truth from mythical tales, religious rituals, and philosophical ponderings on pre-existence, immortality and reincarnation? And who was the 'Thou', we wonder, whose death called forth these strivings in 1851?

We do know, however, that the principal task in that year which demanded tormented poetic effort was the attempt to turn the drafts he had brought back from Venice into a satisfactory poetical drama. The creation and revision of *Dipsychus* was to occupy him for years to come, and yet it was a task which was never finished. At his death he left behind only disjointed fragments which his wife and subsequent editors have struggled to present in structured form.

The basis for any reconstruction of *Dipsychus* is a series of five notebooks containing, between them, drafts for some 14 scenes. Sometimes it is not clear whether scene B is meant to be subsequent to, or an alternative for, scene A, so that it is uncertain how many scenes the drama is intended to contain. No two editions agree on the order in which the scenes are to be presented. The first published version of the poem (1869) and the modern standard edition (1974) agree in offering 14 scenes, but the earlier text unlike the later divides the poem into two parts (one of five scenes and one of nine).

Between the first drafts written in Venice and the texts left to posterity three stages of revision can be identified. There are two notebooks which are, collectively, called by editors and critics 'The First Revision': the first notebook, which has seven leaves cut away at the beginning, contains the scenes which appear in the middle of the published editions, and the remainder of the later scenes, including an epilogue, are entered into the second notebook. A third notebook, known as 'The Second Revision' contains the earlier half of the drama as printed, plus a prologue; it is held to be later than the other two, because it calls the characters in the drama 'Dipsychus and the Spirit' throughout, whereas in the First Revision these names appear only halfway through, replacing 'Faustulus' and 'Mephistopheles' which appear in the first few scenes. 'The Third Revision' is a fair copy of a much reduced version of the opening scenes of the drama (see P, 682).

On this basis editors have constructed versions of *Dipsychus* which differ greatly in length and in tone. Given Clough's changes of mind, and ultimate failure to complete the drama, there is no such thing as *the* text of the poem. Ideally, a biographer should present each revision separately as evidence for the poet's intellectual development at a particular period. This, however, is not possible as there is not sufficient evidence to date the individual notebooks. Most scholars have believed that they were written close together, in the course of 1851. Recently evidence has been presented that the process of revision continued at least until 1854.[1] In the light of these problems, I shall first describe the poem in the form which I believe makes a most coherent whole, and then later return to individual passages in order to throw light on the chronology of revision.

'Dipsychus', the title of the poem and the final name of one of its two characters, is a Greek word taken from the Epistle of St James in the New Testament. In the authorized version it is translated 'double-minded', as in Jas 1.8, 'A double-minded man is unstable in all his ways.' In his undergraduate diaries it was a word which Clough often used to describe the unsatisfactory state of his own soul. The theme of the drama is the difficulty found by the character Dipsychus in making up his mind about the kind of life he is to lead.

The structure which I adopt follows the first edition of the poem in 1865 more closely than it follows the standard edition of 1974. In my reconstruction, the first part of the poem consists of six scenes. (I attach in brackets the number which shows where the scene is placed in the 1974 edition.)

1. The Piazza (= I and VIII)
2. The Public Garden (= II)
3. The Quays (= III)
4. The Hotel (= IV)
5. The Insult (= VII)
6. The Lido (= VI)[2]

The very first scene of the poem, set in the piazza S. Marco in Venice, makes clear that the Dipsychus of the poem is not a fully fictional character like Claude in *Amours de Voyage*, but is much closer to the poet himself. His opening speech goes thus:

> The scene is different, and the place: the air
> Tastes of the nearer North: the people too
> Not perfect southern lightness. Wherefore then
> Should those old verses come into my mind
> I made last year at Naples?
>
> (P, 218)

Dipsychus then quotes at length from *Easter Day*, and having surveyed the scene concludes that Christ is not risen in Venice any more than in Naples. We are clearly invited to identify him with the author of *Easter Day* – though he quickly goes on to disown that poem as 'a thing ill worked, a moment's thought', and refuses to comment on its meaning. 'Interpret it I cannot. I but wrote it.'

The other character in the drama, called in early drafts 'Mephisto' and later 'the Spirit', sometimes appears to be the devil, in his traditional role as tempter; sometimes appears to be simply a projection of Dipsychus' own imagination. The poem – as is stressed in an epilogue – even leaves it ambiguous whether the Spirit is, taken all in all, good or evil. The Spirit pulls in more than one direction, and Dipsychus recognizes more than one force in himself reacting to the Spirit's challenges. 'O double self!' he exclaims at one point 'And I untrue to both'.

The uncertain nature of the Spirit is remarked upon by Dipsychus at the beginning of the poem's second scene.

> What is this persecuting voice that haunts me?
> What? Whence? of whom? How am I to detect?
> Myself or not myself? My own bad thoughts,
> Or some external agency at work
> To lead me who knows whither?
>
> (P, 222)

Up to this point, the Spirit has simply tried to detach Dipsychus from his theological pondering, and encouraged him to take part in the harmless pleasures of the piazza – coffee, ices and the music of Rossini. In succeeding scenes he appears much more clearly in the role of tempter. When Dipsychus is accosted by a woman in the public gardens, the Spirit encourages him to follow her home along the quays. 'Come now!' he says of the prostitutes in the third scene 'how many times per diem / Are you not hankering to try 'em?'

Dipsychus expresses high Victorian disgust:

> Why, why in wisdom and in grace's name,
> And in the name of saints and saintly thoughts,
> Of mothers, and of sisters, and chaste wives,
> And angel woman-faces we have seen,
> And angel woman-spirits we have guessed,
> And innocent sweet children, and pure love,
> Why did I ever one brief moment's space
> To this insidious lewdness lend chaste ears?
>
> (P, 225)

This overwrought protest is mocked by the Spirit in a down-to-earth manner. He is an honest purveyor of sex, and does not wish to paint its delights in too-glowing colours. Casual fornication is not an apple from the tree of knowledge. Whatever virginal curiosity may imagine, for better or worse, it leaves one much as before.

> I know it's mainly your temptation
> To think the thing a revelation
> A mystic mouthful that will give
> Knowledge and death – none know and live!
> I tell you plainly that it brings
> Some ease; but the emptiness of things
> (That one old sermon Earth still preaches
> Until we practice what she teaches)
> Is the sole lesson you'll learn by it
> Still you undoubtedly should try it.
> If not this itch will stick and vex you
> Your live long days till death unsex you
> Hide in your bones, for all I know
> And with you to the next world go.
>
> (P, 226)

After the idealism of his first response to temptation, Dipsychus now offers a more realistic counter, by describing the effects of prostitution on the street-walker herself.

> Look, she would fain allure; but she is cold,
> The ripe lips paled, the frolick pulses stilled,
> The quick eye dead, the once fair flushing cheek
> Flaccid under its paint.

The woman's own capacity for sexual pleasure has been extinguished 'in hot fruition's pawey fingers'. He cannot believe, Dipsychus says,

> that any child of Eve
> Were formed and fashioned, raised and reared for nought
> But to be swilled with animal delight
> And yield five minutes' pleasure to the male.
>
> (P, 228–9)

The Spirit tells Dipsychus that even religious people will not admire his fastidious rejection of the prostitute: they will 'show as pious people can /

Their feeling that you are not quite a man'. But if he will not sample the pleasures of the street, he must try the drawing room. So, for the fourth scene, the two characters move into the hotel.

Hitherto, while Dipsychus has spoken in blank verse, the Spirit's interventions have been in jerky tetrameters. Now as he encourages Dipsychus into more socially acceptable forms of flirtation he moves into heroic couplets.

> Those lovely, stately flowers, that fill with bloom
> The brilliant season's gay, parterre-like room,
> Moving serene yet swiftly through the dances;
> Those graceful forms and perfect countenances,
> Whose every fold and line in all their dresses
> Something refined and exquisite expresses
>
> (P, 236)

The duties of a gentleman may be martial as well as social: chivalry demands that one should defend the honour of oneself and one's womenfolk. In the next scene[3] a Croatian soldier, laying his hand on his sword, tells Dipsychus to get out of his way. The Spirit urges that such an insult calls for a challenge, but Dipsychus says that the matter is too trivial for a duel. Would he say the same, the Spirit asks, when walking with his sister 'if some foul brute step up and kissed her?' He mocks the belief of Christian pacifists that the teaching of the Gospel

> Shall bring the light of inward day
> To Caffre fierce and sly Malay
> Soften hard pirates with a kiss,
> And melt barbarian isles with bliss –
> Leaving in lieu of war and robbing
> Only a little mild stock jobbing.
>
> (P, 260)

The Spirit moves on to general mockery of Christian evangelism, which will stop at nothing until it is ready 'to send up missions per balloon / To those poor heathens in the moon'.

The Spirit now proposes that they should take a *barchetta* to the Lido. In this scene the verses address the question: does God exist? As the boat runs before the wind, Dipsychus relates a dream.

> I dreamt a dream; till morning light
> A bell rang in my head all night,
> Tinkling and tinkling first, and then
> Tolling; and tinkling; tolling again.

So brisk and gay, and then so slow!
O joy and terror! mirth and woe!
Ting, ting, there is no God; ting, ting –
Dong, there is no God; dong,
There is no God, dong, dong!

This opening stanza sets out the structure of the seven that succeed it. The first half of each stanza sets out the joyful and mirthful consequences of the hypothesis that there is no God, the second portrays its consequences of woe and terror. The contrasts between the two halves are built up by devices of rhythm and rhyme: the bell first tinkles out in short tripping syllables atheism's liberating aspects, and then tolls out in long dragged syllables its more miserable consequences.

The second stanza illustrates this pattern:

Ting, ting, there is no God; ting, ting;
Come dance and play, and merrily sing –
Ting, ting a ding; ting, ting a ding!
O pretty girl who trippest along
Come to my bed – it isn't wrong
Uncork the bottle, sing the song!
Ting ting a ding: dong, dong.
Wine has dregs, the song an end
A silly girl is a poor friend
And age and weakness who shall mend?
Dong, there is no God; Dong!

In this balance sheet of wine, women and song, the tinkling lines are overloaded with syllables (we have to read 'merr'ly' in the second line and 'tripp'st' in the fourth), while the tolling lines have less than the regulation eight (we have to drag out 'wine' into a whole foot before reaching the 'dregs') (P, 247).

The other stanzas of the poem explore the consequences of atheism for war and peace and civil order. If there is no God, then there is no one to hold the powerful to account and justice becomes simply the interests of the stronger. The best that the weak of the earth can hope for is that there is some happiness in accepting subjection to the powerful. Stanza six anticipates Nietzsche:

Ring, ting: to bow before the strong,
There is a rapture too in this;
Speak, outraged maiden, in thy wrong
Did terror bring no secret bliss?
Were boys' shy lips worth half a song

Compared to the hot soldier's kiss?
Work for thy master, work, thou slave
He is not merciful, but brave.
Be't joy to serve, who free and proud
Scorns thee and all th'ignoble crowd.
(P, 249)

These stanzas may be set beside Matthew Arnold's well-known treatment of the consequences of disbelief. *Dover Beach* offers human love as the only consolation for the melancholy long withdrawal of faith.

Ah, love, let us be true
To one another! for the world, which seems
To lie before us like a land of dreams
So various, so beautiful, so new
Hath really neither joy, nor love, nor light
Nor certitude, nor peace, nor help for pain . . .
(OA, 136)

The consolation surely fails: if in reality there is no such thing as love, what will keep the poet and his partner true to one another?

Clough's treatment of love in *Dipsychus* is more consistent: it too is a delusion without faith:

O Rosalie, my lovely maid,
I think thou thinkest love is true;
And on thy faithful bosom laid
I almost could believe it true
The villanies, the wrongs, the alarms
Forget we in each other's arms
No justice here, no God above;
But where we are, is there not love?
What? What? thou also go'st? For how
Should dead truth live in lover's vow?
What, thou? Thou also lost? Dong
Dong; there is no God; dong!
(P, 250)

Dipsychus' dream is more consistent than Arnold's poem, but Arnold's pessimism is more complete than Clough's. For the final stanza of Dipsychus' musings weakens the effect of the whole by insisting that the sombre tolling of the bell of atheism is, after all, only a dream.

On the path to heaven the Christian's traditional enemies are the world, the flesh and the devil. The earlier scenes of the drama have shown the Spirit's temptation to sins of the flesh and sins of worldliness. One might have expected the darling task of the devil to be the encouragement of atheism. But the Spirit, on the contrary, reveals himself as an observant, if undogmatic, Anglican.

> The Church of England I belong to
> But think Dissenters not far wrong too;
> They're vulgar dogs; but for his creed
> I hold that no man will be d——d.
>
> (P, 251)

The Spirit's own contribution to the theological debate is a sprightly ditty which can well stand on its own. It did so indeed in the earliest editions of the poems, attributed not to any Mephisto, but to Clough himself.

> 'There is no God' the wicked saith
> 'And truly it's a blessing,
> For what he might have done with us
> It's better only guessing.'
>
> 'There is no God' a youngster thinks,
> 'Or really, if there may be,
> He surely didn't mean a man
> Always to be a baby.'
>
> 'There is no God, or if there is,'
> The tradesman thinks, 'twere funny
> If he should take it ill in me
> To make a little money.'

In the next two verses the poet describes groups who treat God's existence as a matter of indifference. Three more list categories who believe in God: country folks, clergy, married couples and young lovers. Finally:

> And almost every one when age
> Disease or sorrows strike him
> Inclines to think that there is a God
> Or something very like Him.
>
> (P, 251)

This miniature poem is both economic and fluent: Clough chose for it eight verses out of many more which he drafted and rejected. In its final form it makes a pair with Dipsychus' dream: it examines the motives, as the earlier poem examines the consequences, of belief and disbelief in God. It is notable that in each poem belief in God is treated more kindly than disbelief.

As the Spirit ends his song, the *barchetta* reaches the Lido. Dipsychus leaps joyously into the buffeting waves. The Spirit worries about his watch, complains about the thistles, and wishes they had brought a towel. From the beach he observes sardonically

> But you – with this one bathe, no doubt,
> Have solved all questions out and out
> 'Tis Easter Day, and on the Lido
> Lo, Christ the Lord is risen indeed, O!
>
> (P, 254)

So ends the first part of the drama. The six scenes, placed in the order of the 1865 edition, make up a coherent whole. Dipsychus is tempted to unchastity, to violence and to irreligion, and, after varying degrees of hesitation and with various strengths of motivation, he resists each temptation. The three temptations accord with the classical triad of forms of life presented in the texts of Aristotle which Clough taught in Oxford and London: the life of pleasure, the life of honour and the life of thought. Each form of life gives primacy to one of the three parts of the soul anatomized by classical tradition: the appetitive part, the irascible part and the rational part. Each part of Dipsychus' soul is tested in turn and emerges, on the face of it, victorious.

* * *

The second part of the drama differs from first in several ways. Whereas the temptations of part one are such as beset all human beings, the problems of the second part concern the specific choice of a career for an individual with the gifts, ideals and history of Clough himself. Is there any career which can be chosen without a betrayal of ideals? Can an idealist frame a life for himself without fitting into any of the slots provided by the world?

Again, we follow an Aristotelian pattern. Having begun his *Nicomachean Ethics* by discussing the choice between the three lives, Aristotle in the final book of that treatise narrows the choice to one between an active, and a contemplative, exercise of the rational virtues. Here in the poem, the choice is between opting for an ideal, self-chosen exercise of one's gifts, and coming to terms with the opportunities the world has to offer them. Whereas in the first part Dipsychus rejected the three temptations, in the second part he ends by submitting to the Spirit's proposals. Clough is looking his own mundane future in the face: he will have to earn his living, and do so on the world's terms.

Before the second part commences, however, we are offered an entr'acte which, instead of being a consecutive dialogue or argument, is rather an album of loosely connected poems. Entitled *In a Gondola* and located on the Grand Canal, it commences with a poem we have already met, 'Ah were life but as the gondola'. Dipsychus next sings three solemn quatrains on the evil of treating men as means and not ends, and proceeds to a pair of self-quotations. First there are a dozen lines from *Amours de Voyage*, embellished with some new internal rhymes, denouncing 'the demon of craving'. Then there is a solipsistic poem from the Lamech notebook 'Let me love my love unto myself alone'.[4]

At the end of the entr'acte, Dipsychus is given two original poems. The first, 'Better it were, thou sayest to consent' describes two different ways of responding to the mismatch between ideal and real. One can either pretend that the actual shoddy world is already ideal, or claim that there is another world elsewhere in which the defects of the here and now are remedied. Both responses are rejected: 'Play no tricks upon thy soul, O man; let fact be fact, and life the thing it can'. The second poem 'Where are the great, whom thou wouldst wish to praise thee' urges that the praise, love and commands of others are irrelevant to one's own true worth. 'Seek, seeker, in thyself; submit to find / In the stones bread; and life in the blank mind' (P, 240–1).

All the best verses in the entr'acte are given to the Spirit. The longest is a song *As I sat at the café, I said to myself*. In the standard edition this song has 13 verses. Clough kept rewriting it up to his death, and composed more than 20 others, full of lovingly plotted detail. Two stanzas will suffice to give the flavour.

> I sit at my table *en grand seigneur*,
> And when I have done, throw a crust to the poor;
> Not only the pleasure, one's self, of good living
> But also the pleasure of now and then giving.
> So pleasant it is to have money, heigh ho!
> So pleasant it is to have money
>
> I drive through the streets and I care not a d——n
> The people they stare, and they ask who I am
> And if I should chance to run over a cad
> I can pay for the damage if ever so bad
> So pleasant it is to have money, heigh ho!
> So pleasant it is to have money.
>
> (P, 242)

Other stanzas take us through a Parisian banquet, course by course and wine by wine, followed by a trip to the Opera and a fashionable ball. These Gilbertian topper-and-cane verses would, in fact, be more effective if they were part of an opera libretto, with the insistent refrain borne by a genuine chorus. But they carry an implicit message for Dipsychus: the spiritual independence of the world that he craves is possible only for those who have financial independence in the world.

It is hard to trace a single theme through the entire entr'acte. Perhaps the only general moral the reader is meant to draw is spelt out in a brief doggerel lyric sung by the Spirit halfway through.

> The world is very odd we see
>   We do not comprehend it;
> But in one fact can all agree
>   God won't, and we can't mend it
>
> Being common sense it can't be sin
>   To take it as we find it;
> The pleasures to take pleasure in,
>   The pain, try not to mind it.
>
> (P, 241)

The second part of the drama consists in the Spirit's ultimately successful effort to get Dipsychus to accept this 'common sense'. In the reconstruction I prefer, this second part has five scenes.

1. The Academy (= IX)
2. In San Marco (= X)
3. The Piazza at Night (= XI)
4. On a Bridge (= XII)
5. In the Piazza (= XIV)

The first scene begins with another self-quotation: the poem we have already encountered in which in the Accademia a canvas of Byron at Missolonghi is contrasted with Titian's *Assumption of the Virgin*. The two paintings present the contrast between the active and the contemplative life, with the bias in favour of the former. 'If live we positively must,' the poem ends 'God's name be blest for noble deeds' (P, 264).

Dipsychus admits authorship of the verses, but immediately disowns them – indeed, resolves to give up poetry altogether.

Verses! well, they are made, so let them go;
No more if I can help. This is one way
The procreant heat and fervour of our youth
Escapes, in puff, and smoke, and shapeless words
Of mere ejaculation, nothing worth,
Unless to make maturer years content
To slave in base compliance to the world.
(P, 265)

Perhaps, in Clough's mind, the whole of *Dipsychus* was to serve the purpose spelt out in those last lines.

Relations between Dipsychus and the Spirit now take a new turn. Hitherto, the scenes have consisted of soliloquies with interruptions by the Spirit, overheard, but not answered, by Dipsychus. Henceforth, the two engage in dialogue, and indeed in bargaining. Dipsychus is willing to negotiate a Faustian bargain with the Spirit (whom he addresses, initially, as Mephistopheles).

Dipsychus begins the negotiations cautiously.

Should I conceive (not that at all I do,
'Tis curiosity that prompts my speech) –

A wish to bargain for your merchandise,
Say, what were your demands? what were your terms?
What should I do? What should I cease to do?
What incense on what altars must I burn?
And what abandon? What unlearn, or learn?
Religion goes, I take it.
(P, 266)

Not at all, says the Spirit. Devoutness is merely vague emotion, and theology merely leads to suits in ecclesiastical courts. But churchgoing is different, and is quite essential. Indeed, all things considered, Dipsychus might do well to take orders. When this suggestion is rejected, the Spirit offers his help and influence in a legal career. ('Twould do me good / to fig you out in robe and hood. / Wouldn't I give up wine and wench / To mount you fairly on the bench!') Most importantly, he offers to find a suitable lady for Dipsychus to propose to, for marriage is almost a sine qua non for worldly respectability.

Dipsychus retires (scene 2) to meditate on the Spirit's advice, in a soliloquy of 160 lines of blank verse. A legal career disgusts him: lawyers make their money out of the dirt in other people's lives.

Shall I go about,
And like the walking shoeblack roam the flags
With heedful eyes, down bent, and like a glass
In a sea-captain's hand sweeping all around
To see whose boots are dirtiest?

(P, 268)

As for marriage, he had hoped for something better than an arranged match. He had dreamt of a 'love, the large repose / Restorative, not to mere outside needs skin-deep, but thoroughly to the total man'. But such love, though possible, is so rare that it is 'A thing not possibly to be conceived / An item in the reckonings of the wise'.

It is so difficult to be sure one has met the right person: it would be tragic 'to seat some alien trifler on the throne / A queen may come to claim'. In any form of action, the hardest thing is the choice of the right moment. Dipsychus, in trying to decide on his own future, is torn between the dangers of precipitation and procrastination. Perhaps the right moment cannot be chosen by ratiocination; perhaps one should leave its choice to instinct – like a mountain stream bursting through rocks or a hunter leaping over hedge and ditch.

Ah, if I had a course like a full stream,
If life were as a field of chase! No, no;
The age of instinct has, it seems, gone by
And will not be forced back. And to live now,
I must sluice myself into canals
And lose all force in ducts. The modern Hotspur
Shrills not his trumpet of 'To Horse, To Horse!'
But consults columns in a railway guide;
A demigod of figures; an Achilles
Of computation.

(P, 271)

Modern life does not leave room for individual action; everything nowadays is anonymous and collective:

In all those crowded rooms of industry
No individual soul has loftier leave
Than fiddling with a piston or a valve.
Well, one could bear that also: one could drudge
And do one's petty part, and be content
In base manipulation, solaced still
By thinking of the leagued fraternity

And of co-operation, and the effect
Of the great engine. If indeed it work,
And is not a mere treadmill! Which it may be;
Who can confirm it is not? We ask Action,
And dream of arms and conflict; and string up
All self-devotion's muscles; and are set
To fold up papers.

(P, 272)

These lines seem eerily predictive of Clough's later service to Florence Nightingale, as maliciously summed up by Lytton Strachey: 'parcels to be done up in brown paper, and carried to the post'.

Dipsychus accepts that his hope of individual, unselfish, heroic action was a romantic dream; there is no alternative to taking a humble part in the world's work.

I must slave, a meagre coral-worm
To build beneath the tide with excrement
What one day will be island, or be reef
And will feed men, or wreck them. Well, well, well
Adieu, ye twisted thinkings, I submit.

Off stage, the Spirit echoes 'Submit, submit! / Tis common sense, and human wit / Can claim no higher name than it / submit, submit' (P, 278).

In the third scene of the second part, Dipsychus looks back over the life he is to lead, symbolized by Venice and St Mark's piazza. Like Claude who fell in love with the Rome he despised, Dipsychus now fondly describes the townscape he scorned in the first scene of all, reconciled to the people and the architecture of the city. Even the temptations it presents may be the opening out of paths for ampler virtue; one should not regard everything strange as therefore sinful. 'To leave the habitual and the old, and quit / the easy chair of use and wont, seems crime / to the weak soul, forgetful how at first / sitting down seemed so too.'

Dipsychus recalls the alternating moods of despair and contentment in his past life.

Oh, there are hours
When love, and faith, and dear domestic ties,
And converse with all friends, and pleasant walks,
Familiar faces, and familiar books,
Study and art, upliftings into prayer,
And admiration of the noblest things,

Seem all ignoble only: all is mean,
And nought as I would have it. Then at others,
My mind is on her nest; my heart at home
In all around; my soul secure in place,
And the vext needle perfect to her poles.

(P, 275)

The Spirit, fearing that Dipsychus is about to relapse from his resolve of submission, paints a damaging picture of his way of life.

To moon about religion; to inhume
Your ripened age in solitary walks,
For self discussion; to debate in letters
Vext points with earnest friends; past other men
To cherish natural instincts, yet to fear them
And less than any use them.

Uncomfortably close to Clough's own spiritual biography!

Venice has become, for both Dipsychus and the Spirit, a symbol of that leisured life of principled indecision that is to be renounced if anything is to be achieved in the world.

Stay at Venice, if you will;
Sit musing in its churches hour on hour
Cross-kneed upon a bench; climb up at whiles
The neighbouring tower, and kill the lingering day
With old comparisons; when night succeeds,
Evading, yet a little seeking, what
You would and would not, turn your doubtful eyes
On moon and stars to help morality;
Once in a fortnight, say, by lucky chance
Of happier-tempered coffee, gain (great Heaven!)
A pious rapture: is it not enough?
O that will keep you safe. Yet don't be sure –
Emotions are so slippery. Aye, keep close
And burrow in your bedroom; pace up and down
A long half hour; with talking to yourself
Make waiters wonder; sleep a bit; write verse,
Burnt in disgust, then ill-restored, and left
Half-made, in pencil scrawl illegible.

(P, 277)

The accuracy of this description of the *Dipsychus* Nachlass has been flagged by many an editor.

In the next scene the Spirit insists that there is no alternative to coming to terms with the world of business. How else would Dipsychus earn his living? Poetry? 'The strong fresh gale of life will feel' the Spirit mocks 'the influx of your mouthful of soft air.' Philosophy? Can you 'live in metaphysic / with transcendental logic fill your stomach / Schematise joy, effigiate meat and drink'? Pupil teaching? 'Well, old college fame / The charity of some free-thinking merchant / Or friendly intercession brings a first pupil / But not a second' (P, 284).

Dipsychus has to concede the futility of these proposals, and once again submits to the Spirit:

> Welcome, wicked world
> The hardening heart, the calculating brain
> Narrowing its doors to thought, the lying lips
> The calm-dissembling eyes; the greedy flesh,
> The world, the Devil – welcome, welcome, welcome.
> (P, 281)

The scene that follows is weak, and perhaps Clough would have dispensed with it had he completed his revisions. In it Dipsychus claims, quite unconvincingly, that his submission is only pretence: once the Spirit has given him entry to the Philistine world he will, like Samson, bring it all down in a suicidal catastrophe. The scene's only memorable lines use the imagery of Genesis to reinforce the Spirit's message that acceptance of the world is the sign of maturity:

> 'The man his parents shall desert'
> The ordinance says 'and cleave unto his wife'.
> O man, behold thy wife, the hard naked world
> Adam, accept thy Eve.
> (P, 287)

The bargain is clinched in the final scene, and the Spirit reveals that his name is indeed Mephistopheles. But he has a score of other names too: his favourite is the one given him by St Paul in the Epistle to the Ephesians: *Cosmocrator*. He is the ruler of the darkness of this world – the world that Dipsychus has at last made up his mind to enter.

An epilogue in prose takes the form of a dialogue between the author of the poem and an uncle. It is largely a debate whether the teaching and preaching of Arnold at Rugby had a good or a bad effect. But the part of the dialogue that throws most light on the poem comes near the beginning. The uncle complains (with justice) that some of the later soliloquies in the poem are soporific. However, he did think some of the devil's remarks were quite sensible. 'But sir' the poet replies 'perhaps he wasn't a devil after all. That's the beauty of the poem; nobody can say. You see, dear sir, the thing which it is attempted to represent is the conflict between the tender conscience and the world' (P, 292).

This holds the key to the understanding of the poem. One reader may see Dipsychus' original innocence as admirable, and read the poem as the narrative of his corruption. Another may think his conscience absurdly tender, and welcome the Spirit's injections of common sense. Either interpretation is legitimate: most readers, in fact, will take a position somewhere between the two. Clough himself, in different moods, will have adopted different positions along the spectrum of possible readings, sometimes identifying himself more with the ethereal idealism of Dipsychus, sometimes with the jaunty worldliness of Mephisto. But in the drama as presented the criticism which each, by juxtaposition, makes of the other is as much an utterance of the authorial voice as is either of the positions criticized. That, as the poet says in the Epilogue, is the beauty of the poem.

Just as Dipsychus' spiritual journey can be seen as one of corruption or one of maturation, so can Clough's own biography, depending on whether it is seen from a religious or from a secular viewpoint. Few poets have written poems which are so self-revealing: revelatory indeed, as the poet insists, of more than one self. Dipsychus' verses are often literal echoes of the utterances, public and private, of an earlier Clough; and from the mouth of the Spirit we often hear the sentiments of Clough's mentors over many years. The last word, perhaps, is with one of these mentors. In 1833 Emerson wrote into his diary a sentiment which could stand as a headline for the poem. 'No man can have society upon his own terms. If he seeks it, he must serve it too.'

One of Clough's most often quoted – or misquoted – poems survives on a single undated sheet of paper. From its content, it might well have been intended for *Dipsychus*. Entitled 'The Latest Decalogue', its two-edged satire would make it sit well in the mouth of Mephisto.

Thou shalt have one God only; who
Would be at the expense of two?
No graven images may be
Worshipped, except the currency.
Swear not at all; for for thy curse
Thine enemy is none the worse.
At church on Sunday to attend
Will serve to keep the world thy friend.

Honour thy parents – that is, all
From whom advancement may befall.
Thou shalt not kill, but needs't not strive
Officiously to keep alive;
Do not adultery commit:
Advantage rarely comes of it.
Thou shalt not steal – an empty feat,
When it's so lucrative to cheat.
Bear not false witness; let the lie
Have time on its own wings to fly.
Thou shalt not covet, but tradition
Approves all forms of competion.

The sum of all is, thou shalt love,
If any body, God above:
At any rate shall never labour
More than thyself to love thy neighbour.
(P, 205)

Notes

1 By J. P. Phelan, 'The Textual Evolution of Clough's *Dipsychus and the Spirit*', *Notes and Queries*, 2000, pp. 230–9.

2 I have presented substantial arguments for this pattern in my book *God and Two Poets*, London 1988, ch. 10.

3 As set out above, I follow the 1865 edition in placing the insult scene at this point. In the 1974 edition it is scene VII.

Chapter Nine
Transatlantic Engagement

Whatever Clough may have felt when planning *Dipsychus* in Venice, by the time he was rewriting the drama in London the situation it represented was exactly the reverse of his own true position. So far from needing persuading, by Mephistophelean wit and subtlety, that he ought to find a profession and seek a bride, he was, by the end of 1851, as good as engaged to be married and desperately hoping for a job of any kind.

He had first met the woman who was to become his fiancée, in 1850 at the house of Richard Monckton Milnes, the Liberal MP for Pontefract, a patron of literature and a friend of Tennyson and Thackeray. The two men had met each other in revolutionary Paris in 1849, and had quickly found interests in common. Milnes for a number of years paid court, in vain, to Florence Nightingale. When Clough was invited to his house party at Fryston Lodge he found among the other guests a cousin of the Nightingales, Blanche Smith. Blanche was the daughter of Florence's Aunt Mai, and of Samuel Smith, an Examiner of Private Bills in the House of Commons. The Smiths were well-to-do, and Samuel's father William had been Whig MP for Norwich. The family had an ample country house at Combe Hurst near Kingston, and Blanche also spent long periods with the Nightingales at their house in Embley.

Blanche was born in 1828 and so was nine years younger than Arthur. From the ages of 12 to 15 she had been brought up by the Martineau family, and from 15 to 17 she had lived with a very Calvinist family in Lausanne and Geneva. Two further years with the Martineaus had restored her to a broadly Unitarian view of religion, and for the two years before she met Clough she had been living in one or other of the Smith-Nightingale households. By 1853 she was lamenting that she had very little religion at all, but she continued to feel that God was 'a dear friend that one trusts' (B, 645). The strongest intellectual influence in her family was her Aunt Julia, who was often to be found curled up with a German idealist volume (B, 651, 662).

By the spring of 1851 it was clear, at least to Florence Nightingale, that Clough was seriously interested in Blanche. On 20 March she wrote to Milnes – who was by now engaged to another lady, Annabel Crewe – asking him to give Clough a favourable introduction to her family.

Will you forgive me for asking a favour from you? I believe you are acquainted with Mr A. H. Clough. If you like him enough to speak a good word for him, that good word spoken at Embley might save a good deal of suffering.

There will be six objections in the minds of my people:

1. An instructor of youth
2. Without a sous
3. Or a relation
4. Or orthodoxy
5. Shy
6. 'Bothie'

Might I ask you to be his introducer to my people, did it happen conveniently? I would not have asked it in this formal way, if I had thought it likely that I should see you.

Florence Nightingale.

Since Blanche's name did not appear in the letter, it is understandable, if comic, that Milnes took the request as meaning that Florence herself intended to marry Clough. She had to write a follow-up letter five days later explaining that Clough did not want to be her husband but 'to be my son-in-law'.[1] (She was actually one year younger than Clough.)

We do not know how Milnes acted on this letter, but by May Clough felt confident enough to tell Tom Arnold in a letter that he was familiar with the Smiths and that he had a liking for the (male) members of the family (M, 291). Meanwhile, Matthew Arnold's wooing had taken a more favourable turn. In January, after 90 days of courtship by letter alone, Judge Wightman lifted the veto on meetings between the pair. But it was only in April that he gave permission for an engagement, when Arnold was appointed Inspector of Schools, through the good offices of his employer Lord Lansdowne, and his former Balliol tutor Ralph Lingen, now Education Secretary.

Clough was not overjoyed by Matt's engagement: marriage, he complained, forced old friends to make a graceful withdrawal. Matt himself was later to say that 'being in love generally unfits a man for the society of his friends'. 'I consider Miss Wightman' Clough told Tom 'as a sort of natural enemy. How can it be otherwise – shall I any longer breakfast with Matt twice a week?' But he was one of a very select group of friends, including Walrond and Edward Arnold, who attended the wedding on 10 June. The bride, he told Tom, was 'small with aquiline nose, and very pleasing eyes, fair in complexion . . . She seems, as Matt calls her, a charming companion' (M, 291). Matt did not wait for the wedding breakfast but set off with his bride towards the Continent, to write – if tradition is to be believed – *Dover Beach* in his hotel on the wedding night.

If Clough was to follow Arnold into matrimony he needed something like Arnold's inspectorship to live on. Towards the end of the year an opportunity presented itself. A new college was to be set up in Sydney, New South Wales. Clough decided to apply for the Professorship of Classics which was united with the Principalship. He sought references from Hawkins (who declined), from Shairp (who begged him not to 'go to bluster and bully among gold-digging Australians') and from Matt – who turned on his best eloquence. 'In patience, in self-control, in disinterestedness, in clearness of mind and dignity of character, Mr Clough, even as a young man stood above and apart from other young men. That superiority he has continued to retain' (L, 228).

Clough asked the Council of University Hall to allow him to apply for the Sydney post on the understanding that, if elected, he would give up his present position in February. The members of Council saw this as a wonderful opportunity to rid themselves of their difficult Principal, and refused permission for him to apply unless he immediately resigned from London. They wished, they said, to 'make an opening for a gentleman whose connexions might perhaps restore this Institution to some prosperity'. They refused to allow even a week's delay, but they offered to allow him to reside within the Hall until the end of the Session. Faced with this ultimatum, Clough resigned unconditionally with effect from the end of the year, and declined the offer of accommodation. Council minuted its 'sense of the consideration he has shown at all times for the interests of the institution' (M, 300).

On 31 December, the day he became unemployed, Clough made a proposal of marriage to Blanche and was accepted. Two days later he learnt from Sir John Herschel, the chair of the electoral board, that another candidate had been appointed to the Sydney professorship.

The urgent search for alternative employment was placed in the capable hands of Lady Ashburton. She declared herself relieved at the failure to obtain the Sydney chair. 'Something must turn up here that would be better than such expatriation.' She wrote to Lord Lansdowne, whom Clough had met at the Grange, asking him to consider him for a vacant examinership in the Department of Education. Lansdowne's reply held out little immediate prospect of a job, and in forwarding it to Clough Lady Ashburton felt the need to console him by describing the beauty of the snowdrops and aconites at the Grange (M, 303, 305).

In the meantime, Clough was reduced to supporting himself from his savings and from fees for two hours a day coaching. He also drew a meagre stipend from the Professorship at University College which he had retained after resigning as Principal of University Hall. In March he jumped at the chance of a Chair in Classics at the University of Aberdeen, but fell back when he found that to take it up he would have to subscribe to the Westminster Confession, the Kirk's test of orthodoxy.

The engagement to Blanche got off to a bad start. The exact date of her acceptance of Clough is not known, but it seems to have been between Christmas of 1851 and New Year of 1852. In July 1852 Arthur recalled to Blanche the 'line of trees where we walked six months and a half ago, where the man in the cart asked if we had lost our way and you told him we had not'. In December 1852 Blanche wrote to Arthur in America 'Do you remember last Christmas Day, dear? It is very nearly a year now since we began our pilgrimage together and certainly less like going together down stream then than it was a kind of forward and back step' (B, 604).

Clough's very first letter after the engagement, on 1 January 1852, was a severe step backward. It contained sentiments with which the reader is by now familiar, but which were news to Blanche. The apple which tempted Eve, the new fiancé wrote, was the belief that love is everything.

> Women will believe so, and try and make men act as if *they* believed so, and straightway, behold, the Fall, and Paradise at an end etc. etc. Love is not everything, Blanche; don't believe it nor make me pretend to believe it. '*Service*' is everything. Let us be fellow-servants. There is no joy nor happiness nor way nor name by which men may be saved but this. (M, 300)

Ever afterwards, Blanche referred to this as 'the terrible letter', and 15 months later she said 'it is all I can do, even now, to forgive that'. It made her question, briefly, whether she had done well to accept the proposal. But Arthur's next letter was just as unyielding.

> Do you think that though you and all womankind together cast me off that Truth would not be true, earth beautiful, the sky bright, honour honour and work work – only a little harder. I tell you, yes; take it as you will. I ask no girl to be my friend that we may be a fond foolish couple together all in all each to the other . . . I will ask no one to put off her individuality for me; nor will I, weak and yielding as I am, if I can help it, put off mine for anyone. (M, 301)

When, hard on these first letters, came the news that the prospect of employment at Sydney had disappeared, no one could have blamed Blanche if she had broken off the engagement. Arthur himself said 'What I had rather looked forward to originally in case of not going to Sydney was unmarried poverty and literary work.' But Blanche found that she already loved this strange man so much that she was prepared to wait, years if necessary, until he found a post in England which would enable him to support her. Her father, Samuel Smith, insisted that the minimum income on which he would permit the marriage was 500 pounds a year (M, 303, 447).

During the next few months, Clough gradually mastered the art of writing love-letters. Between January and October he wrote 82 letters and received 39 in return. In them he relived his childhood and boyhood for Blanche, confessed his faults and recalled their trysts. He reported on the health of the flowers she sent to grace the dingy apartment off Bedford Square to which he moved at the end of February. He told her about his moods and the weather ('rain, rain, rain, and universal umbrellas travelling churchward' one Sunday) and kept her informed about his social engagements (a lecture by Mazzini for instance, followed by dinner with Charles Darwin 'pretty fair fun, with a spice of cynicism, champagne and moselle'). From time to time he felt that the improbability of his obtaining an appropriate income meant that they should part from each other (M, 306; PPR, 174–7).

Blanche responded to such a letter in March

> Do you not think that whatever outward circumstances come we may allow ourselves to rejoice in the feeling of our mutual attachment and possession, that we may look on it as a bright port, a refuge when life looks difficult, a haven where one may find comfort and strength for fresh work?

She encouraged Arthur to hope that he might make her life happier and 'more real', and in his turn he told her 'my dearest child, you shall, please Heaven, bring me back into the real warm life'. 'My child' was his favourite endearment: it would be wrong to read into it any condescension, since it was a standard Victorian term of affection between friends of either sex on equal terms. Clough wrote of himself 'I wish and hope that I may, in spite of the hard unpromising look-out before us, always continue to be your child.' And Blanche herself preferred that form of endearment to any other: she rebuked Arthur when he addressed her as 'dear Blanche' (M, 308, 339).

From the start of the engagement Blanche seems to have been suspicious, or perhaps jealous, of Matthew Arnold's influence. In an early letter Clough admitted that he did not expect her to like *The Strayed Reveller*, the only volume of Arnold's poems so far published. 'It had a great effect on me though, it and its writer, but it is over I hope, and I don't mean to let it have any more' (M, 301). Arnold had returned from a lengthy honeymoon trip in October 1851 and had since then been travelling round the country in his new capacity as Schools Inspector, leaving his now pregnant wife alone, except for weekends, in their new house in Eaton Place. He had offered advice on Clough's abortive application for an examinership in the Council Office ('hard dull work low salary stationariness'). After that the two poets seem to have lost contact with each other for two months.

At the end of March Matt was back in town, and Clough joined him and his wife at the Lyceum theatre, and went with them a day later to the house of John Blackett, now a *Globe* journalist. He clearly felt some guilt about this. 'Considering that he is my most intimate friend (or has been)' he wrote defensively to Blanche 'it is not a great deal to have seen of him during the ten days that he has been here and hereabout, – to have spent an hour with him at a theatre last night; with perhaps a couple of hours more this evening at a party?' (M, 311).

Early in April Clough spent some time at Combe Hurst, the Smiths' country house. There he wrote out for Blanche a fair copy of a dozen of his recent poems. We do not know how much of his verse she had read before they met: it may be that she is the subject of a verse written in 1851 (of which she made a special fair copy in her own hand):

Because a lady chose to say
I know not what long months away
A lady charming fair and young
En passant, in the crowd one night
She'd read my verse with such delight –
For this is it and not for more
My brain I ransack o'er and o'er
And consecrate, to make and mend
Each busy workday's scanty end,
With labour long and service hard
To win some future word's reward?
Ah folly, folly, folly

(P, 318)

By now she had already read, at least in part, *The Bothie* and *Ambarvalia*: Arthur had some difficulty in persuading her that *The Bothie* was quite innocent – even if 'a little boyish' (M, 338). He now offered an anthology chosen from the poems he had written since 1849: biblical poems like 'Lamech' and 'Jacob', the Chamonix poem 'Les Vaches, Say not the struggle, Peschiera, Hymnos Aumnos' and a number of short pieces that were to find their final home in *Dipsychus*.[2]

At Easter Clough paid his usual visit to Rugby and stayed with the Shairps. There he found Benjamin Jowett as a fellow guest. On Easter Monday the two of them escorted a couple of ladies on horseback to the Civil War battlefield of Naseby, following 'Shairp on his hunter, the pride of his heart, leading the way, and opening the gates, and commanding in chief'. Arthur described the ride and the Northamptonshire countryside for Blanche with a wealth of geological detail: blue lias, red sandstone, yellow-brown oolite (PPR, 176). Matthew Arnold invited him to join him the following weekend at Derby, where he was staying on his course of inspection. But once again the two failed to make contact.

The engagement to Blanche was not publicly announced, because Arthur felt so uncertain of ever being in a position to marry her. More than once in May he wrote to her that since he had so little chance of success in his profession of education – 'because of the stigma of the abjured xxxix articles' – it would be better if they separated. Blanche urged that whatever might come, their attachment was 'a bright point, a refuge when life looks difficult, a haven where one may find comfort and strength for fresh work'. Clearly, she had now found his wavelength. Arthur responded that he could not do otherwise than feel 'happy in your goodness and kindness and tenderness'.

Despite Clough's desire for secrecy, rumours abounded among his friends. Matt knew about the courtship, but was discreet (L, 232); other close friends like Walrond were left guessing. Clough visited Oxford in May and introduced him to the Smith family, including Blanche and her sister. On his departure Walrond speculated that he was engaged to one or other of the two young ladies. Max Müller the orientalist, just beginning his long academic career at Oxford, overheard Walrond and passed on the guesswork to J. A. Froude, who had now settled in comfortable domesticity in Wales. Writing to Clough to tell him of the birth of his second daughter, Froude wrote that unless Muller was entirely mistaken 'I and all your friends have reason to rejoice with all our hearts for you.' He was ready to offer his house Plasgwynant as a honeymoon cottage (B, 569).

Clough was indignant and reproached Müller for the indiscretion. Müller wrote a letter of apology on 21 May, and described the meeting with Walrond and the Smiths:

> I volunteered no conjecture at the time, but when I was told your friend's name and that he resided near Richmond, I said that I had heard about him before and that I had been told he was a Liberal in politics, very rich, and that you were likely to marry one of his daughters. (B, 568)

Clough now had to write to Froude to tell him that the wedding was at best a distant prospect: he took the opportunity to ask how much was the minimum sum a prudent man might live on. Froude came out with the same sum as Papa Smith. 'With £500 a year of only income a man who can do without a horse and a tailor's bill, and a lady who can do without a lady's maid may in my opinion marry with prudence in any part of England' (B, 569).

By the end of May Blanche was despairing of Arthur finding a job in England. Why not, she suggested, try his fortune in America? Arthur was at first intimidated by the prospect, but on 17 June (Blanche's birthday) he wrote to Emerson 'Is there any chance, do you think, of earning bread and water, if not bread and flesh, anywhere between the Atlantic and the Mississippi, by teaching Latin, Greek, or English.' At the same time he asked what 'people of decent habits' in New England thought it was possible to marry on (M, 315).

Emerson replied encouragingly from Concord. 'Do you take the first ship or steamer for Boston, come out and spend two or three months here in my house. I will defend you from all outsiders, initiate you step by step into all the atrocities of republicanism. You shall look about you, know all the inlets and capabilities of country and town; have good milk, eggs, coffee, and not-so-good-as-English mutton.' Many a decent family in Boston, he was sure, lived on a thousand dollars a year. His report on teaching prospects was not quite as inviting. Perhaps the best initial prospect was private tuition for young men rusticated from Harvard for idleness or misbehaviour. 'The College authorities' Emerson reported 'are always looking round them for instructors in safe country towns, on a radius of 10 or 20 miles from Cambridge, to whose supervision they may assign these *mauvais sujets*' (M, 316).

While Emerson's reply was on its way across the Atlantic, Clough continued to look for English employment. He was by now so desperate that in July he even applied for an inspectorship of Roman Catholic schools, writing for support to Ward, who was teaching in a Catholic seminary at Ware. Ward replied warmly, offering a testimonial and applauding Clough's engagement; but his actual influence on the appointment, he reported, was little above zero. Monckton Milnes, too, warned that the post would almost certainly go to a Roman Catholic. Clough consoled himself by telling Blanche that the job would have been 'restrictive and dependent, requiring silence and extreme discretion, and something of suppression' with 'a life of perpetual motion over the whole of England' (M, 318).

Blanche, meanwhile, was travelling in Somerset and Devon with her family, and kept Arthur informed, day by day, of their movements. She was delighted to tell Arthur that on the way to Ilfracombe her mother, in the corner of a very roomy carriage, 'informed me that you were a most excellent person in a manner that rejoiced my heart'. Meanwhile, Anne Clough was warning her that Arthur could write letters that were 'like a box on the ear'. Arthur told Blanche that she would get on very well with his family: '[they] are good plain uncritical people only apt I suppose as you say to think a great deal about "their wonderful son and brother"'.

Emerson's letter arrived early in August, and Clough at once resolved to accept his offer, showing the letter to Matthew Arnold, with whom he dined on 2 August. He did not stay long after dinner, he reported to Blanche 'because of Fanny Lucy, who wants him to be with her'. It seems that the new Mrs Arnold, no less than the future Mrs Clough, was finding the Arnold–Clough relationship difficult to swallow. Nonetheless, Clough saw Matt again the next day and borrowed £10 from him. Matt approved of the plan to settle in America, and told his mother that it might be a good idea if his brother Tom, now thinking of returning from the Antipodes, followed suit (L, 21).

Emerson followed up his invitation with a letter that could not have been warmer. 'In coming to America you cannot come wrong' he wrote. 'My wife and my children and some good neighbours are made happy by the expectation of quickly seeing you, and your chamber is all ready.' Clough found that the earliest steamer he could take sailed on 30 October. In August he spent a few farewell days with Matt during one of his inspection tours in Wales. and wrote to Blanche describing his farewell visits to his aunts at Min-y-Don, St Asaph and Mold. Lady Ashburton, recovering from a lengthy bilious fever, invited him to a valedictory house-party on 15 October: 'Give us as long a visit as your Ladie Love and lordly preparations for *being sea-sick* will permit'. All the usual suspects were to be there – Carlyle, newly returning from inspecting Frederick the Great's battlefields in Silesia, and Mrs Carlyle, coming separately with the Brookfields. Thackeray was to be Clough's fellow passenger on the transatlantic voyage. Lady Ashburton specially invited Ingersoll, the new American minister, and she wrote letters of introduction to Secretary of State Edward Everett (a former president of Harvard) and to the great orator Daniel Webster (who had ten years earlier negotiated with her father-in-law the treaty settling the boundary between the US and Canada).

The voyage of the Cunarder sail-and-steam packet *Canada* from Liverpool to Boston between 30 October and 12 November 1852 must be one of the best documented transatlantic crossings of all time. Thackeray and Clough both wrote full prose accounts to their lovers in England,[3] and Clough followed this up, later in life, with a semi-fictional account in verse. For the first four days on the ocean the two writers were too seasick to leave their cabins. Clough recovered first, and was able to keep on his legs when the ship hit a gale near Newfoundland and nearly ran into Cape Race. He paid a sick visit to Thackeray's cabin (the best on the ship) and was lent an advance copy of *Henry Esmond* which had been delivered to the author on the Liverpool quayside. As the weather improved, Thackeray described Clough walking the decks in a wide-awake hat and mustard-coloured inexpressibles. Clough told Blanche 'Thackeray and I get on very swimmingly'. The two men showed off their almost identical writing desks, Thackeray's the gift of his publisher, Clough's the gift of Blanche's mother.

Besides *Henry Esmond* Clough had another newly published book with him to read: Matthew Arnold had given him as a farewell present *Empedocles on Etna, and Other Poems, by* A. 'Write me from America concerning them' he wrote on 28 October 'but do not read them in the hurry of this week' (L, 245). During the voyage Clough wrote a number of verses of his own. While the ship was leaving the Mersey he composed 30 lines of farewell to Blanche ('Farewell, farewell, her vans the vessel tries') on the following pattern:

The docks, the streets, the houses past us fly
Without a strain the great ship marches by . . .
The billows whiten and the deep seas heave;
Fly once again, sweet words, to her I leave.
(P, 333)

When he recovered from his four days in bed – and from a temporary loss of his engagement ring – Arthur penned another three stanzas to the 'sweet eyes in England, dear to me'. In the poem 'Lie here, my darling, on my breast', written in his berth at dawn off Nova Scotia, he tells Blanche how he dreams of her lying beside him, kisses the empty air, and in imagination touches the parting of her hair. The poems were sent off to England by the first steamer that crossed the path of the *Canada*, off the coast of Nova Scotia. Blanche kept them and published them posthumously under the title *Songs in Absence* – but she omitted 'Lie here, my darling' as being 'too warm'. The poems are inferior to Clough's love poems of the 1840s, but they are just good enough to be useful for other lovers, homesick like him but lacking his talent, to send as missives to their distant beloveds.

More successful was a poem inspired by the days of seasickness.

Ye flags of Piccadilly
Where I posted up and down
And wished myself so often
Well away from you and Town

Are the people walking quietly
And steady on their feet?
Cabs and omnibuses plying
Just as usual in the street? . . .

This squally wild north-wester
With which our vessel fights
Does it merely serve with you to
Carry up some paper kites?

Ye flags of Piccadilly,
Which I hated so, I vow
I could wish with all my heart
You were underneath me now!
(P, 336)

Clough presented a copy of these verses to Thackeray, who adorned them with an impromptu sketch of their author (P, 744).

The voyage also produced some more serious verses. One beginning 'Come home, come home! and where a home hath he / whose ship is driving o'er the driving sea?' evokes well, at the literal level, the migratory life of the seafarer, while also hinting at a deeper level of cosmic homelessness. 'Come back, come back! behold with straining mast' takes the headwind that blew the ship off course near Newfoundland as an emblem of Clough's own hesitation about emigration, and is in effect a self-exhortation to perseverance. Here is the final one of its eight vigorous stanzas:

> Come back, come back!
> Back flies the foam; the hoisted flag streams back;
> The long smoke wavers on the homeward track;
> Back fly with winds things which the winds obey:
> The strong ship follows its appointed way.
>
> (P, 337)

Once he found his sea legs, Clough enjoyed the life aboard the steamer, even if by the end of the trip he found the enforced intimacy with fellow passengers a strain. Years later, in the prologue to *Mari Magno*, he recalled the pleasures of the voyage (placed, significantly, in August, not November) in a set of heroic couplets.

> Delight to me was in that wondrous force
> Ceaseless impelling on the appointed course,
> Delight that burning and victorious will
> Mid winds and waves that held its purpose still,
> Delight at noon on each succeeding day
> To hear the ship had won upon her way
> Her sum of miles – delight were mornings grey
> And gorgeous eves, – nor was it less delight
> On each more temperate and favouring night
> Friend with familiar or with new-found friend,
> To pace the deck, and o'er the bulwarks bend,
> And the night watches in long converse spend.
>
> (P, 374)

One of the new-found friends was the Harvard poet James Russell Lowell, author of a satirical *Fable for Critics*, and later to be the founding editor of the *Atlantic Monthly*. He advised him to set up a school to prepare boys for college. Accompanying him was his wife, Maria White Lowell, an ardent campaigner against slavery, whom Thackeray found excessively priggish. Clough gave Lowell a walking-on part in *Mari Magno* and described him thus:

> Of the New England ancient blood was one;
> His youthful spurs in letters he had won;
> Unspoilt by that, to Europe late had come, –
> Hope long deferred, – and went unspoilt by Europe home.
> (P, 374)

At dinner on the last day of the voyage healths were drunk. Thackeray was proposed first. Then a passenger proposed 'Lowell, the American poet'. In returning thanks, Lowell proposed 'Clough, the English poet'. It was Arthur's first intimation that his reputation was higher in the US than in Britain.

Clough arrived in New England at an auspicious time for American literature, often called the American Renaissance. The previous two years had seen the publication of several classic novels: Nathaniel Hawthorne's *The Scarlet Letter* and *The House of the Seven Gables*; Herman Melville's *Moby Dick* and Harriet Beecher Stowe's *Uncle Tom's Cabin*. A little earlier, W. Prescott had published *The Conquest of Peru* and H. D. Thoreau had published his tract on civil disobedience. Henry Wadsworth Longfellow, Edgar Allen Poe and Oliver Wendell Holmes, as well as Emerson and Lowell, had all recently published volumes of verse.

This ferment of literary activity was centred around the city of Boston, and its leaders were to go down into history as the Boston Brahmins. The name 'Brahmins', said Oliver Wendell Holmes, who was one of them, indicated 'the harmless, inoffensive, untitled aristocracy' of New England 'which has grown to be a caste by the repetition of the same influences generation after generation'. Boston, according to Holmes, was 'the intellectual hub of the Universe'.

Several of the Brahmins, of course, lived not in Boston itself but in nearby Cambridge. Holmes himself, the future 'Autocrat of the Breakfast Table' and father of the famous judge, was at this time Professor of Anatomy and Dean of the Harvard Medical School. His colleague as Professor of Modern Languages was Longfellow, who was yet to write *Hiawatha*. Their publisher, William Ticknor, was a foremost figure in Massachussetts society and owned the Old Corner Bookstore which is still a place of pilgrimage in Boston.

A few miles away in the country was Concord, where Emerson lived and held court. Close by him lived Henry Thoreau, who had earlier built himself a hut on Walden Pond. At Concord too lived Bronson Allcott, a vegetarian mystic best known to posterity as the father of Louisa May Alcott, who already, at the age of 14, was beginning to be his main financial support.

This talented and generous intellectual community immediately took Clough to its heart. He had long been on close terms with Emerson and his seaboard friendship with Lowell endured. His brief encounter with Margaret

Fuller stood him in good stead with a community that revered her memory and in this same year brought out her *Memoirs*. *The Bothie*, he discovered, was well known and was to be seen on many a drawing-room table. Sir Charles Lyell, the doyen of British geology, had arrived on the previous steamer for an American lecture tour. He and his wife were generous in providing introductions to their friends in Boston.

The social whirl into which Clough was plunged is described in daily detail in his letters to Blanche. On the day of his arrival, 12 November, a message from the Lyells was waiting at his hotel. Next day, Saturday, Lady Lyell took him to pay his respects to the Ticknors. He visited Dr Samuel Howe, editor of the Boston *Commonwealth* and head of an institute for the blind, and met his wife Julia Ward Howe, later to be famous as the author of *The Battle Hymn of the Republic*. At the Howes' he was introduced to the son of a Harvard professor, young Charles Eliot Norton, 'with whom' he reported 'I swear eternal friendship'. This was to be the most important of Clough's American friendships: it lasted until death and beyond, with Norton providing warm support to Blanche as a widow.

Clough took the evening train to Concord – escorted by the mystic Allcott – to take up Emerson's invitation. He found on arrival that he had been expected to arrive by a different ship, and that Emerson was shortly to take off for a lecture tour. Accordingly he stayed only for the weekend, but enjoyed 'loads of talk', was charmed by Emerson's 11-year-old daughter, and walked with him 'to a bit of a wood with a prettyish pool' – no doubt Walden Pond. In the evening Thoreau called for tea, and Arthur plucked some birch bark as a memento to send to Blanche.

Concord was not everyone's ideal community. A few years before, in *Mosses from an Old Manse* Hawthorne had written:

> Never was such a poor little country village infested with such a variety of queer, stangely dressed, oddly behaved mortals, most of whom look upon themselves to be important agents of the world's destiny, yet were simply bores of a very intense water.

Clough was never bored by Emerson, but he regarded his Swedenborgian wife as a poor housekeeper. 'Dinner is a sort of mess of cocoa, bread and butter, and stawberries and cream.' In particular he disapproved of the Irish servants doing the washing up in a bucket in the dining room. Altogether, he did not fancy the wooden houses in the Concord countryside even though they cost only £500 to buy. But he found Boston 'very tolerably English'. 'The Yankees' he told Blanche 'are a singularly human-hearted set of people and I expect to get on well enough with them. I am in very good spirits at present, I assure you' (M, 330, 334, 450).

By the end of the next week Arthur was so enthusiastic about America that – only half in jest – he urged Blanche to bring her whole family over, including the Nightingales. Norton had introduced him to Felton the Professor of Greek ('a thoroughly kind-hearted worthy man', though too fond of Dickens), who promised to find him some pupils. Lady Lyell had taken him to see Prescott. Emerson had given a dinner in Boston in his honour, at which the other guests included Mr and Mrs Longfellow (beautiful but boring, he found her) and Nathaniel Hawthorne, whose most recent novel, *The Blithesdale Romance* Clough had read (two volumes in two and a half hours) in his London club in preparation for his voyage (M, 318, 338, 399).

Among the other guests was the Massachusetts anti-slavery senator Charles Sumner. Clough soon became aware of the political tensions on the issue of slavery, exacerbated by the Fugitive Slave Law which mandated Federal police in non-slave states to capture and return to their owners slaves who had fled from the Southern states. This law was detested in Boston, and Clough soon decided that it was 'a piece of truckling to the South' (M, 354). Even in Boston, few people, at this stage, were for the absolute abolition of slavery, but most believed that slaves entering a slave-free state should remain free. Emerson and Sumner were 'free-soilers' of this kind; Hawthorne, on the other hand was a Democrat: he had just written the campaign biography for Franklin Pierce's bid for the presidency. Prescott and the Ticknors were conservatives or 'Old Hunkers'.

The keen abolitionists among Clough's new friends were the Howes, who fulminated against slavery in their *Commonwealth*. The Lyells and Ticknors warned Clough against being too familiar with them: he might be tarred with the abolitionist brush. He himself, who had spent his childhood in slave-owning Charleston, had no firm conviction that it should be compulsorily abolished. He was happy to follow the free-soil lead of Emerson, though he differed from him in believing that the Federal Government should, by offering compensation, encourage slave states to get rid of slavery (M, 354). On the other hand, the Howes were friends of the Nightingales, and Mrs Howe, he soon found, was much the cleverest of the Boston womenfolk. So while he looked for an apartment in Cambridge he accepted the Howes' hospitality.[4] He was disturbed by some of the abolitionist literature he found there, and even more shocked when he discovered later that the Howes were engaged in the 'Underground Railway' for smuggling fugitive slaves to Canada. On Julia Howe he made a great impression. 'In appearance' she wrote in her reminiscences 'I thought him rather striking. He was tall, tending a little to stoutness, with a beautifully ruddy complextion and dark eyes which twinkled with suppressed humour. His sweet, cheery manner at once attracted my young chidren to him.'[5]

He was glad to find accommodation of his own at 2 Garden Street, Cambridge, at a bed and breakfast establishment kept, confusingly, by another

American scroll featuring Holmes, Alcott, Lowell, Emerson, Hawthorne and Longfellow.

Mrs Samuel Howe. He was later surprised to find that his landlady, though she opened doors herself and did her own washing up, moved in polite society. She too turned out to be an abolitionist. For dinner and tea he signed on at a nearby boarding house at two and a half dollars per week (M, 336, 340).

Besides slavery, another contentious issue was temperance. Massachusetts had recently followed the example of Maine and become a dry state. Dr Howe served no wine; a few others provided sherry and madeira from stocks they held before Prohibition. Clough soon adapted to this. 'Wine and spirits' he told Blanche 'are certainly not required where there is so much stimulant in the air; even tea and coffee may well be dispensed with.' Cocoa, he decided, was the best drink for the climate (M, 335).

Clough spent Thanksgiving (25 November) with the Nortons. The Nortons, he explained to Blanche 'belong to a rather exclusive tip-top conservative set, that of the Ticknors'. Mr Norton and Mr Ticknor had married two sisters. 'They are high Whigs, which means Tories, and quite aristocratic, so to say.'[6] Clough went to church with the Nortons at 11, dined with them at 2, took tea with them at 7 and then went with them to Boston for an evening party at the Ticknors, attended by 50 cousins. After games, a charade, and 'a very good supper' he was back home in Cambridge by midnight, in time to write up the day for Blanche. Next day he dined on English grouse and pheasant at the Longfellows' and then went up to the Norton house at Shady Hill, where the family acted *Box and Cox*. He wrote an epilogue, his first American composition, in which he lamented the fate 'of those in bachelor estate / condemned to traverse o'er and o'er again / The world of lodgings let to single men' (P, 339).

Norton senior, a respected biblical scholar, was a pillar (some said 'the Pope') of orthodox Unitarianism, having made his reputation with a tome of 'Reasons for not believing the Doctrines of Trinitarianism' (1821). Clough felt he had to attend church with the Nortons from time to time. Cambridge's 'tall Gothic church' he wrote to Carlyle 'is altogether a make-belief, being wooden in material and unitarian in doctrine' (M, 344). During the sermon he composed a poem 'while the preacher, much perplext / to pieces pulls the weary text' recalling 'the darling figure of my love' and imagining the sound of her voice and the rustle of her purple silk. (P, 339). It went off to Blanche with the next letter: he apologized for the quality of the verse, complaining that the sermon had ended to soon. He had lain awake all morning, he explained, fancying himself with her 'in the garden, going up to the greenhouse'.

Clough was disconcerted by the strength of Unitarian feeling in Cambridge. 'They are so awfully rococo in their religions notions that were I much in the way of hearing them expressed I should infallibly speak out and speak strongly' he told Blanche, to her considerable alarm (M, 360; B, 666). In general he avoided church-going, and justified this in a cliché-ridden poem 'Amid these crowded pews must I sit and seem to pray?' (P, 350).

Respectable people, he found, looked askance at Emerson and his friends like Alcott and Fuller, who had given up Unitarianism and taken to forms of spirituality even further from orthodox Christianity, such as transcendentalism. Emerson, he reported 'stinks in the nostrils' of all except Longfellow and Howe. A particular *bête noire* of such respectable people was the minister Theodore Parker, whose new Congregational Society of Boston tried to occupy a position between Unitarianism and transcendentalism. Clough dined with him *chez* the Howes, and found him congenial. 'Theodore Parker has been preaching some very infidelical sermons' he later reported to Blanche 'proclaiming disbelief in Miracles and all that – by which the genteel Boston mind is a good deal disturbed, poor thing' (M, 340, 355).

On the last day of November all Boston turned out to mourn at the funeral of Daniel Webster, whose death had coincided with Clough's arrival. The letter of recommendation from Lady Ashburton was now worthless – but in any case, he wrote rather heartlessly, 'Webster could not have done much for me – he was head over ears in debt, ambition, and disappointment' (M, 337). On the same day the Lyells returned to England from New York. By Lady Lyell's kind hand Clough sent a parcel of bonnets to Blanche.

At the beginning of December Clough at last made an effort to make some money. In an advertisement in the Boston *Daily Advertiser* he offered tuition to individual pupils. The notice was accompanied by a list of 14 referees, beginning with President Sparks of Harvard, and including Mr S. G. Ward, the Boston representative of Baring's (the Ashburtons' Bank). The advertisment did not produce any response, but private recommendation brought a single pupil, the 17-year-old Lindell Winthrop, a nonchalant, aristocratic six-footer. He was due to come for three hours a day until July and pay 300 dollars for the year and Clough quickly calculated that with three such pupils a year he would have enough to live on. Winthrop, however, was irregular in attendance, and soon revealed himself as a 'mere rowing, pleasure hunting, youngster' and in February he quit, and his family decided that the best place for him was Canton (M, 341, 383).

The connection with S. G. Ward, however, lasted longer. It turned out that his wife was a former friend of Margaret Fuller. She and Mrs Howe and a group of other women constituted a feminist set. In general Clough did not like them: he disapproved of Mrs Howe's style of singing, and as for the others 'they do the satirical, and the sarcastic, and the ill-natured, and the fastidious, and the intellectual, and all that' – it was as bad as being back in London. In his dislike of transcendentalist females he was for once in agreement with Charles Dickens, who ten years earlier, in *Martin Chuzzlewit*, had parodied the effusions of a literary lady in a wig:

> Mind and matter glide swift into the vortex of immensity. Howls the sublime, and softly sleeps the calm Ideal, in the whispering chambers of the imagination. To hear it, sweet it is. But then, outlaughs the stern philosopher, and saith to the Grotesque 'what ho! Arrest for me that Agency! Go bring it here! and so the vision fadeth'. (p. 467)

Altogether Clough found the position of women in America somewhat puzzling.

> Ladies carve a great deal, and bring you things even at great suppers . . . No man seems expected to carve for a lady, and they don't get up when the ladies leave the dining room, nor open the door, except casually. Only, in omnibuses and the cars (as they call railway trains) they expect you to give your place up and are very impudent about that, any woman whatever – and some of them I believe will even ask. (M, 360)

He approved, however, of the high standard of female education, and reported admiringly to Carlyle 'Girls in Boston of the richer classes all learn Latin and Algebra. They have all read Virgil and Caesar' (M, 396).

In his dislike of feminists, Clough made an exception for Mrs Ward. He went to her house for the first ball of the season on 8 December, but he did not dance, finding, so he told Blanche, the Bostoniennes excessively plain. At a party two nights later he met 'a very pretty charming-looking Miss Otis'. She was, he hastened to add, 'the first person here that has at all reminded me of you' – though it emerges from his detailed description that there was no resemblance at all between the two ladies. He was on safer ground describing a meeting with James Lowell's aged and deaf father:

> He began by saying that he was born an Englishman, i.e. before the end of the Revolution. Then he went on to say 'I have stood as near to George III as to you now. I saw Napoleon crowned Emperor . . . I saw the present Sultan ride through Constantinople on assuming the throne' – and so on – all in a strong clear voice and in perfect sentences which you saw him making beforehand. And all one could do was only to bow and look expressive. (M, 348)

The younger Lowell continued to suggest to Clough that he should run a school. So too did the Harvard Professors Longfellow and Felton. Twelve scholars at $200 a year would provide ample funds for a couple to live on. A possibility opened up at Milton, seven miles from Boston, with school buildings available free and the prospect of 20 scholars. The problem was that eight of the scholars would be boarders: Clough could not manage these alone, and would Blanche be willing to take them on? Better, he thought, keep a day school in Boston with hours from nine to twelve, like a cousin of Emerson's who kept one of those admirable ladies' schools there.

If there were problems about keeping a school, Blanche inquired, and if private pupils did not present themselves, why not give lectures?[7] Arthur replied that people would only attend courses, which must have made her wonder why he had not brought with him his lecture courses from London. In mid-December he did give one lecture at Harvard, but received no fee. He consoled himself with the thought 'One lecture may be read as much as 100 times. The usual fee is 15 to 20 dollars, and expenses' (M, 349). But as time went on, he began to think that schoolkeeping, preferably a girls' school, was the most realistic prospect, and he kept inquiring whether Blanche would be willing to share such a life. If all went well and she agreed, he could cross the Atlantic in April, marry her, and bring her back to start term in September (M, 350).

Though a diligent correspondent where Blanche was concerned, Clough wrote little to any of his old friends in England. To Carlyle he sent a letter enclosing a two-dollar bill, so that he could see what Harvard looked like ('red-brick old fashioned buildings, rather inclined to tumble down'). By the same post he wrote Matthew Arnold a letter describing briefly but enthusiastically his new circle of friends. Matthew's response, which arrived around Christmas time, contained a douche of well-deserved cold water.

> I have no doubt that you will do well *socially* in the U.S.: you are English, you are well introduced – and you have personal merit – the object for you is to do well *commercially*.
>
> Value the first only so far as it helps the second. It would be poor consolation for having not established oneself at the end of a year and a half to be able to say – I have got into the best American Society. (L, 249)

This, Arthur complained to Blanche, was the only letter he had received from any of his friends, other than Carlyle, since coming to America (M, 365).

Clough's new friends were less demanding than Matt. James Lowell, in compliment to *The Bothie*, sent him an invitation to Christmas dinner couched in hexameters. Clough (who was studying geometry in preparation for schoolteaching) replied to his brother hexametrist:

> Is it not given, or am I confusing, as an axiom in Pierce
> Or postulate in Euclid, that a monad in space cannot eat
> Two several dinners at the same hour of the day and in two different houses;
> He therefore, who is engaged to partake of turkey and pie
> With Mr and Mrs Longfellow at Mr Appleton's table
> Cannot, he grieves to infer, hope also to take them at Elmwood.
>
> (M, 252)

The Appletons hung a present for him on their Christmas tree: a penwiper shaped like a butterfly. Possibly Clough felt the gift was a little close to the bone, for he left it behind and had to call again to collect it on New Year's Eve.

At Christmas time Blanche and Arthur looked back over a year of engagement. It is clear from their letters that each was very much in love with the other. The letters as published in the standard edition of Clough's correspondence do not give an adequate indication of the degree of affection, since the repeated endearments have, very reasonably, been omitted. But the full texts are replete with what Margaret Fuller would have called the 'dish and spoon' aspect of life. There are many kisses attached to each letter before departure, and each arriving letter is carried about as a treasure. There are many countings of days to the next possible meeting, and many nostalgic recallings of happy moments of intimacy during the earlier part of the year.

> This time last year – when you sat in the drawing room between the table and the fire and I was before you, and you asked 'will you love me' – O my dear Blanche do not let me be unworthy of what was then in your heart. (B, 618)

From time to time Blanche, too, expressed herself as totally unworthy of Arthur: 'How odd you should like me. I am so poor and horrid.' By contrast, there are also between the pair lots of misunderstandings, reproaches and perceived failures to respond adequately to the other's expressions of affection. Such troubles, normal with any engaged couple, were exaggerated by the extreme slowness of the exchange of letters across the Atlantic: a letter that had given offence could be three weeks old before any apology caught up with it. Blanche found Arthur exasperatingly hard to please. 'I wonder whether all your life you will go on, when you're unhappy, unhappy for this cause, and when you're happy, dissatisfied because you're happy' she wrote on 17 December. At one point she was tempted to wonder whether love was perhaps 'only a little spell to bring people into a noose which they cannot get out of'. But every letter, on either side, ended with expressions of intense longing.

Within the bounds of Victorian propriety the expressions of desire are quite physical. Arthur is always imagining himself stroking Blanche's hair and likes to recall kneeling in front of her and putting his head in her lap. Blanche from time to time recalls, with reproachful delight, some violent wooing by Arthur at Swedenbridge near Ambleside The theme of fellow service has not been forgotten – in the very first letter aboard ship Arthur wrote 'one way or other whatever happens we shall, I trust, be each other's, and work out our little work together'. But the early emphasis on the value of suffering is revoked: 'O dear child, now that I have gone away from England for your dear sake you may forget the old letters of this time last year.' On the last day of the year, by way of an anniversary present, he sent a poem 'Were I with you, or you with me' – I quote two of its five quatrains:

> My darling's face I cannot see,
> My darling's voice is mute for me,
> My fingers vainly seek the hair
> Of her that is not here but there . . .
>
> The mere assurance that she lives
> And loves me, full contentment gives;
> I need not doubt, despond, nor fear,
> For she is there, and I am here.
>
> (P, 343)

On New Year's eve he attended another ball at Mrs Ward's. American dancing, he considered, was more cheerful than graceful: the young men waltzed very ill, and the music was too loud to talk over (M, 361, 368). He danced a quadrille with Miss Ticknor, but otherwise sat the evening out. However, he took careful notes on the young ladies' dresses 'for the benefit of my young lady far away' to whom he despatched detailed descriptions. Mrs Howe, he reported 'dresses so low that I'm always in terror lest she should come up bodily out of it, like a pencil out of a case'. Mrs Howe, he was later to discover, had an ambiguous reputation, quite apart from her abolitionism: she liked to think of herself as Becky Sharp, and published a set of compromising verses. For the moment, however, Clough decided that she was at bottom a good creature. 'Peace be to her shoulders, therefore' (M, 356).

Later in January he was invited to the Longfellows, along with Emerson, Lowell and Norton, for a farewell dinner for Hawthorne, who had been appointed by the new President Pierce as consul in Liverpool. Wherever he went, Clough inquired about the minimum sum for a couple to live on. The answers he was given depended on the wealth of his informants: Hawthorne and his wife, he was told, had lived for an entire year at Concord on one hundred dollars. In Cambridge the Nortons thought the minimum was two thousand dollars, but Professor Felton's wife thought $1200 adequate. Clough kept calculating ways in which he could achieve at least the lower target, and was encouraged to be told by Thackeray that one could secure a 6 per cent secure return on some American stocks. But he had so far earned almost nothing at all, and had been living on the £50 which he had brought with him out of his total assets of some £500. Though his expenses were modest – 8 dollars a week – he could not claim, even as late as April, to have covered them: he had earned only $45 since his arrival (M, 369, 389, 424, 439).

His American friends kept repeating that he should start a school.[8] The more he looked at this prospect, the less he liked it, and whenever an opportunity presented itself he found some reason for turning it down. The school at Milton was impossible because it involved keeping a boarding-house. A classics post in an existing academy offered only $800, and required a three-year commitment. A school that offered at Concord did not pay enough and would have been lonely for Blanche (M, 383, 390, 411, 425). Once March had gone past, there was no prospect of opening a school until next September. As the year went on, the nearest possible starting date moved to 4 March 1854 (M, 411, 436). Clough was reluctant to admit it to himself or to others, but it soon became clear to his friends, such as Lady Lyell, that he had no intention of starting a school in America until Blanche joined him (M, 426). But without starting a school, how could he afford to marry Blanche and bring her over?

The prospect of lecturing was more attractive. No doubt, not being a best seller, he could not make the enormous sums that Thackeray had reported. But Oliver Wendell Holmes, the local 'pet lecturer', was said to make $1,500 a year, and Clough, having attended one lecture which made him 'burn with indignation and contempt' thought he ought to be able to do no worse (M, 408). Homer seemed a suitable topic, so in preparation for lectures he began translating him. 'If I can get through this first book of the Iliad, I think that will make a capital thing for a Lecture. These people have a great idea of Verse' he wrote on 9 January (M, 361).

The translation of foreign classics was coming into fashion at Harvard – later to culminate in Longfellow's rendering of Dante. *Evangeline* had brought English hexameters into vogue, but among the Boston circle some regarded Clough's versification as superior. James Lowell, a great admirer of *The Bothie*, had written of Longfellow in his *Fable of Critics*:

> I'm not over-fond of Greek metres in English.
> To me rhyme's a gain, so it be not too jinglish,
> And your modern hexameter verses are no more
> Like Greek ones than sleek Mr. Pope is like Homer.
>
> (Lowell 1848: 66)

But a good hexameter version of the *Iliad* and the *Odyssey* in modern English, a more authentic rendering than sleek Mr Pope, would be welcomed on both sides of the Atlantic. So Arthur's enthusiasm for Homer translation in the new year of 1853 was not so perverse as it may have seemed at the time to Blanche.

At the end of January, however, Clough was offered two more immediate opportunities to earn some money. A Harvard senior called Guild – a nephew of Mrs Ticknor and Mrs Norton – presented himself as a pupil and proved intelligent and diligent. Clough, he reported, taught as he had never been taught before, and he recruited other young men until Clough had a class of seven pupils to lecture to on Aristotle's *Ethics* on Tuesdays and Thursdays at $6 a week (M, 391, 394, 421). Even more promising, Mr Brown, of the booksellers Little Brown, wanted to publish a new edition of Plutarch, and offered Clough $350 to revise the standard translation of the *Lives*. Clough reckoned that this would take six months, and quickly settled down to regular work on this task, which he said he liked better than 'anything which requires distinct statements of opinion or the like' (M, 367, 376).

This was all very cheering news, and there was also an article worth $35 to be written for the *North American Review* on the Report of the Oxford University Commissioners. At the same time Arthur tried to prepare Blanche for a life of poverty – which he defined as cold meat six days out of seven. She would not have to do drudgery, he told her, but if she was to avoid the appalling Irish servants she should bring over one English girl and a boy. Blanche queried the arithmetic on which Arthur was basing his hope of setting up house, but she responded that she would not at all mind 'a little of the pie and pudding world'. She began to take instructions in the more menial aspects of housekeeping. For some while she had been learning how to play the violin, and she offered to give music lessons to help make ends meet in Boston. She was quite firm that she could not do without a piano. At the same time she was also taking lessons in Italian from a flatmate of Mazzini's – but she found the smell of his cigar smoke hard to stomach (M, 383, 393, 404–5).

Throughout the early months of 1853 Blanche kept Arthur informed of events in England, both domestic and political. Home life was initially rather drab: everyone, she complained, made mountains out of molehills.

> Aunt Ju goes on in her own way, and Papa gets into an excitement about the least thing, and we get out of temper, and Mama is not much of a head, so we make a great mess sometimes. But it is much better when Mama is at home, though, with Papa, and she never minds any troubles.

Florence Nightingale was at this stage a family problem rather than a national monument. She was desperately seeking some useful employment outside the household. But her attempts to do so only acquired her the reputation of being an interfering busybody. Blanche thought the allegations quite unjust. 'It is so unlike Flo to interfere with anybody' she wrote (B, 654).

The Smiths' domestic life, however, soon took a dramatic turn. Mr Farrer, a friend of Arthur's, became a regular visitor to the Smith household, and took an interest in Blanche's sister Bertha – a young lady to whom Arthur had been dutifully sending across the Atlantic presents such as a tomahawk. In February he told Samuel Smith that he wished to marry her, but he confessed that there was a problem: he had a lunatic sister. The Smiths made investigations and were told that the insanity was not hereditary but 'accidental'. However, after a few weeks Farrer withdrew his proposal, of which Bertha was still in total ignorance (B, 660). Less than a month later it was discovered that he was to be married to someone else. 'Fancy' Blanche wrote to Arthur 'Bertha being given to a man ready a month afterwards for someone else' (B, 666). Bertha herself was more interested in working in a sanatorium with Florence.

Early in 1853 the death of Wellington stimulated Clough to write a poem, *Last Words*, comparing the Duke favourably to Napoleon, whom in other moods he much admired (P, 269, 343). The poem was published in *Fraser's Magazine* in February. Still in a bad humour with his English friends, Clough sent Blanche a moping little poem 'That out of sight is out of mind'. 'They were my friends' he wrote ''twas sad to part / almost a tear began to start' – but he had discovered that, excepting for the blind, what is out of sight is indeed out of mind.

> But love *is* as they tell us blind
> So out of sight and out of mind
> Need not, nor will, I think, be true
> My own and dearest love, of you
> (P, 347)

His friends in England, however, *were* thinking of him, and to some purpose. On 20 December 1852 the conservative government of Lord Derby resigned. It was followed by a coalition government under Lord Aberdeen, in which Disraeli was succeeded by Gladstone as Chancellor of the Exchequer. Lady Ashburton wrote to Carlyle 'One of the great joys at the present time in the formation of this Govt is that *we* are not in it, and another that I think it will go very hard if I get nothing for Clough' (M, 355). Her friend Lord Granville, the Lord President of the Council, promised to propose Clough for the next vacancy for an Inspectorship such as Matthew Arnold's (M, 386). Carlyle sent Granville's letter across the Atlantic; but Clough was not greatly encouraged. There were only three such posts, he told Blanche 'so before any opening occurs, the Administration may be an Opposition'. Later, however, worn down by the New England winter, he found the prospect more attractive, and asked Blanche to sound out her family about the possibility of his returning. By mid-May he had decided that he would prefer an assured £700 a year in England than depend on 'Yankee papas and mamas in a Boston school'. On the other hand, rather than be an Inspector in England his first preference would be to take pupils and live on literary earnings in Cambridge (M, 397, 423, 433).

When letters did arrive from other friends, Clough did not always like them. Shairp wrote in January and February urging him to give up 'the faiths of the philosophers and literateurs' and return to Christianity. 'How I have longed that Christ the Spirit might be revealed in your spirit, your heart of hearts' (M, 368, 377). We do not possess Clough's reply, but in it he accused Shairp of hypocrisy and self-deceit. 'I will not hide from you that your letter gave me great pain' replied Shairp, 'Nothing you can say will make me change my holdings; but I wish not to quarrel with you and therefore beg that you will write no more on these subjects' (M, 402, 412).

Arnold's Christmas letter, as we have seen, contained a serious rebuke. In response Clough accused him of a falling off in friendship. Matt replied 'I cannot say more than that I really have clung to you in spirit more than to any other man – and have never been seriously estranged from you at any time.' The period of his own development, he said, coincided so exactly with their friendship 'that I am for ever linked with you by intellectual bonds – the strongest of all'. Clough was still not sufficiently mollified. Before leaving England he had given Matt a text of *Amours de Voyage* and he complained about his lack of enthusiasm for it. 'We will not discuss what is past any more' Matt replied on 21 March, 'as to the Italian poem, if I forebore to comment it was that I had nothing special to say' – and changed the subject (Laing, 252–4).

Shortly after this, Clough wrote for *The North American* a review of Arnold's *Empedocles on Etna*. The poem, as he summarizes it, tells how Empedocles, weary of misdirected effort, and incapable of doing anything that shall be true to his proper interior sense, wandering forth with no determined purpose into the mountain solitudes, flings himself into the boiling crater of Etna. The review was disdainful of 'the high, and shall we say, pseudo-Greek inflation of the philosopher musing above the creator, and the boy Callicles singing myths upon the mountain'. The only moral Clough can find to the story is 'the deceitfulness of knowledge and the illusiveness of the affections, the hardness and roughness and contrariousness of the world, the difficulty of living at all, the impossibility of doing anything – *viola tout*'. He must surely have known that the same deflationary summary could be made of his own *Dipsychus* – but that, he could plead, was not a published work. At this time it lay in a trunk confided to the care of Blanche – who one day took a look at it, and asked if she could read it all. This drew an anguished response 'please don't read Dipsychus yet – I wish particularly not. You shall see it sometime – but now, not, please – dear, I beg not, please' (M, 350, 417; PPR, 368ff).

Whether Blanche, after this, was able to resist a further peek, we do not know. The only misdemeanour she confessed to was deleting, from a letter she was to forward to Matthew Arnold, some unflattering references to her own family. But her distaste for *Dipsychus* had its effect on Arthur. He wrote a couple of hundred lines of *Dipsychus Continued* to give the drama a moral ending. Dipsychus, 30 years on, is now Lord Chief Justice. He is confronted by a beggar woman who turns out to be the prostitute he enjoyed in Venice. 'In old times' she tells him 'You called me pleasure: my name now is – Guilt.' Blanche had worked upon his innate inability to leave well alone.[9]

Of Clough's English friends no one worked more energetically for his welfare than Frederick Temple. On 10 May Temple wrote to notify him that a reconstruction of the Education Committee of the Privy Council provided for a Secretary, two Assistant Secretaries, and six Clerks of the first Class. Lord Granville (inspired of course by Lady Ashburton, and backed by Lingen, the Secretary of the Committee) was willing to offer one of these clerkships to Clough. This would be a six-hour-a-day job worth £300 a year, rising yearly by £25 to £600. The duties of the office, it seemed, were to supervise and standardize the examinations of candidates for teaching posts in schools. It would not pay as well as an inspectorship of the kind held by Matthew Arnold, but at least according to Lady Ashburton, it would be more interesting and carry more prestige (M, 432).

Temple realized that if Clough accepted the post he would have a long wait to marry. So he proposed a second alternative. Palgrave, his Vice-Principal at Kneller Hall, was also interested in the job. Suppose he were to take it, and Clough were to become Vice-Principal in his place? The post was paid £400 a year, rising in three years to £500; it carried with it the obligation of residence, but that meant that board and lodging came free.

Clough's friends urged him to accept the examinership. 'Write at once to Lord Granville and say Yes' wrote Carlyle. 'Prefer us to America' urged Lady Ashburton. Shairp, too, in a letter that began 'Don't let us wrangle any more across the wide Atlantic' urged him to return. 'I suppose your income would soon rise after you had shown yourself a useful man.' Temple, in a second letter, pointed out candidly that it was doubtful whether Clough would make a success of a school in America. 'You are, as you know, fond of putting a fine point on things and you would not be satisfied unless you could teach in a very superfine way.' He urged him to return speedily in order to decide (M, 432, 441).

The offer placed Clough in a quandary. His main object in life was to marry Blanche as soon as possible: questions of salary and domicile were utterly secondary to that. The one thing he would not do for her was to found a school without her at his side. It was clear that the examinership would not by itself allow him to marry for another eight years, and his repugnance to accept this was reinforced by a letter from his prospective father-in-law recommending against acceptance. Samuel Smith held out instead the prospect of financial support to assist the couple to settle in America.

Clough agreed that the examinership held out the prospect of too long a delay before marriage. However, he was attracted by Temple's alternative Kneller Hall proposal. He made this clear in his reply to Samuel Smith, urging him not to 'exaggerate the blessings and the hopes of New England life'. But he had little hope that Smith would agree. 'Nothing but their own pet plan would satisfy dear Papa and Mama' he told Blanche. 'I am quite content that

Cabinet offices

he should decide for America' since 'you my dearest are for it.' To Lady Ashburton he wrote saying that he left it to be settled between his friends whether or not to accept the Council Office position.

Blanche did, as he had guessed, favour the American alternative: in a letter which crossed with his she wrote 'my £4,000 would give us in America at least 200 a year, on which we would not starve; while in England it would be diminished to nothing, by insurance and low interest'. But she worried whether Arthur would really commit himself to earning enough. 'You see you hardly do anything till you are driven to it by outward pressure.' She also reported that if Arthur decided for America her father would allow them to get married as soon as they wished.

Blanche, as her letter shows, was already exasperated with Arthur's lack of enterprise. He had now outraged Samuel Smith and Temple by suggesting that they should, between them, decide on the response to be given to Granville. Temple wrote 'I have seen the Smiths. The conclusion to which Mr Smith has come is: not to decide. Obviously the natural conclusion. He merely upholds his original conditions: £500 a year before marriage in England.' He went on to say 'My dear fellow you *cannot* have this matter decided for you . . . There is nothing left for it but immediate return to England, to choose for yourself' (M, 447).

While this letter was crossing the Atlantic, Arthur continued to write to Blanche as if it was a foregone conclusion that they would be living in America. In bed with a cold, he sulked at her 'sermon' ('I don't think it is quite good for me, do you know, to be spurred and lashed in that wicked way'). But by her 25th birthday, 18 June, his mind was more focused on the generosity of her Papa's offer of funding a settlement in America. He was looking forward to moving into the Norton's house at Shady Hill when they moved to their summer residence at Newport, and he began planning for his next year's pupils. He had just made a significant addition to his circle of friends, a young Harvard rhetoric professor and future editor of Chaucer, named Francis J. Child, who professed himself willing to collaborate in the setting up of a school (M, 425–6). But within eight hours of receiving Temple's letter, he dropped everything and took the next steamer from New York, leaving books and clothes in Cambridge and a valise at Concord.

In the end he was not, after all, left to make his own decision. Already on 11 June Blanche told Temple to accept the examinership on his behalf. She was willing, in two years time, if Arthur had not been promoted to an Inspectorship, to move to America. But she had been persuaded by her family not to let him turn down the last chance he was likely to be offered of a career in England. Sam Smith rendered the Kneller Hall proposal irrelevant by renewing his offer of £200 a year, without any longer attaching American residence as a condition (M, 454). Clough acquiesced in the decision that had been taken for him. 'With the offer of such money-assistance as will enable us to marry within the course of a year I could hardly do otherwise,' he told Norton. By the end of July he had formally accepted the post and taken up his position in the office ('up two pair at the very corner of Downing St and Whitehall'). 'If I refused it' he told Emerson 'I seemed to have no further chance of England whereas in taking it I do not forfeit all chance of America. At least I hope not' (M, 455, 457).

For a while he nursed hopes of returning. His spirits were lowered, he said, 'returning from the young and hopeful and humane republic to this cruel, unbelieving, inveterate old monarchy' (M, 460). He kept up a regular, if somewhat impersonal, correspondence with his American friends, bringing them up to date with literary and political gossip. But by Christmas all his books and belongings, sent by the ever-obliging Norton, were in Liverpool, where Hawthorne was now the US consul. 'We all bewail our Lycidas' Lowell wrote 'with Emerson at the head' (M, 464).

Clough resumed – for the time being – his friendship with Matthew Arnold, who seemed surprisingly untroubled by his review of *Empedocles*. 'At Fox How' Matt wrote at the end of August 'they think that your article on me is obscure and peu favorable – but I do not myself think either of these things.' On a tour of inspection in Wales he wrote 'If you knew the refreshment it was to me to think of you in London again' (L, 269, 271). But Clough found his old friends had become very *churchy*. Froude had now repented of *The Nemesis of Faith*, and Shairp, according to Jowett, was wickedly 'fallen back into the most uncompromising Scotch orthodoxy'. Arnold's wife ('a little Belgravian', according to Blanche) was quite religious, and even Matt himself was now recommending that most people – though not the elite – should stick to the old religious dogmas (M, 412, 460). Only Carlyle could be relied upon to be congenially unorthodox.

At the end of October Matthew Arnold brought out the first volume of poems he had published under his own name. It included many of those already published anonymously and some substantial new ones, notably *Sohrab and Rustum*. It was introduced by a preface disowning *Empedocles*: perhaps Arnold had been more affected than he let on by Clough's negative response to the poem. The preface became a classic statement of Arnold's own poetical theory: Clough confessed to friends that he did not at all agree with it. One poem in the collection *The Scholar Gipsy* evoked the days of Oxford undergraduate wanderings. For once Matt had produced a poem that Clough really liked. 'It is *so* true to the Oxford Country' he wrote to Norton, urging him to secure an American edition by Ticknor and Fields. Arnold deprecated his compliments, saying that the poem did no more than awake a pleasing melancholy (L, 282).

During his brief Christmas break Clough visited the Ashburtons at the

Grange, and stayed with the Nightingale family at nearby Embley Park, which was their winter home. In the new year he sent regular batches of Plutarch material across the Atlantic to honour his contract with Little Brown. Charles Norton suggested an American edition of his poems. 'I don't think I can set to work to unravel my weaved-up follies at this present moment' Clough said at first; but after a couple of months he warmed to the idea and sent a text of *Amours de Voyage* along with the May consignment of Plutarch (M, 477, 482).

The marriage of Arthur and Blanche took place on 13 June. They were married from Embley and honeymooned at the Nightingales' other home, Lea Hurst, near Matlock. We do not know who attended the ceremony, but the wedding presents are well documented, at least those from America.

Emerson and Norton and the others of the group decided to fill, between them, a trunk of gifts. 'I will go to sleep tonight' Emerson wrote to a friend 'I will go to sleep tonight taking order to dream what I shall put in the box. I wish we could forge the hook that would bring him here –where he was really content to live, I inferred, in the last days before his departure' (Ralph 1939 IV: 443). The Longfellows sent Blanche a Florentine mosaic brooch, Lowell sent the pair a silver creamer, and Felton a pair of ice-tongs. Emerson, in spite of not having recovered 'from the grief of your astonishing desertion of me' sent a silver candlestick 'emblematic of the light of Philosophy'.

During a sweltering July the Cloughs lived at Combe Hurst, looking for a house which they eventually found in St Mark's Crescent near Regent's Park. After a honeymoon in Switzerland, they lived there for five years, and their first two children were born there.

On the basis of the documentation that survives it is difficult to form a clear picture of the Clough's marriage. Because Blanche, during the engagement, was distressed by what she saw when she peeped into Arthur's old poems and letters ('I did hardly know that good men were so rough and coarse') some writers have rushed to the conclusion that the marriage was not sexually satisfactory. The circumstances of their engagement, however, meant that the couple learnt each other's virtues and faults at an early stage: when Blanche took Arthur on she knew exactly what she was getting. ('As for being unsoiled in the past' he had written 'it were mere deception to claim anything like it'.) She had become willing to accept that 'men's love . . . is less spiritual and depending more on juxtaposition'; but she had warned him 'I am intensely proud, and my independence is almost necessary to me' (B, 646). After the marriage, visitors always remarked on their happiness. On the appearance of Coventry Patmore's poem *The Angel in the House*, celebrating an idyllic marriage, many in America including Emerson believed that Clough was the author (M, 402–4).

During his married life Clough published no poems in England, and until his final illness he did not produce even privately anything original. Critics have blamed his marriage for impoverishing him intellectually. If one takes the view, as Clough himself sometimes did, that verse is a safety valve for the expulsion of diseased and depressive humours, then it seems hard to blame Blanche for healing him of the necessity for such relief. But in fact, Clough was, so far as his day job and other commitments allowed, quite active poetically during the years of his marriage. He continued to work on *Dipsychus*, and he revised *Amours de Voyage* for publication in Lowell's new journal *The Atlantic Monthly*. Right up to his last illness he was gathering and revising other poems for an American collection.[10]

Blanche, after his death, affirmed it as a good thing that after his marriage there was none of the 'enforced and painful communing with self alone' that had hitherto marked his life. 'The close and constant contact with another mind' she wrote 'gave him a fresh insight into his own, and developed a new understanding of the wants of other people.' She is correct in saying that there is in his poems plenty of evidence for his appreciation of family relations, and for his love of children. Had his health held out, she assures us, 'a long life of happiness and usefulness was clearly open to him' (PPR, 44ff).

A widow is not on oath when describing departed domestic bliss. But there is no good reason to doubt the essential truth of her account. The pair, united in marriage after so many trials, probably did live happily ever after – or rather, lived happily until Arthur's life was brought to a tragically early end.

Notes

1 The letter is among the Houghton papers at Trinity College, Cambridge.
2 The fair copy is in the Bodleian library: Ms. Eng. Poet d.128.
3 For Thackeray, see Gordon N. Ray, *The Letters and Private Papers of William Makepeace Thackeray*, 4 vols, Oxford 1945–6, III, pp. 146ff.
4 In spite of the Nightingale connection, Blanche was disturbed by this when she heard of it. 'I hope you won't get involved in abolition; not being one it would be a pity' she wrote, with dubious syntax. 'I read an anti-slavery paper, wherein it seemed to me the free-soilers are right'.
5 Blanche was not so great an admirer of Arthur's portliness. In a letter written at this time she says 'Don't go and get any older yet, or greyer, and don't get fat, mind that' (B, 357).
6 Blanche, on receipt of this letter, remarked that she did not like the sound of aristocratic democrats.
7 Thackeray, when he ran into Clough in the New Year told him that on his tour he had already got a hundred a year for his family. 'Dollars you mean?' 'No – Pounds'.
8 An exception was Longfellow, who wrote 'Clough thinks of opening a school for boys in Boston. Think of that! With all his sensitiveness and poetic softness!'
9 An American dating for *Dipsychus Continued* was established by Katherine Chorley, *Arthur Hugh Clough: the Uncommitted Mind*, Oxford 1962, pp. 264–6.
10 This is well brought out by P. Scott in his unpublished Ph.D dissertation on Clough, Edinburgh University 1976.

Chapter Ten

Marriage and Fellow Service

Most of what we know of the last seven years of Clough's life is derived from his correspondence with his transatlantic friends. Norton, Lowell and Child were now to him what Burbidge, Gell and Simpkinson had been in his youth. There was now little communication with Matthew Arnold: the two writers exchanged books with each other, and no doubt they passed each other by from time to time in the Council Office, but there were no more shared breakfasts and few more letters. Clough no longer shared holidays with Matt, as Walrond continued to do.[1] Of the old brigade only Tom Arnold, who returned from the antipodes a Roman Catholic and took a job at John Henry Newman's University in Dublin, kept in touch with all the old affection (M, 522, 558).

The 1850s were overshadowed in the US by the events leading up to the civil war between North and South, in the UK by the actual war, in alliance with France and Turkey, against Russia. In the letters of Clough's American correspondents one can read of the steps that led to the outbreak of hostilities. In March 1854 Longfellow wrote deploring the 'infamous Nebraska Bill' which permitted the extension of slavery beyond its previously agreed northern limit. Clough, though still not an out-and-out abolitionist, wrote to Norton 'I hope to heaven you'll get rid of slavery.' He was an admirer of Harriet Beecher Stowe, whom he had met at the Longfellows in February 1853. In this he was at odds with Carlyle, who was greatly annoyed when Mrs Stowe was fêted by upper-class British ladies: the Duchess of Sutherland presented her with a gold bracelet shaped like a shackle, and other noblewomen brought golliwogs, the currently politically correct kind of doll (M, 383, 431). In 1854 Child wrote to warn of 'Know Nothings', the new anti-Catholic, anti-foreigner party (M, 493). In 1856 Clough corresponded with Lowell about that year's presidential election and about the celebrated case of Dred Scott, a Virginian slave long resident in Illinois who was refused free status by the Supreme Court (M, 519).

John Brown's seizure of the federal arsenal at Harper's ferry, an unsuccessful attempt to start a slave insurrection, divided Clough's friends. Some thought him justly hanged as a murderer. But Howe and Parker had been members of the 'secret six' who supported him, and Emerson saluted him as 'the new saint who will make the gallows glorious like the cross'. When the war finally broke out in 1861 Emerson described it as 'the most wanton piece of mischief that bad boys ever devised'. Clough in a letter that was to be his last lamented that even from Concord young men were sent to the battlefield and to pestilence. 'People here are brutally ignorant and unfeeling about the matter – so far at least as they express their mind by the newspapers – but there is a vast deal of mute fellow-feeling with the North' (M, 586).

Clough was much more directly affected by the Crimean war of 1854, though he was very nonchalant about it when he first he passed news of it to Norton (M, 476). He was drawn close to it by Blanche's cousin, Florence Nightingale. Shortly after his return from America, she had overcome family opposition to become the superintendent of a Harley Street Establishment for Gentlewomen during Illness. She had travelled in Germany and France to acquaint herself with continental methods of nursing and had quickly become an expert on hospital administration. In August 1854 she was engaged in dealing with an epidemic of cholera in Soho.

In the same year a series of articles in *The Times* revealed the shocking condition of soldiers wounded in the Crimean war and neglected by the medical authorities. In October, the war secretary, Sidney Herbert, decided to send a party of nurses to Scutari, on the Bosporus, and asked Florence to lead it. Within a few days she assembled a group of 38 who set off on 21 October.

Clough had initially disliked Flo, as he made clear to Blanche during their engagement. 'I suppose I am something like her' he admitted 'in my unsympathetic unloving sort of temper; not so upright, perhaps and, I will venture to say, *softer* in both senses.' Flo, he thought, was unimaginative, though intelligent; arithmetical rather than creative; arid and lacking in tenderness, but 'of a high steady benevolence' (M, 307). By now he had overcome his dislike and had become a great admirer. He accompanied her to Calais on the first part of her journey to the Bosporus. He had become thoroughly alarmed about the war 'I passed some recruits the other day, and a man looking on said "They'll all be killed, every man jack of them." I'm sorry for it' (M, 491).

Nightingale arrived in Scutari a few weeks after the battle of Balaclava, well known for the loss of the Light Brigade that Tennyson mourned in a famous poem.[2] The battle produced an enormous number of casualties. By November 1855, Nightingale and her team were nursing four miles of patients, and she had to act as quartermaster general as well as head nurse. Since May she had herself been ill with 'Crimean fever' – typhus, she believed – caught inspecting hospitals in the field. In September she had been joined at Scutari by her Aunt Mai, Clough's mother-in-law. Clough learnt from her that 'the nurses in general have been only too faithful to their old metropolitan habits of drinking, thieving and the like' (M, 506). Herbert sent out another contingent of nurses led by Mary Stanley: relations between the two groups of nurses became

Florence Nightingale

strained, leading to a stiff correspondence between Clough and Mary's brother Arthur Stanley (M, 507ff). The war continued until June 1856. Nightingale stayed until the end, made famous by a verse of Longfellow:

Lo! in that hour of misery
A lady with a lamp I see
Pass through the glimmering gloom
And flit from room to room.

In her honour a national appeal set up a Nightingale Fund and Clough was put in charge of its administration.

After the war ended Clough visited Paris, Berlin and Vienna as secretary to a commission to inspect military schools. His American friend Charles Eliot Norton was taking a prolonged tour of Europe in 1855–6 and paid two lengthy visits to England. He had visited the Clough household in December and found it happy in spite of the loss of the first child (M, 512). When he returned in the following summer Clough gave him a rather chilly letter of introduction to Matthew Arnold at Fox How. Clough's mother and sister were now neighbours of the Arnolds, having moved in 1852 from Liverpool to Eller How in Ambleside.

During the war Clough continued work on his revision of the Plutarch translation, and sent regular packets across the Atlantic to his publisher: the final one was despatched in October 1857, a few months after the first printed volume had appeared (M, 525). There were plans for an American edition of *The Bothie*. 'Surely if Browning can be printed the Bothie ought to go off by ten thousands' Child wrote. But the plans proved abortive (M, 512). Clough liked *Hiawatha* when it appeared, even though Child declared it unreadable; but he shared Child's low opinion of Browning. He read in proof Tennyson's 1855 volume of poems, and thought only *Maud* had any merit. It was perhaps no coincidence that Matthew Arnold declared that *Maud* had been influenced by Clough's own style. 'He seems to be coming to your manner in *The Bothie* and the Roman poem' (L, I, 322). In October the Cloughs spent a holiday at Freshwater on the Isle of Wight, near the Tennysons' house, where the laureate was at this time working on *The Idylls of the King*. 'I like him personally better than I do his manner in his verses' Clough told Child. 'Personally he is the most unmannerly simple big child of a man that you can find.' Rather than any contemporary poet, he reported, he had become fascinated by Crabbe, as the most purely English of poets (M, 522).

Florence Nightingale had returned to England determined to reform the Army Medical Service, and for this purpose she created a network from the Queen and Prince Alfred downward. For a royal commission, set up under Sidney Herbert, she wrote a report of 830 pages entitled *Notes on Matters*

Affecting the Health, Efficiency and Hospital Administration of the British Army, showing by statistics the great extent to which military mortality was caused by inadequate hospital treatment. 'Our soldiers are enlisted' she wrote 'to die in barracks.'

While preparing this report Florence relied greatly on the support of Clough and his family. In 1857, confined to bed on doctor's orders, she moved into rooms in the Burlington Hotel and installed Arthur, along with his mother-in-law, as her gatekeeper. Blanche and Papa Smith had to console each other at Combe Hurst for the absence of their spouses. July of that year was spent by Arthur at Ambleside and much of his holiday was devoted to sub-editing the text of the Nightingale report (M, 529ff). The *Notes* were privately circulated in 1858. Their principal immediate effect was to improve and standardize the method of collecting hospital statistics.

For two years after 1858 Clough and Sidney Herbert were much preoccupied with negotiations about the use of the memorial fund in connection with the rebuilding of St Thomas's hospital. In 1860 their efforts bore fruit in the establishment at St Thomas's of the Nightingale School and Home for nurses. The work was exhausting. According to the family tradition Arthur 'would come home to St Mark's Crescent after a day at the education office, settle down in his chair, and then, inevitably a message would arrive from Florence: would he please take a cab and go up to Hampstead'.[3] But it must be said that he was a willing co-operator in wearing himself out: in September 1857 he had written to Flo 'My work here is I am glad to say beginning to relax a little. So if you have any more commissions – pray consider me.'

The precise nature of the relationship between Florence and Arthur remains an enigma. In her grief at his death she compared their love to that between David and Jonathan, 'greater than the love of women' and implied that she had been the closest to him of all his friends. But this was typical of her self-dramatization, and the evidence suggests that Arthur, devoted as he was to her, saw the two of them as engaged together in what was essentially a business operation. He felt, he once told Florence, that God was working out a scheme in which he was taking part with her. Blanche, though she resented the demands Florence made on Arthur's time and energy, never displayed the jealousy which would have been natural if there had been a romantic element to their partnership.

One of Clough's most significant services to Florence was unconnected with her work on nursing and sanitation. Rarely, the two talked together of religious matters. Florence shared much of Arthur's scepticism. At Easter in 1859 she remarked to him that all the world was celebrating a thing that they might be pretty sure had never happened. By the end of the year she had compiled an enormous book on theological, philosophical and social issues entitled *Suggestions for Thought*. She sent it for criticism to John Stuart Mill who urged her to publish it. When she sent it to Arthur, however, he side-stepped by sending it (without revealing its authorship) to Benjamin Jowett. Jowett did not consider the work publishable as it stood, but was sufficiently intrigued to write a letter of detailed criticism. This was the beginning of a vast correspondence and a warm friendship which played an important role in the lives of both correspondents. Initially, Florence was so much in awe of Jowett that, as Blanche told Arthur, her letters to him were largely composed by Aunt Mai (B, 1061).

Despite the overwork his career prospered: he was able to save enough to invest several hundred pounds in Scottish railway shares and in American stocks (M, 535). Blanche, after a difficult pregnancy, was delivered of a healthy daughter in February 1858 (M, 543). In 1859 he was promoted to being private secretary to Robert Lowe, once his science tutor, now secretary of the committee on education. In preparation for the birth of their second child, Arthur and Blanche moved with the one-year-old Florence into a larger house at 21 Campden Hill Road, Kensington. Their son Arthur was born in December of that year.

In 1856 Lowell, Emerson, Longfellow and others of their circle had resolved to found a new periodical, *The Atlantic Monthly*. The first issue appeared in October 1858, and it and its successors carried, in instalments, *Amours de Voyage* (M, 535, 543). To Clough's surprise it brought in money, the first he had ever earned by his verse: he asked Norton to add to his American holdings. He continued to keep his American friends informed about English literary events. Matthew Arnold's tragedy *Merope* he found devoid of pleasure or interest: in this he anticipated the unanimous opinion of succeeding critics. *The Idylls of the King* he thought superior to Tennyson's earlier works. In December 1859 he asked Norton 'Are your people reading Darwin on Species, published by Murray? It is a very remarkable book I believe' (M, 574).

In the same month Clough suffered an attack of scarlatina, and never fully regained his health. He was laid up for a while with a lame leg, and in the following year broke a toe and was once again immobile – though in May he was well enough to travel to Oxford for a rare meeting with Matthew Arnold, who was now Professor of Poetry, lecturing on the translation of Homer. In June his mother died after several years of paralysis; his sister Anne moved in for a while with the family at Campden Hill.

An autumn holiday in Scotland failed to restore Arthur's health. On 25 October he wrote to Norton from the Council Office 'I think very likely we shall go to Malvern for a week and for a little gentle water cure for me, who am a little out of order and not quite in vigour for the 10 months campaign shortly to commence' (M, 581). Finding that 'water curing is a very lazy thing' he stayed on for five weeks instead of two, and after the wedding of his sister-in-law Bertha at Christmas he went back to Malvern for a further five weeks, having obtained six months leave from the Council Office (PPR, 50).

He returned to London early in February 1861.[4] 'You don't know what a pleasure, what a change it is' he told Blanche 'to be at home & see a few friends quietly'. But after celebrating the third birthday of his daughter Florence ('a chatterbox of the first water') he moved with his family to Freshwater on the Isle of Wight. There, according to Blanche, 'he soon improved and regained his spirits, and for the last time really enjoyed his family life with his wife and children'.

Arthur liked walking on the beach, carrying on his shoulder the baby Arthur who was just beginning to talk and say 'Papa'. He began work again on his translation of Homer. When Florence Nightingale heard that he had brought his books with him, she told Blanche 'He'd better burn them all.' Arthur's response was 'Flo does not know that I am doing this Homer: it's a pleasure she takes no account of. It makes a great difference to me'. A further letter from Flo was 'horrid' and made Blanche weep: it took all Arthur's tact to calm her down. In return she rubbed him regularly to soothe his rheumatism and neuralgia.

In March the couple were invited to stay with the neighbouring Tennysons. They had been invited in time for dinner, but when they arrived Alfred said that he could not entertain them since the Dean of Chichester was coming. However they persisted, and were rewarded by hearing the laureate reading *Maud* aloud. The reading took three hours, and as they went up to bed Arthur whispered to Blanche 'That was rather a debauch, wasn't it.'

Arthur got on famously with the two young Tennyson boys: he helped their tutor Dakyns to teach them chess. After his death Blanche treasured one particular memory. 'At luncheon they had a plum pudding and a flag in it, and this flag was rushed after by one and another. The boys tried to get it from Arthur. I remember so well his face laughing at them.'

Tennyson and Clough discussed the recently published *Essays and Reviews*, an anthology of liberal theology which led to charges of heresy against some of its authors, notably Benjamin Jowett. On 19 March Clough went to London and brought Jowett back with him. He joined the family on walks, and helped Arthur pull Blanche up the steeper hillsides. It was the longest time Jowett had spent with Clough since his departure from Oriel, and it left him with a favourable impression of Blanche. 'I have always considered his marriage as the real blessing and happiness of his life' he wrote to her six months later (M, 604).

Jowett, however, did not like to see Clough translating Homer: he felt that he should be doing something original instead. Clough was crestfallen. Perhaps he received more encouragement from Matthew Arnold who came down to Freshwater one Sunday in April. We cannot be sure, because Matt had taken a long time to get round to reading the sample translations he had been sent (L, II, 51). This was the last recorded meeting between the two poets.

The doctors were now urging Clough to travel to a warmer climate. On 19 March the family decided to go to Florence, but a few days later Blanche discovered that she was pregnant again. Plans were changed, and Arthur decided to go to Athens, alone. He left England at the end of April. For the last time he kept, in the minuscule version of his handwriting, a travel diary which enables us to trace his movements. He visited Greece and Constantinople, whence he wrote his last letter to Matt. 'No sooner was he again at leisure and in solitude', Blanche tells us 'than the old fountain of verse, so long dry within him, reopened afresh' (PPR, 587). Just before he left England, Emerson had written 'Your muse is silent and too long' (M, 585).

Clough rose to the challenge by writing a poem entitled *Primitiae*: a love story in the style of Crabbe. It was later to figure in a suite of poems entitled *Mari Magno*.[5] The first-person hero of the story, at the age of 12, meets a cousin, Emily, two years his senior, in a Welsh rectory, which by its description is sited in Beaumaris. He and Emily are marooned on a haystack, and, when kissing on a beach, are joined by a senior schoolfellow, Helston, in his yacht. The hero at age 18 visits the family again, in the vicar's retirement rectory, for a ball which he finds boring. The next day, however, he finds that he is attracted to Emily and has missed an opportunity. A year later he returns, and shows off his university learning. He appears all head and no heart, and the visit is a failure. Emily, now Emilia, becomes more distant, and the poem ends with the hero, on the grand tour after his degree, meeting her at the Giesbach falls with her new husband Helston. He stays with her at her new home, and describes the college fellowship that he has won. She says he'll waste his talents as a don, and that if he gives it up he will rise above her and his family. He takes her advice and the poem ends.

As has been pointed out earlier, the milieu described in the poem clearly reflects childhood experiences of Clough. Whether or not the story reflects an actual love for a cousin, rendered abortive through shillyshallying, must remain uncertain. The poem contains also some more recent autobiographical elements, reflecting current travels.

> From Rome with joy I passed to Greece
> To Athens and the Peloponnese;
> Saluted with supreme delight
> The Parthenon-surmounted height;
> In huts at Delphi made abode,
> And in Arcadian valleys rode . . .
>
> (P, 390)

And so on for another 15 lines.

On this tour, Blanche tells us, he also perhaps wrote 'the second of the Mari Magno stories'. This story in the standard edition is called the 'Clergyman's First Tale': it tells of a couple called Edmund (20) and Emma (18). The two play games on a summer night in the northern mountains, where Edmund makes too free with Emma's Christian name. Having been too serious at school, Edmund now enjoys riding, swimming and hiking. But 'With all his eager motions still there went a self-correcting and ascetic bent.' The poem then purports to quote passages from a notebook written beside Wordsworth's wishing-gate. Should impulse be law? Or should one's wishes be winnowed? Surely love must be all-conquering if it be love at all, and it must include lofty fellowship of mind with mind. Edmund feels that he cannot really be in love with Emma because he is not totally overwhelmed. Whether he really loves her; only absence will show, and so he goes away on tour. On his return he finds his father sick and has to drudge to provide for his family. Worn out, he is sent to the seaside for his health, and there meets Emma by chance on the shore. The two fall into each other's arms and are married within weeks. The poem ends with a stanza to the effect that love is fellow-service.

The poem is not a success, in spite of containing some fine lines. The notebooks of the hero and heroine are not well-integrated into the story; the final reunion and marriage is a hasty and unconvincing episode; and the concluding piece about love as fellow service is bafflingly ill-attached. The story does, however, have a clear message: marriage should *not* be based on a romantic idea of love as an all-conquering obsession (lines 97–109). In an earlier chapter I have argued that the early part of the poem may have reference to an unsuccessful courtship of Jane Arnold.

In June Clough returned to England, bringing with him his poetic output. His health at first appeared much improved. Blanche met him at Camford, near Lea Hurst. 'He ran down the Station Hill, looking so well, very much sunburnt, with a black moustache and beard, very grimed.' He sat for his portrait to Hilary Bonham Carter, a connection of the Nightingale clan, and visited J. A. Froude, now with an established reputation based on the first two volumes of his classic *History of England*. Froude, widowed in 1860, was about to marry his deceased wife's half-sister, and Clough gave him *Primitiae* as an engagement present.

On 6 July Clough crossed the channel again and travelled to Paris via Dieppe and Rouen. He paid a number of visits there and wrote a letter to Blanche about applying for possible jobs which would be less demanding than his present post: perhaps an examinership for Woolwich, or for London University. It was important that the salary should not fall below £400: she should take advice from Matthew Arnold (who had written a helpful letter on 5 July) and she should keep away from Florence Nightingale (B, 1053).

Later in the month he went to Bourges by train and reached Clermont on Sunday 14 July. There he walked to Royat, where the Tennysons were staying.

Tennyson and his family in the 1860s

A diligence then took him over the mountains to a watering place at 3,000 feet called Mont Dore, a village built around a square with hotels on three sides and on the fourth a bathing establishment with a number of hot springs issuing from the volcanic rock. To Blanche Arthur described his hotel – a vast one with 20 rooms to a corridor.

> 'Tis an odd enough place to be in – dejeuner at 10, dinner at 5.30 – two tables of about 25 people all French –we also have a drawing room where we meet before meals and sit generally (only I don't) gentlemen unbeknownst to ladies give their arms to ladies aforesaid to conduct 'em into dinner and occasionally out from dinner. I sat near some pleasantish people at dinner – a Parisian (?) of the Parisians on one hand, and a Marseilles opulent-seeming seeming-merchant with a wife, a sister, and some children on t'other. (B, 1060)

He recorded an entertainment by a poetic improviser. This performance, and the free and easy relations between the sexes, seem to have stimulated Clough's own poetic vein, and he wrote a story about how easy it was in a large hotel to go to the wrong room. In the poem two sisters share a bed; one of them goes downstairs to get her watch, and returns to a different room. Unknowingly, she gets into bed beside a young man. Discovering her mistake in the morning she runs away. In due course the young man returns the watch, and the pair get married and live happily ever after. This slight and tawdry piece was eventually to figure in *Mari Magno* as 'The American's Tale'. But it is clear from a study of the manuscripts that any American flavour was added later. The poem was first called 'Marriage' and later 'Juxtaposition'.

While Arthur was staying at Mont Dore, Blanche was negotiating with his superiors at the Council Office for an extension of his leave until March 1862. Arthur, when he found out, was annoyed: he was determined to return to work in November. The correspondence follows the same pattern as that of 1853 with Blanche taking the decisions, and Arthur, initially angry, eventually coming round. On 28 July he wrote to his superior Lingen along the lines Blanche had suggested. But this was not before he had received from her a long and stern letter:

> You do not know how much grief it gave me to feel sure you had done yourself harm this time, and all through these months since your health failed I have had the feeling that you *would* not look forward, that you would only plan when the decision was so imminent as to be too late. *Quem Deus vult perdere prius dementat*. Sometime I have been afraid the first process has begun. (M, 594)

Meanwhile Clough's temper had been much improved by his meeting the Tennysons once again. He shared their walks, and was downhearted when they left on 23 July. He decided to follow them to the Bagneres de Luchon, and 'ride about' in the Pyrenees. He travelled southward by diligence on 25 July and wrote a lively verse account of the journey, full – like all his longer poems – of detailed and accurate geographic description. It gets off to a good jog-trot:

A little after one with little fail
Down drove the diligence that bears the mail;
The *courier* therefore called, in whose *banquette*
A place I got, and thankful was to get:
The new postillion climbed his seat, *allez*
Off broke the four cart-horses on their way.

The interest of the poem is in the description of the companions on the journey: the *conducteur* himself, a soldier invalided out of the Italian wars, a peasant abusing an illiterate mayor, a priest with a tale of a sick child healed by the Virgin; the postilion caps this by telling of the remarkable cure of his own ailing ass.

It was some time after writing this poem that Clough had the idea of incorporating into a sequence the poems so far written on his sick leave: *Primitiae*, *Edmund and Emma*, *Juxtaposition* and *A La Banquette*. He would produce a suite of poems like Chaucer's *Canterbury Tales*: but instead of pilgrims to a shrine, his narrators would be transatlantic voyagers such as he and Thackeray had been in 1852. In a preface to the suite he described the passengers on the vessel: a lawyer, a rural dean and a returning American tourist. Of his companions of 1852 only Lowell is clearly recognizable behind the masks. A number of features of the machinery, however, recapitulate closely the 1852 voyage: the near-collision with Cape Race, and the fog in Halifax, for instance.

The different stories of the voyagers are all to have a single theme.

Of marriage long one night they held discourse,
Regarding it in different ways, of course.
Marriage is discipline, the wise had said,
A needful human discipline to wed;
Novels of course depict it final bliss,
Say, had it ever really once been this?

(P, 376)

The title of the sequence, as so often in Clough, bears a double meaning. *Mari Magno* is a natural title for a series of tales on seaboard; but it also echoes a famous passage of Lucretius, beginning 'Suave mari magno', which describes the pleasure that watching ships battling with the elements at sea can give to someone safe on shore. This suggests that the poem is meant to represent, from the point of view of someone happily married, the various things that can go wrong before or after a wedding.

Having decided on this theme and this structure, Clough went on to add two new stories. The mate of the ship tells how a French governess returning to France from her Anglo-Irish family is stranded on Liverpool pier after missing her connection to Bordeaux. The ship's captain takes her in and marries her out of pity. An artillery officer on board questions whether the captain is not merely adding another to his collection of wives in every port. He tells his own story of a Crimean marriage between a wounded soldier and his nurse.

It is clear how these new stories, and three out of the original quartet, illustrate different motives for marriage and different consequences they may have. But in what way does the account of the coach journey, 'A la Banquette', fit in? In the sequence it appears under the title 'My Tale'. Is it merely keeping a place for an eventual account of his own marriage? Or is it intended, in some oblique way, to portray it already?[6]

August was largely taken up with a farcical pursuit of the Tennysons, resembling Claude's chase of Mary Trevellyn in *Amours*. Clough reached Bagneres de Luchon and found no sign of them. Perhaps they had instead gone to Luchon. After eight days of solitary walking he learnt they were at Bigorres. He decided to follow them and booked a coach thither for 10 August. But on the evening of 9 August the Tennyson family turned up in Luchon.

Meanwhile, important news had come from London. On 5 August the newspapers reported the death of Sidney Herbert. The letter from Blanche which gave a fuller account ('Flo was very overpowered and cried') also carried the announcement, in her mother's hand, of the birth of a baby daughter. Clough at once decided that she should be called 'Blanche Athena'. He resisted a suggestion from Flo that 'Sidney' should be somehow incorporated in the name.

Clough spent the second week of August in the foothills of the Pyrenees. In bed with diarrhoea on 13 August he wrote a poem 'Currente Calamo' that describes a graceful olive-skinned girl driving a donkey. Justly proud of the poem, he sent it in his next letter to Blanche. More mysteriously he added it to 'A la Banquette' to make up 'My Tale'.

At Luz, on the feast of the Assumption, he learnt that the Tennysons were due on the following Monday, 19 August, so he decided to stay. Once again they failed to appear, and once again he set off in pursuit, and found them at noon on 25 August. The boys, it seemed, had been ill and Mrs Tennyson had been confined to the house. Once contact had been made he was very helpful, finding suitable accommodation in Luz, escorting Mrs Tennyson on walks, encouraging the boys' convalescence, arranging dinner for the family, persuading Alfred to make the most of the scenery. ('He is helpless by himself and thinks himself more helpless than he is.')

While with the Tennysons he wrote the next of the *Mari Magno* stories, the one which was eventually published as 'The Clergyman's Second Tale'. In the story, Edward and Jane get married at 21 and have nine years of blissful marriage.

> Fonder she of him or he of her
> Were hard to say . . .
> Their busy days for no ennui had place,
> Neither grew weary of the other's face.
>
> (P, 416)

Edward, however, falls ill and is sent abroad for his health, while his wife goes to her mother in Surrey. He finds solitary wandering dismal. He wants to return, but his wife says it is all too soon. At his table d'hôte he falls for a beautiful Junoesque woman who entices him into her bedroom. He is full of remorse for this lapse, and resolves that he cannot ever come home to his wife. She will remain with her mother, he will take lodings by his office and support her financially each quarter day. Later in London he meets his partner in adultery, now a streetwalker. He is summoned home to the sickbed of a daughter. The daughter recovers, and he resumes earlier married life.

Of all the series, this poem was the one most admired when first published, and most reviled in the twentieth century. The admiration and the detestation may both be based on a false premise: namely that we are meant to admire the egotistical penitence of the husband. The clerical narrator seems to do so; but the poet surely meant us to accept rather the view of the Artillery Captain that the husband's leaving his family was no less sinful than his adultery.

It does not seem to have been remarked how closely autobiographical is the setting of the tale. Clough's letters to Blanche of 23 July (from Mont Dore) and 30 July (from Bagnères de Luchon) show that he was at that time in exactly the same condition as Edward in the tale. Edward, while travelling abroad for his health's sake is staying at a watering place, and utterly bored.

> He wrote to say, he thought he now could come,
> His usual work was sure he could resume,
> And something said about the place's gloom
> And how he loathed idling his time away.
> O, but they wrote, his wife and all, to say
> He must not think of it, 'twas quite too quick.
>
> (P, 418)

On 26 July Blanche wrote to Arthur saying 'Why on earth you should come back in September I don't see – after we settled that it was *better* not.' Clough, as we have seen, yielded to her pressure in a letter written to the Secretary of Education from Tarbes on 28 July. In the poem Edward yields, but shortly afterwards has his adulterous affair. Three days later a letter

> Came from his wife, the little daughter too
> In a large hand – the exercise was new –
> To her papa her love and kisses sent.
> (P, 420)

Just such a letter from little Florence is pasted into Clough's letter-book about this time.

Four days after his fall Edward writes to his wife and confesses his adultery. In Clough's letter of 30 July to Blanche from Luchon he complains that it is not easily endurable 'to stay poking about abroad for more than two or three months at a time, all by oneself or something no better *or perhaps worse*' (my italics). For Clough, as for Edward, 'criminal conversation' with Ms Juno would of course be far worse than keeping to himself.

If, for a moment, we adopt the hypothesis that Clough did have an affair with a fellow-guest during his last days at Mont Dore, we find no lack of supporting evidence. The journey that is recorded in 'My Tale' would then have occurred immediately after he had, in his own mind, shattered a marriage that had begun so happily. All that he is left with are the banal shards of solitary life and chance companionship that are described in 'My Tale'.

If we take the 'Clergyman's Second Tale' as literally autobiographical, then the journey of 'My Tale' is one and the same as the remorseful Edward's journey. Four days after his fall:

> late in the night at a provincial town
> In France a passing traveller was put down
> Haggard he looked, his hair was turning grey,
> His hair, his clothes, were much in disarray.
> (P, 420)

The tale was written in a single night, when Clough was with the Tennysons soon after the journey of 'My Tale'. When he read the poem aloud to them, we are told, he was reduced to tears. It would be very typical of Clough to be initially overwhelmed with remorse for any wrong he had done. The poem and its conclusion may be aimed to persuade himself, as much as anyone else, that adultery need not be an end to a marriage. His own marriage had just produced a new baby. The letter which he wrote on learning of this was unusually affectionate (beginning, uniquely, 'My *dearest* love' and containing extra endearments (M, 597; B, 1073).

It is, no doubt, unwise to place much reliance on the hypothesis that Clough had an affair at Mont Dore such as the one he assigns to Edward. It is usually the background, rather than the actual events, that can be shown to be autobiographical in Clough's poems. At most, the poem may recall a fantasy entertained while he was in the bad temper with Blanche that the late July letters record. 'So she doesn't want me back, doesn't she? Does she realise what temptations she is leaving me to cope with? Suppose, to teach her a lesson, I went to bed with that dark attractive woman across the table in my *pension*!'

On 15 September Clough learnt that Blanche, recovered from childbirth, planned to cross the channel to take care of him. He left the Tennysons and travelled by Pau and Bordeaux to Paris, where he met Blanche off her omnibus on 18 September. 'I was soon struck' she records 'by his general languor, by the half pain which it gave him to talk of things at home, partly as if he longed to be among them, partly as if he could not bear the effort of mind.'

The pair visited the Parc Monceau, inspected the new Boulevard Sevastopol, and admired the Venus de Milo. They took the train to Dijon, Arthur selecting from the station bookstore a novel for Blanche to read. Following the honeymoon footsteps of Matthew Arnold they found their way up to the Grande Chartreuse 'a long long building in a pretty half wild garden'. Arthur admired St Bernard's drinking cup. He was irritated with Blanche for spending too much time in the shop, but showed his usual good nature when she left her keys behind there. 'He never tormented me' she recorded 'for my forgets.' She carried off a fir cone, later to sow the seeds at Combe.

The couple proceeded by diligence to Pontarlier and to Neufchatel by train. An accident delayed them for an hour. 'We sat together on the weary station bench' Blanche wrote 'and I just remarked my joyful feeling of being always together again.' At Villeneuve they were joined by another English couple, Sir John and Lady Colville. The railway ended at Sion, and Arthur had to bargain to find a coachman to take them to Brig and over the Simplon pass to Domodossola.

From Sion they diverted briefly into the Valais – a lighthearted trip, with Arthur walking in the woods near Visp, pulling up grass of Parnassus and telling Blanche of his travels in Greece. On the way to Brig they passed the coachman's house, and he asked permission to stop and greet his wife. He was away a long time. Arthur was greatly amused. 'A most sentimental man' he said.

The ascent of the Simplon began at Brig; the steeper parts had to be travelled on foot. A night was spent beside a fire in the salon of an inn at Berisal, half way up. On the next day the snow came down so thickly that the horses could hardly move and it looked as if the party might be marooned at the hospice. But they were able to reach Simplon village for lunch, where they found the name of one of the Clough cousins in the inn book. From then on the snow cleared and they were able to enjoy the views of the peaks. Arthur bought chunks of black crystal to take home for the children. He went off alone to see the waterfall. 'That is the kind of thing Tennyson would admire' he told Blanche. 'He would stay for an hour looking at it.'

After walking across the frontier, the couple celebrated their arrival at Domodossola with a glass of Asti Spumante. Arthur kept 'expressing his pleasure at being once more in the South'. They spent a number of days in the towns around Lago Maggiore. Arthur would dawdle by day and lie on the sofa in the evenings covered with plaids. He much appreciated a supply of port which Blanche had brought over. But on Monday 30 September, she reports: 'I had a catastrophe, in carrying our precious port, and spilt it over my shawl. A. was much distressed about the shawl – that got well but the port was an irreparable loss.'

After a few days boating on the lake, which tired Arthur, they travelled to Milan. On the train between Magenta and Novara there were 'two Italians, husband and wife, with a pair of lovebirds in a cage which they said were "indivisible" in a kind of positive way as if they had said green or red. The young lady was very handsome, a good sort of face, with clear pure brow and well cut dark eyes and wavy hair. Arthur admired her and several times we talked of her afterwards as "the pretty young mother".'

Once in Milan, Arthur revived sufficiently for an extensive tourist trail – to Sant'Ambrogio, S. Lorenzo and the tomb of Galla Placidia, thrice to the Duomo, twice to the Brera, where Arthur paid court not only to Raphael's *Sposalizio* but also to the paintings of Bernadino Luini. He 'was particularly struck by a Bonifazio. He sat opposite it and laughed till he almost cried. It was the Inn at Emmaus. The host was so exactly like a burly innkeeper. That is what amused him.' The main problem in Milan was avoiding too much company with the effusive Dr Burgon of Oriel, who was leading a party of High Church ladies on a pilgrimage to Jerusalem. At La Scala they saw Donizetti's *Roberto Devereux*; Arthur was full of contempt for the plot.

The next stop was Parma, where Arthur was enchanted by the effects of distance and the serenity of light in the Correggios in the Belle Arti. He stayed a long time in the convent of San Paolo, with its surprisingly erotic frescoes of Diana. Diana had been the subject of his most recent self-standing poem, a rendering of the legend of Actaeon, who was transmuted into a stag and savaged by his own hounds, because he peeped at the goddess while she was bathing. It ends:

> He fled, an antlered stag wild with terror to the mountain
> She, the liquid stream in, her limbs carelessly reclining,
> The flowing waters collected grateful about her.
>
> (P, 361)

Arthur copied into his pocket book the mysterious Pythagorean inscription which the Abbess had placed over her fireplace: 'Ignem gladio ne fodias': do not poke the fire with your sword.

The final stage of the journey took them first to a bad hotel in Bologna. Though racked with rheumatic pain, Arthur visited the Academia and a brace of churches. But despite his enthusiasm for the Risorgimento he did not accompany Blanche to watch Victor Emmanuel take the salute at a military parade. Two more days and one more horrible night brought them to Florence, where they arrived at the same time as a family of friends, the Horners.

They secured lodgings in the Casa Fabiani, opposite the Pitti Palace. Arthur now took to his bed with a high fever: reluctantly, he agreed to see a physician, Dr Wilson. Joanna Horner slept with Blanche, and a maid was hired. On 22 October the landlady tried to turn the family out, but the doctor provided a certificate to say that Arthur should not be moved.

Nonetheless, they moved shortly afterwards to the Piazza Independenza, where Arthur was tended by a nurse who had looked after Elizabeth Barrett Browing. In the last days of October his fever departed, but he was paralysed on one side. Blanche read him some of Wordsworth, but he could not attend for long. It was clear that he had not long to live, and his sister Anne was summoned. She arrived just a few days before Arthur died on 13 November.

Entries in Blanche's diaries convey the atmosphere of these last days.

> During the time we were at Casa Fabiani he gave me his blue book of poems. I read Actaeon to him: he liked it and made me read it again.
>
> Once he took hold of my two hands in his and said 'my hands are whiter than yours now'. I said 'because you have been ill, dear'.
>
> He always used to call me Blanchie then, not Mama, as he did at home.
>
> Once I was sitting on the bed in the evening and he said 'we've been very happy together, haven't we dear'. He used often to say just that in common times as if it was the one thing at any rate which had been successful.
>
> I unpacked his trunk. I found one book nicely bound most carefully done up. I hoped it was something good to read, and it was a new Liddell and Scott lexicon.
>
> I used to read a little bit out of the Golden Treasury. It was really the only book we had.

> Once I asked him something about religion and he said 'Really dear I am too tired to think about those things'. I very seldom asked him a direct question but used to listen to what he said to other people.
>
> (On 10 November) I said 'do you send your love to the children' he said 'I always send my love to the children, dear' and he breathed once or twice quite quietly and it was all over.

In these last days Clough continued, frenetically, to compose poetry. He kept a small book below his pillow into which he scribbled. During the last days of October he got out of bed and began making a fair copy. 'I've written 450 lines while I've been ill' he told Blanche triumphantly. When he was no longer able to write, he began to dictate to her.

The poem that he was writing was the one which finally became, in *Mari Magno* the 'Lawyer's Second Tale'.[7] A 25-year-old Oxford college fellow, Philip, staying in a Highland inn after a reading party falls in love with a parlourmaid, Christine. He attempts to resist temptation, but finally seduces her. He escorts her by sea to Glasgow, gets her cabin upgraded and teaches her astronomy. At Glasgow he takes lodgings with her family. He plans to marry her, but reveals to her family that it would mean forfeiting a fellowship worth £300. He attends the college audit in Oxford, and on his return to Glasgow finds that the family, disbelieving his promise and anxious to get the girl out of his clutches, has emigrated to Australia. He follows them across the ocean but cannot trace them. On his return be becomes a successful journalist, serves on government commissions, and marries a Lady Mary who is childless. Later, his former love, now married with a family, turns up in England from Australia. The two women make friends with each other, and Christine hands over her eldest son – Philip's – to the childless Lady Mary.

Blanche, taking dictation, was horrified by the heartlessness of the Scottish family who had deceived Christine into emigration by pretending that Philip had deserted her. 'Couldn't you get him away in time?' she said: but Arthur told her to wait to see how the story turned out. In the course of dictating, he was much moved by the passage where Christine renounces her boy.

> She smiled, and kissed her boy, and 'Long ago
> When I was young I loved your father so
> Together now we had been living too
> Only the ship went sooner than he knew
> In loving him you will be loving me
> Father and mother are as one you see.'
>
> (P, 436)

When Philip in response says 'Oh love, this little let me call you so' Clough broke down and could dictate no more. Blanche had to copy the rest of the story, posthumously, from the pencil scribbles in his diary.

The poem completes the sequence of *Mari Magno* poems. The theme of the seduction of a Scottish girl is, as we have seen, a common one in Clough's *oeuvre*, and once again the setting of the first part of the poem hints at a fragment of autobiography. Whatever history lay behind the fiction, there is something very moving about Clough's anxiety to complete, with his dying breath, a story in which a wife gives absolution for her husband's sins. But whether, in his own case, these were sins in thought or sins in deed is a secret which he and his wife both carried to their graves.

Notes

1 After Clough's death Matt wrote to his widow, apologizing for his slight acquaintance with her and regretting how much 'circumstances have in the last few years separated me from him' (L, II, 105).

2 Matthew Arnold took a more detached view of the losses: they would be felt, he opined, more on the parade ground than on the battlefield (L, II, 298).

3 Katherine Chorley, *Arthur Hugh Clough: the Uncommitted Mind*, Oxford 1962, p. 316.

4 Much of the rest of this chapter is based on a day-by-day diary written up by Blanche shortly after Arthur's death. A copy is in Balliol library.

5 It appears in the final published version as the *Lawyer's First Tale*.

6 Such is the thesis of Mr Philip Stewart, 'Has the poet told us his secret?' *The Oxford Magazine*, No. 166, p. 6.

7 See the fuller description of the story on p. 120 above.

Epilogue

Arthur Hugh Clough was buried in the Protestant cemetery in Florence, near his American friend Theodore Parker. His wife and sister returned to England and lived for a while with the Nightingales before starting their lives afresh. Anne Jemima continued on the educational career which had begun with her schools in Liverpool and Ambleside, and became ever more ambitious in her projects for the higher education of women, which culminated in her becoming the founding principal of Newnham College, Cambridge. Blanche devoted her widowhood to the education of Arthur's children and to the publication of his literary remains.

Clough's *Nachlass* consisted of a vast and bewildering collection of loose sheets and manuscript notebooks, with some poems written out in fair copy and others extant only in preliminary scribble. Three substantial works lay unpolished and incomplete: *The Mystery of the Fall*, *Dipsychus* and *Mari Magno*. Many fine shorter poems were still unpublished including the biblical lays based on Genesis, the Browning-like monologue on Louis XV ('Sa Majesté tres Chretienne') and the two poems most often anthologized, 'Say not the Struggle Naught Availeth' and 'The Latest Decalogue'. To bring these remains into publishable form called for dedication and critical acumen.

Fortunately, Arthur in his last years had been working with Charles Eliot Norton on the preparation of a volume of poems to be published in Boston. It was to contain a revised *Bothie*, *Amours de Voyage*, the best of the *Ambarvalia* poems, and a number of shorter poems written since 1849. Arthur did not live to see it through the press; but Blanche used it as the basis for the first collected edition of the poems, published in 1862. She added to the material in Norton's hands some more short poems, a few extracts from *Dipsychus*, and a brief version of *Mari Magno* containing only three tales: 'Love is fellow-service' (Edmund and Emma), 'My tale' ('A La Banquette'), and the untitled tale of the adulterer Edward and his forgiving wife Jane. The collection was published simultaneously by Macmillan in London, with a memoir by Palgrave, and by Ticknor and Fields in Boston, with a memoir by Norton.

During the rest of the 1860s Blanche brought out further and fuller collections of her husband's verse. In 1863 a new edition of *Poems* included a much fuller *Mari Magno*, and a volume of *Letters and Remains* privately circulated in 1865 contained a complete version of *Dipsychus*. The most ample collection appeared in 1869 under the title *Poems and Prose Remains*: two volumes that contained as well as the earlier material many unpublished poems, a number of pieces in prose, a generous sampling of correspondence and a memoir written by Blanche herself. The volume of poems was reprinted 13 times in the Victorian period, and did not go out of print until 1932.

The first modern edition of the poems appeared in 1951, and a fuller, critical edition, in 1974. These superseded Blanche's editions. In addition to providing a scholarly apparatus, the editors often, on the face of the text, varied from the decision made in the 1860s.

Blanche has been criticized, in particular, for omitting, in the interests of propriety, significant passages in *Dipsychus* and other poems. The criticism is misplaced. In private life she was no prude: careful reading of the correspondence of 1861 shows that, long before Lady Chatterley, she had a conjugal nickname for her husband's private parts. Arthur himself, before his death, had clearly had second thoughts about much of the material that she omitted to publish. The 1865 edition of *Dipsychus* is closer than the 1974 one to his own latest revision. Many of Blanche's detailed decisions about the presentation of Clough's texts are, I have argued earlier, preferable to those made by later more scholarly editors.

It was a challenging task to publish for a general public the complete works of a poet who expressed views on religion and sex that were far removed from the mainstream of Victorian orthodoxy. It was no mean feat to have placed almost all of Clough's poetry in the public domain within a decade, and to have secured for it general critical and popular acclaim. Blanche's achievement compares favourably with that of another Victorian who was faced with responsibility for the *Nachlass* of an original and difficult poet. Robert Bridges did not get the collected verses of Gerard Manley Hopkins into print until nearly 30 years after his death.

Blanche did, however, do a disservice to Arthur's memory by fostering the legend that his *ouevre* was inadequate to his talents, so that as a poet he was somehow incomplete and maimed. Certainly, the output that had been published before he died did no sort of justice to his many-faceted poetical gift; hence the judgements of many critics, at the time of his death, that he had failed to fulfil the potential of his early life. Moreover it was natural for a young widow to dream of what might have been if only her husband had lived a full span of years. But by the time Blanche herself had collated, organized and presented to the public the substantial works of the period 1849–53 it was clear that Clough, on the basis of what he had written in his short life, deserved to rank among the major poets of the century. Most obviously, he compared well as a poet with Matthew Arnold – undoubtedly in the quantity of his verse, and arguably in its quality.[1]

Arnold himself gave further currency to the legend of Clough's inadequacy. The elegy *Thyrsis* which he wrote in 1866 in Clough's memory recalls with great beauty the Oxford scenery that provided the background to the two poets' juvenile companionship. But there is a grave distortion in his comparison of Clough's search for truth with the wanderings of the Scholar Gipsy of his own earlier Oxford poem.

> Thou, too, O Thyrsis, on like quest wert bound,
> Thou wanderedst with me for a little hour!
> Men gave thee nothing, but this happy quest,
> If men esteem'd thee feeble, gave thee power
> If men procured thee trouble, gave thee rest
> And this rude Cumner ground
> Its fir-topped Hurst, its farms, its quiet fields,
> Here cam'st thou in thy jocund youthful time,
> Here was thine height of strength, thy golden prime!
> And still the haunt beloved a virtue yields.
>
> What though the music of thy rustic flute
> Kept not for long its happy, country tone;
> Lost it too soon, and learnt a stormy note
> Of men contention-tost, of men who groan
> Which task'd thy pipe too sore, and tired thy throat –
> It fail'd and thou wert mute.
>
> (OA, 246)

This stanza is a reversal of the truth in its suggestion that Clough's talent declined after the years of Oxford companionship. Clough's Oxford verse is mainly mediocre and sombre; it is the poems that he wrote after breaking with Oriel that show his powers at their height. It is the years 1848–51 that constitute Clough's poetic prime, not the years of his Berkshire rambles. Arnold knew, in fact, that his elegy did not do Clough justice: he was (with good reason) reluctant to send it to Blanche, and she, when she read it, did not like it. Benjamin Jowett too thought it a most inadequate tribute. Matthew Arnold, he told Florence Nightingale, was not a bad fellow, but he had no real depth of feeling.

Earlier chapters have, I hope, brought out the complicated nature of the relationship between Arnold and Clough. Neither of them could be brought to appreciate the other's work with any warmth; each looked at the other's poems for something that was not there. Important though their friendship was to each in personal terms, I believe that it was, from a literary point of view, damaging. Each would shrug off, cheerfully enough, the other's criticisms; but the taunts had their silent effects, so that Clough hesitated to publish 'the Roman poem' that Arnold despised, and Arnold, after reading Clough's tart review, discarded, in favour of inferior poems, *Empedocles on Etna*.

As a poet, Clough was anything but a failure – but as a person? From the point of view of orthodox religion, his loss of faith shows that his character was flawed and that his life ended in disaster. But critics who have never themselves had any faith also seem ready to regard his personality as defective and his life as tragic. This is odd, since during his life all those who knew him regarded him as uncommonly virtuous, and all those who were close to him found him eminently lovable.

Undoubtedly, Clough suffered from an incapacity to take decisions promptly, and an inability to perform well on demand, whether it was a matter of passing examinations or of surmounting professional hurdles. These defects were the downside of his ability to see both sides of a question, and his reluctance to compromise his integrity on serious issues. They exasperated his closest friends, and brought him the reputation of being the kind of person who had to have all important decisions taken for him by other people.

In fact, in poetry and in life, Clough was his own man. Having experimented in the style of many masters, from Crabbe to Tennyson, he emerged from his apprenticeship as a poet with a style that was uniquely his own. In his metrical experiments he anticipated Hopkins, and in his handling of intertextuality he anticipated Eliot. He established himself as the most intellectual British poet of the nineteenth century.

Worshipping an iconic headmaster who is also a surrogate for an absent father is no doubt not a good start for a life of independence. But the influence of Thomas Arnold served Clough as an inoculation against many an infectious charisma. At Oxford he held his own against Ward and resisted the enchantments of Newman. In London and in Boston he inhaled the cloudy fumes breathed forth by Carlyle and Emerson, but he emerged from the experience with a head clearer than either of them.

The major life decisions – to leave Oriel and Oxford, to give up belief in Christian dogma, and to marry Blanche Smith – were all taken by Clough himself, in opposition to the advice of his friends and difficulties raised by families. All three decisions proved correct: departure from Oxford led to poetic flowering, abandonment of dogma led to religious tranquillity, marriage to Blanche led to matrimonial happiness. When W. G. Ward's biographer wrote that Clough 'never recovered the peace of such religious convictions as had been shaken in him' Blanche protested 'As a fact he had the truest peace of mind, which I felt as the peace of religious trust. That he did not recover his early beliefs is true.[2]

The one case which supports the belief that Clough could never make his own decisions is his departure from Boston in 1853 to take up a position in the

Education department. This is held out as a classic case of his shilly-shallying, brought to an end only when Blanche and Temple insisted on his returning to England to take responsibility for a decision which they had already taken for him. In fact, a study of the correspondence shows that it was not Clough, but the Smith family, who shilly-shallied. Right up to the last moment Blanche and her father led Clough to believe that they wished him to continue to seek his fortune in Massachussetts. His prospects were indeed, after a difficult start, very promising. He had collected a number of pupils who admired him and who would encourage others to come to him for tuition and provide the quantum of fees necessary for him to support a wife. If this hope proved deceptive, he had found a friend who was willing to join him in the second-best method of providing for a family, namely the foundation of a school. These hopes were dashed when there came from Combe Hurst the peremptory command, backed with financial sanction, that he should return to England.

Arthur was so much in love with Blanche, and so anxious to marry her as soon as possible, that he did not question the wisdom of her friends' decision. But was the return across the Atlantic really in his best interests? His literary reputation was much higher in the US than in England, and his new American acquaintances appreciated his talents more generously than any of his English friends. Teaching pupils in Cambridge, holding forth on the Massachusetts lecture circuit, and publishing in the burgeoning American literary journals might well have earned Clough a greater competency, with less drudgery, than the post in the education office secured by his return to England.

Had the Cloughs settled in Cambridge Arthur would not have been subjected to the excessive demands of Florence Nightingale which, so she and others believed, significantly shortened his life. But a lifelong sojourn in America, it might be argued, would have deprived Arthur of his opportunity for the philanthropic work which he saw as a vocation higher even than the writing of poetry. Sadly, however, one can be sure that the horrors of the Civil War would have provided the same kind of opportunities for selfless service in Boston that the Crimean War provided in London. Taking one counterfactual with another, we may regret that Clough did not follow his own inspiration and persuade Blanche to follow him westward where the land was bright.

Notes

1 The *New Oxford Book of Victorian Verse*, ed. Christopher Ricks, Oxford 1987, devotes 43 pages to Clough and 13 to Arnold.

2 St Andrew's University archives, MS 36347.

Florence. The Protestant Cemetery, March 1862. Reproduced with kind permission of the Master and Fellows of Balliol College, Oxford.

Bibliography

A comprehensive bibliographical guide to works by and about Clough appeared in 1968: Gollin, Richard M., Houghton, Walter E., and Timko, Michael, *Arthur Hugh Clough: a Descriptive Catalogue*, the New York Public Library. This is annotated and is divided into three parts: Poetry, Prose, Biography and Criticisim. The critical section contains 500 items.

I list below works most often used while writing this biography.

Allot, M. and Super, R. H., *The Oxford Authors: Matthew Arnold*, Oxford 1986.

Bergonzi, Bernard, *A Victorian Wanderer: the Life of Thomas Arnold the Younger*, Oxford 2003.

Bertram, Jim (ed.), *New Zealand Letters of Thomas Arnold the Younger*, London and Wellington 1939.

Biswas, R. K., *Arthur Hugh Clough: Towards a Reconsideration*, Oxford 1972.

Brock, M. C. and Curthoys, M. C., *The History of the University of Oxford*, Vol. 7, *The Nineteenth Century*, Oxford 1997.

Chadwick, Owen, *A History of the Popes, 1830–1914*, Oxford 1998.

Chorley, Katherine, *Arthur Hugh Clough: the Uncommitted Mind*, Oxford 1962.

Christiansen, Rupert, *The Voice of Victorian Sex: Arthur Hugh Clough*, London 2001.

Clough, Blanche Athena, *A Memoir of Anne Jemima Clough*, London 1897, 1903.

Clubbe, J. (ed.), *Froude's Life of Carlisle*, Columbus 1979.

Faber, Geoffrey, *Jowett: a Portrait with Background*, London 1957.

Greenberger, E. B., *Arthur Hugh Clough: the Growth of a Poet's Mind*, Harvard University Press 1970.

Honan, Park, *Matthew Arnold: a Life*, London 1981.

Hughes, Thomas, *Tom Brown's Schooldays*, London 1857.

Jenkins, Roy, *Churchill*, London 2001.

Kenny, A., *God and Two Poets*, London 1988.

Ker, Ian, *John Henry Newman: a Biography*, Oxford 1988.

Knight, William, *Principal Shairp and his Friends*, London 1888.

Lake, K. (ed.), *Memorials of William Charles Lake*, London 1901.

Lowell, James, *A Fable of Critics*, Boston 1848.

McCrum, M., *Thomas Arnold, Headmaster*, Oxford 1989.

Monsarrat, Ann, *An Uneasy Victorian: Thackeray the Man*, London 1980.

Murray, Nicholas, *A Life of Matthew Arnold*, London 1996.

Newman, J. H., *Letters and Diaries*, Vols VII–VIII, ed. G. Tracey, Oxford 1995, 1999.

Phelan, J. P., 'The Textual Evolution of Clough's *Dipsychus and the Spirit*', *Notes and Queries*, 2000, pp. 230–9.

Prothero, R. G. and Bradley, G. G., *The Life and Correspondence of Arthur Penrhyn Stanley*, 2 vols, London 1893.

Ray, Gordon N., *The Letters and Private Papers of William Makepeace Thakeray*, 4 vols, Oxford 1956–6.

Risk, Ralph, *The Letters of Ralph Waldo Emerson*, 6 vols, New York 1939.

Rouse, W. H. D., *A History of Rugby School*, London 1898.

Scott, Patrick, *Victorian Texts I: Amours de Voyage by Arthur Hugh Clough*, St Lucia, Queensland 1976.

——*Victorian Texts IV: The Bothie by Arthur Hugh Clough*, St Lucia, Queensland 1976.

Stanley, A. P., *The Life of Thomas Arnold D. D.*, London 1844; 1903.

Strachey, Lytton, *Eminent Victorians*, London 1918.

Thorpe, Michael (ed.), *Clough: the Critical Heritage*, New York 1982.

Veyriras, Paul, *Arthur Hugh Clough (1819-1861)* Paris 1964.

Ward, Maisie, *Young Mr Newman*, London 1948.

Ward, Wilfrid, *William George Ward and the Oxford Movement*, London 1889.

Williams, David, *Too Quick Despairer: the Life and Work of Arthur Hugh Clough*, London 1969.

Ziegler, Philip, *The Sixth Great Power: Barings 1762–1929*, London 1992.

Index